MULTI-SOURCED EQUIVALENT NORMS IN INTERNATIONAL LAW

Recent decades have witnessed an impressive process of normative development in international law. Numerous new treaties have been concluded, at global and regional levels, establishing far-reaching international legal and regulatory regimes in important areas such as human rights, international trade, environmental protection, criminal law, intellectual property, and more. New political and judicial institutions have been established to develop, apply and adjudicate these rules. This trend has been accompanied by the growing consolidation of treaty norms into international custom, and increased references to international law in domestic settings. As a result of these developments, international relations have now reached an unprecedented level of normative density and intensity, but they have also given rise to the phenomenon of 'fragmentation'.

The debate over the fragmentation of international law has largely focused on conflicts: conflicts of norms and conflicts of authority. However, the same developments that have given rise to greater conflict and contradiction in international law, have also produced a growing amount of normative equivalence between rules in different fields of international law. New treaty rules often echo existing international customary norms. Regional arrangements reinforce undertakings that already exist at the global level; and common concerns and solutions appear in many international legal fields. This book focuses on such instances of normative parallelism, developing the concept of 'multisourced equivalent norms' in international law, with contributions by leading international law experts exploring the legal and political implications of the concept in a variety of contexts that span the full spectrum of international legal norms and institutions. By concentrating on situations governed by a multitude of similar norms, the book emphasizes the importance of legal contexts and institutional settings to international law-interpretation and application.

Volume 32 in the series Studies in International Law

Studies in International Law

Volume 1: Between Light and Shadow: The World Bank, the International Monetary Fund and International Human Rights Law
Mac Darrow

Volume 2: Toxics and Transnational Law: International and European Regulation of Toxic Substances as Legal Symbolism
Marc Pallemaerts

Volume 3: The Chapter VII Powers of the United Nations Security Council
Erika de Wet

Volume 4: Enforcing International Law Norms Against Terrorism
Edited by Andrea Bianchi

Volume 5: The Permanent International Criminal Court
Edited by Dominic McGoldrick, Peter Rowe and Eric Donnelly.

Volume 6: Regional Organisations and the Development of Collective Security
Ademola Abass

Volume 7: Islamic State Practices, International Law and the Threat from Terrorism: A Critique of the 'Clash of Civilizations' in the New World Order
Javaid Rehman

Volume 8: Predictablity and Flexibility in the Law of Maritime Delimitation
Yoshifumi Tanaka

Volume 9: Biotechnology and International Law
Edited by Francesco Francioni and Tullio Scovazzi

Volume 10: The Development of Human Rights Law by the Judges of the International Court of Justice
Shiv Bedi

Volume 11: The Environmental Accountability of the World Bank to Third Party Non-State Actors
Alix Gowlland-Gualtieri

Volume 12: Transnational Corporations and Human Rights
Edited by Olivier De Schutter

Volume 13: Biotechnologies and International Human Rights
Edited by Francesco Francioni

Volume 14: Human Security and International Law: Prospects and Problems
Barbara Von Tigerstrom

Volume 15: The Arms Trade and International Law
Zeray Yihdego

Volume 16: Africa: Mapping New Boundaries in International Law
Edited by Jeremy Levitt

Volume 17: Forced Migration, Human Rights and Security
Edited by Jane McAdam

Volume 18: The Use of Nuclear Weapons and the Protection of the Environment during International Armed Conflict
Erik Koppe

Volume 19: The Shifting Allocation of Authority in International Law: Considering Sovereignty, Supremacy and Subsidiarity
Edited by Tomer Broude and Yuval Shany

Volume 20: Counterterrorism: Democracy's Challenge
Edited by Andrea Bianchi and Alexis Keller

Volume 21: Amnesty, Human Rights and Political Transitions
Louise Mallinder

Volume 22: Property Rights and Natural Resources
Richard Barnes

Volume 23: Human Dignity and the Foundations of International Law
Patrick Capps

Volume 24: Sovereignty and the Stateless Nation: Gibraltar in the Modern Legal Context
Keith Azopardi

Volume 25: The International Court of Justice and Self-Defence in International Law
James A Green

Volume 26: State Liability in Investment Treaty Arbitration: Global Constitutional and Administrative Law in the BIT Generation
Santiago Montt

Volume 27: Reappraising the Resort to Force: International Law, Jus ad Bellum and the War on Terror
Lindsay Moir

Volume 28: International Law and Dispute Settlement: New Problems and Techniques
Edited by Duncan French, Matthew Saul and Nigel White

Volume 29: The Democratic Legitimacy of International Law
Steven Wheatley

Volume 30: Reflections on the UN Declaration on the Rights of Indigenous Peoples
Edited by Stephen Allen and Alexandra Xanthaki

Volume 31: Contracting with Sovereignty: State Contracts and International Arbitration
Ivar Alvik

Multi-Sourced Equivalent Norms in International Law

Edited by
Tomer Broude
and
Yuval Shany

·HART·
PUBLISHING

OXFORD AND PORTLAND, OREGON
2011

Published in the United Kingdom by Hart Publishing Ltd
16C Worcester Place, Oxford, OX1 2JW
Telephone: +44 (0)1865 517530
Fax: +44 (0)1865 510710
E-mail: mail@hartpub.co.uk
Website: http://www.hartpub.co.uk

Published in North America (US and Canada) by
Hart Publishing
c/o International Specialized Book Services
920 NE 58th Avenue, Suite 300
Portland, OR 97213-3786
USA
Tel: +1 503 287 3093 or toll-free: (1) 800 944 6190
Fax: +1 503 280 8832
E-mail: orders@isbs.com
Website: http://www.isbs.com

British Library Cataloguing in Publication Data
Data Available

ISBN: 978-1-84946-145-0

Typeset by Hope Services Ltd, Abingdon
Printed and bound in Great Britain by
Lightning Source UK Ltd

Foreword

It has become common to highlight the risks arising from the fragmentation of international law. These risks are related, first, to increased conflicts between different norms and between different international legal regimes and, second, to inconsistencies in the application of international law. To a large extent this book addresses the same risks from a rather different perspective: similar rules or, as the authors put it, normative parallelism. By the latter, the authors refer to the multiplication of similar rules arising from different legal sources; the expression they have coined for this being multi-sourced equivalent norms.

One of the first virtues of this book is to map this often neglected reality and to better conceptualize the phenomena. To put it simply, these multi-sourced equivalent norms lead to competing (but similar) norms regulating the same situations of fact. To a large extent, this phenomenon can still be presented as a form of fragmentation in international law. At the core of this fragmentation is the existence of competing legal sources whose coordination within a single legal order is, at the minimum, contested and which are, in fact, applied by multiple legal regimes. The difference with respect to the traditional fragmentation discussion is that the focus is not on different competing rules but on competing equivalent norms. One might expect the latter not to be a source of tension but of harmony. That would ignore the fact that norms only acquire meaning in their context and that meaning is ultimately determined by who interprets and applies them. At the core of the issues raised by multi-sourced equivalent norms is the interpretation and application of equivalent norms to the same situations by different legal systems. This creates potential substantive conflicts in the resolution of the same or similar situations. One first question is whether there is a legitimate normative claim to have those conflicts arbitrated and solved by the law? In other words, does the rule of law require eliminating these inconsistencies and legal uncertainties in international law? Can we, in fact, talk about inconsistency and legal uncertainty in such cases? Aren't these concepts only to be assessed within a legal order? If so, can we talk about an international legal order composed of a plurality of international legal regimes and is it subject to the rule of law? The answers to these questions depend on our underlying assumptions of the nature of international law and the role to be played by different actors. One of the emerging trends is the central role to be played by courts. There are increased appeals for judicial bodies to actively promote integration and coordination between different legal orders. This could be done either by international judicial bodies integrating, through interpretation, the rules of a particular international legal regime into another international legal regime or by domestic courts increased reliance on international law arguments in deciding domestic disputes. But that raises important institutional and legitimacy questions.

One of the attractions of the book is therefore that of presenting the current discussions on the nature and fragmentation of international law from a rather different perspective. The background is that of increased legal pluralism. First, increased economic and political integration has led to a multiplication of international legal regimes and jurisdictional fora. Second, there are increased conflicting jurisdictions among different legal orders (state, supranational and international). These conflicts may not necessarily be legal in formal terms but they are de facto. They generate instances of what we could label as interpretative competition and adjudication among courts. This context also gives rise to possible externalities (where the decision taken in a certain jurisdiction has a social and an economic impact, albeit not a binding legal impact, in another jurisdiction). Both of these phenomena can be constructed as being at the origin of fragmentation in international law. But this fragmentation is not simply a product of differentiation as the current book demonstrates. Pluralism may also lead to approximation by the contacts it promotes between different legal orders and their respective legal communities. This feeds a cross-fertilization of legal concepts. To a large extent, multi-sourced equivalent norms are a product of these two competing forces in pluralism: one pulling towards differentiation and the other towards harmonization.

The book is empirically thorough and normatively diverse. At the empirical level it describes the phenomena of MSEN, its different forms and shapes and how context matters in identifying different types of MSEN and their differentiated effects. But it also discusses the approaches adopted by different actors towards MSEN and how to address the potential problems they raise. At the normative level, the book addresses the challenges but also the opportunities raised by MSEN. Multi-sourced equivalent norms embody a paradox: they are, simultaneously, a source of approximation between different international legal regimes and of possible inconsistencies and conflicts between them. The book describes how different normative approaches to deal with MSEN are possible under international law while constantly highlighting that paradox. In this way, the book is a uniquely powerful and original contribution to the current debates on the future of international law.

Miguel Poiares Maduro

Acknowledgements

This book is the result of a group effort. It contains the products of the work of a study group that met four times over the course of a year and a half, for the purpose of exploring the concept of MSENs in international law. These meetings benefited from the participation of a number of world class experts, who presented to the group their work and thoughts on related subjects. The concepts and insights developed by the group were ultimately shared with other scholars at a broader conference that took place in Jerusalem in the spring of 2009 and generated, in turn, additional contributions for the present collection of essays. Obviously, the present publication would not have been possible without the intellectual and financial support of many people and institutions that supported the work of study group.

First and foremost, we would like to thank our academic collaborators – the other members of the study group – Dr Lorand Bartels, Dr Guy Harpaz, Professor Moshe Hirsch, Professor Andre Nollkaemper, Professor Joost Pauwelyn and Dr Isabelle Van Damme; the experts who participated in the three meetings leading up to the final conference – Professor Georges Abi-Saab, Professor Laurence Bossion de Chazournes, Professor James Crawford, Dr Zachary Douglas, Professor Ralf Michaels (who also participated in the final conference) and Dr Marieke Oderkerk; the rest of the participants in the project's concluding conference – Professor Eyal Benvenisti, Claire Charters, Professor Tarcisio Gazzini, Professor Robert Howse, Gil Limon (who also participated in two study group meetings), Professor Miguel Maduro, Martins Paparinskis, Professor Ruti Teitel; and other contributors to this volume – Dr Erik Denters, Professor Jurgen Kurtz and Dr Nikolaos Lavranos. During its work, the study group held meetings with the support of hosting institutions and faculties at the Lauterpacht Centre at the University of Cambridge, at the Amsterdam Centre for International Law (University of Amsterdam) and at the Graduate Institute in Geneva. We are grateful to these institutions and local interlocutors for hosting us (special thanks are due in this regard to Professor James Crawford for his gracious hospitality).

Overall, the project was funded by the Davis Institute for International Relations at the Hebrew University of Jerusalem. We are extremely appreciative for the support of Professor Alfred Tovias, the Institute's Director, as well as for the work of the Institute's administrative staff – Anat Ilouz, Hani Mazar and Meital Levy – who helped with the logistics of the work of the study group and the concluding conference.

Additional thanks are due to Oren Tamir and Erin Gray, who served as the Study Group's administrative coordinator at different stages of its work; Michele Manspeizer provided excellent editorial support in the book production process; and Professor Ruth Lapidoth was, as always, a constant source of support and advice. Finally, we would like to thank the team at Hart Publishing, especially Richard Hart and Rachel Turner, whose continued support has been indispensable.

TB and YS
Reut, Israel
2010

Contents

PART II
MSENS IN JUDICIAL PRACTICE

PART III
MSENS IN SPECIFIC NORMATIVE AND INSTITUTIONAL CONTEXTS

List of Contributors

Lorand Bartels University lecturer in Law and Fellow of Trinity Hall, University of Cambridge.

Tomer Broude Senior lecturer in the Faculty of Law and Department of International Relations, and the Academic Director of the Minerva Center for Human Rights at the Hebrew University of Jerusalem.

Claire Charters Ngati Whakaue, Ngati Tuwharetoa, Tainui and Nga Puhi. Fellow, New Zealand Centre for Public Law at Victoria University of Wellington and PhD Candidate, University of Cambridge.

Erik Denters Associate Professor, Faculty of Law, Vrije Universiteit Amsterdam.

Tarcisio Gazzini Associate Professor, Faculty of Law, Vrije Universiteit Amsterdam.

Guy Harpaz Senior lecturer and Jean Monnet Lecturer, Law Faculty and Department of International Relations, Hebrew University of Jerusalem; President of the Israeli Association for the Study of European Integration.

Moshe Hirsch Maria Von Hofmannsthal Chair in International Law, Faculty of Law and Department of International Relations, Hebrew University of Jerusalem; Global Faculty, Centre for Energy, Petroleum, Mineral Law and& Policy, Faculty of Law, University of Dundee.

Robert Howse Lloyd C. Nelson Professor of International Law, New York University School of Law.

Jürgen Kurtz Senior lecturer and International Investment Law Research Programme Director, Institute for International Law and the Humanities, University of Melbourne Law School, Australia. Email: j.kurtz@unimelb.edu.au.

Nikolaos Lavranos Dr iur, LLM, former Max Weber Fellow (2008–2009) EUI; currently senior trade policy adviser, Dutch Ministry of Economic Affairs.

Luis Miguel Poiares Maduro Joint Chair, Robert Schuman Center for Advanced Studies and Department of Law, European University Institute, Florence; formerly, Advocate General to the European Court of Justice.

Ralf Michaels Professor of Law at Duke University School of Law and currently Visiting Professor and Research Fellow at the Program in Law and Public Affairs, Princeton University

André Nollkaemper Professor of Public International Law, the Faculty of Law, University of Amsterdam.

Martins Paparinskis D Phil candidate, University of Oxford, the Queen's College; Hauser Research Scholar, New York University. Previously, Arts and Humanities Research Council and Commercial Bar Scholar at the University of Oxford.

Joost Pauwelyn Professor of International Economic Law and WTO Law at the Graduate Institute of International Studies in Geneva, Switzerland and Director of its Centre for Trade and Economic Integration.

Benedikt Pirker Teaching Assistant, College of Europe, Bruges.

Yuval Shany Hersch Lauterpacht Chair in Public International Law at the Faculty of Law of the Hebrew University of Jerusalem and a director in the Project on International Courts and Tribunals.

1

The International Law and Policy of Multi-Sourced Equivalent Norms

Tomer Broude and Yuval Shany

But let judgment run down as waters,
and righteousness as a mighty stream.

Amos 5:24[1]

I THE PUZZLE OF NORMATIVE PARALLELISM IN INTERNATIONAL LAW

THE EPIGRAPH, A passage now almost three millennia old, is a plea for social justice and the rule of law that reverberates with equal force in our day and age. However, we cite it here not only for its substance, but mainly for its rhetorical structure. The phrase reflects the puzzle of parallelism that is analogous to the set of legal problems that this book is devoted to. The verse is a simple couplet, and its two constituent phrases obviously echo each other. But what is the true logical relation between them? Repetition? Augmentation? Differentiation? Contradi(stin)ction? Some combination of all the above? Surely the two parts of the verse are equivalent, but they are neither identical, nor fully equal. The prophet's intentions are effectively and independently captured in each part of the verse, yet there is a supplementary effect in their separate existence, as the two parts appear to reflect upon each other somehow.

Such parallelism has long been the object of study among scholars of the Bible, who not only identify several distinct types and dynamics of parallel relationships between verses, but use this 'parallelism of members' – *parallelismus membrorum*[2] – as an aid in interpreting one part of a verse in

[1] King James Bible translation. The original script in Hebrew is written: 'ויגל כמים משפט וצדקה כנחל איתן'

[2] The term was first used by Robert Lowth in *De Sacra Poesi Hebraeorum* (1753), translated into English by G Gregory in *Lectures on the Sacred Poetry of the Hebrews* (1787). Lowth identified three species of parallelism in biblical verse: the synonymous, the antithetic and the

the light of the other.[3] Moreover, these verses are not only part of ancient Hebrew poetry; they often contain a strong normative element. If viewed as legal imperatives or prescriptive rules, do the two branches of the sentence copied above – deceptive in their likeness – simply repeat the same rule, or do they provide subtly different commands, whose divergence might become decisive in particular circumstances? What is the legal significance of this parallelism and how does one rule reflect on its erstwhile equivalent? What, indeed, is the relationship between two norms that are so similar to each other, yet different? Do they create normative inconsistency, and if so, what is the consequent effect on legal certainty and the political legitimacy of law?

This book is about normative parallelism and equivalence, as it exists – and this is increasingly the case – in contemporary international law, bringing with it a slew of legal questions regarding the relationship between equivalent norms. We have opted to label the situations in which equivalent rules co-exist in the international legal sphere as 'Multi-Sourced Equivalent Norms' or MSENs for short. They are 'equivalent' because like the parallel parts of a biblical couplet, they are not always identical, and an understanding of their interrelationship requires deeper study. They are 'multi-sourced' because unlike the biblical 'parallelism of members', equivalent international norms are rarely conjoined like the analogous parts of a verse. Rather, equivalence is found between distant sources of international law, and across fields of international law that otherwise might have little in common with each other.[4] Furthermore, normative parallelism often exists unnoticed and unacknowledged, although pregnant with problems of law and policy, that lie dormant until unexpected contexts and unintended developments bring them to the fore.[5] In this chapter we will define and discuss MSENs as a conceptual introduction to the particular studies that follow.

synthetic. We shall return to these distinctions shortly. At this stage we only emphasize that parallelism and equivalence are not always of a synonymic nature.

[3] An interpretative technique used by Lowth himself in *Isaiah: A New Translation with a Preliminary Dissertation and Notes* (London, J Dodsley for J Nichols, 1778) (reprinted with an introduction by D Reibel); *Robert Lowth [1710-1787]: The Major Works* (1995). See also A Berlin, *The Dynamics of Biblical Parallelism* (Bloomington, Indiana University Press, 1985).

[4] Eg, in her study of MSENs relating to Indigenous peoples' rights, Claire Charters refers to the work of diverse international institutions, and a broad range of otherwise unrelated international instruments, ranging from the United Nations Human Rights Council to the World Bank. See in this volume, C Charters, 'Multi-Sourced Equivalent Norms and the Legitimacy of Indigenous Peoples' Rights under International Law' in T Broude and Y Shany (eds), *Multi-Sourced Equivalent Norms in International Law* (Oxford, Hart Publishing, 2011) p 189.

[5] Eg, one of the most intensely debated international MSEN instances in recent years – the relationship between the customary plea of necessity, as expressed in art 25 of the ILC 'Draft Articles on State Responsibility' (2001) GAOR 56th Session Supp 10 UN Doc A/56/10 on the one hand, and the 'public order' and 'essential security interests' exceptions in bilateral investment treaties on the other – might have remained a hypothetical issue of purely academic interest, if not for the 2001–02 financial crisis in Argentina. For detailed analysis, see in this volume, J Kurtz, 'Delineating Primary and Secondary Rules on Necessity at International Law'.

II THE RISE OF MSENS IN FRAGMENTED INTERNATIONAL LAW

Normative parallelism is not unique to international law and exists in a variety of domestic legal settings. The same behaviour – assault or wilful killing – is often prohibited under criminal statutes and at the same time gives rise to liability under tort law.[6] An administrative agency may regulate the conduct of private actors through regulations, licences and contracts, as different sources whose normative content may be similar or identical.[7] A national legal system may refer to religious law to determine whether a marriage has been consummated, establishing a parallelism between religious and civic personal law.[8] The 'kitchen sink' strategy of private litigation leads to lawsuits in which the same act is allegedly in violation of rules and obligations from a broad range of legal sources. These equivalences are commonplace and are rarely considered problematic and can be attributed to the normative unity and institutional integrativity of domestic legal systems. After all, parallel domestic norms are typically promulgated by the same legislative system and/or adjudicated by the same courts. MSENs may, however, have a very different effect in the 'anarchical' international legal system,[9] which is characterized by a lack of institutional integration.

The lack of integration at the international level and the growth in lawmaking underlies the problem of normative fragmentation. Indeed, recent decades have witnessed an impressive process of normative development in international law: Numerous new treaties have been concluded, both on the global and regional levels, establishing far-reaching international legal and regulatory regimes in important issue areas such as human rights, international trade, environmental protection, criminal law, environmental protection, intellectual property and more. This trend has been accompanied by the growing consolidation of treaty norms into international custom. As a result of these developments, international relations have now reached an unprecedented level of normative density and intensity. While these developments are clearly a response to an increased demand for international law and institutions, and have many positive implications –

[6] On this parallelism see, eg, JC Coffee, 'Does "Unlawful" Mean "Criminal"?: Reflections on the Disappearing Tort/Crime Distinction in American Law' (1991) 71 *Boston University Law Review* 193.

[7] See, eg, S Arrowsmith, 'Government Contracts and Public Law' (1990) 10 *Legal Studies* 231, at 231, noting that 'the government uses contract as a method of controlling behaviour as an alternative to enacting regulations'. In practice, government contracts and licences are used to reinforce rather than substitute statutory regulation.

[8] As is the case in Israel and India see, eg, M Galanter and J Krishnan, 'Personal Law and Human Rights in India and Israel' (2001) 34 *Israel Law Review* 101.

[9] 'Anarchical' here refers to the absence of central authority in international relations. See generally, H Bull, *The Anarchical Society: A Study of Order in World Politics* 3rd edn (New York, Columbia University Press, 1977).

such as the promotion of the international rule of law, the advancement of important values and the facilitation of interstate cooperation – they also present several theoretical and practical challenges in law and legal policy that are worthy of further investigation.

One such major challenge specifically identified by the International Law Commission (ILC) is the fragmentation of international law. According to the 2006 ILC report on the subject, in the absence of a central authority in international relations, the rapid normative development by different and uncoordinated legal regimes might lead to 'conflicts between rules or rule-systems, deviating institutional practices and, possibly, the loss of an overall perspective on the law'.[10] The report then goes on to discuss a variety of phenomena, which contribute to normative fragmentation (for example, self-contained regimes and regionalism) and considers different legal principles that may improve upon existing levels of coordination between different international norms (*lex specialis, lex posterior, jus cogens,* systemic integration through harmonizing interpretation).[11]

The debate over the fragmentation of international law, epitomized by the work of the ILC, has largely focused on conflicts: conflicts of norms[12] and conflicts of authority.[13] However, the same developments that have given rise to greater conflict and contradiction in international law have also produced a growing amount of normative equivalence between rules in different fields of international law. New treaty rules often echo existing international customary norms; regional arrangements reinforce undertakings that already exist at the global level; and common concerns and solutions appear in many international legal fields. In its report, the ILC took brief note of this phenomenon that we refer to here as parallelism or

[10] ILC, 'Report of the Study Group of the ILC, Fragmentation of International Law: Difficulties arising from the Diversification and Expansion of International Law' (2006) UN Doc A/CN.4/L.682, 11 (Fragmentation Report).

[11] Note, however, that the report only briefly touched on the relation between the normative and institutional dimensions of fragmentation and did not explore the potential impact of consolidation or dispersion of law-making and law-applying powers among international organizations and institutions on normative fragmentation. For a discussion of links between normative and institutional fragmentation; see T Broude, 'Fragmentation(s) of International Law: On Normative Integration as Authority Allocation' in T Broude and Y Shany (eds), *The Shifting Allocation of Authority in International Law: Considering Sovereignty, Supremacy and Subsidiarity* (Oxford, Hart Publishing, 2008) and T Broude, 'Principles of Normative Integration and the Allocation of International Authority: The WTO, The Vienna Convention on the Law of Treaties and the Rio Declaration' (2008) 6 *Loyola University Chicago International Law Review* 173.

[12] See generally, J Pauwelyn, *Conflict of Norms in Public International Law: How WTO Law Relates to Other Rules of International Law* (Cambridge, Cambridge University Press, 2003).

[13] See Y Shany, *The Competing Jurisdiction of International Courts and Tribunals* (Oxford, Oxford University Press, 2003). See also, N Lavranos, 'Concurrence of Jurisdiction between the ECJ and other International Courts and Tribunals' (2005) 14 *European Environmental Law Review* 213, 213–25; N Lavranos, 'Towards a Solange Method between International Courts and Tribunals?' in Broude and Shany (eds), *The Shifting Allocation of Authority*, above (n 11); I Canor, 'Exercise in Constitutional Tolerance? When Public International Law Meets Private International Law: Bosphorus Revisited' and A Cohen, 'Domestic Courts and Sovereignty' in Broude and Shany, *The Shifting Allocation of Authority in International Law*, above (n 11).

equivalence, in its mention of fragmented international rules that nonetheless 'point in the same direction'.[14] These rules are MSENs, and it is on the difficulties associated with their legal effects that the contributions in this book have focused.

III DEFINING AND CHARACTERIZING EQUIVALENCE

To better understand the problems raised by MSENs, the International Law Forum of the Hebrew University of Jerusalem, with the financial support of the Davis Institute for International Relations, established in 2008 an international academic study group on MSENs, involving a group of international law experts from a variety of backgrounds and perspectives. The group met several times – at Cambridge, in Amsterdam, Geneva and finally on Mount Scopus in Jerusalem – for a series of working sessions in which the study group's participants presented their works in progress on the law and policy of MSENs in international law. The mandate of the study group was deliberately quite broad: to examine the issues and problems that arise from the existence of MSENs in a fragmented international legal order, and to consider methodologies for their resolution.

For the purposes of the study group's work, MSENs were understood as situations where distinct international legal rules direct *similar or identical behaviour*; more specifically, MSENs were defined as

> two or more norms which are (1) binding upon the same international legal subjects; (2) similar or identical in their normative content; and (3) have been established through different international instruments or 'legislative' procedures or are applicable in different substantive areas of the law.[15]

Despite its limitations, this definition allowed for a very wide range of cases to be examined; viewed through the MSEN lens, international law appeared refreshingly harmonious, rather than conflictual. A few examples will suffice. Consider the obligation to prevent transboundary pollution, which may be considered by many European states as a MSEN, since it is firmly grounded in international custom,[16] a number of global

[14] ILC, Fragmentation Report, above (n 10) 52.

[15] Many of the contributions in this book make specific reference to this definition.

[16] This is reflected, eg, in the 1941 *Trail Smelter* case and the 1972 Stockholm and 1992 Rio Declarations. *Trail Smelter (US v Canada)* (1938/1941) 3 RIAA 1905; Declaration of the United Nations Conference on the Human Environment (June 1972) UN Doc A/CONF.48/14, 2; Rio Declaration on Environment and Development (Rio de Janeiro 3–14 June 1992) UN Doc A/CONF.151/26 (vol I).

and regional environmental treaties,[17] European Union (EU) law[18] and human rights law.[19] The obligation not to pollute might even be viewed as a general principle of international law.[20] Other examples include the legal defence of necessity, which may in many cases, such as those involving non-international armed conflicts under human rights law, co-exist in international humanitarian law and the general laws of state responsibility;[21] the prohibition of the use of force (and the self-defence exception thereto) that exists under both international customary law and the UN Charter, as well as under regional instruments and some bilateral agreements;[22] the concurrent national treatment obligations in regional trade agreements and under the World Trade Organization (WTO), which may overlap with non-discrimination norms applicable to foreign labourers under human rights law and certain provisions of international investment law;[23] and the prohibition of torture that exists under a number of human rights treaties and in international humanitarian law; substantive EU norms that overlap with norms existing under WTO law, the laws of the European Economic Area (EEA) and the European Convention on Human Rights.[24] In short, international law, in spite of (and indeed because of) its fragmentation, is characterized by equivalence as much as it is by conflict.

The study group attempted to look at the theoretical and practical dimensions of MSENs. It aimed to explore how MSENs have been treated by law-applying agencies, such as international tribunals and domestic courts applying international law,[25] and to consider the relative degrees of success offered by different courses of action. Its work also tried to assess the criteria for identifying points of similarity and difference among MSENs and the tendency to attribute to them either independent or mutually-subsumed existence. From the outset, it was clear to the study group that MSENs are not monolithic. They differ with respect to the types of

[17] See, eg, the Climate Change and Ozone Treaties and the 1979 Long-Range Transboundary Air Pollution Treaty. United Nations Framework Convention on Climate Change (adopted 9 May 1992, entered into force 21 March 1994) 1771 UNTS 107; Convention on Long Range Transboundary Pollution (adopted 17 November 1979, entered into force 16 March 1983) (1979) 18 ILM 1442.

[18] See eg, Council Directive (EC) 84/360/EEC [1984] OJ L188/20.

[19] See eg *Lopez Ostra v Spain* (App no 16798/90 (1994) ECHR 46.

[20] This could derive from the good-neighbourliness principle. See UN Charter, art 74.

[21] See, eg, *Legal Consequences of the Construction of a Wall in the Occupied Palestinian Territory* [2004] ICJ Rep 136.

[22] See the 1955 Treaty of Amity, Economic Relations and Consular Rights between the United States and Iran, explored in the ICJ *Oil Platforms* case: *Oil Platforms (Iran v US)* [2003] ICJ Rep 161.

[23] See, eg, N DiMascio and J Pauwelyn, 'Nondiscrimination in Trade and Investment Treaties: Worlds Apart or Two Sides of the Same Coin?' (2008) 102 *American Journal of International Law* 48.

[24] See, eg, C Foley, *Combating Torture: A Manual for Judges and Prosecutors* (Colchester, Human Rights Centre, 2003) 8–10.

[25] See, in this volume, A Nollkaemper, 'The Power of Secondary Rules to Connect the International and National Legal Orders', below p 45.

legal sources that gave rise to normative parallelism (for example, overlapping treaty-regimes; different sources of international law, such as custom or treaty law; different substantive branches of international law). In addition, different MSENs will often have different 'background' principles and rules (dispute settlement provisions, reservations, applicability prerequisites and principles of interpretation) and different institutional framework for application. The way MSENs are treated may also differ between specific normative regimes.

While addressing these MSEN-related issues, a central question that emerged was whether there exist unifying characteristics that cut across the various categories and expressions of multi-sourced obligations. There is no 'neat' answer to this question, but the following three features could be discerned in most, if not all, of the study group's discussions (and are further expressed in the specific studies included in this book).

First, MSENs are never fully equal, and it is the differences among them that are particularly interesting. Different political, institutional and legal contexts – the background on which MSENs are created and upon which they operate – are often determinative of the ways in which they act and relate to each other. While the nucleus of all MSENs is their equivalence, the accompanying contexts accentuate the differences between them.

Secondly, the contextual and other differences between otherwise equivalent MSENs present international legal actors (including judicial decision-makers) with choices to be made regarding the relative emphasis placed on each relevant MSEN in analysis, interpretation, application, argumentation and adjudication. These choices provide actors with flexibility, allowing them to pursue their goals by shifting between regimes relatively easily.[26] However, this can cause the legal framework of some MSENs to be weakened or neglected, or create conflict when different actors disagree about the relationship between applicable MSENs. In many MSENs, the line between smoothly-running normative equivalence on one hand, and conflictuality between norms or institutions, that stems from the contextual differences embedded in equivalence on the other, can be very thin indeed.

Thirdly, with all the eclectic diversity of MSENs, the analytical menu of methods through which international law can treat normative equivalence and resolve the operative difficulties that it raises appears to be restricted to a number of discrete strategies, that should be carefully studied in each case.

Let us now elaborate on these features.

[26] Used broadly, the term 'regime shifting' describes a range of situations in which international actors opt to shift the focus of legal and political activity relating to a certain issue, to the institutional forum or normative regime whose context and background rules better serve their interests or goals. This shift can impact processes, outcomes and the relevant regimes as well. See LR Helfer, 'Regime Shifting: The TRIPs Agreement and New Dynamics of International Intellectual Property Lawmaking' (2004) 29 *Yale Journal of International Law* 1.

IV SAME, SAME, BUT DIFFERENT? CONTEXT AND THE DIFFERENCES EMBEDDED IN MSENS

One cross-cutting theme examined by the study group is that MSENs are in fact never fully equal, and that it is the differences between them, such as in their contexts that create their complexity. Similar MSENs may differ in their precise formulation, but even identically phrased norms entail different normative consequences resulting from the distinct political, normative and institutional environments in which they function.[27] On the normative plane, MSENs are influenced by different background principles and rules such as reservations, dispute settlement provisions, exemptions from liability and interpretative principles that apply directly to some, but not all equivalent instruments or regimes. In addition, MSENs may come under the jurisdiction of different institutions, which may serve only partly overlapping constituencies and different political agendas through distinct decision-making processes.[28] This is the case, for example, when a norm becomes 'multi-sourced' and equivalence is established by way of direct incorporation, such as when a regional trade agreement directly references and incorporates rules from the WTO,[29] or when the TRIPS Agreement incorporates provisions of non-WTO intellectual property treaties.[30]

This observation, of the differences embedded in MSENs, is crucial to our understanding of MSENs. It is the varying political, normative and

[27] For a clear exposition of this notion, see *MOX Plant (Ireland v UK)* (2002) 41 ILM 405, 413 ('Considering that, even if the OSPAR Convention, the EC Treaty and the Euratom Treaty contain rights or obligations similar to or identical with the rights or obligations set out in the Convention, the rights and obligations under those agreements have a separate existence from those under the Convention; considering also that the application of international law rules on interpretation of treaties to identical or similar provisions of different treaties may not yield the same results, having regard to, inter alia, differences in the respective contexts, objects and purposes, subsequent practice of parties and travaux preparatoires'). For additional discussion of different aspects of the MOX Plant dispute, see in this volume, N Lavranos, 'The OSPAR Convention, the Aarhus Convention and EC Law: Normative and Institutional Fragmentation on the Right to Access to Environmental Information', below p 143.

[28] For an analysis of the impact of different jurisdictional provisions on MSENs, see in this volume, L Bartels, 'Jurisdiction and Applicable Law Clauses: Where does a Tribunal find the Norms Applicable to the Case before it?', below p 115.

[29] See eg, North American Free Trade Agreement (NAFTA) (adopted 17 December 1992, entered into force 1 January 1994) art 103, (1993) 32 ILM 289.

[30] See eg, Agreement on Trade Related Aspects of Intellectual Property Rights, Marrakesh Agreement Establishing the World Trade Organization, art 1(3) (adopted 15 April 1994, entered into force 1 January 1995) (1994) 33 ILM 81. For a discussion of other examples of cross-regime incorporation, see in this volume, B Pirker, 'Interpreting Multi-Sourced Equivalent Norms: Judicial Borrowing in International Courts', below p 93 and G Harpaz, 'EU Review of UN Anti-Terror Sanctions: Judicial Juggling in a Four-Layer, Multi-Sourced, Equivalent-Norms Scenario', below p 171. For a discussion of the interplay between TRIPs and investment treaties, see in this volume, M Paparinskis, 'Equivalent Primary Rules and Differential Secondary Rules: Countermeasures in WTO and Investment Protection Law', below p 259.

institutional contexts that make MSENs truly equivalent, rather than equal – like the parts of a biblical verse. In every set of MSENs, there is a core of equivalence, but also a measure of difference. In many cases – perhaps even most cases – this difference will have little practical effect. After all, the conduct mandated or prohibited by the MSENs is basically the same (ie, pointing in the 'same direction'). Nevertheless, one cannot foresee the entire universe of cases that arise in the relations between parties, and at some step along the way, a circumstance may arise in which the contextual difference between MSENs may become crucially dispositive.

Certainly, this suggests that there is no such thing as 'perfect' or 'true' MSENs (that are equivalent in every aspect, including context), as opposed to 'imperfect' or 'false' MSENs, whose equivalence is greatly reduced by contextual differences.[31] The existence of some differences is in fact inherent in MSENs.[32]

One might therefore wish to refine the definition of MSENs somewhat by stipulating that they encompass norms that are prima facie similar or identical in their normative content. This might be useful, because the differences between MSENs – and more importantly, those contextual differences that might give rise to difficulties of application – might not be self-evident or apparent from a casual review. This does not necessarily mean that the eventual revelation that a meaningful difference, even a conflict, exists between the normative or contextual elements of two particular MSENs, causes them to lose their 'MSEN'-ness. These differences do not turn them into conflicting norms, whose relationship presumes conflict. In contrast, MSENs are norms which on their face are presumed to be mutually reinforcing, even though at some level of analysis and with certain factual patterns there might emerge an inconsistency between them.

V OIL OR SAND IN THE GEAR SHIFT? MSENS AS THE TRANSMISSION SYSTEM OF INTERNATIONAL LAW

Acknowledging the inherent gaps between MSENs highlights the indeterminacy of the relationships between them and their normative outcomes.

[31] E Denters and T Gazzini distinguish between 'identical MSENs' and 'similar MSENs' (see in this volume, 'Multi-Sourced Equivalent Norms from the Standpoint of Governments', below p 69). The former would still be distinct on the basis of differences in background principles.

[32] Indeed, as a general matter, one might treat the idea of *effet utile* or 'effective interpretation' as a general principle of interpretation (see, eg, I Van-Damme, *Treaty Interpretation by the WTO Appellate Body* (Oxford, Oxford University Press, 2009) 275–78), and argue that there must be some difference of consequence between two identical norms governing relations between the same parties, even if the difference is not apparent on its face, because the parties to the MSENs saw fit to enact the same rule not in order to create redundancy, but rather to add to the normative environment that governs the relations between them.

This indeterminacy means that international actors engaged with MSENs – states, non-state actors, international organizations, domestic and international tribunals – are granted alternatives and posed with dilemmas that add important dimensions to the regular palette of legal and policy choices. When differences emerge – especially contextual or 'second-order' differences – between otherwise equivalent norms, actors may opt to privilege or emphasize one norm (or regime) over another, or to couch the relationship between these norms in ways that are conducive to their interests, needs or values (such a choice may also be influenced by sociological factors).[33] These are choices to be made, and with implications, at both the legal-normative level and the political-governance level. What set of secondary rules should be invoked or given precedence and why? Which normative or institutional regime will ultimately govern the conduct in question and emerge as the more influential one? Of course, these questions may be considered from a variety of theoretical perspectives: legal, rational choice, or social-constructivist perspectives, and diverse practical ones.[34] The important general point to be made here is that MSENs provide actors with a flexibility that would not exist otherwise.

One aspect of this flexibility, that has pros and cons, is the facilitation of regime shifting – the transfer of relative weight between normative or institutional settings. MSENs can act in this regard like the transmission system of a car, transmitting power from one regime to another. However, the inherent differences between MSENs, in conjunction with the preferences of actors, determine where the centre of gravity eventually lies, potentially changing some of the legal and political balances which originally underplayed some of the relevant international norms. For example, if both international human rights law and international humanitarian law include an obligation to minimize civilian casualties during armed conflicts,[35] but only the former provides individuals who were harmed with effective remedies, one might expect gradual attempts to apply human rights norms also in dispute settlement proceedings relating to armed conflict situations, thereby putting the traditional equilibrium between the rights and obligations of the parties to armed conflicts under

[33] For a discussion, see in this volume, M Hirsch, 'The Interaction between International Investment Law and Human Rights Treaties: A Sociological Perspective', below p 211.

[34] For a related discussion, see in this volume, R Michaels and J Pauwelyn, 'Conflict of Norms or Conflict of Laws? Different Techniques in the Fragmentation of International Law', below p 19.

[35] See, eg, Protocol Additional to the Geneva Conventions of 12 August 1949, and Relating to the Protection of Victims of International Armed Conflicts (adopted 8 January 1977, entered into force 7 December 1978) 1125 UNTS 3, art 51(2) (AP I). ('The civilian population as such, as well as individual civilians, shall not be the object of attack. Acts or threats of violence the primary purpose of which is to spread terror among the civilian population are prohibited'); International Covenant on Civil and Political Rights, (adopted 16 December 1966, entered into force 23 March 1976) 999 UNTS 171, art 6 (ICCPR).

increased pressure.[36] This may also have implications for the allocation of power among institutions, as institutional frameworks more sympathetic to human rights issues would be incrementally empowered by interested parties, at the expense of humanitarian law applying institutions.

This may be viewed as a positive development, but clearly, such a shift from one regime to another – that is both possible and legitimate because of the equivalence of the two – entails legal complications resulting from other contextual differences between them, that may sow the seeds of undesirable legal conflict (for example, in the methods of interpretation of human rights and humanitarian norms, gaps in the expertise of human rights courts in humanitarian law, unavailability of defences existing in humanitarian law in human rights litigation, etc). Moreover, while the capacity to manipulate MSENs as a normative 'transmission system' between rules and regimes can empower and enhance certain MSENs (as in the civilian casualties example above), it also provides parties to MSENs and other law-appliers with the ability to evade the application of important sets of background principles or other elements of MSENs, and to attempt to bypass significant institutions (and thereby the political frameworks they represent). This increased flexibility also carries considerable risks, making differences between MSENs act as sand in the same gear shift oiled by normative equivalence. Generally, the work of the study group demonstrates that there are two main problems that may arise in this respect, ie: (a) that different parties or other actors will select mutually incompatible background principles and institutions, thus creating a potential for normative or institutional confusion and conflict; and (b) that regime shifting on the basis of MSENs will upset some of the more delicate equilibriums underlying the primary norms in question. The problems are highly interrelated.

The first type of problem occurs when different actors with different preferences or decision-making patterns use the same MSENs to move in different directions. This might have quite legitimate causes. For example, as Denters and Gazzini demonstrate in their contribution to this volume, tribunals and governments have different perspectives and approaches to the resolution of differences between MSENs that derive from their distinct institutional roles.[37] As a result, a court might use normative equivalence in order to retain the discussion of a particular question within its

[36] See, eg, B Bowring, 'Fragmentation, *Lex Specialis* and the Tensions in the Jurisprudence of the European Court of Human Rights' (2009) 14 *Journal of Conflict and Security Law* 485; Y Shany, 'Human Rights and Humanitarian Law as Competing Legal Paradigms for Fighting Terror' in O Ben Naftali (ed), in XIX/1 *Collected Courses of the Academy of European Law: Human Rights and International Humanitarian Law* (forthcoming 2010).

[37] See Denters and Gazzini, above (n 31). See also Lavranos, above (n 27).

jurisdiction, (as in the ICJ *Nicaragua* case,[38] or in *Oil Platforms*[39]) or in order to preserve the normative exclusivity of its system of allegiance (like the WTO Appellate Body did with respect to the precautionary principle in the *Hormones* dispute).[40] Different tribunals can interpret the relationship between the same MSENs in different ways (indeed, a tribunal might try to sidestep the entire incidence of MSENs by choosing a restrictive approach to the issue before it; nevertheless, the potential for confusion does not necessarily disipate).[41] Still, governments may view MSENs as tickets to 'selective compliance',[42] through which they too can follow one MSEN and detract from another. Overall, when one focuses only on the differences between MSENs – the sand in the gear shift box – these institutional gaps make MSENs very similar to simple normative or institutional conflicts, which is the subject-matter of fragmentation.

The second type of problem occurs when a shift facilitated by an MSEN creates conflict between contextual, second-order norms. For example, if a reservation to a treaty could be circumvented through the invocation of a parallel customary norm or another treaty norm that is not technically covered by the reservation, then the object and purpose of the original reservation has been frustrated. Similarly, it is questionable whether a party would have accepted a specific primary norm belonging to one legal regime had it anticipated at the time that the norm would be subject to the jurisdiction of another institution operating under a different legal regime, which represents a less politically hospitable forum for the party in question. At the same time, a reverse approach of excessive restraint in the application of MSENs across regimes may raise comparable difficulties. For example, refusing to apply an MSEN to which no reservation had been attached, just because the parallel MSEN had been subject to reservation, extends, in effect, the reservation to the parallel regime and disrupts the internal equilibrium of the first regime. In the same vein, depriving institutions from jurisdiction over parallel MSENs undermines their powers to definitively pronounce on the legal rights and obligations of the parties.

In sum, international MSENs are comprised of equivalences and differences that create legal and political alternatives for actors and law-appliers. These alternatives can be seen as enhancing flexibility and enabling regime shifts that may in some cases strengthen international normativity. Conversely, this flexibility can provide states with fertile ground for pursuing self-interested and manipulative behaviour, manoeuvring between

[38] *Military and Paramilitary Activities in and against Nicaragua* (*Nicaragua v US*) [1986] ICJ Rep 14, 94.

[39] *Oil Platforms*, above (n 22) 181–82.

[40] WTO, *European Communities-Measures Concerning Meat and Meat Products (Hormones) – Report of the Appellate Body* (16 January 1998) WT/DS26/AB/R, Pt VI.

[41] See Lavranos' analysis of the OSPAR arbitration panel in Lavranos, above (n 27).

[42] See Denters and Gazzini, above (n 31).

MSENs in ways that accentuates conflicts between second-order norms. This diversity of possible dynamics creates a complex environment in which difficult choices concerning the needs and methods of regulating and harmonizing MSENs must be taken.

VI WHAT'S ON THE MENU? WAYS OF REGULATING INTERACTION BETWEEN MSENS

Finally, although the MSEN phenomenon is prevalent in international law across many fields and norm types, and in interaction with many actors and institutions, the study group found a high degree of correlation between the methods that have been employed in different cases in order to regulate normative equivalence. Three principal models of regulation emerge, and although it is difficult, if not impossible, to predict which model will be used by which actor and under which circumstances, these models constitute the operative menu for dealing with MSENs.

A The 'Dominant Norm/Regime' (or *Lex Specialis*) Model

In this model, MSENs are deemed to be in a *lex specialis* type of relationship, in which the differences between them are resolved by opting to exclusively apply the terms of the dominant or particular norm. This model is typified by the *Southern Bluefin Tuna* case,[43] in which an arbitral tribunal held that the parties' jurisdictional obligations under the United Nations Convention on the Law of the Sea (UNCLOS) are subsumed by a regional fisheries agreement that constituted a UNCLOS-implementing arrangement (and therefore, in substance, created an MSEN situation of global/ regional equivalence). In reaching that decision, the tribunal compared the competing legal prescriptions found in the two relevant instruments and selected, pursuant to rules of interpretative precedence, the most influential norm. The dominant norm then governed all situations over which it was potentially applicable, and its contextual attributes crossed over to other regimes and overrode the background rules which would have otherwise applied (in that case, the dispute settlement provisions of UNCLOS).

B The Cumulative Model

In this model, MSENs are viewed as constituting parts of the same fabric, although contextual differences may apply only to parts of it. This

[43] UNCLOS, Arbitral Tribunal (4 August 2000), *Southern Bluefin Tuna* (2000) 39 ILM 1359.

model may be demonstrated by the 1986 *Nicaragua* judgment,[44] in which the ICJ held that a US reservation, which barred the Court from relying on the UN Charter for the purpose of jurisdiction, did not have the effect of blocking reliance on an equivalent customary norm that established jurisdiction through another instrument. This decision thus represents a *cumulative* model, ie, it views MSENs as simultaneously applicable in substance, while there is no crossover of background rules (in the *Nicaragua* case, reservations) from one regime to the other (in contrast to the dominant norm regime, in which only one regime applied, period).

C The Integrative Model

This model may be illustrated by the *Legality of Nuclear Weapons* Advisory Opinion,[45] in which the ICJ reached the conclusion that one of three alleged grounds of illegality of nuclear weapons – international humanitarian law – constituted *lex specialis,* but that all relevant norms should be construed in light of the parallel norms coming from other branches of law (in the circumstances of the case, international human rights law and international environmental law, which contain norms potentially governing the lawfulness of nuclear weapons) This opinion therefore represents an approach that seeks to harmonize, using interpretative means, between overlapping parallel regimes.[46] Another example of an integrative approach to MSENs can be found in *Oil Platforms,* where the ICJ resorted to the customary law of self defence in order to construe a parallel norm – the 'essential security interests' exception in the Iran-US Treaty of Amity.

The rules of interpretation in international law appear to be flexible enough to entertain these three approaches, even in the same situation, leaving decision-makers with considerable leeway in determining the normative path that they intend to follow.

VII CONCLUSIONS

Normative equivalence is as ubiquitous in international law as poetic parallelism is in biblical poetry. Although we do not expect MSENs to become a frequently used term in international legal discourse, we have found the idea of (re-)formulating international law and politics in their mould to be a very clear prism through which to view problems of normative

[44] *Military and Paramilitary Activities,* above (n 38).

[45] *Legality of the Threat or Use of Nuclear Weapons* (Advisory Opinion) [1996] ICJ Rep 226.

[46] Essentially the same approach has been embraced in WTO cases such as the 1998 *Shrimp/Turtle* case. *US–Import Prohibition of Certain Shrimp and Shrimp Products* (1998) 38 ILM 118 (AB Report).

fragmentation and institutional governance in international law today – no less so than the more commonly referred to problems of normative contradiction and institutional competition. Indeed, as we have shown in this introduction, MSENs are not free from either conflict or competition; still, they have strong, at times dominant equivalent features. Ultimately, it may very well be that MSENs offer a more frequent and complicated challenge to the coherence of international law than directly clashing norms.

In this book there are many analyses of various MSENs, with discussions of both their normative and institutional aspects, the problems that they give rise to and the different solutions that can be provided. By no means, however, are these analyses exhaustive. Indeed, many questions remain unexplored and unanswered. The task of mapping and typifying the different responses to problems raised by MSENs is too vast to be covered by a single study group and a single collection of studies. It is our hope, however, that legal researchers who encounter scenarios that conform to MSEN formats will find the methodology and analytical language developed in this book useful in approaching their own research. It is our even greater hope that this exploration of normative equivalence will, however modestly, contribute to the vision of justice and righteousness, as waters and streams.

Part I

MSENs and the Fragmentation of International Law

2

*Conflict of Norms or Conflict of Laws?: Different Techniques in the Fragmentation of International Law**

Ralf Michaels and Joost Pauwelyn

I INTRODUCTION

'INTERNATIONAL LAW IS a legal system'. Thus begins the first of 42 conclusions formulated by the ILC study group on the fragmentation of international law.[1] The sentence is more a postulate than an actual conclusion, and a disputed one at that. After all, much of the current discussion on the fragmentation of international law is motivated precisely by the suspicion that international law might actually not be a system, at least not an internally coherent one the way we think of domestic legal systems. The study group thus postulates an answer to an *ontological* question – whether international law actually is a system – in order to answer the *technical* question of how to deal with conflicts and interrelation between its rules.

This is difficult enough for the kind of conflicts that the report identifies as the most relevant ones: conflicts between 'principles that may often point in different directions . . . new types of treaty clauses or practices that may not be compatible with old general law or the law of some other specialized branch'.[2] The discovery of Multi-Sourced Equivalent Norms

* This chapter is an attempt to see whether we can find common ground from our different starting points. For Ralf Michaels, this starting point lies in a project, currently pursued with Karen Knop and Annelise Riles, on Private International Law as a general theory of law. Some thoughts in this chapter draw on discussions from that larger project. For Joost Pauwelyn, this work emerges from his earlier work on conflict of norms in International Public Law.

[1] International Law Commission (ILC), 'Conclusions of the Work of the Study Group on the Fragmentation of International Law: Difficulties arising from the Diversification and Expansion of International Law, Report of the 58th Session' (2006) GAOR 61st Session UN Doc A/61/10, ch XII, 400–23, paras 233–51 (ILC, Fragmentation Report); see also 'Conclusions of the Study Group', *ibid*, para 251 (conclusion no 1) (at 407).

[2] ILC, 'Fragmentation of International Law: Difficulties arising from the Diversification and Expansion International Law. Report of the Study Group of the International Law

(MSENs)[3] suggests that the challenge is even more fundamental: even where rules in different regimes do *not* point in different directions, the question which of them is applicable remains. This suggests that the fragmentation of international law does not only imply a plurality of values; it also implies a plurality of techniques.

The assumption for many participants in the debate, what we call here the ontological question – whether international law is a coherent system – has not only technical but predominantly normative implications, or is even itself, really, a normative question. There exists a widespread normative preference for coherence over fragmentation, order over disorder, system over plurality. We do not go so far as to claim that the question of whether international law is a coherent system or not is normatively irrelevant. However, we do think that its normative implications are overrated, and that the main problems with fragmentation are technical, not normative, in nature. If the resolution of conflicts were only possible within a coherent system, then the question of whether international law is such a system would have direct normative implications. If, by contrast, it could be shown that conflicts can be resolved also in the absence of one coherent system, then what looked like a normative question would become a technical one: the prime question is then, which of the different types of technical rules do we have to apply to deal with the conflict?

The ILC report rightly points out that, in order to deal with fragmentation, 'it is useful to have regard to the wealth of techniques in the traditional law'.[4] The rules it refers to, and limits its inquiry to, are rules concerning conflicts *within* a legal system. We refer to this approach as 'conflict of norms', with reference to the title and type of analysis conducted by one of us in an earlier book.[5] These rules are rules on hierarchical relations, presumptions of statutory interpretation and principles of balancing (for example, on how different rules *within* Belgian law interrelate). Use of these rules appears to presuppose that international law is a system comparable to a domestic legal system. Indeed, it appears scholars often *want* to see international law as a system (rather than a pluralist or fragmented agglomeration) in part because this makes it possible to apply traditional conflict-of-norms rules (such as the principles of *lex posterior* or *lex specialis*). When the report of the ILC study group discusses ideas of legal pluralism, for example, it does so with the concern that such plural-

Commission. Finalized by M Koskenniemi' (13 April 2006) UN Doc A/CN.4/L.682, 14, para 15 (Koskenniemi Report).

[3] See in this volume, T Broude and Y Shany, 'The International Law and Policy of Multi-Sourced Equivalent Norms' in T Broude and Y Shany (eds), *Multi-Sourced Equivalent Norms in International Law* (Oxford, Hart Publishing, 2011) p 1.

[4] ILC, Fragmentation Report above (n 1) 406, para 250.

[5] J Pauwelyn, *Conflict of Norms in Public International Law: How WTO Law Relates to Other Rules of International Law* (Cambridge, Cambridge University Press, 2003). Note that 'norms' is here not opposed to law.

ism will be incompatible with the systematic approach and the rules on conflict of norms it encompasses.[6] Its main author, Martti Koskenniemi, has elsewhere expressed his normative concerns over such pluralism.[7]

As a matter of fact, rules to deal with pluralism exist, and conflict-of-norms rules are not the only set of rules for conflicts. Another set of rules in 'traditional law' concerns conflicts *between* legal systems (which we will refer to as 'conflict of laws' or 'private international law solutions'). These rules are typically rules of domestic law that determine which of several domestic substantive laws should apply (for example, whether Belgian or German law applies to a fact pattern), according to certain factors, for example, the location of the object in question or the nationality of the parties.

Both sets of rules – 'conflict-of-norms' rules and 'conflict-of-laws' rules – were traditionally developed with regard not to international law, but to domestic legal systems. Rules on hierarchical relations between rules and on systematic statutory interpretation were created within the context of domestic legal systems. Rules on conflict of laws are also mostly rules of domestic law (though they have at least in part been derived from principles of international law),[8] but they have been applied to conflicts between the laws of different states, not to conflicts between different treaties. Such conflict-of-laws rules have occasionally been considered for public international law, too. In 1953, Wilfred Jenks argued that 'some of the problems which [conflicts of law-making treaties] involve may present a closer analogy with the problem of the conflict of laws than with the problem of conflicting obligations within the same legal system'.[9] Philip Jessup, in his famous lectures on transnational law, also discussed the problem of applicable laws before international tribunals as one of choice of law and compared it explicitly with the task of the national judge in determining which law to apply.[10] More recently, Andreas Fischer-Lescano and Gunther Teubner have developed the idea that the national differentiation of law is now overlain by a sectorial differentiation and that conflicts

[6] Koskenniemi Report, above (n 2) 247, para 488.

[7] M Koskenniemi, 'Global Legal Pluralism: Multiple Regimes and Multiple Modes of Thought' (2005) 20–21: www.helsinki.fi/eci/Publications/MKPluralism-Harvard-05d%5B1%5D.pdf. A more positive assessment of such International Law pluralism is offered in D Kennedy, 'One, Two, Three Many Legal Orders: Legal Pluralism and the Cosmopolitan Dream' (2007) 3 *New York University Review for Law and Social Change* 641. See more generally, R Michaels, 'Global Legal Pluralism' (2009) 5 *Annual Review of Law and Social Science* 243, 249 and passim; see also I Voina-Motoc, 'Conceptions of Pluralism and International Law' in H Ruiz Fabri, E Jouannet and V Tomkiewicz (eds), *Select Proceedings of the European Society of International Law* 401 (Oxford, Hart, Publishing, 2008).

[8] A Mills, 'The Private History of International Law' (2006) 55 *International & Comparative Law Quarterly* 1; see also, R Michaels, 'Public and Private International Law: German Views on Global Issues' (2008) 4 *Journal of Private International Law* 121 with references.

[9] CW Jenks, 'The Conflict of Law-Making Treaties' (1953) 30 *British Yearbook of International Law* 401, 403; see also, *ibid*, 405–06.

[10] P Jessup, *Transnational Law* (New Haven, Yale University Press, 1956) 72 ff; see especially 96–97.

between sectorial laws – regimes – must, like conflicts between national laws, be dealt with through a system of conflict of laws.[11] One of us, in a relatively early book on the subject, briefly considered but rejected, for the time being, a private international law approach.[12]

That said, extensive discussions of when and how a private international law approach would actually work to resolve public international law conflicts do not exist. Jenks discusses conflict avoidance more than conflict resolution. Jessup uses tools that are not those of conflict of laws. Fischer-Lescano and Teubner argue that the special character of conflicts among regimes requires the development of substantive norms, without a satisfactory explanation as to why exactly this should be so.[13] Moreover, there is relatively little discussion on which of these two approaches is to be preferred under what circumstances. The reason may be that scholars writing in the field start from a certain assumption on the ontological challenge – namely, that international law is or should be a coherent system, or that it is not – and derive rules from that assumption.

In this chapter, we do not set out to place the ontological question of whether international law is a system at the beginning of the research. Rather, we begin with a presentation of the two different approaches and a discussion of the prerequisites for their respective applicability (sections II and III). We then discuss how these two approaches map on to the discussion of fragmentation of international law, without actually, at this stage, prioritizing one over the other. If anything, our claim would be that public international law conflicts are likely *sui generis*, with aspects of both conflict of norms and conflict of laws, and that to resolve this type of conflicts one can learn and borrow from both approaches (section IV). Finally, we take on the question of what this means for the systematic nature of international law (section V). All through this chapter, we do not offer a systematic analysis, but rather a number of examples to demonstrate the existence, and usefulness, of two very different sets of conflict rules.[14]

An important message of this chapter for public international lawyers is this: the now frequently voiced unease among public international

[11] A Fischer-Lescano and G Teubner, 'Regime Collisions: The Vain Search for Legal Unity in the Fragmentation of Global Law' (2004) 25 *Michigan Journal of International Law* 999.

[12] Pauwelyn, above (n 5) 8–10.

[13] Fischer-Lescano and Teubner, above (n 11) 1022–23.

[14] In all of this, we restrict our analysis to questions of applicable law. That is, we are not concerned with the question of which tribunal, if any, has jurisdiction. Nor do we address here the extent to which the jurisdictional question affects the question of the applicable law or vice versa. On questions of jurisdiction, *forum non conveniens* and other domestic law principles, see Y Shany, *The Competing Jurisdictions of International Courts and Tribunals* (Oxford, Oxford University Press, 2003); T Broude, 'Fragmentation(s) of International Law: On Normative Integration as Authority Allocation' in T Broude and Y Shany (eds), *The Shifting Allocation of Authority in International Law: Considering Sovereignty, Supremacy and Subsidiarity* (Oxford, Hart Publishing, 2008); J Pauwelyn and L Eduardo Salles, 'Forum Shopping Before International Tribunals: (Real) Concerns, (Im)Possible Solutions' (2009) 42 *Cornell International Law Journal* 77.

lawyers with traditional conflict-of-norms rules[15] is best answered with private-international-law solutions. Although certain traditional conflict-of-laws rules cannot be used *tel quel* because the connecting factors they rely on – places, people, governmental interests – cannot be applied to regimes, functionally refined conflict-of-laws rules promise to be more helpful. Another core message of this chapter, targeted this time at a private international law audience, is that conflict of laws can operate not only between the laws of states, but to resolve public international law conflicts, but not all of them and in a contextually adapted fashion.

II INTERACTIONS WITHIN LEGAL SYSTEMS: CONFLICT OF NORMS

A Solutions in Domestic Law

Legal systems provide their own tools to establish their internal coherence.[16] More than one rule may a priori be applicable to a set of facts. Institutionally, internal coherence is established mainly through highest courts. Doctrinally, the solution lies in legal rules that determine the relation between different norms. European law in the civil law tradition (which historically relied less on courts to establish internal coherence procedurally) has been particularly robust in developing a number of presumptions of statutory interpretation to resolve conflicts between norms, but similar solutions are found in the common law.

A first set of conflict rules acts at the level of hierarchy of norms. Thus, under the rule of lex superior *derogat legi inferiori*, the hierarchically superior rule trumps the hierarchically inferior. It is for this reason that constitutional law trumps ordinary statutory law, which in turn trumps common law rules; mandatory rules of contract law trump party agreements, and these agreements in turn trump subsidiary rules of contract law.

Where no such hierarchy of sources exists and rules are enacted in the same field, for example in contract law, a second set of conflict rules must be developed. As between more general and more specific rules, for example, the one with the more specific scope of application applies (*lex specialis derogate lege generali*). Thus, general contract law is trumped by the specific rules on consumer contracts on the one hand, or by those on commercial

15 See, eg, Pauwelyn, above (n 5) 367–80 (referring to 'the fiction of "legislative intent"' and difficulty of putting a time-label on a treaty in the context of the *lex posterior* principle as it applies in public international law) and Koskenniemi Report, above (n 2) 130, para 255 ('the argument from *lex posterior* or *lex specialis* [both conflict-of-norms rules] seems clearly more powerful between treaties within a regime than between treaties in different regimes. In the former case, the legislative analogy seems less improper than in the case of two treaties concluded with no conscious sense that they are part of the "same project"').

16 See K Kress, 'Coherence' in D Patterson (ed), *A Companion to Philosophy of Law and Legal Theory* (Oxford, Blackwell, 1996) 533.

contracts on the other. Under the rule of *lex posterior derogat lege anterior*, a later rule is presumed to trump an earlier rule. Both *lex specialis* and *lex posterior* are presumptions as to the intent of the lawmaker or legislator on the issue in question. Presumably, a lawmaker, in regulating a specific area, wants to create special rules that trump the general rules in the field. As a consequence, the presumption is that the latest and/or most specific legislative expression matters and prevails. According to the literal rule, similar terms in different statutes are in principle presumed to have the same meaning.

Finally, where rules with different functions are in conflict, the above, second set of conflict rules is of limited use. For example, rules of intellectual property may conflict with rules of antitrust law. Intellectual property rules give the owner a monopoly over a certain intangible good, whereas antitrust law sets out to combat monopolies. Rules on freedom of speech may conflict with rules on personal dignity. The solution in most legal systems is one of balancing of interests, though this has frequently been criticized.

B Prerequisites

All of this is well known. What is sometimes underappreciated is the extent to which the above 'conflict-of-norms' rules work smoothly only insofar as we can assume that (1) all legal rules in play coexist within a single overarching system and (2) the decision which rule to apply can be imputed, albeit by fiction, to a unitary lawmaker with a coherent legislative intent. This is why these rules are traditionally applied within legal systems, not between legal systems, and in a universe with a unitary lawmaker, not with many lawmakers.

Thus, the *lex superior* principle requires a common system within which a hierarchy of norms can be established; it does not function between systems. Take, for example, the famous Yahoo! case decided in 2000.[17] In that case, French courts decided, essentially, that Yahoo!, a Californian company, could be banned from enabling the auctioning of Nazi literature on its internet auction site, even though such a ban would be in conflict with the First Amendment of the US Constitution. Some authors have criticized this decision with the suggestion that the conflict between a statute and a constitutional rule must be resolved in favour of the Constitution.[18] Such reasoning would be perfectly adequate if the conflict had arisen within one legal system, either between the French Constitution and a French statute,

[17] *L'Union des Etudiants Juifs de France v Yahoo! Inc*, TGI Paris, 20 November 2000, *JurisClasseur Periodique*, édition générale – La Semaine Juridique, 2000 Actualités 2219 with note by J Gomez: www.juriscom.net/txt/jurisfr/cti/tgiparis20001120.pdf.

[18] A Ben-Ezer and AL Bendor, 'Conceptualizing Yahoo! v LCRA: Private Law, Constitutional Review, and International Conflict of Laws' (2004) 25 *Cardozo Law Review* 2089, 2111–12.

or between the US Constitution and a US statute. By contrast, where the conflict exists between a statute and a Constitution of two different legal systems (with two 'lawmakers' independent from each other), the argument becomes unconvincing, because no hierarchical relation exists: the French legislator is not subject to the requirements of the US Constitution, and the US Constitution does not, on its own force, reach into France. This does not mean that the French court should not have considered the US Constitution at all, or that the status of the US Constitution should play no role; only that the basis for this cannot be found in the *lex superior* principle.

Presumptions of statutory interpretation, which work well among rules on the same level of hierarchy within one system, are similarly dependent on the presumption of a uniform legislator, even if this presumption is fictitious. As between legal systems, they lose much of their plausibility. For example, the *lex specialis* rule is grounded in the presumption that a legislator, in regulating a specific case, wants to carve out an exception from the general rules existing for a set of matters.[19] As between countries or between national laws, it is hard to make a similar presumption. The French hate speech statute is more specific than the First Amendment, but it does not follow at all that it should therefore take priority as an exception to the First Amendment. Similar limitations exist for the *lex posterior* rule. The rule makes sense within one legal system, because the legislator can be presumed to legislate with knowledge of prior laws and thus with reference to those laws. This assumption is less warranted between legal systems.[20] It seems quite implausible to argue, for example, that the US Constitution must stand back merely because it is older than the French statute in question. Similarly, the assumption that similar terms in different statutes have a similar meaning (the 'literal rule') makes sense within one legal system that strives for internal consistency, because we can presume that the unitary lawmaker means the same thing with similar terms. The assumption is much harder to make between different legal systems. For example, as comparative lawyers have often warned us, contract in English law is not the same as *contrat* in French law;[21] it is not even the same in English law as in US law.

Finally, the balancing between rules serving different functions (for example, Belgian intellectual property law versus Belgian antitrust law)

[19] *Cf* B Simma and D Pulkowski, 'Of Planets and the Universe: Self-Contained Regimes in International Law' (2006) 17 *European Journal of International Law* 483, 489.

[20] A partial exception exists where statutes are written in explicit reaction to foreign laws, eg, British blocking clawback statutes against US judgments (see L Collins, 'Blocking and Clawback Statutes: The United Kingdom Approach' in L Collins (ed), *Essays in International Litigation and the Conflict of Laws* (Oxford, Oxford University Press, 1997) 333). Here, it is clear that these statutes trump US law within the British legal system, though this in itself is obviously not binding on US law.

[21] C Valcke, 'Divergence and Convergence among English, French, and German Conceptions of Contract' (2006) 16 *European Review of Private Law* 29.

is in principle linked to intra-systemic reasoning as well. Rational balancing requires an objective standard for the respective weight of each principle to be balanced.[22] If that standard cannot be derived from the intent of a unitary legislator, it must come from somewhere else, for example, a uniform standard of welfare maximization. As between legal systems, the problem is that the difference between the conflicting norms is typically a consequence of the fact that each of the systems uses a different 'objective standard' to define, weigh and ultimately balance the conflicting principles within its own system. Simplistically speaking, the US values freedom of speech higher than the need to ban anti-Semitic speech; the result of balancing speech and dignity within French law is different. Since balancing is a function of the relative weight of different principles, and this relative weight may be different within different legal systems, balancing between legal systems will often not resolve the conflict between these different balancing results.[23] Brainerd Currie in particular, as the inventor of the governmental interest analysis in the field of conflict of laws, opposed such balancing between legal systems precisely for this reason, because it ignored the policy choice made by the forum's legislator. In his view, a judge cannot balance the interests of its own legislator against those of another.[24] Indeed, most methods of conflict of laws (though not all)[25] oppose open balancing of interests and instead focus on the relative strength of policies. Similarly, the idea of finding a mix between different regimes, which Fischer-Lescano and Teubner propose for public international law conflicts, has been proposed occasionally as a solution for traditional choice-of-law problems.[26] However, most conflict-of-laws approaches eschew a mixture or compromise between different laws and instead designate either one or the other state's law to apply.

III INTERACTIONS BETWEEN LEGAL SYSTEMS: CONFLICT OF LAWS

A Solutions in Domestic Law

One reason, then, why conflicts between different legal systems are governed by different rules than are conflicts within one legal system, is that

[22] R Alexy, 'Balancing, Constitutional Review, and Representation' (2005) 3 *International Journal of Constitutional Law* 572, 575.

[23] See also, J Bomhoff, 'Balancing the Global and the Local: Judicial Balancing as a Problematic Topic in Comparative (Constitutional) Law' (2008) 31 *Hastings International & Comparative Law Review* 555.

[24] B Currie, 'Notes on Methods and Objectives in the Conflict of Laws' (1959) *Duke Law Journal* 171, 177.

[25] See, eg, JHC Morris, 'The Proper Law of a Tort' (1951) 64 *Harvard Law Review* 881, 890.

[26] AT von Mehren, 'Special Substantive Rules for Multi-State Problems' (1974) 88 *Harvard Law Review* 347; GB Dinwoodie, 'The Development and Incorporation of International Norms in the Formation of Copyright Law' (2001) 63 *Ohio State Law Journal* 733.

the rules developed for intra-systemic conflict do not work well in the context of inter-systemic conflict. There is no hierarchy between different legal systems, except for the relative hierarchy that each system may claim for itself over others. There is no overarching system within which rules on statutory interpretation could achieve coherence. There is no uniform legislative intent on which the resolution could be based. There is no neutral or mutually accepted standard under which different values could be balanced.

The alternative is not anarchy but private international law. In private international law, several methods exist on how to resolve conflicts *between* legal systems. With gross simplification, it may be appropriate to present three methods: the 'traditional method', 'governmental interest analysis' and 'functional analysis'. While the first two are tied to conflicts between state laws, the third one is more promising for international law.

The first method, here called the 'traditional method', exists in both Europe and the United States, with some differences that need not concern us here.[27] Under the traditional method, the applicable law is determined on the basis of conflict-of-laws rules designed for different areas of law in the abstract, without regard to the content of the substantive law. Essentially, determining the applicable law is a three-step endeavour. In a first step, the matter in question must be characterized as one of contract law, tort law, procedure, etc, so the applicable choice-of-law rule (for example, that for contract or tort) can be determined. In a second step, application of this choice of law leads to the determination of the applicable law on the basis of a connecting factor. Most of these connecting factors are either territorial (the place of the tort for matters of tort, the place of performance for matters of contract law, etc) or personal (the law of nationality or of domicile for matters of personal status, etc). In a third and final step, the law so determined is applied unless its application would violate the public policy of the forum law.

A good example of this three-step analysis is provided by the Supreme Court of Delaware in *Folk v York-Shipley*, which applied this inter-systemic method to a conflict between the laws of different US states.[28] The plaintiff, a Delaware domiciliary whose husband had died in a car collision in Pennsylvania, sued for loss of her husband's consortium. Such a cause of action existed in Delaware's law but not in Pennsylvania's law. The Court first had to characterize this issue as one of tort law (liability for a car accident) or one of family law (injury to a marriage): a tort claim would be governed by the law of the place of the injury, whereas a family law claim

[27] On differences, see R Michaels, 'The New European Choice-of-Law Revolution' (2008) 82 *Tulane Law Review* 1607, 1610–16.

[28] *Folk v York-Shipley* 9 NY 2d 34, 211 (1961). Note that private international law rules apply not only among the laws of different nation states, but among the laws of different states of the United States.

could arguably have been governed by the law of the common spousal domicile, which was Delaware. Once the issue was characterized as one of tort law, in a second step the place of the injury had to be determined and was determined to be the place of the car accident (Pennsylvania), not the place where the wife lived and where arguably her consortium was lost (Delaware). In a third step, finally, the Delaware court determined that the law of Pennsylvania applied. The court did not discuss, though it could have, whether Pennsylvania law should remain inapplicable because it violated a fundamental policy of Delaware so it would.

A second approach, developed in opposition to the traditional method described above, is called 'governmental interest analysis'. The starting point for this method is the 'governmental' interest of a state in having its own law applied. Hence, the substance of the respective laws provides the starting point of the analysis (though their respective quality or desirability is not normally a criterion). Here, the first step is to determine which rules of law claim applicability, in view of both their text and of whether the respective legislative intent would be furthered by their application. If more than one state is interested in having its law applied and their laws differ, the resulting 'true conflict' must be resolved, and various suggestions have been made for how such a conflict can be resolved.

Perhaps the most important solution is that of 'comparative impairment': as between two conflicting laws, the judge should apply the law that would be more impaired by non-application.[29] An example can be seen in *Tucci v Club Méditerranée SA*.[30] Tucci, a Californian citizen, had been injured during his employment at a vacation camp operated by French defendant Club Méditerranée in the Dominican Republic. Under California law, Tucci had a tort claim because Club Méditerranée had no insurance with a company authorized in California. Under the law of the Dominican Republic, by contrast, workers' compensation was the only available remedy. The court held that the law of the Dominican Republic established a quid pro quo between employers and employees by giving employees easy access to compensation while shielding employers from tort liability. This quid pro quo would be severely impaired if Tucci was granted a tort claim under Californian law. By contrast, if the law of the Dominican Republic applied and Tucci's claims were limited to those under workers' compensation, California's interest would be insignificantly impaired: California's interest in making sure that employees are adequately insured was fulfilled because Club Méditerranée in fact had insurance, albeit with a French, not a Californian insurer. Except for the insurance requirement, California provides for a quid pro quo comparable to that in the Dominican Republic. As a result, the law of the Dominican

[29] WA Baxter, 'Choice of Law and the Federal System' (1963) 16 *Stanford Law Review* 1.
[30] *Tucci v Club Mediterranee*, SA. 89 Cal.App.4th 180 (2001).

Republic was applied. Note that the court was not balancing policies; it balanced governmental interests.

Finally, more recent methods of conflict of laws adopt variants of a 'functional' perspective, even though the meaning of such a term and the method discussed under it differ among different authors and courts. In England, this means that the court should look for the proper law, the law most appropriate to govern the issue in question.[31] In the United States, Arthur von Mehren and Donald Trautman developed a multifaceted method to determine the applicable law on the basis of a number of factors, including the relevant strength of the policies of the involved states, a comparative evaluation of the asserted policies, a commonly held multi-state policy and the degree of effective control each state has over the matter.[32] In Europe, a functional approach led not to a rejection but a refinement of the traditional approach.[33] The three steps of the European approach outlined above were maintained but disentangled from the idea that the applicable law should be based on the power of the state over its territory and its citizens. In all of these functional approaches, the search is ultimately for the most appropriate law, the law with the closest connection to the facts, considering a variety of factors.

B Prerequisites

The above conflict-of-laws methods are quite closely linked to relations between different legal systems. They do not function well for intra-systemic conflicts. To explain why this is the case we must engage in a somewhat more elaborate discussion because the reasons are slightly different for each of the approaches discussed.

The traditional method is hard to apply to intra-systemic conflicts for two reasons. First, the approach presumes that the conflict occurs between two legal orders that are essentially complete, insofar as each of them must have rules in the same area of law: tort law, contract law, etc. Where, for example, the issue is characterized as one of tort law, the conflict is between two tort laws (for example, those of Pennsylvania and Delaware). Although such situations exist also, occasionally, within legal systems (for example, between general contract law and consumer contract law), a second reason makes the traditional approach difficult to apply to almost all intra-systemic conflicts. Under the traditional approach, the applicable law is determined through

31 FA Mann, 'The Proper Law in the Conflict of Laws' (1987) 46 *International and Comparative Law Quarterly* 437.

32 AT von Mehren and DT Trautman, *The Law of Multistate Problems* (Boston, Little, Brown, & Co, 1965); summarized in SC Symeonides, *The American Choice-of-Law Revolution: Past, Present and Future* (Leiden, Martinus Nijhoff Publishers, 2006) 28–29.

33 See Michaels, 'The New European Choice-of-Law Revolution', above (n 27) 1616.

either a territorial or a personal connecting factor, and such factors are often absent within legal systems.[34] The distinction between general contract law and consumer contract law, for example, cannot be made on the basis of territorial factors because they are not territorially distinct. It can be made on the basis of personal factors, depending on whether one party is a consumer or not.[35] Yet other conflicts – that between nuisance as a tort and property, for example – cannot.

Governmental interest analysis, in turn, is hard to apply to intra-systemic conflicts for a related reason: it assumes the coexistence of two governments whose interests are in question and potentially in conflict. As between two systems, each with its own government, it may be possible to determine which government has the greater interest. Within one legal system, this is impossible, as long as, at least in theory, the same government or 'lawmaker' is concerned.

The relative inadequacy of conflict-of-laws approaches for intra-systemic conflicts is no coincidence. Both the traditional method and governmental interest analysis are catered specifically to conflicts between states. The choice of connecting factors – territory, citizenship, governmental interests – mirrors closely the classical definition of the state as based on three elements: a territory, a population, a government structure.[36] In international law, by contrast, even where we can speak of different sub-systems or branches of international law (say, World Trade Organization (WTO) law and human rights law), these are not defined by territory or personality, and neither WTO law nor human rights law has its own government with conceivable governmental interests, so the criteria developed in these particular conflict-of-laws approaches are not applicable as such. Moreover, in conflicts between states, the use of such factors makes it possible to allocate issues among states precisely because these states resemble each other structurally and functionally – each state displays these abstract criteria, and each state generally performs the same functions. Within one system this method is often inapplicable because different statutes, different sectors of the law, do not display the same structure and do not perform the same function. If, for example, Belgian general contract law and Belgian consumer law performed the same functions one of them would be redundant and likely abolished.

The functional approach to conflict of laws appears to be less open to such criticism. The search for the proper law (or norm), the designation

[34] They have become problematic also for conflicts between domestic laws because of the diminished role of territoriality; see R Michaels, 'Globalizing Savigny? The State in Savigny's Private International Law and the Challenge of Europeanization and Globalization' in M Stolleis and W Streeck (eds), *Aktuelle Fragen politischer und rechtlicher Steuerung im Kontext der Globalisierung* (Baden-Baden, Nomos, 2007) 114: www.lsr.nellco.org/duke_fs/15/.

[35] Strictly speaking, the relevant factor is not a personal one, because what is characterized is not the person (is the person a consumer or not?) but the transaction (is it a consumer contract or not?).

[36] Michaels, 'Globalizing Savigny?' above (n 34) 121, 128–37.

of the applicable law (or norm) on functional grounds, appear, to some extent, to be possible regardless of whether we are within one system or between systems. Indeed, in this sense the functional approach to inter-systemic conflicts is in many ways not so different from the functional approach to intra-systemic conflicts discussed above. However, differences do exist. First, in intra-systemic conflicts the focus is on balancing laws (recall the IP versus antitrust law example); in inter-systemic conflicts it is on balancing respective regulatory interests (recall the notion of comparative impairment). Secondly, in intra-systemic conflicts, the functional approach aims at coherence; in inter-systemic conflicts, it aims at coordination. Thirdly, in intra-systemic conflicts, a functional approach can lead to mixed or compromise solutions; in inter-systemic conflicts, the aim is to maintain the internal integrity of each system by designating one or the other, and to minimize the consequences of frictions.

IV INTERACTIONS IN PUBLIC INTERNATIONAL LAW

Which of the above approaches is more adequate for conflicts within public international law or for fragmented public international law? At first sight, the core question may seem to be whether international law is more like one system or more like the combination of several systems: if it is one system, we should use a conflict-of-norms approach; if it is a combination of systems, we should use a private international law approach.

We do not think this is the most useful order of steps. Whether international law behaves like a system or not is in no small part determined by the very way in which relations between rules are handled. If we choose intra-systemic rules to govern relations between, say, the international trade and climate change regimes, this very choice constructs international law as a system. If we choose inter-systemic rules to address interactions, this constructs public international law as a plurality and a uniform system of public international law no longer emerges. This suggests, however, that we need not start with the ontological question – is public international law one system or not? Instead, we can start by addressing the pragmatic question of which rules work best for different contexts – conflict of norms or conflict of laws? – and determine in light of the answers how to understand public international law.

A General International Law and Treaties

One important type of interaction between rules of international law is that between treaties and general international law. Treaties, ratified by explicit consent by a certain number of states, are akin to contracts or contractual regimes. For example, the WTO treaty[37] and the Kyoto Protocol[38] are binding (only) on the states that agreed on and ratified these treaties. General international law (to some extent akin to codes and statutes or common law) encompasses the rules that states are 'born into' and that are binding on all states irrespective of explicit consent and subject matter. For example, general international law rules on treaty interpretation or state responsibility are by default applicable in both the context of the WTO and the Kyoto Protocol. General international law includes customary international law and general principles of law. To some extent, it includes also quasi-constitutional norms, in particular, *jus cogens*, from which no treaty can deviate.

For interactions and conflicts between treaties and general international law, intra-systemic conflict rules work well. The reason is simple but deserves repeating: this type of interaction closely resembles the interaction of rules within a single legal system. If general international law and, in particular, rules of *jus cogens* exist at all, they must by necessity, in order to be general, exist within – or constitute – a legal system. Denying the systemic character of international law implies denying the existence of general international law. Notably, the absence of a unitary lawmaker or source of authority is no counterargument – the unitary lawmaker is assumed as a fiction, as in Article 53 of the Vienna Convention on the Law of Treaties (Vienna Convention), which refers, to the 'international community of States' as the creator of *jus cogens*.[39]

In this intra-systemic constellation, the *lex superior* rule as we know it within domestic legal systems can be used for hierarchical relations. *Jus cogens* is then the 'higher law' prevailing over all other rules of the international law 'system'. In this sense, Article 53 of the Vienna Convention, which provides that '[a] treaty is void if, at the time of its conclusion, it conflicts with a peremptory norm of general international law', states little more than a definitional truism. This hierarchical structure – *jus cogens* trumps treaties – does not, in and of itself, resolve conflicts, because it does not define whether a given rule of general international law is *jus cogens* (and thus trumps treaties) or not. The notion of hierarchy itself does not even implicate that there must be any rules of *jus cogens* at all. However, it does capture

[37] By 'WTO treaty' we mean the final act embodying the results of the Uruguay Round of Multilateral Trade Negotiations, concluded in Marrakesh, Morocco, on 15 April 1994, published in WTO Secretariat, *The Results of the Uruguay Round of Multilateral Trade Negotiations, The Legal Texts* (Cambridge, Cambridge University Press, 2008).

[38] Kyoto Protocol to the United Nations Framework Convention on Climate Change, UN Doc FCCC/CP/1997/7/Add.1 (10 December 1997); 37 ILM 22 (1998).

[39] Vienna Convention on the Law of Treaties (adopted 23 May 1969, entered into force 27 January 1980) 1155 UNTS 331 (VCLT). For the counterfactual nature of international community, see DC Ellis, 'On the Possibility of "International Community"' (2009) 11 *International Studies Review* 1; see also, B Bliesemann de Guevara and FP Kühn, 'The "International Community" – Rhetoric or Reality?' (2009) 27 *Sicherheit und Frieden/Security and Peace* 73.

that to the extent that rules belong to *jus cogens*, conflicts between them and treaties are questions of hierarchy within a legal system.

Similarly, *lex specialis*, another intra-systemic conflict rule discussed above, works well for interactions between general international law and specific treaties (such as the WTO treaty). This is made explicit, for example, in Article 55 of the ILC 'Draft Articles on State Responsibility' (generally considered part of customary international law), which explicitly confirms, under the heading of '*lex specialis*', that

> [t]hese articles [ie, the ILC Draft Articles] do not apply where and to the extent that the conditions for the existence of an internationally wrongful act or the content or implementation of the international responsibility of a State are governed by special rules of international law.[40]

Finally, the presumption against conflict and the principle of 'systemic integration', as they are known in international law,[41] are (much like the intra-systemic literal rule discussed earlier) built on the premise that the legislator or specific group of contracting states must be presumed not to want to deviate from, or contradict, an earlier expression or rule. Again, for the intra-systemic type of interaction between general international law and treaties this presumption fits well: we can presume that, for example, two states that conclude a treaty did so with the background of general international law, to which they are both bound, in mind.

B Conflicts within One Branch of International Law

Similar considerations apply to norm relations within one branch of international law, such as within the WTO system or within the realm of the law of the sea.[42] For example, pursuant to Article 16(3) of the Marrakesh Agreement Establishing the WTO, this Agreement prevails over all other agreements within the WTO – an application of the intra-systemic *lex superior* principle.[43] Pursuant to the *lex specialis* rule, specific agreements on trade in goods (say, agriculture) prevail over the more general rules in the GATT. Article 311(1) of the 1982 UN Convention on the Law of the

[40] ILC, 'Draft Articles on State Responsibility, International Law Commission, Report of the 53rd Session' (2001) UN Doc A/56/10, 26 ff. See the commentary, *ibid*, 140–41.

[41] See VCLT, above (n 39) art 31(3)(c), directing that treaties must be interpreted 'taken into account, together with the context: . . . (c) any relevant rules of international law applicable in the relations between the parties'. On systemic integration, see also ILC, Fragmentation Report, above (n 1) paras 17 ff.

[42] We leave open the question what exactly constitutes a sub-branch of international law.

[43] 'In the event of a conflict between a provision of this Agreement and a provision of any of the Multilateral Trade Agreements, the provision of this Agreement shall prevail to the extent of the conflict'. See Marrakesh Agreement Establishing the World Trade Organization (adopted 15 April 1994, entered into force 1 January 1995) 1867 UNTS 154.

Sea (UNCLOS)[44] confirms the *lex posterior* principle when stating that '[t]his Convention shall prevail, as between States Parties, over the Geneva Conventions on the Law of the Sea of 29 April 1958'. In these cases, it is possible to assume a fictitious WTO or UN law of the sea 'legislator'. Granted, the actual negotiating parties change constantly – countries join and leave treaties as the United States did with UNESCO, withdrawing in 1984 and rejoining in 2003, or China, which left the GATT in 1950 and joined the WTO in 2001. Nonetheless, there is still enough institutional coherence, continuity and memory to make the fiction of a unitary law-maker plausible.

A broader application of the intra-systemic *lex posterior* rule is found in Article 30 of the Vienna Convention: for parties bound by two treaties, 'the earlier treaty applies only to the extent that its provisions are compatible with those of the later treaty' (Article 30(3)). Interestingly, the very title as well as paragraph 1 of Article 30 state explicitly that this *lex posterior* rule applies only between 'treaties relating to the same subject matter'. This suggests that the rule was written mainly with intra-systemic conflicts in mind, that is, successive treaties, within the same field or branch of international law, broadly speaking.[45] Indeed, although the *lex posterior* rule has occasionally been used to resolve conflicts between two branches of international law, this creates some unease. Take GATT: the original GATT[46] was concluded in 1947 so that the later Treaty of Rome[47] or Montreal Protocol[48] would arguably prevail over it; yet, when GATT 1994[49] was concluded, did this mean that GATT rules now all of a sudden trump the earlier EC Treaty or Montreal Protocol? And that with the recent Lisbon Treaty[50], GATT must again give way? One way to alleviate this unease is

[44] 'This Convention shall prevail, as between States Parties, over the Geneva Conventions on the Law of the Sea of 29 April 1958'. See United Nations Convention on the Law of the Sea (adopted 10 December 1982, entered into force 14 November 1994) 1833 UNTS 3 (UNCLOS).

[45] That said, the 'same subject matter' in art 30 could also be interpreted more broadly as covering any situation where two norms conflict or overlap including, eg, norms from different branches, such as trade and environmental treaties or NAFTA and WTO law: if they so conflict, can one not presume that they cover the 'same subject matter'? See Pauwelyn, above (n 5) 364. However, when applying the *lex posterior* rule to successive treaties in different fields or branches, the rule is often less convincing (*ibid*, 377 and Koskenniemi Report, above (n 2) para 255, quoted above in n 15).

[46] General Agreement on Tariffs and Trade 1947 (adopted 30 October 1947, entered into force 29 July 1948) 55 UNTS 194 (GATT).

[47] Treaty Establishing the European Economic Community (adopted 25 March 1957, entered into force 1 January 1958) 298 UNTS 11 (Treaty of Rome).

[48] Substances that Deplete the Ozone Layer (adopted 16 September 1987, entered into force 1 January 1989) 1522 UNTS 3 (Montreal Protocol).

[49] General Agreement on Tariffs and Trade 1994 (Annex 1A of the Marrakesh Agreement Establishing the World Trade Organization, adopted 15 April 1994, entered into force 1 January 1995) 1867 UNTS 187.

[50] European Union, Treaty of Lisbon amending the Treaty on European Union and the Treaty establishing the European Community, 13 December 2007 OJ (C 306) 50.

to rank the *lex specialis* principle above the *lex posterior* rule, so the more specific EC Treaty then prevails over GATT irrespective of GATT's timing. Yet, on what basis is one to decide that a treaty or specific norm is 'more specific'? Another option is to deny that in those situations we are talking about successive treaties in the first place by qualifying either or both of these treaties as 'continuing' or 'living' treaties (so that Article 30, by its very terms, does not apply).[51] Another, perhaps easier, explanation follows from our discussion earlier: Article 30 and *lex posterior* should presumptively not apply to interactions between different branches of international law because those interactions are more akin to inter-systemic conflict, a type of conflict not well suited for application of the *lex posterior* principle.

C Conflicts between Branches of International Law

The most pressing problems of public international law fragmentation concern conflicts between functional sub-systems or branches of international law – trade and environment, finance and human rights, etc. This is the context in which traditional intra-systemic conflict rules have proven unsatisfactory. As noted earlier, the mechanical *lex posterior* rule does not work well for conflicts between EU and WTO law or between GATT and multilateral environmental treaties and leads to surprising and often unconvincing results. The same is often true with respect to the *lex specialis* principle: how is one to decide whether, for example, a restriction on trade in an endangered species is more specifically covered by a WTO rule (as a trade matter) or by a CITES provision (as an environmental matter), given that no neutral higher authority exists to make this decision? And should treaty parties be able to undermine their WTO obligations merely by formulating a specific rule? This is, in our view, in no small measure due to the fact that this type of conflict is more akin to inter-systemic conflict for which intra-systemic conflict rules such as *lex posterior* and *lex specialis* were not designed.

There are two reasons why intra-systemic rules may be inadequate. The first is that the fiction of the unitary lawmaker, a prerequisite of these rules as we saw earlier, becomes increasingly implausible in the modern context of highly specialized, functional regimes. International trade, investment, environment and human rights law, each with their own international institution and/or club of negotiators, enforcement mechanisms, epistemic communities, related national ministries, NGOs and even academics, make it increasingly difficult to assume a unitary lawmaker with a

[51] See Pauwelyn, above (n 5) 489–90; J Pauwelyn, 'Bridging Fragmentation and Unity: International Law as a Universe of Inter-Connected Islands' (2004) 25 *Michigan Journal of International Law* 903, 908–09.

sufficient sense of institutional coherence, continuity and memory across these different branches. As a result, application of the intra-systemic rules of *lex superior, lex posterior* or *lex specialis* and the related quest for the genuine intent of international law's 'unitary lawmaker' have become increasingly strenuous.[52] This raises the obvious question whether and when to shift from such conflict-of-norms rules to conflict-of-laws rules.

The second reason, related to the first, is that when it comes to tensions between branches of international law it becomes difficult to devise a neutral perspective from which neutral conflict solutions could be formulated. Instead, each branch typically has its own rules or perspective for dealing with conflicts, and these rules or starting points often differ. For example, as noted earlier, there may be little point in trying to define the *lex specialis* in the interaction between trade agreements and environmental agreements: from the perspective of the trade agreement, the trade rule will be more specific (as in 'trade in' environmentally sensitive goods); from the viewpoint of the environmental treaty, the environmental rule will be more specific (as in 'environmental concerns' related to trade).

Sometimes, this neutrality problem becomes explicit in the text of conventions. GATT Article XXIV, for example, states that regional trade agreements such as NAFTA are subject to certain GATT principles, thereby setting up the GATT as *lex superior*. Article 103 of NAFTA, in contrast, explicitly states that in the event of conflict between GATT and NAFTA, NAFTA prevails. A similar tension exists between Article 103 of the UN Charter, setting up Charter obligations as *leges superiores*, and the WTO rule that WTO panels may not 'add to or diminish' from WTO covered agreements which some have read as a conflict rule defining WTO law as *lex superior*.[53] Other examples illustrating the problematic nature of *lex superior* in inter-systemic type conflicts encompass interactions between UN and EC treaties, EC law and the European Convention on Human Rights, UNCLOS and WTO law, etc. The problem of applying *lex superior* in this context is reminiscent of the Yahoo! example discussed earlier and the impossibility to establish a hierarchy between a French statute and a US constitutional rule.[54]

Sometimes, balancing is suggested as a solution. However, as discussed earlier, balancing as a conflict rule may work well within a system but not between sub-systems or branches of international law. If both international trade tribunals and environmental tribunals each engage in rational balancing, in the absence of a common, objective standard (available essentially only within a single 'system') the value judgments involved in balancing are likely to lead to different results, depending on the values or

[52] *Cf* Simma and Pulkowski, above (n 19) 483, 489.

[53] L Bartels, 'Applicable Law in WTO Dispute Settlement Proceedings' (2001) 35 *Journal of World Trade* 499.

[54] *L'Union des Etudiants Juifs de France v Yahoo! Inc*, above (n 17).

perspectives inherent in the trade system as opposed to the environmental system. For example, when the WTO balances trade as against environmental protection under GATT Article XX, the environment is set up as an exception for which the burden of proof rests on the country attempting to protect the environment. In addition, environmental measures may only trump trade liberalization rules in case they are 'necessary' and there is no 'less trade restrictive alternative' available. Before an environmental tribunal, the opposite would likely be true, with, for example, environmental protection as the rule, and trade liberalization as the exception.

This suggests that to the extent conflicts between sub-branches of international law become more akin to inter-systemic conflicts, applying the intra-systemic conflict rules of *lex superior, lex specialis, lex posterior* or balancing becomes more strenuous. If scholars have clung to such rules nonetheless, the reason may well be their fear that the alternative would be some unorganized legal pluralism. If it can be shown that inter-systemic rules, if and where appropriately applied, can provide a certain degree of coordination, such fears might be alleviated.

Here, we can only sketch some such possibilities. One would be to develop private-international-law rules on the basis of connecting factors, except that these connecting factors cannot be those of territory or personality (as in domestic inter-systemic conflict rules) but must be functional, institutional and/or procedural connecting factors pointing toward one branch of international law rather than the other (for example, as the 'proper law'). Fischer-Lescano and Teubner, who advocate a somewhat comparable approach, argue that any solution of the conflict cannot result in an either/or decision but must somehow combine aspects of both regimes, because most conflicts have relevant effects within more than one sub-system.[55] But effects within more than one system are characteristic of traditional private-international-law situations between states, too. In the example from the Delaware court discussed earlier,[56] the claim for loss of consortium undoubtedly has effects in both tort and family law, and in both Pennsylvania and Delaware. Here, the goal is not to determine whether the issue is 'really' one of tort or one of marriage law (it clearly touches on both), but instead which law is more appropriately applied. Similarly, in international law, we would not ask whether an issue 'really' belongs to trade or environmental law, but rather, which regime is more appropriate to be applied to the particular fact pattern. Applying the trade rather than the environmental regime is not a simple preference of trade interests over environment interest, but a preference of the decision in the trade regime on the role of environmental concerns over the decision within the environmental regime on the role of trade. This is a question not

[55] Fischer-Lescano and Teubner, above (n 11) 1021–22.

[56] See *Folk v York-Shipley*, above (n 28).

confined to 'true conflicts'; it is a question also where the different regimes provide norms that are equivalent, in other words, the case of MSENs.

Arguably, this is what really goes on when international tribunals exercise the jurisdiction to 'interpret the submissions of the parties' so as to 'isolate the real issue in the case and to identify the object of the claim'.[57] We can also find such a search for the 'closest connection' in the decision in *Southern Bluefin Tuna.* The tribunal in that case did not think the conflict belonged only to one or the other regime, as 'it is a commonplace of international law and State Practice for more than one treaty to bear upon a particular dispute'.[58] Nonetheless, because the dispute was 'centred' in the 1993 Convention for the Conservation of Southern Bluefin Tuna, that Convention became the basis for the decision. The tribunal did not deny that the conflict also 'arose' under UNCLOS. Rather, it concluded that '[t]o find that, in this case, there is a dispute actually arising under UNCLOS which is *distinct* from the dispute that arose under the [1993 Convention] would be artificial'.[59]

Another example of an inter-systemic conflict rule operational in international law can be derived from Article 22 of the Convention on Biological Diversity (CBD), which holds that

> the provisions of this Convention shall not affect the rights and obligations of any Contracting Party deriving from any existing international agreement, except where the exercise of those rights and obligations would cause a serious damage or threat to biological diversity.[60]

The provision shows that the CBD does not claim absolute superiority over other treaties (as noted earlier, in inter-systemic type conflicts this self-positioning as *lex superior* would likely be futile). The CBD does claim priority only where a serious damage or threat to biological diversity must be expected. This rule can be explained as an application of the public policy exception. Article 22 does not resolve conflicts universally, because the competing treaty might simultaneously claim priority, but it does provide a structure for addressing these conflicts from the perspective of one regime in a way to minimize the conflict.

A different kind of hands-off-approach-within-limits for inter-systemic type conflicts can be found in the now well-established *Solange II* approach to the interaction between German constitutional law and EC law, as well

[57] *Nuclear Tests (Australia v France)* [1974] ICJ Rep 262, para 29; *Nuclear Tests (New Zealand v France)* [1974] ICJ Rep 466, para 30; and *Fisheries Jurisdiction (Spain v Canada)* [1988] ICJ Rep 437.

[58] See also, UNCLOS, Arbitral Tribunal (4 August 2000), *Southern Bluefin Tuna* (2000) 39 ILM 1359, para 52.

[59] *Ibid*, para 54 (emphasis added). But see the forceful separate opinion by Sir Kenneth Keith, *ibid*, paras 1, 10–13, 30–31.

[60] Convention on Biological Diversity (adopted 5 June 1992, entered into force 29 December 1993) 1760 UNTS 79.

as between the European Court of Justice (ECJ) and the European Court of Human Rights (ECtHR) in the *Bosphorus* case.[61] Each of those regimes could have a legitimate claim to superiority; yet, as discussed, when faced with inter-systemic conflicts, such claim risks having little effect. Instead, a certain accommodation was found where each of these regimes or courts recognized the other but added that where the encroachment becomes too serious, superiority will be reclaimed – not with binding force for the other regime, but only by each side for itself. Where the encroachment is not serious, there is a presumption of equivalence among the different regimes (a case of MSEN) that facilitates deference.

Consider finally the Preamble of the Cartagena Protocol on Biosafety.[62] The Preamble first invokes the principle of mutual support among trade and environment agreements. Applying this principle, it maintains that the Protocol 'shall not be interpreted as implying a change in the rights and obligations of a Party under any existing international agreements', especially the WTO. However, in the very next paragraph, we find that the Protocol is not subordinated to the WTO. This text displays a desire to maintain intra-systemic coherence and consistency, and in its great abstraction also shows the limits of such a desire. It may, at times, be more appropriate to treat the conflict between trade and environment as one more akin to inter-systemic conflict. From this perspective, the principle of mutual support could then be read as the principle of comity which provides the historical basis for conflict of laws between states. Conflict of laws has become much more refined; an invocation of comity is rarely necessary in view of the fine-grained conflict-of-laws rules approaches we have.[63] A similar development may be more attractive for the relationship between trade and environment, instead of the solutions centred in interpretation and hierarchical subordination, which the Protocol has in mind, and which tend towards circularity.

D Multi-Sourced Equivalent Norms

Finally, what does all of this mean for multi-sourced equivalent norms (MSENs)? In our view, a method borrowed from conflict of laws appears particularly fruitful for MSENs, because the problem addressed by MSENs is familiar in that field. MSENs have been defined as rules that are '(1) binding upon the same international legal subjects; (2) similar or

[61] *'Solange II'*, BvR 2, 197/83, (1987) 3 *Common Market Law Reports* 225; *Bosphorus Hava Yollari Turizm v Ireland* (2006) 42 EHRR 1; *cf* K Knop, R Michaels and A Riles, 'International Law in Domestic Courts: A Conflict of Laws Approach' 2009 *ASIL Proceedings* (forthcoming).

[62] Preamble of the Cartagena Protocol on Biosafety (29 January 2000), 39 ILM 1027 (2000).

[63] See, eg, Michaels, 'Public and Private International Law', above (n 8); but see now DE Childress, *Comity as Conflicts: Resituating Comity as Conflict of Laws* (forthcoming).

identical in their normative content (in the words of the ILC, "point in the same direction"); and (3) have been established through different international instruments or "legislative" procedures or are applicable in different substantive areas of the law'.[64] In focusing on rules that point in the same direction, they fill a gap left open by the ILC Fragmentation Report that is addressed almost exclusively at rules pointing in different directions.[65] This distinction between rules pointing in different directions and rules pointing in the same direction is discussed, in governmental interest analysis (explained earlier), as the distinction between true and false conflicts. True conflicts describe situations in which the policies of different states are in conflict. (This definition is in accordance with more recent definitions of conflict in international law, which go beyond rules that cannot be obeyed at the same time and include rules that pursue different goals.)[66] False conflicts, by contrast, describe situations in which either only one of the two policies is implicated, or – and this makes for the parallel with MSENs – where the policies of both states or of both regimes are congruent.[67] The typical solution is then for the court to apply forum law.

MSENs exist both within and between sub-systems of international law. For example, 'national treatment' as a MSEN can be found in the WTO and in NAFTA, spread across the branches of trade and investment law. At the same time, national treatment is also sprinkled as a principle in various WTO agreements within the WTO regime. Equivalent rules on the use of force, as addressed in the Nicaragua case,[68] are set out in custom and in treaties, within the same 'system' or in the intra-systemic interaction between general international law and treaties defined earlier. In the context of investment arbitration, similar principles may be set out in an investment contract under domestic law as well as in the bilateral investment treaty (BIT) under international law, that is, across the national and international 'systems'. Yet, we submit that the problem dealt with under the title of conflict of norms or conflict of laws is structurally capable of accounting at least for some types of MSENs as well.

One example for the treatment of MSENs can be found in Article 189.4(a)–(c) of the EC Chile Free Trade Agreement (FTA):[69]

[64] Broude and Shany, 'The International Law and Policy of Multi-Sourced Equivalent Norms', above (n 3) 5.

[65] Koskenniemi Report, above (n 2) paras 23–24.

[66] E Vranes, 'The Definition of "Norm Conflict" in International Law and Legal Theory' (2006) 17 *European Journal of International Law* 395.

[67] For discussion and a different application in International Law, see AJ Colangelo, 'Universal Jurisdiction as an International "False Conflict" of Laws' (2009) 30 *Michigan Journal of International Law* 881.

[68] *Military and Paramilitary Activities in and against Nicaragua (Nicaragua v US)* (Jurisdiction and Admissibility) [1984] ICJ Rep 392.

[69] Agreement establishing an association between the European Union and its Member States, of the one part, and the Republic of Chile, of the other part (3 October 2002): www.trade.ec.europa.eu/doclib/docs/2004/november/tradoc_111620.pdf (emphasis added).

(a) When a Party seeks redress of a violation of an obligation under the WTO Agreement, it shall have recourse to the relevant rules and procedures of the WTO Agreement, which apply notwithstanding the provisions of this Agreement.
(b) When a Party seeks redress of a violation of an obligation under this Part of the Agreement, it shall have recourse to the rules and procedures of this Title.
(c) Unless the Parties otherwise agree, when a Party seeks redress of a violation of an obligation under this Part of the Agreement which is *equivalent in substance* to an obligation under the WTO, it shall have recourse to the relevant rules and procedures of the WTO Agreement, which apply notwithstanding the provisions of this Agreement.

The rule seems to have been written under the assumption of a relation of hierarchy vis-à-vis the WTO. Such a relation is not necessary, as the example of NAFTA–WTO showed. And indeed, rules 4(a) and 4(b) display a strong sense of an inter-systemic approach more prone to conflict of laws rules than conflict-of-norms rules. Thus, both Articles 4(a) and 4(b) base the applicable law on the close connection between obligations under a Treaty and the rules and procedures connected with them, an approach in tune with the traditional method of conflict of laws that designate entire legal systems, not just individual norms, to apply.

The most interesting provision in this context, however, is Article 4(c) of the FTA with its special regime for MSENs. Here, the otherwise necessary connection between rule and context is given up. Instead, the provision adopts an approach comparable to governmental interest analysis of laws, where the situation described would be viewed as a false conflict: not a situation in which only one regime is interested in the application of its law, but a situation in which the application of one law in fact furthers the interests of the other regime as well. Under governmental interest analysis, such situations are typically resolved in favour of forum law: New York is free to apply its own wrongful death statute if doing so furthers also the policies of Massachusetts. Here, the resolution is in favour of the rules of the WTO, but structurally this is not different. In both cases, one law – forum law in the domestic conflict-of-laws analysis, WTO law in the WTO-FTA context – is presumably applicable, but under certain conditions, in particular a difference in the relevant policies, a deviation can be justified.

This example suggests more generally that, at least for some types of MSENs, a conflict-of-laws approach may be appropriate. The idea that equivalent rules exist in different regimes (such as national treatment in the WTO and Chile-EU FTA) is familiar from an inter-systemic context, namely from comparative law: in comparative law, the functional method presumes that different legal systems will contain if not similar then at least functionally equivalent rules (for example, on contracts or tort), because each legal system is internally complete and thus needs to respond to essentially the same challenges as every other legal system.[70] Both French and English law have rules dealing with questions of enforcing contractual consensus; the question in conflict of laws is which of the two is applicable. The same situation occurs in international law, for example, as between NAFTA and the WTO, or the Chile-EU FTA and the WTO: both aim at resolving, essentially, the same challenges (in this case, nationality-based discrimination in an economic context). They contain MSENs because they are not perfectly integrated. Thus, to the extent international law develops more or less complete regimes in parallel (albeit centred on limited principles such as national treatment or non-discrimination), a conflict-of-laws approach seems most promising. This is the link between MSENs, the general topic of this volume, and the conflict-of-laws alternative, suggested in this chapter.

V CONCLUDING THOUGHTS: IS INTERNATIONAL LAW A SYSTEM?

So far, we have deliberately discussed the technical question – the respective adequacy of different sets of rules for different types of public international law conflicts – without addressing the ontological question whether international law is a system. The result has been that international law can actually borrow rules from both, and that different sets of rules are better for different types of conflicts. This means that the normative implications of whether international law is a system are actually not that great. Nonetheless, the question remains relevant, and some implications emerge from our analysis.

One tendency seems to be this: interactions between treaty-regimes (for example, the WTO) and general international law (for example, the law of treaties or state responsibility) are better resolved with rules made for intra-systemic conflicts and relate to international law as a 'system'. Similarly, conflicts *within* branches of international law, for example within the WTO Treaty, appear to benefit from intra-systemic rules and thereby suggest that it makes sense to conceive of the WTO as a (sub-)system.

In contrast, for interactions between specialized treaty regimes (say, environmental law versus trade law), traditional intra-systemic rules do not always provide satisfactory frameworks for analysis. However, as we demonstrate above, this emergence of different sub-systems or legal pluralism need not result in anarchy. Rather, coordination between these

[70] See R Michaels, 'The Functional Method of Comparative Law' in M Reimann and R Zimmermann (eds), *The Oxford Handbook of Comparative Law* (Oxford, Oxford University Press, 2006) 339, 367–72; for criticism of this assumption see, eg, J de Coninck, 'The Functional Method of Comparative Law: Quo Vadis?' (2010) 74; *Rabels Zeitschrift für ausländisches und internationals Privatrecht* Issue 2 (forthcoming) and the response by Michaels, *ibid.*

branches or sub-systems can occur, albeit imperfectly, through inter-systemic conflict-of-laws rules. This suggests that in these aspects international law is better seen as an unsystematic plurality of systems or regimes, without the need of conceiving these systems as self-contained.

What does this mean for the question whether international law is a system or not? First, we have seen that the question is far less important than the drafters of the ILC Fragmentation Report appear to have thought, because the technical question – which set of rules is adequate for which type of interaction between rules – can be answered without recourse to this ontological question. Secondly, to the extent that the answers to the technical question allow for conclusions, they suggest that it is useful to conceive of international law as a system for some aspects and as the interaction of various systems in others. It suggests that one set of conflicts rules – conflict-of-norms rules – is appropriate for one set of conflicts, and another set of conflicts rules – conflict-of-laws rules – is appropriate for the other. The criticism of international law as a system thus has it half right: international law is not a full-fledged system, and traditional conflict-of-norms rules are not always appropriate to resolve public international law conflicts. However, this finding does not lead to anarchy but instead into another set of conflicts rules.

International law may, therefore, be a system at some level (in the sense, for example, that all of its rules and branches interact and are governed by certain general rules without there being so-called self-contained regimes),[71] but a universe of different systems, sub-systems or branches at another level (in the sense, for example, that rules within the WTO Treaty interact differently than a WTO rule interacts with the Kyoto Protocol). The outcome is not chaos and anarchy but a more sophisticated legal landscape, consequence of, to use the very title of the ILC study group, 'the diversification and expansion of international law'. Put differently, applying private international law solutions to public international law conflicts – or recognizing that certain conflicts of international law may be more akin to a conflict between Belgian and German law than a conflict between one Belgian norm and another – need not mean the end of international law. On the contrary, it highlights the increased maturity and complexity of international law and its unique, hybrid features as a *sui generis* type of legal order.

If all of this is correct, then the first question for relations between international law norms, or regimes, is neither whether international law is a system or not, nor which norm or which regime should prevail, if any. The first question is which approach should be used to resolve the conflict, that of conflict of norms or that of conflict of laws. This question cannot

[71] Or as the ILC Study Group puts it: 'Its rules and principles (ie, its norms) act in relation to and should be interpreted against the background of other rules and principles'. See 'Conclusions of the Study Group' above (n 1) 407, para 251 (conclusion 1).

and need not be determined with regard to an ontology of international law; it must be established anew for many new conflicts. The dynamic and evolutionary character of international law makes it unlikely that the internal differentiation of international law either is static or follows a predetermined path. The dependence of international law on its actual practice suggests that how we resolve certain conflicts has an effect on the very nature of these conflicts. How we resolve conflicts determines what international law is. This is one more reason why we should think hard before blindly applying the conventional wisdom of conflict of norms. As international law diversifies and matures, some public international law conflicts may well be best resolved through private international law solutions. This chapter opens the way for such alternative approach. Elaborating specific conflict-of-law rules for certain public international law conflicts is the logical next step.

3

The Power of Secondary Rules to Connect the International and National Legal Orders

André Nollkaemper

I INTRODUCTION

WHEN STATES MAKE international norms part of the national legal order, whether through automatic incorporation or transformation, such norms start to lead a double life and exist simultaneously at both international and national levels. For instance, fundamental human rights are both part of international law and of the law of most, if not all states, in the world.[1] War crimes and the crime of genocide are both part of the (international) law to be applied by the International Criminal Court (ICC)[2] and part of national law of many states of the world.[3] In such cases, we can properly speak of Multi-Sourced Equivalent Norms (MSENs).[4] As international law increasingly regulates matters that also are covered by national law,[5] the existence of MSENs across the international/national divide will increase.

[1] See, for instance, JA Frowein, 'The Interaction between National Protection of Human Rights and the ECtHR' in R Wolfrum and U Deutsch (eds), *The European Court of Human Rights Overwhelmed by Applications: Problems and Possible Solutions, International Workshop* (Heidelberg 17–18 December 2007) (New York, Springer Law Publishing, 2009) 51.

[2] Rome Statute of the International Criminal Court (adopted 17 July 1998, enforced 1 July 2002) 2187 UNTS 90 (ICC).

[3] See, eg, C Kreß and F Latlanzi (eds), *The Rome Statute and Domestic Legal Orders, vol. I: General Aspects and Constitutional Issues* (Baden Baden, Nomos, 2000); W Burke-White, 'Proactive Complementarity: the International Criminal Court and National Courts in the Rome System of International Justice' (2008) 49 *Harvard International Law Review* 53.

[4] See general definition in this volume: T Broude and Y Shany, 'The International Law and Policy of Multi-Sourced Equivalent Norms' in T Broude and Y Shany (eds), *Multi-Sourced Equivalent Norms in International Law* (Oxford, Hart Publishing, 2011) p 5.

[5] JHH Weiler, 'The Geology of International Law: Governance, Democracy and Legitimacy' (2004) 64 *Heidelberg Journal of International Law* 547; LF Bravo, 'International and Municipal Law: The Complementarity of Legal Systems' in RSJ Macdonald and DM Johnston (eds), *The Structure and Process of International Law: Essays in Legal Philosophy, Doctrine, and Theory* (The Hague, Martinus Nijhoff, 1984) 715; RY Jennings, 'The Judiciary, International and National, and the Development of International Law' (1996) 45 *International and Comparative Law Quarterly* 1.

If international norms and their national counterparts are fully identical, no problems of inconsistency, or conflicting prescriptions, or authorizations need arise. Both norms will prescribe or authorize the same behaviour. Performance of the international obligation will imply performance of national law, and vice versa. That may be the case in situations of automatic incorporation,[6] use of specific rules of reference,[7] or literal transformation (or as it is sometimes called: 'legislative ad hoc incorporation') of an international obligation in national law.[8]

However, identity between an international norm and its national counterpart is not guaranteed. For one thing, in case of 'legislative ad hoc incorporation' the content of a national norm frequently is not fully identical to the underlying international norm. For instance, many national criminal laws are either broader or narrower in terms of the definition of international crimes than the international definition of such crimes.[9] Frequently, the same will hold true for fundamental rights. Moreover, even if the contents of a domesticated norm is identical to the international original at the moment that that international norm becomes part of the national legal order, over time that identity may be lost. Subjected to differing normative systems and institutions, the international and the national variant of a norm may start to differ, leading to different and perhaps even competing prescriptions or authorisations.

At a systemic level, the separate existence of international norms and their national counterparts may have implications for the unity of international law. That unity is already limited at the international level.[10] These limits are multiplied by diverging interpretations at the national level. National laws and national organs interpret and apply international obligations in multiple ways and often contradict or even override them. This undermines not only uniform interpretation, but essential features of the rule of law, notably generality, equality of application and certainty.[11]

To some extent, divergent interpretations at national level are an inevitable and even necessary consequence of the structural dualistic relationship between the international and the national legal order. The margin of

[6] A Cassese, *International Law* 2nd edn (Oxford, Oxford University Press, 2005) 220.

[7] WN Ferdinandusse, *Direct Application of International Criminal Law in National Courts* (The Hague, TMC Asser Press, 2006) 7.

[8] Cassese, above (n 6) 221.

[9] Ferdinandusse, above (n 7) 117.

[10] M Koskenniemi, 'The Politics of International Law – 20 Years Later' (2009) 20 *European Journal International Law* 7; M Koskenniemi and P Leino, 'Fragmentation of International Law? Postmodern Anxieties' (2002) 15 *Leiden Journal of International Law* 553. See also, AL Paulus, 'Subsidiarity, Fragmentation and Democracy: Towards the Demise of General International Law?' in T Broude and Y Shany (eds), *The Shifting Allocation of Authority in International Law: Considering Sovereignty, Supremacy and Subsidiarity* (Oxford, Hart Publishing, 2008) 99.

[11] BZ Tamanaha, *On the Rule of Law: History, Politics, Theory* (Cambridge, Cambridge University Press, 2004) 131.

appreciation doctrine is one of many reflections of this divide.[12] Indeed, it might be argued that the aspiration of unity of international law is and should be confined to the international level proper. However, given the frequent interactions between international and national law, surely some limits to national variations have to be set? The very rationale of an increasing part of international law lies precisely in the meaning and application it is given at national level. To limit the ambition of unity to the international level would make that a sterile and esoteric notion, devoid of much practical relevance.

This chapter will address one set of rules that may help to moderate the divergence between international norms and the national versions of such norms, and the resulting divergence of interpretations between states. It will discuss to what extent secondary rules of international law can induce convergence between international norms and domesticated international norms. I use the term 'secondary rules' to refer to those rules that define the normative context within which primary norms function and that thereby affect the operation of such primary norms.[13] Secondary rules include rules of interpretation, rules of change and rules of responsibility.[14] Whether two identical primary norms are given the same interpretation, or applied in a similar manner, depends in part on the question of whether they are governed by the same secondary rules.

The question then arises whether national courts, or other national organs that interpret or give effect to an international obligation that has been made part of national law, are to give effect to the same secondary rules that guide the interpretation and application of that norm in the international legal order. Should a national court interpret and apply national rules that are equivalent to an international norm, in light of (secondary) international principles of interpretation? Or should it apply them as national rules in light of national principles of interpretation? Should, for instance, a national court that considers individual criminality for genocide consider questions of intent in light of the relevant international principles, or should it only consider national law?[15]

[12] Y Shany, 'Toward a General Margin of Appreciation Doctrine in International Law?' (2005) 16 *European Journal International Law* 907.

[13] HLA Hart, *The Concept of Law* (Oxford, Oxford University Press, 1961) 91.

[14] See for a definition of secondary norms including such aspects: TM Franck, *The Power of Legitimacy Among Nations* (Oxford, Oxford University Press, 1990) 184. In international law the term 'secondary rules' is generally limited to the last form, following Ago's use of the concept, in which primary norms lay down rights and obligations ('rules of conduct'), secondary norms provide the consequences for breaches of primary norms. See the discussion by J Combacau and D Alland, 'Primary and Secondary Rules in the Law of State Responsibility: Categorizing International Obligations' (1995) 16 *Netherlands Yearbook of International Law* 81.

[15] The question arose in the *Van Anraat* case. Van Anraat, a Dutch businessman, was charged with providing chemicals to Saddam Hussein who used these chemicals in attacks in northern Iraq in the late 1980s. The Court of Appeal had to consider whether the criterion of intent as an element of complicity was to be assessed in accordance with domestic law or

In considering this question, it should be taken into account that secondary rules are constitutive of legal systems.[16] They inform and determine the connection between different primary rules and it is precisely by virtue of such secondary rules that, despite the wide variety of norms adopted in different institutions by different actors, we can still speak of a legal system.[17] It is for this reason that the international and the national legal systems have in principle their own secondary rules and indeed constitute separate systems.[18]

It thus may be thought that the operation of secondary norms of international law is limited to the international system itself. International obligations that have been domesticated have become part of a different normative universe.[19] They lead a separate life as national law, governed by separate secondary norms.[20] The point can be illustrated by *R v Safi (Ali Ahmed)*, in which the Court of Appeal held that national defences are available for international crimes that have been made punishable in national law.[21] This is likely to lead to varying interpretations, governed by national law, and to the possibility that a person is convicted of an international crime in one state on the basis of conduct which would not lead to a conviction for the same crime in another, even though that latter state may have enacted the same prohibition for that crime.[22]

Indeed, there is ample practice where national courts apply principles of national (statutory) interpretation without referring to international

in line with the corresponding rules of international law. Court of Appeal, The Hague, *Public Prosecutor and ors v Van Anraat*, LJN BA4676, 2200050906-2; ILDC 753 (NL 2007).

[16] Hart, above (n 13).

[17] ILC, 'Report of the Study Group of the ILC, Fragmentation of International Law: Difficulties arising from the Diversification and Expansion of International Law' (2006) UN Doc A/CN.4/L.628, para 35.

[18] Of course, Hart did not consider that the secondary rules of international law had matured in a way that allowed international law to be qualified as a legal system; Hart, above (n 13) 208. See for the term system in regard to international law, eg, G Abi-Saab, 'Cours Géneral de Droit International Public' (1987) 207 *Receuil des Cours: Collected Courses of the Hague Academy of International Law* 105. See also ILC, 'Conclusions of the Work of the Study Group on the Fragmentation of International Law: Difficulties arising from the Diversification and Expansion of International Law, Report of the 58th Session' (2006) GAOR 61st Session Supp 10 UN Doc A/61/10, 407, para 1 (stating that 'International law is a legal system. Its rules and principles (ie, its norms) act in relation to and should be interpreted against the background of other rules and principles. As a legal system, international law is not a random collection of such norms. There are meaningful relationships between them. Norms may thus exist at higher and lower hierarchical levels, their formulation may involve greater or lesser generality and specificity and their validity may date back to earlier or later moments in time').

[19] M Hakimi, 'Secondary Human Rights Law' (2009) 34 *Yale Journal of International Law* 596.

[20] See, eg, with regard to treaty interpretation, A Mestre, 'Les Traités et de droit interne' (1931-IV) 38 *Receuil des Cours* 299 (arguing that national courts should interpret treaty law in the same way as domestic law). Also, with respect to English practice, CH Schreuer, 'The Interpretation of Treaties by Domestic Courts' (1971) 45 *British Yearbook of International Law* 257.

[21] *R v Safi (Ali Ahmed)* [2003] EWCA Crim 1809; 74 BYIL (2003) 471.

[22] R O'Keeffe, commenting on *R v Safi (Ali Ahmed)*, *ibid*.

principles of interpretation.[23] While, for instance, the United States' legal system has developed specific principles of treaty construction, these are not generally the same as rules of international treaty interpretation.[24] To the extent that the question should be answered in the latter sense and national organs are not guided by international secondary norms, the national interpretation and application of international norms indeed may undermine the unity of international law as it is received at domestic level.

However, it might also be argued that secondary rules of international law remain applicable to the interpretation, modification and termination of corresponding rules at national level. An international norm, while transformed or incorporated into national law, may remain under the guidance of the international legal order. International law then can have a normative impact on the national legal order that to some extent may contribute to a unity in the interpretation and application of international law. There is a substantial amount of state practice, referenced below, that supports the latter model and which seeks to maintain secondary level connections between an international norm and its national manifestations.[25]

Of course, the single fact that two or more states, or their courts, will be guided by the same secondary norms will not ensure uniformity of interpretation and application. The principles of treaty interpretation, for instance, are of a general nature. Given the dominant role of auto-interpretation, their application is likely to differ between states.[26] But at least it can then be said that there is a normative pull towards convergence.

In this chapter I review the foundations, scope and consequences of the application of secondary rules of international law at the national level, in particular by national courts, so as to preserve some connection between the international and national manifestations of a norm. The chapter proceeds as follows: I first provide an overview of the type of situations in which the question of the application of international secondary norms

[23] See, eg, Supreme Court of Pakistan, *Societe Generale de Surveillance S.A. v Pakistan*, ILDC 82 (PK 2002) para C5. See for a critical review of treaty interpretation by the US Supreme Court, short of what international law would require, JK Setear, 'A Forest with no Trees: The Supreme Court and International Law in the 2003 Term' (2004) 91 *Virginia Law Review* 579, 614.

[24] DJ Bederman, 'Revivalist Canons and Treaty Interpretation' (1994) 41 *University of California at Los Angeles Law Review* 953; JF Coyle, 'Incorporative Statutes and the Borrowed Treaty Rule' *Virginia Journal of International Law* (forthcoming) 41 (discussing 'treaty canons'): www.ssrn.com/abstract=1373028. See also, G Gaja, 'Italy' in FG Jacobs and S Roberts (eds), *The Effects of Treaties in Domestic Law* (London, Sweet & Maxwell, 1987) 107; Supreme Court of Norway, *Hans-Jürgen Hartman M/S Kvitnes GmbH & Co KG v Ministry of Fisheries and Coastal Affairs*, Final decision on civil interlocutory appeal, Case No HR-2007-00325-A; ILDC 818 (NO 2007).

[25] See the references in Schreuer, above (n 20) 272 et seq. See also, FG Jacobs, 'Introduction' in *The Effects of Treaties in Domestic Law*, *ibid*, xxix.

[26] L Gross, 'States as Organs of International Law and the Problem of Autointerpretation' in G Lipsky (ed), *Law and Politics in the World Community* (Berkeley, University of California Press, 1953) 59–88; P Weil, 'Le droit international enquête de son identité. Cours général de droit international public' (1992) 237 *Recueil des Cours* 220–23.

to domesticated international norms may arise (section II); I then discuss whether, as a basis for application of international secondary rules, it is possible to construe the application of secondary rules of international law in terms of obligations (section III). In section IV, I discuss, as an alternative foundation, the proposition that there exists an essential connection between primary and secondary norms that can survive the migration of a primary norm into a different legal system. Given that it is not possible to fully construe the effects of secondary norms in terms of obligations, in section V I present a perspective in which secondary rules of international law function as a normative penumbra that guides the interpretation and application of international norms in a different legal system. Finally, I examine to what extent different national (constitutional) arrangements governing the effect of international law in the national legal order may affect the impact of the normative penumbra of secondary rules of international law in the national legal order (section VI). Section VII contains conclusions.

II SITUATIONS IN WHICH THE APPLICATION OF SECONDARY RULES OF INTERNATIONAL LAW MAY MAKE A DIFFERENCE

Secondary rules of international law may become relevant to the interpretation and application of domesticated international norms in at least five situations. First, and perhaps most importantly, they can affect the interpretation of national rules that emanate from or correspond to international law. It is a not uncommon for national courts to interpret a national norm that directly or indirectly reflects an international norm in the light of that international origin, taking account of the international principles that are relevant for determining the meaning of the original.[27] That practice recognizes that international obligations, also when these have been made part of national law, should be given the meaning ascribed to them by the system in which they originate.[28]

[27] See, eg, *King v Bristow Helicopters Ltd*, Re M (on the application of CM [2002] 2 AC 628; ILDC 242 (UK 2002), para 80; *NEC Semi-Conductors Ltd and ors v Inland Revenue Commissioners*, First instance claim for restitution [2003] EWHC 2813 (Ch); ILDC 260 (UK 2003); *Attorney-General v Zaoui*, ILDC 81 (NZ 2005), para 12 (Supreme Court of New Zealand); *Sabanci v Erdal*, Appeal in cassation, No P 05 1491 N, (2006) Journal des Tribunaux 642; ILDC 592 (BE 2006) (Court of Cassation of Belgium); *Office of the Public Prosecutor v Lariz Iriondo*, Ordinary Appeal Judgment, L.845.XL, vol 328; ILDC 125 (AR 2005) (Supreme Court of Argentina). See further R Gardiner, *Treaty Interpretation* (Oxford, Oxford University Press, 2008) 128–38. See also the examples given in E Criddle, 'The Vienna Convention on the Law of Treaties in US Treaty Interpretation' (2004) 44 *Virginia Journal of International Law* 431. The Supreme Court of Israel adopted a similar approach in a 1980s case concerning the interpretation of the Warsaw Convention on Carriage by Air FH 36/84 *Teichman v Air France* IsrSC 41(1) 589.

[28] See, eg, *R (Al Fawwaz) v Governer of Brixton Prison* [2001] UKHL 69, para 39 (in which Lord Slynn states that 'to apply to . . . treaties the strict canons appropriate to the construction of domestic statutes would often tend to defeat rather than to serve [their] purpose'). See

The national practice that falls in this category can be further divided into two categories. One category takes a narrow approach and confines international principles of interpretation to rules of national law that incorporate or transform a particular treaty obligation in national law. This category includes, in states with a system of automatic incorporation, international obligations as they have become part of national law and, in states with a system of transformation, statutes that expressly transform an obligation into national law – so-called 'borrowed treaty rules'.[29]

A broader approach is to also apply international interpretive principles to national rules that in substance overlap with international obligations, but are not necessarily a result of incorporation or transformation of international obligations. Indeed, they may predate the entry into force of international obligations. An example is the interpretation of fundamental constitutional rights that in substance largely overlap with subsequently adopted international human rights, although they originated independently from the international obligation in question. Such rights are also properly regarded as MSENs. Yet, they differ from the first category (that limits the international principles of interpretation to those rules of national law that incorporate or transform a particular treaty obligation) in that it is impossible to base the application of international interpretive rules on the assumption that the legislature intended to maintain conformity with an international obligations.

A second set of international secondary rules may affect the application and interpretation of domesticated international obligations consists of rules of change, that is: rules specifying how primary rules are changed.[30] These rules are determinative for the evolution of the original international norm at the international level, through amendment, modification, subsequent practice or termination. They may also be relevant for the existence and application of norms at national level. That is most obvious in the case of automatic incorporation or in the case of an express *renvoi* to international law (for example, a national war crimes statute that criminalizes violations of the international laws of war). Once the original international norm has changed, or has been overtaken by a different international norm, that necessarily will affect the identity of the domesticated international norm. Indeed, national courts frequently have assumed a role in making determinations on the invalidity and termination of treaties.[31]

also, J Wouters and M Vidal, 'Non-Tax Treaties: Domestic Courts and Treaty Interpretation' in G Maisto (ed), *Courts and Tax Treaty Law* (Amsterdam, IFBD, 2007) 3, 5–6. See below, section VI.

[29] Coyle, above (n 24).

[30] Hart, above (n 13) 93.

[31] See for a review of practice of domestic courts in respect of invalidity and termination, B Conforti and A Labella, 'Invalidity and Termination of Treaties: The Role of National Courts' (1990) 1 *European Journal of International Law* 44.

A third set of secondary rules that might be relevant for the application of equivalent norms across the international/national divide consists of conflict rules that, in case of competing obligations, determine which obligation should prevail. At the international level, questions arising out of the concurrent applicability of conflicting obligations obviously are to be answered on the basis of the conflict rules of international law, such as the rules relating to successive treaties,[32] the principle of *lex specialis*,[33] etc. The question is whether, when a domesticated international norm conflicts with another domesticated international norm, that conflict remains subject to the same international conflict rules. There is some practice suggesting that where treaties are part of national law, international principles will be taken into account in determining how a conflict is to be resolved.[34]

A fourth secondary rule provides a conflict rule governing conflicts between international and national law. In the case of a conflict between international and national law the principle of supremacy of international law proclaims that international law is to set aside national law – a principle that in certain respects can be considered as a secondary rule.[35]

In principle, the claim to supremacy of international law is confined to the international level. It is at that level that states cannot invoke national law to justify the non-performance with an international obligation, and it is at that level that international courts, by virtue of their establishment under international law, have to give precedence to international law over national law.[36]

However, some states have given effect to the international secondary (conflict) rule and have perceived the principle of supremacy as requiring that international law – once duly introduced in national law – also in the *domestic* legal order prevails over national law. For instance, the open nature of the Dutch legal system can be traced to the legislature's belief that international law required that Dutch law be set aside whenever it

[32] The Vienna Convention on the Law of Treaties (adopted 23 May 1969, entered into force 27 January 1980) 1155 UNTS 331, art 30 (VCLT); see also, ILC, 'Conclusions of the Work of the Study Group', above (n 18) 416, para 24.

[33] ILC, 'Conclusions of the Work of the Study Group', *ibid*, 408.

[34] Poland, Supreme Court, Resolution of the Supreme Court, Question of law brought by the Court of Appeal in Gdansk, I KZP 47/02; ILDC 273 (PL 2003); France, Council of State, *Abderrahmane Zaïdi v France*, Decision on annulment, No 206902; ILDC 764 (FR 2000), 21 April 2000.

[35] G Fitzmaurice, 'The General Principles of International law Considered from the Standpoint of the Rule of Law' (1057) 92 *Recueil des cours* 68; C Santuli, *Le Status International de L'Ordre Juridique Étatique* (Pedone, Paris, 2001) 427.

[36] J Verhoeven. 'Article 21 of the Rome Statute and the Ambiguities of Applicable Law' (2002) 33 *Netherlands Yearbook of International Law* 3.

conflicts with treaty law.[37] Courts in Belgium,[38] Indonesia[39] and Latvia[40] have set aside national law that conflicted with international law, expressly referring to Article 27 of the Vienna Convention on the Law of Treaties (VCLT). There are also cases in which courts have suggested that national conflict rules that grant precedence to international law were appropriate, since they respect the supremacy claimed by international law, or by particular international treaties or courts, such as the European Court of Human Rights (ECtHR).[41]

Fifthly, secondary rules of international law that are used to determine the consequences of breaches of international obligations may, directly or indirectly, influence the consequences that at national level are or should be attached to breaches of the national manifestations of that obligation. In many states national courts have followed international principles of attribution or reparation.[42] Thereby, at the national level some degree of unity is maintained between the application of an international norms and its domestic manifestation.

Each of these five manifestations can help to maintain a certain unity between international obligations, on the one hand, and the domestic manifestations of such obligations, on the other. Thereby they may counteract the pull to fragmentation that is the natural result of the combination of the dualistic relationship between international and national law[43] and the principle of auto-interpretation.[44]

[37] A Nollkaemper, 'The Application of Treaties in the Netherlands' in D Sloss (ed), *The Role of Domestic Courts in Treaty Enforcement: A Comparative Study* (Cambridge, Cambridge University Press, 2009).

[38] *ING België v B I*, Appeal Judgment, 2 March 2007, Nr C.05.0154.N; ILDC 1025 (BE2007). This builds on the Court of Cassation's judgment in the case *Franco-Suisse Le Ski*, Hof van Cassatie/Cour de cassation, 21 May 1971, Pas. 1971, I, 886, in which it was established case law that a directly effective treaty provision had primacy over a conflicting legislative act.

[39] *Constitutional Review of Law No 22 of 1997 on Narcotics*, 23 October 2007, No 2-3/PUU-V/2007; ILDC 1401 (ID 2007).

[40] *Judgment of the Constitutional Court of the Republic of Latvia on a Request for Constitutional Review*, ILDC 189 (LV 2004). The Court had to consider whether the Latvian Code of Administrative Penalties was compatible with the International Convention on Facilitation of International Maritime Traffic, which provides that states shall not impose any penalty upon ship owners if their passengers possess inadequate control documents. The Court derived from the obligations of Latvia under the VCLT, in particular, the obligation to perform treaties in good faith that in a case of contradiction between rules of international law and national legislation, the provisions of international law must be applied. Hence, the Court set aside the domestic law.

[41] Eg, *Al-Nashif v National Police Directorate at the Ministry of the Interior*, Judicial review, Judgment No 4332; ILDC 608 (BG 2003) 10–11 (Supreme Administrative Court of Bulgaria).

[42] See the examples given in A Nollkaemper, 'Internationally Wrongful Acts in Domestic Courts' (2007) 101 *American Journal International Law* 760.

[43] G Arangio-Ruiz, 'Dualism Revisited: International Law and Interindividual Law' (2003) 86 *Rivista di Diritto Internazionale* 909; G Gaja, 'Dualism: A Review' in G Gaja (ed), *New Perspectives on the Divide between National and International Law* (Oxford, Oxford University Press, 2007) 57.

[44] Gross, above (n 26); Weil, above (n 26).

III OBLIGATIONS TO GIVE EFFECT TO SECONDARY NORMS

In some cases, the justification for giving effect to international secondary norms may be found in express obligations. Such obligations may exist under either international law (see below, section III A) or national law (see below, section III B).

A International Obligations to give effect to Secondary Norms

Some secondary rules contain an obligation to give effect to such rules. Of the five types of rules discussed above in section II, this holds in particular for the principles of responsibility and, more controversially, supremacy. It is difficult to conceive of principles of interpretation or change in terms of international obligations, even though it may be argued that the interpretation to be given to domesticated norms should be affected by a more general obligation to ensure conformity between international and national law.[45]

A brief overview of secondary obligations pertaining to international responsibility may illustrate how international secondary obligations may be relevant to the national level. General international law formulates several obligations of states in relation to international wrongs that may be relevant to national courts. Examples are the obligation of states not to recognize as lawful a situation created by a serious breach of an obligation arising under peremptory norms of international law and the obligation not to render aid or assistance in maintaining that situation.[46] Article 41 of the Articles on State Responsibility was for instance relied on by the Italian Court of Cassation as an argument for denying the immunity of Germany in a case involving alleged violations of *jus cogens* (forced labour in the Second World War).[47]

[45] See below, section V.

[46] Art 41(2) of the Articles on the Responsibility of States for Internationally Wrongful Acts (Articles on State Responsibility) are contained in the Annex (28 January 2002) UN Doc A/Res/56/83.

[47] *Ferrini v Federal Republic of Germany*, ILDC 19 (IT 2004) 9 (holding that the recognition of immunity from jurisdiction for a state that is responsible for breaches of peremptory norms would be in contrast with, inter alia, the obligation of states not to recognize situations determined by its commission, the prohibition to provide help or assistance for the maintenance of situations that originated from such violations and the obligation to use legitimate means to bring about the end of illicit activities); see also A Bianchi, 'Italian Court of Cassation ruling on immunity from suit for damages for deportation and forced labor during World War II (Comment to decision)' (2005) 99 *American Journal of International Law* 242; and, critically, A Gattini, 'War Crimes and State Immunity in the Ferrini Decision' (2005) 3 *Journal of International Criminal Justice* 224, 236. The question whether this case law conforms to international law is now before the ICJ in *Jurisdictional Immunities of the State* (*Germany v Italy*).

Another example is the obligation not to aid or assist another state in the commission of an international wrong.[48] This principle, that may in fact have more a character of a primary than of a secondary norm,[49] was considered by the German *Bundesverfassungsgericht* in a decision granting extradition of a Yemeni national to the United States. The German authorities had arrested the person in question, based on an arrest warrant issued by the United States District Court for the Eastern District of New York. The United States' prosecution authorities charged the complainant with having provided (financial) aid to terrorist groups, in particular Al-Qaeda and Hamas, and with having recruited new members for these groups. The complainant travelled to Germany as a result of conversations that a Yemeni citizen had had with him in Yemen, but this was part of an undercover mission of United States' authorities. The complainant alleged that the 'abduction' by means of trickery constituted an obstacle precluding extradition. The *Bundesverfassungsgericht* said that the administrative authorities and the courts of Germany are prevented from participating in a decisive manner in acts by (non-German) organs of state authority that are performed in violation of general rules of international law. Since tortuous action on the part of the United States would establish the responsibility of the United States under international law vis-à-vis Yemen, 'there would be the risk that by extraditing the complainant, Germany would support a United States' action that is possibly contrary to international law, which would make Germany itself responsible under international law vis-à-vis Yemen'.[50] The Court expressly referred to Article 16 of the Articles on State Responsibility. Even though the Court eventually allowed the extradition,[51] this example shows obligations that at the international level are part of a set of secondary rules can be relevant at national level.[52]

Principles of cessation[53] and reparation[54] provide obligations that may be binding on a state that has committed an internationally wrongful act

[48] Articles on State Responsibility, above (n 46) art 16.

[49] B Graefrath, 'Complicity in the Law of International Responsibility' (1996) 2 *Revue Belge de Droit International* 370, 371.

[50] *Al-M, Individual constitutional complaint procedure, Bundesverfassungsgericht,* BVerfG, 2 BvR 1506/03 Order of 5 November 2003; ILDC 10 (DE 2003) 47.

[51] The Court held that 'the general rule of international law that is alleged by the complainant, ie, the existence of an obstacle precluding extradition in the case of an "abduction" by means of trickery, does not exist', *ibid*, 48. It thus considered the matter under the question whether or not the primary rule would preclude extradition, rather than under the general principle of complicity.

[52] Another example is a decision by the *Bundesverwaltungsgericht* of 21 June 2005, in which the Court considered that the attacks on Iraq by the United States and the United Kingdom in 2003 were unlawful and that aid or assistance to that international wrong by Germany would in itself constitute a wrongful act, expressly referring to art 16 of the ILC Articles (ILDC 483 (DE 2005); see discussion by N Schultz, 'Case Note – Was the War on Iraq Illegal? – The Judgment of the German Federal Administrative Court of 21 June 2005' (2006) 7 *German Law Journal* 25.

[53] Articles on State Responsibility, above (n 46) art 30.

[54] *Ibid*, arts 31 and 35–37.

and that as such may also be as legally relevant for a national court as the primary norms that were breached in the first place. In this context, it is relevant that the Articles on State Responsibility suggest that secondary obligations are not only owed to states, but to individuals;[55] what in many cases will be a precondition for national courts' willingness to consider international claims. Indeed, several treaties which provide for international primary rights of individuals, also grant individuals a right to reparation vis-à-vis the state, which may apply if these primary rights are breached. These treaties thus recognize that a primary right of individuals can be matched by a secondary right and a corresponding obligation of the state.[56]

The national relevance of secondary obligations of reparation is particularly clear for treaties that recognize a right to substantive reparation, such as a right to compensation or to material restitution. Examples are Article 13 of the Torture Convention,[57] Article 5(5) of the European Convention on Human Rights (ECHR),[58] Article 9(4) of the International Covenant on Civil and Political Rights (ICCPR)[59] (providing for a right of compensation to be awarded by national court in cases of unlawful detention) and Article 14(6) of ICCPR (providing for a right to compensation in case of a miscarriage of justice). Like the underlying primary norms, such remedies are to be given effect before national courts.[60] One may doubt whether such rules are properly to be considered as secondary rules – since they are treaty-based obligations – but this is an example of a situation where the distinction between primary and secondary rules has little legal relevance. The abovementioned treaty regimes couple a breach of an internationally protected right with the right to reparation. For a state or (national court), it is immaterial whether the remedy is part of a primary or a secondary rule. While the classification of treaty-based remedies as primary

[55] Crawford noted that 'in form a saving clause, it nonetheless clearly envisages that some "person or entity other than a State" may be directly entitled to claim reparation arising from an internationally wrongful act of a state'. J Crawford, 'The ILC's Articles on Responsibility of States for Internationally Wrongful Acts: A Retrospect' (2002) 96 *American Journal of International Law* 874, 887. Similarly, J Crawford, *Restatement of the Law. Foreign Relations Law of the United States* vol 2 (Philadelphia, American Law Institute, 1986) para 906.

[56] C Tomuschat, 'Individual Reparation Claims in Instances of Grave Human Rights Violations: the Position under General International Law' in A Randelzhofer and C Tomuschat (eds), *State Responsibility and the Individual* (The Hague, Martinus Nijhoff Publishers, 1999) 7.

[57] Convention against Torture and Other Cruel, Inhuman or Degrading Treatment or Punishment (adopted 10 December 1984, enforced 26 June 1987) 1465 UNTS 85.

[58] Convention for the Protection of Human Rights and Fundamental Freedoms (adopted 4 November 1950, enforced 3 September 1953) 213 UNTS 222 (ECHR). See generally on right to reparation under the ECHR; see, eg, M Pellonpää, 'Individual Reparation Claims under the European Convention on Human Rights' in Randelzhofer and Tomuschat, above (n 56).

[59] International Covenant on Civil and Political Rights 999 UNTS 171 (adopted 16 December 1966, enforced 23 March 1976) 999 UNTS 171 (ICCPR).

[60] See generally, D Shelton, *Remedies in International Human Rights Law* 2nd edn (Oxford, Oxford University Press, 2006) ch 9.

rules may have been a convenient tool for the codification exercise of the International Law Commission (ILC), it adds little to the resolution of legal questions before national courts.[61]

The practice outside the scope of treaty regimes in support of a customary principle that a state would be obliged to provide in its national legal order remedies for individuals whose international rights have been violated, is limited. Some support can be found in the adoption by the General Assembly in March 2006 of the 'Basic Principles and Guidelines on the Right to a Remedy and Reparation for Victims of Gross Violations of International Human Rights Law and Serious Violations of International Humanitarian Law'.[62] These principles provide that victims of such violations would have a right of access to (domestic) justice as well as to adequate, effective and prompt reparation for harm suffered, enforceable in the national legal order. However, customary international law has not (yet) followed the example of EC law, which has established that an individual who suffers damage as a result of a failure of a Member State to respect his or her obligations under Community law enjoys a right of reparation for the damage caused by such unlawful behaviour, which must be allowed to be exercised in the national legal order.[63]

Obligations to provide reparation frequently are formulated by international courts that have determined that reparation is due, in particular when the constituent treaty provides that judgments of that court are binding on the state concerned.[64] On this basis, a decision of an international court relating to the (non-)performance of an international obligation, may, depending on the national law of the state concerned, have effects at national level. Indeed, the Italian Court of Cassation has said that when the ECtHR established a violation of rights under the ECHR, individuals might rely on a right to reparation, either of a pecuniary nature or as *restitutio in integrum*, which the national courts were obligated to enforce.[65]

The conclusion is thus that if a national court determines that an international obligation has been breached, certain secondary obligations may

[61] The savings clause of art 33 of the Articles on State Responsibility, above (n 46) appears to be introduced precisely with a view to such treaty-based rights or reparation, without concern for their status as primary or secondary rules.

[62] UN Doc A/Res/60/147 (2006). See discussion by M Zwanenburg, 'The Van Boven/Bassiouni Principles: An Appraisal' (2006) 24 *Netherlands Quarterly of Human Rights* 641.

[63] Joined Cases C-6/90 and C-9/90 *Francovich* and *Bonifaci* [1991] ECR I-5357; Tomuschat, above (n 56) 9.

[64] See, eg, art 94 of the Charter of the United Nations; art 59 of the Statute of the International Court of Justice (adopted 26 June 1945, entered into force 24 October 1945) 3 Bevans 1179; ECHR, above (n 58), art 46 and art 62 American Convention on Human Rights (adopted 21 November 1969, entered into force 18 July 1978) 1144 UNTS 123.

[65] *Dorigo*, Appeal Judgment, No 2800/2007; ILDC 1096 (IT 2007). See also, *Al-Nashif v National Police Directorate*, above (n 41). Of course, this is not a universally accepted construction; see the different approach taken by the US Supreme Court in *Medellín v Texas*, Appeal Judgment, No 06-984; 552 US; ILDC 947 (US 2008).

be applicable, particularly in the sphere of reparation. Such secondary rules may result in a convergence between the meaning and application of equivalent norms at international and national level.

However, basing the application of secondary principles by national courts on express secondary obligations has only limited explanatory or normative power for our present inquiry. Its power would seem to be confined to principles of reparation and will not easily cover other types of secondary rules. Many other principles of international responsibility (such as principles of attribution and circumstances precluding wrongfulness) are not easily phrased in terms of obligations binding on a state. The same is true for principles of interpretation or rules of change. It is for that reason that we have to consider (in sections IV–V below) alternative bases for the application of secondary rules at national level.

B National Obligations to give effect to Secondary Norms

Before discussing alternative normative foundations of the domestic effect of secondary rules, it is relevant to point out that in certain cases, national law provides for such effect. An illustration is the *Al-Jedda* case. The House of Lords considered international principles of attribution of acts to international organizations. The basis thereof did not lie in international law, however. Under the UK Human Rights Act, the rights of Al-Jedda depended on this right under the ECHR. He could have no better rights under the Act than he would have had under the Convention.[66]

An alternative national law argument is that as a result of domestic constitutional law, courts may have to respect the will or intent of the legislature. When the political branches of a state have allowed automatic incorporation, or chose to enact legislation that incorporates the terms of a treaty, they make a decision to conform national law to international law. Considerations of separation of powers then may require that national courts that are to interpret or give effect to the national manifestation of the international obligation, do so in a manner that keeps close to that intention and thus maintains the conformity between international and national law. If the courts do not interpret that treaty in light of an underling treaty, they would overturn the decision of the political branches.[67] Likewise, if they would not consider the impact in subsequent modifications of a rule at international level, they would disconnect the link between the international and the national domain that the legislature sought to establish. The same could be said for the application of secondary principles of responsibility.

[66] *Al Jedda v The Secretary of State for Defence* [2007] UKHL 58, [2008] 2 WLR 31.
[67] Coyle, above (n 24) 19.

The normative effect of international secondary rules may also flow from the fact that secondary rules themselves may be part of national law. That will be the case when such rules are part of a treaty that, through automatic incorporation or legislation, have been made part of national law, for instance the VCLT in relation to treaty interpretation or the ECHR in relation to remedies flowing from a breach of the Convention. It also may be the case for secondary rules that are part of customary law, and that as such have become part of national law. This would, for instance, be relevant for a state that is not a party to the VCLT, but that is bound by the customary rules of the law of treaties As many states in the world accept the national effect of customary rules of international law, their courts would be empowered and perhaps obliged to give effect to domesticated international obligations in light of such secondary rules.

However, the domestic status of secondary rules does not seem to be a necessary or sufficient condition for the effect of such rules. While sometimes national courts have determined that a particular rule of treaty interpretation or responsibility was part of national law,[68] the application of the international normative context does not necessarily depend on the formal status of secondary rules in the national legal order.[69] In many cases, courts have given effect to secondary rules of international law without considering the domestic status of such norms. An example is a decision of the District Court of The Hague that applied secondary rules of attribution to review responsibility of a claim based in part on international rules.[70]

IV THE ESSENTIAL CONNECTION BETWEEN PRIMARY AND SECONDARY NORMS

The proper basis for giving domestic effect to secondary rules of international law is the essential connection between such norms, on the one hand, and primary norms, on the other. Secondary norms determine the existence and meaning of a primary norm and the consequences of its breach. It may be argued that the fundamental connection between primary and secondary norms should not be broken when a primary norm is transplanted into a national legal system. If a court gives effect to an international obligation disconnected from its secondary context, it does not give effect to that obligation, but to another norm.

[68] *The Republic of Ecuador v Occidental Exploration & Production Co* [2006] EWHC 345 (Comm) 90 (Aikens J).

[69] See Crawford, 'The ILC's Articles on Responsibility of States', above (n 55) 890 (noting that 'the secondary rules of state responsibility are only indirectly applicable in domestic courts, and they do not require legislative implementation').

[70] *HN v Netherlands (Ministry of Defence and Ministry of Foreign Affairs)* First instance judgment, LJN: BF0181/265615; ILDC 1092 (NL 2008).

This is both relevant to the application of national norms by an international court and to the application of international norms by national courts. As to the former, the Permanent Court of International Justice (PCIJ) said:

> Once the Court has arrived at the conclusion that it is necessary to apply the municipal law of a particular country, there seems no doubt that it must seek to apply it as it would be applied in that country. It would not be applying the municipal law of a country if it were to apply it in a manner different from that in which that law would be applied in the country in which it is in force.[71]

As to the latter, the essential connection between primary and secondary norms may help explain national cases that are guided by corresponding secondary norms of international law, regarding both interpretation[72] and remedies.[73] A particularly far-reaching, though rarely followed example, is the decision of the District Court of Rotterdam in the Netherlands, that in adjudicating claims of Dutch farmers who had suffered damage as a result of discharges of chlorides into the river Rhine by French mines near Strasburg, based its conclusion that a tort had been committed directly on the general principle of (international) law that a wrongful act entails responsibility.[74] Even though such cases are rare, there are a large number of other cases by which courts gave a more modest application to secondary rules and thereby maintained some convergence between the international and the national legal order. It is also this consideration that underlies the significant practice of judicial dialogues between national and international courts, even when decisions of international courts are not binding on the forum state,[75] as well as the practice of national courts to refer to interpretations of the courts of different states concerning the interpretation of international obligations.[76]

[71] *Brazilian Loans, France v United States*, Judgment PCIJ Series A no 21; ICGJ 261 (PCIJ 1929) para 72. See also, G Schwarzenberger, *International Law vol I International Law as Applied by International Courts and Tribunals* (London, Stevens & Sons, 1945) 25.

[72] Gardiner, above (n 27) 128; Criddle, above (n 27) 431.

[73] *Republic of Kenya v Minister For Home Affairs & 2 Others Ex parte Leonard Sitamze*, Miscellaneous Civil Case 1652 of 2004, (2008) eKLR, ILDC 1094; 18 April 2008 (High Court at Nairobi) (holding that where Kenya is a party to an international instrument whose provisions are not reflected in the Constitution, the Court must interpret the to address, recognize, and give remedies under that instrument provided that the instrument is not inconsistent with the Constitution).

[74] See, District Court of Rotterdam, 8 January 1979, NJ 1979, nr 113, *Id.*, 16 December 1983, NJ 1984, nr 341.

[75] See, eg, *Scattergood v Attorney General*, Appeal decision, Civil Appeal No 12/2005; ILDC 921 (CY 2005) (Supreme Court of Cyprus) (granting interpretive effect of to decisions of the ECtHR in cases to which Cyprus was not a party); *Callao Bar Association v Congress of the Republic*, Constitutional Review, Case No 00007-2007-PI/TC; ILDC 961 (PE 2007) (Constitutional Court of Peru) (granting interpretive effect of to decisions of the Inter-American Court of Human Rights in cases to which Peru was not a party).

[76] See, eg, MA Waters, 'Mediating Norms and Identity; The Role of Transnational Judicial Dialogue in Creating and Enforcing International Law' (2005) 93 *Georgetown Law Journal* 487;

Decisive in this approach is the qualification of the international or national nature of the obligation. If an obligation is qualified in international terms, it follows that international secondary rules should be applied. In the Advisory Opinion on the *Reparation for Injuries Suffered in the Service of the United Nations*, in reply to the question whether the United Nations has the capacity to bring an international claim against the responsible government to obtain reparation for damage to the United Nations, the International Court of Justice (ICJ) stated:

> As the claim is based on the breach of an international obligation on the part of the Member held responsible by the Organisation, the Member cannot contend that this obligation is governed by municipal law, and the Organisation is justified in giving its claim the character of an international claim.[77]

Likewise, an English court held that when an arbitral tribunal addressed the rights of Occidental Exploration & Production Co (OEPC) in international law vis-à-vis Ecuador, that

> if the tribunal concluded that international law rights of OEPC had been violated by Ecuador, or the latter was in breach of its international law obligations, then the tribunal will have to consider what remedies are available *in international law* to repair any damage caused to OEPC by Ecuador's breach of OEPC's international law rights (emphasis added).[78]

V SECONDARY RULES AS A NORMATIVE PENUMBRA

Given the essential connection between primary and secondary norms, the effect of secondary norms for the national legal order follows from the general principle of effective interpretation and application of international obligations.[79] The principle of effectiveness of performance serves to coordinate and ensure some degree of convergence between two legal systems. While states are not obliged to implement or copy all rules of international law into their national legal order, they should make those alterations and adjustments, and resort to those interpretations, that are necessary to ensure an effective application of their international

ME Adjami, 'African Courts, International Law, and Comparative Case Law: Chimera or Emerging Human Rights Jurisprudence?' (2002) 24 *Michigan Journal of International Law* 103; E Benvenisti, 'Reclaiming Democracy: The Strategic Uses of Foreign and International Law by National Courts' (2008) 102 *American Journal of International Law* 241.

77 *Reparation for Injuries Suffered in the Service of the United Nations* [1949] 174 ICJ Rep 180.

78 *The Republic of Ecuador v Occidental Exploration & Production Co* [2006] EWHC 345 (Comm) 122 (Aitkens J).

79 See on the former principle, H Lauterpacht, 'Restrictive Interpretation and the Principle of Effectiveness in the Interpretation of Treaties' (1949) 26 *British Yearbook of International Law* 67.

obligations.[80] This effect can also be based on the principle of good faith, as enshrined in Article 26 VCLT.[81] The ECtHR followed the same principle when it noted that 'it follows from the Convention, and from article 1 in particular, that in ratifying the Convention the Contracting States undertake to ensure that their national legislation is compatible with it'.[82] This effect also is related to the principle of effective treaty interpretation.

The principle of effective performance of international obligations thus should not be confined to the substantive principles in question, but should extend to the secondary rules that inform the meaning and application of the primary norms, to the extent that this would be necessary to ensure effective application of the international norm in question. A failure to make secondary rules part of national law will not in itself result in an internationally wrongful act. But a failure to give effect to an international obligation with the meaning and contents it has at the international plane may constitute a wrong. For giving effect to an international norm devoid of its international normative context, may well be to give effect to a different norm.

In the event that a state would have to answer for an alleged wrong before an international tribunal, it would have to convince that tribunal that it did not only give effect to an isolated international norm, but that that norm was interpreted and applied in the meaning that international law ascribed to it. It is this consideration, and the resulting need to give domestic effect to an international obligation in its international context, that explains the tendency of national courts to refer to the interpretative practice of international and foreign courts.[83]

In one respect, however, the power of this argument based on effective performance is limited. The scope of the principle of effective treaty interpretation and application, in principle is limited to the scope of the primary obligations. Secondary obligations are primarily relevant where it is necessary to perform an international obligation.

The situation is essentially different for cases where national courts seek guidance on international norms in areas where no obligation exists, for instance in regard to the adoption of national criminal laws that copy the provisions of the ICC Statute. Many states considered it desirable to follow the Statute, perhaps to enhance the chances that national trials would be respected under the complementarity principle. In doing so, they may

[80] The PCIJ referred to the principle according to which 'a State which has contracted valid international obligations is bound to make in its legislation such modifications as may be necessary to ensure the fulfillment of the obligations undertaken': *Greco-Bulgarian Communities* (Advisory Opinion, 1930) PCIJ Rep Series B No 17 at 20; G Schwarzenberger, *International Law* (Sweet & Maxwell, London, 1976) 68; S Kadelbach, 'International Law and the Incorporation of Treaties in Domestic Law' (1999) 42 *German Yearbook of International Law* 66.

[81] M Virally, 'Review Essay: Good Faith in Public International Law' (1983) 77 *American Journal of International Law* 130, 132.

[82] *Maestri v Italy* (App No 39748/98) (2004) 39 EHRR 832.

[83] See above (nn 65 and 66).

be inclined to interpret provisions of the ICC Statute in line with secondary rules of international law, precisely to enhance the prospect that they will apply the same law as the ICC would apply. Yet, that would not be the result of legal obligation.[84] Likewise, the South African Constitutional Court referred to VCLT to interpret provisions of the Constitution that substantively related to, but formally were not connected to international norms.[85] In this context, it is to be recalled that many, though not all, states apply the presumption of consistent interpretation (that is: national law should be construed as much as possible in conformity with international law) not only to legislation post-dating an international obligation, but to legislation that existed independently and perhaps even before an international obligation came into force.[86] In such cases, national courts may still value coherence between national and international law, for instance because they see themselves as part of a larger enterprise in the interest of the international community.[87]

This also means that the normative impact of secondary rules of international law may differ between particular rules of international law. For instance, the normative pull of principles of treaty interpretation may be strongest in the case of treaties that seek to establish a uniform regime.[88] These considerations may be quite different and in fact less relevant than for a treaty such as the ECHR that does not aim to lay down a minimum regime, but only minimum norms.[89]

Given that it is not (always) possible to construe the impact of secondary rules in terms of an international obligation to give effect to such rules, their impact may be explained in less formal terms. A convenient concept to describe the impact of secondary norms is the notion of

[84] G Werle and F Jessberger, *Principles of International Criminal Law* (Cambridge, Cambridge University Press, 2005) 74.

[85] L du Plessis, 'International Law and the Evolution of (Domestic) Human-Rights Law in Post-1994 South Africa' in JE Nijman and A Nollkaemper (eds), *New Perspectives on the Divide between National and International Law* (Oxford, Oxford University Press, 2007).

[86] G Betlem and A Nollkaemper, 'Giving Effect to Public International Law and European Community Law before Domestic Courts. A Comparative Analysis of the Practice of Consistent Interpretation' (2003) 14 *European Journal of International Law* 569.

[87] G Scelle, 'Règles générales du droit de la paix' (1933) 46 *Recueil des Cours de l'Académie de La Haye* 331–703, 356; H Lauterpacht, *International Law: Being the Collected Papers of Hersch Lauterpacht* vol 2 (Cambridge, Cambridge University Press, 1970) 567 (noting that where international law is part of national law – instead of proclaiming the exclusive authority of the national legal system – courts regard themselves, in addition to their normal function – as administering a law of a unit greater than the state); see also, D Halberstam and E Stein, 'The United Nations, the European Union, and the King of Sweden: Economic Sanctions and Individual Rights in a Plural World Order' (2009) 46 *Common Market Law Review* 72 (noting in respect to the ECJ that 'the Court acts not only as a court of the Community, but also as a court of the international legal system').

[88] See, eg, US Supreme Court, *Olympic Airways v Husain*, Appeal Judgment, 540 US 644 (2003); ILDC 703 (US 2003) 124 S Ct 1221 (2003), 24 February 2004, Scalia, dissenting (arguing that the interpretation of the Warsaw Convention should give serious consideration to how foreign courts of other signatories to the Convention had resolved these legal issues).

[89] Jacobs, above (n 25) xxxi.

'normative penumbra'. Penumbra means, literally, 'dim light'. It is the outer filamentary region of a sunspot. A 'penumbra' may be any area of transition around an area of great light. The grey area in between the light and the shadow is the penumbra. This use of this term follows the use of the term by US Supreme Court Justice Holmes, who used the term 'penumbra' to refer to 'outer bounds of authority emanating from a law'.[90] Later the Supreme Court used the concept to find that privacy in the 'marital bedroom' is defined in the 'penumbra' of constitutional rights, which do not specifically define a privacy right, but imply it.[91]

The term 'normative penumbra' is used here to refer to the phenomenon that international norms may exert normative power beyond the international legal system, into its periphery or penumbra. It may be argued that the secondary rules of international law serve as a normative penumbra, that informs the meaning of corresponding rules at national level, and that remain applicable to the interpretation, modification and termination of international obligations at national level.[92] Secondary rules of international law are connected to the primary norms, and when the latter are applied, the former lift along.

VI THE LIMITING EFFECT OF NATIONAL LAW

The degree in which a domesticated international norm will, in any particular case, be determined or influenced by secondary rules of international law will depend to a large extent on the constitutional principles governing the status of international law in the national legal order.

While secondary rules of international law may have a normative impact in all national legal systems, the foundation and the degree to which they will do so will differ between states. Three situations may be distinguished. First, when states have incorporated an international obligation into national law, based on a general rule of reference, such as is the case in the United States[93] or the Netherlands,[94] that obligation generally

[90] *Danforth v Groton Water Co*, 178 Mass. 472, 476–77, 59 N.E. 1033, 1034 [1901] 477. See also, OW Holmes and M Lerner, 'Tax Law and the Prenumbra – Schlesinger v Wisconsin' in OW Holmes and M Lerner (eds), *The Mind and Faith of Justice Holmes: His Speeches, Essays, Letters, and Judicial Opinions* (Edison, Transaction Publishers, 1988) 257 and A Lief, *The Dissenting Opinions of Mr Justice Holmes* (Buffalo, Hein Publishing, 1981) 156.

[91] *Griswold v Connecticut*, 381 US 479 (1965); see also *Roe v Wade*, 410 US 113 (1973).

[92] Nollkaemper, 'Internationally Wrongful Acts in Domestic Courts', above (n 42) 760.

[93] Such as art VI of the US Constitution, providing that 'This Constitution, and the laws of the United States which shall be made in pursuance thereof; and all treaties made, or which shall be made, under the authority of the United States, shall be the supreme law of the land; and the judges in every state shall be bound thereby, anything in the Constitution or laws of any State to the contrary notwithstanding'. CM Vazquez, 'Treaties as Law of the Land: the Supremacy Clause and the Judicial Enforcement of Treaties' (2008) 122 *Harvard Law Review* 599.

[94] JG Brouwer, 'The Netherlands' in JG Brouwer (ed), *National Treaty Law and Practice: Dedicated to the Memory of Monroe Leigh* (Leiden, Nijhoff, 2005) 483.

will remain recognizable as such. A national court that gives effect to that norm, in any case when it is self-executing, will apply that norm, not a domestic 'translation' thereof. The situation is similar in states, like the UK or Israel, where customary law is automatically part of national law.[95] Courts then continue to apply international law (rather than national law) also after its incorporation into the national legal system.[96]

In this situation, secondary rules of international law remain attached to the primary norms and there remains a direct connection between the international origin of a norm and its domestic life. It may not be entirely accurate to say that what national courts apply is exclusively international law, as it is obvious that once the relevant international norms have been made part of national law, they are for all sorts of purposes also part of national law. However, it may at least be said that the domesticated international norm maintains an international quality and that the normative context of the international norms will feed the reception at national level.

To some extent this also applies in another situation, when states use incorporating legislation. This holds both for 'monistic' states (in particular when treaty provisions are not self-executing) and 'dualistic' states, that by necessity rely on such legislation. In such cases, the international origin may still be relatively clear when an implementing statute refers to an international norm without copying it. For instance, the immigration rules of the United Kingdom define an asylum applicant as a person who 'makes a request to be recognised as a refugee under the Geneva Convention on the basis that it would be contrary to the United Kingdom's obligations under the Geneva Convention for him to be removed from or required to leave the United Kingdom'.[97] For the application of this provision, a court will have to interpret the Convention clearly as an international instrument. Another example is the UK Human Rights Act, which clearly is based on the European Convention and that indeed in terms of its interpretation is influenced by the interpretation of the European Convention.[98]

[95] Supreme Court of Israel, *Physicians for Human Rights and ors v Prime Minister and ors, and joined case,* Original petition to the High Court of Justice, HCJ 201/09, 248/09; ILDC 1213 (IL 2009) para 15. An English translation is available at: www. elyon1.court.gov.il/files_eng/09/010/002/n07/09002010.n07.pdf.

[96] MS McDougal, 'The Impact of International Law upon National Law: A Policy-oriented Perspective' (1959) 4 *South Dakota Law Review* 25; reprinted in McDougal and Associates, *Studies in World Public Order* (New Haven, Yale University Press, 1960) 206; R Müllerson, *Ordering Anarchy: International Law in International Society* (The Hague, Martinus Nijhoff Publishers, 2000) 200.

[97] Para 327a of the Immigration Rules, available at: www.ukba.homeoffice.gov.uk/policyandlaw/immigrationlaw/immigrationrules/part1.

[98] See, eg, *R (Ullah) v Special Adjudicator; R (Do) v Secretary of State for the Home Department* [2002] EWCA Civ 1856 (CA); ILDC 249 (UK 2002) para 48 (relying on jurisprudence of the ECtHR).

A different situation arises in a third category, where a treaty is translated into statutes that do not expressly recognize its origin. In these cases, the original international quality may go unrecognized. The international origin then may be clouded and, for all practical purposes, the international norm has indeed started to lead a separate, domestic, life. There may be a certain paradox here; in particular, when an international obligation of non-self executing domestic legislatures will necessarily have to adopt national law to make it effective and give contents to such an obligation. Yet, the more an international obligation becomes embedded in and effective in national law, the more the international origin will be lost.

In each of these three situations, national law is likely to set limits to the degree secondary rules of international law may indeed cast their effect into national law. National law and domestic constituencies may counteract the pull towards normative convergence exercised by secondary rules of international law. The familiar patterns of collisions between primary norms of international law and national law finds its parallel in potential conflicts between secondary norms of international law and national law.

National law will in particular limit the effects of secondary rules of international law in the third situation identified above (incorporation of an obligation in a statute that no longer displays the international origin), but it also holds for the first two categories, in which various methods may be used to limit the power of courts (or other organs) to give full effect to the meaning of an international norms as recognized at the international level, for instance by precluding the self-executing nature of a treaty (thus dis-connecting the link between the national norm and its international origin) or by obliging the courts to defer to the executive. For instance, a US Court of Appeals held that there was no need to resort to a review of the *travaux préparatoires* with regard to an ambiguous treaty provision when enforcement of that provision was controlled by national law.[99] Moreover, in many states, courts tend as a matter of national law to defer to the executive in matters of treaty interpretation.[100] An example is the US Military Commissions Act, conferring on the President the authority for the United States to interpret the meaning and application of the Geneva Conventions that shall be authoritative as a matter of US law, and thus may restrict the scope of interpretation otherwise afforded to the judicial branch.[101]

[99] *Cornejo v County of San Diego and ors*, Appeal Judgment, 504 F3d 853 (9th Cir 2007); ILDC 1080 (US 2007), 24. See also *Kolovrat v Oregon*, 366 US 187, 194 (1961).

[100] United States, Court of Appeals for the Second Circuit, *Mora v New York*, Appeal Judgment, 524 F3d 183 (2d Cir 2008); ILDC 1100 (US 2008), 24 April 2008 (Consistent with the common practice of US courts in treaty interpretation cases, the views of the US government were entitled to substantial deference). See also J Yoo, *The Powers of War and Peace: the Constitution and Foreign Affairs after 9/11* (Chicago, University of Chicago Press, 2005) 190; CR Sunstein, 'Chevronizing Foreign Relations Law' (2007) 116 *Yale Law Journal* 1170.

[101] Military Commissions Act 2006, *Public Law* 109–366 (17 October 2006).

The notion of normative penumbra is not a conflict rule that can resolve conflicts between international law and national law in favour of the former. To the extent that national law indeed pulls in a different direction, similar primary norms, existing at international and national level, will start to lead a different life, each serving different constituencies.

VII CONCLUSION

Within limits set by the domestic legislature, national courts have considerable leeway in placing their application of an international obligation in its international context. There is a not insignificant and probably increasing practice in which national courts do not just apply single international norms, but give effect to the wider normative context. This practice has great potential in allowing national courts to contribute to a normative convergence between international and national law across legal orders. This practice can only be partially explained in terms of obligations of states to give effect to such secondary norms. Rather, the proper explanation and normative basis may be found in the combination of the connection between primary and secondary norms of international law, and the principles of good faith and effective treaty performance. The result is that secondary rules have the power to project, as a penumbra, their meaning into domestic legal orders that, by way of obligation or otherwise, have adopted equivalent norms. However, the power of the penumbra weakens where national law interjects and imposes its own secondary rules, serving its own domestic purposes.

4

Multi-Sourced Equivalent Norms from the Standpoint of Governments

Erik Denters and Tarcisio Gazzini

I INTRODUCTION

SITUATIONS GOVERNED BY Multi-Sourced Equivalent Norms (MSENs) are normally examined in the context of the judicial settlement of disputes. The chapter aims at taking one step back and explores how governments behave when confronted with these situations. This chapter first compares the different perspectives of tribunals and states with regard to the interpretation and application of MSENs (section II). It then examines the two categories of MSENs, namely 'identical' and 'similar' MSENs, introduced by the definition of MSENs adopted for the purpose of this volume (sections III and IV respectively).[1] It finally discusses the governmental decision-making process leading to compliance – or non-compliance – with obligations imposed by MSENs (section V) and considers how and to what extent consistent state practice contributes to the convergence of MSENs and ultimately to the unity of international law (section VI).

This chapter focuses primarily but not exclusively on obligations related to international investment. The choice of substance is due to the density and variety of international commitments in this area and the intense interaction between investment treaties *inter se* and between these treaties and both customary international law and non-investment treaties.

This chapter takes a realist perspective based on the assessment of the positive and negative effects of compliance (or non-compliance)[2] and is

[1] See in this volume, T Broude and Y Shany, 'The International Law and Policy of Multi-Sourced Equivalent Norms' in T Broude and Y Shany (eds), *Multi-Sourced Equivalent Norms in International Law* (Oxford, Hart Publishing, 2011) p 1. The definition reads: 'MSENs can be defined as two or more norms which are (1) binding upon the same international legal subjects; (2) similar or identical in their normative content [in the words of the ILC, "point in the same direction"]; and (3) have been established through different international instruments or "legislative" procedures or are applicable to different substantive areas of the law'.

[2] For a concise and clear discussion of the main international relations approaches to the decision-making process concerning compliance with investment treaties, see M Hirsch,

developed against the background of the debate over the unity of international law, which is primarily concerned with compliance with international rules.

II GOVERNMENTAL *VERSUS* JUDICIAL PERSPECTIVE

Before examining how governments deal with MSENs, it is appropriate to briefly discuss how their perspective is analogous to or different from that of international tribunals.[3] Starting with the similarities, governments and tribunals alike generally interpret MSENs contained in international treaties in accordance with Articles 31 and 32 of the Vienna Convention on the Law of Treaties (VCLT)[4] that reflect customary international law.[5] In particular, governments and tribunals must account for other MSENs that may be applicable between the parties as required under Article 31(3)(c) VCLT that stipulates that treaties are to be interpreted taking into account 'any relevant rules of international law applicable in the relations between the parties'.[6]

Governments and tribunals also share the method used to establish the existence and content of customary rules. They both must be satisfied about the two elements which concur to the creation and evolution of customary rules, namely extensive, uniform and representative state practice (objective element) and *opinio juris* (subjective element).[7] This method has

'Compliance with Investment Treaties: When are States More Likely to Breach or Comply with Investment Treaties?' in C Binder et al, *International Investment Law for the 21st Century. Essays in Honour of Christoph Schreuer* (Oxford, Oxford University Press, 2009) 865.

[3] This chapter focuses on executive bodies, although legislative and judicial bodies may also be confronted with MSENs. For a discussion on interpretation and implementation of treaties within national legal systems see R Gardiner, *Treaty Interpretation* (Oxford, Oxford University Press, 2008) 126–33.

[4] Vienna Convention on the Law of Treaties (adopted 23 May 1969, entered into force 27 January 1980) 1155 UNTS 331 (VCLT).

[5] See *Application of the Convention on the Prevention and Punishment of the Crime of Genocide* (Judgment) [2007] ICJ Rep, para 160; *Case Concerning the Dispute Regarding Navigational and Related Rights* (Judgment, 13 July 2009) para 47: www.icj-cij.org/docket/files/133/15321.pdf.

[6] In the field of foreign investment, see for instance, *Saluka Investments BV (The Netherlands) v Czech Republic* (UNCITRAL Arbitration) Partial Award (17 March 2006) para 254. In general, see C McLachlan, 'The Principle of Systemic Integration and Article 31(3)(c) of the Vienna Convention' (2005) 54 *International and Comparative Law Quarterly* 279; D French, 'Treaty Interpretation and the Incorporation of Extraneous Legal Rules' (2006) 55 *International and Comparative Law Quarterly* 55; U Linderfalk, 'Who are "the Parties"? Article 31, Paragraph 3(c) of the Vienna Convention and the "Principle of Systemic Integration" Revisited' (2008) 55 *New York International Law Review* 343. As maintained by P Sands, 'Treaty, Custom and the Cross-fertilization of International Law (1998) 88 *Yale Human Rights & Development Law Journal* 85, 95 '[t]his rule of interpretation reflects a "principle of integration" [and] emphasizes both the "unity of international law" and the sense in which rules should not be considered in isolation of general international law'.

[7] See International Law Association, Committee on the Formation of Customary (General) International Law, *Final Report* (London, 2000): www.ila-hq.org/html/layout_committee.htm.

been consistently adopted by the International Court of Justice (ICJ)[8] and is generally accepted in literature.[9]

Four main differences concerning the application of MSENs by governments and international courts can be pointed out. First, in judicial proceedings, MSENs may be entangled with jurisdictional questions, as illustrated in the *Nicaragua* case. In that case, the United States unsuccessfully challenged the ICJ's jurisdiction on the basis of the multilateral treaty reservation to the declaration under Article 36(2) of the Statute of Court.[10] Faced with MSENs on the use of force, however, the Court held that it could not dismiss 'claims of Nicaragua under principles of customary and general international law, simply because such principles have been enshrined in the texts of the conventions relied upon by Nicaragua'.[11]

Governments, on the contrary, deal with MSENs as substantive rules which prescribe, allow or prohibit a certain identical or similar conduct. Given their plenipotentiary powers, they are not initially concerned with jurisdictional issues, although the possibility of facing judicial proceedings may influence their conduct.

Secondly, tribunals may apply MSENs only insofar as they are allowed to do so by the provisions governing the law applicable to the dispute they are settling. The applicable law may be found in the relevant provisions contained either in the treaty itself,[12] or in the legal instrument providing for the judicial settlement of the dispute.[13]

[8] See *North Sea Continental Shelf Cases* [1969] ICJ Rep 3, 43 ff; *Continental Shelf* (*Libyan Arab Jamahiriya/Malta*) (Judgment) [1985] ICJ Rep 13, 29–30; *Case Concerning Military and Paramilitary Activities in and against Nicaragua* (Merits) [1986] ICJ Rep 14, 97 ff and 107–08; *Legality of the Threat or Use of Nuclear Weapons* (Advisory Opinion) [1996] ICJ Rep 226, 253 ff. For a critical analysis, see P Haggenmacher, 'La doctrine des deux éléments du droit coutumier dans la pratique de la Cour internationale' (1986) 90 *Revue Générale de Droit International Public* 5; MH Mendelson, 'The Formation of Customary International Law' (1998) 272 *Recueil des Cours de l'Académie de Droit International* 155.

[9] See, in particular H Waldock, 'General Course on Public International Law' (1962) 106 *Recueil des Cours de l'Académie de Droit International* 1, 49; K Wolfke, *Custom in Present International Law* 2nd edn (Dordrecht, Nijhoff, 1993).

[10] Statute of the International Court of Justice, 26 June 1945, available at: www.icj-cij.org. The reservation has been described by HW Briggs, 'Nicaragua v United States. Jurisdiction and Admissibility' (1985) 79 *American Journal of International Law* 373, 378 as 'nonsensical'.

[11] *Case Concerning Military and Paramilitary Activities in and against Nicaragua* (Jurisdiction and Admissibility) [1984] ICJ Rep 392, para 73. See also UNCLOS, Arbitral Tribunal (4 August 2000) *Southern Bluefin Tuna* (2000) 39 ILM 1359.

[12] According to art 26(6) Energy Charter Treaty (ECT) (adopted 17 December 1994, entered into force 16 April 1998) www.enchArticleer.org, for instance, tribunals 'shall decide the issues in dispute in accordance with this Treaty and applicable rules and principles of international Law'. See also, art 1131 North American Free Trade Agreement (NAFTA) (adopted 17 December 1992, entered into force 1 January 2001). For an example among many concerning bilateral investment treaties (BITs), see art10 (4) of the BIT between China and the Netherlands.

[13] See, in particular, art 42(1) of the ICSID Convention on the Settlement of Investment Disputes Between States and Nationals of Other States (adopted 18 March 1965, entered into force 14 October 1966) 575 UNTS 159 according to which 'The Tribunal shall decide a dispute in accordance with such rules of law as may be agreed by the parties. In the absence of such

In contrast, governments are expected to consider all MSENs that are relevant in a given situation. As a result, governments are confronted with MSENs more frequently and intensely than tribunals. Governments' conduct in dealing with other subjects of international law – both in terms of complying with their obligations and enjoying their rights – and of implementing international law within their jurisdiction is often determined by MSENs.

Moreover, governments' conduct may be prescribed by MSENs in *statu nascendi*, especially when they are interested in the evolution of these MSENs into *lex lata*. Tribunals, on the contrary, are prevented from applying *lex ferenda* unless the jurisdictional clause indicates it as applicable law.[14]

Thirdly, the question of applicable law before tribunals may be complicated by the systemic interpretation required under Article 31(3)(c) VCLT. In theory, the two questions – application and interpretation – must be kept distinct. The law applicable by an international tribunal refers primarily to the relevant legal rules governing the substantive issues in dispute. These rules are normally agreed on by the parties and may well belong, especially in the field of investment, to national legal orders.[15] Article 31(3)(c), on the contrary, commands international tribunals to take into account all relevant rules of *international law* applicable in the relations between the parties for the purpose of interpreting an international treaty. Such a command is independent from the consent of the parties and limited to international rules.

Article 31(3)(c) must be applied with caution. A tribunal may be prevented from applying rule A as this rule does not fall within the applicable law and, following the methodology of Article 31(3)(c), simultaneously 'take into account' any relevant rule, including rule A. While 'applying' a rule and 'take into account' a rule are two different exercises, the distinction may not always be easily acknowledged as demonstrated by the ICJ's decision in *Oil Platforms*[16] which was criticized in separate/dissenting opinions

agreement, the Tribunal shall apply the law of the Contracting State party to the dispute (including its rules on the conflict of laws) and such rules of international law as may be applicable'. See E Gaillard and Y Banifatemi, 'The Meaning of "and" in Article 42(1), Second Sentence, of the Washington Convention: The Role of International Law in the ICSID Choice of Law Process' (2003) 18 *ICSID Review – Foreign Investment Law Journal* 375.

[14] In *Ireland v United Kingdom* ('OSPAR' Arbitration), Final Award, 2 July 2003, para 99: www.pca-cpa.org/upload/files/OSPAR%20Award.pdf, the Arbitral Tribunal declined to apply *lex ferenda*, which it referred to as 'almost' law. The tribunal mentioned *Continental Shelf (Tunisia/Libyan Arab Jamahiriya)* (Judgment) [1969] ICJ Rep 18, para 4, as an example of a decision in which the parties mandated the ICJ to apply *lex ferenda*, namely the new accepted trends in the Third Conference on the Law of the Sea.

[15] For the different meanings of applicable law in international commercial arbitration, see A Redfern, M Hunter, N Blackaby and C Partasides, *Law and Practice of International Commercial Arbitration* 4th edn (London, Sweet & Maxwell, 2004) ch 2.

[16] *Case Concerning Oil Platforms (Iran v US)* (Judgment) [2003] ICJ Rep 161.

and in literature.[17] In the case of multilateral treaties, furthermore, it remains to be seen whether the interpreter has to take into account the rules applicable in the relations between all parties to the dispute or rather all parties to the treaty which is being interpreted.[18]

Unlike tribunals, governments are not affected by the risk of blurring the distinction between applicable law and systemic interpretation. Indeed, they are expected to comply with *all* relevant MSENs. By the same token it is immaterial whether all the parties to a multilateral treaty containing one or more MSEN need also be bound by the other treaty for the purpose of Article 31(3)(c).

Fourthly, tribunals are supposed to operate from a strictly legal perspective. In settling international disputes, they apply the legal rules they are mandated to apply by the parties or other relevant legal instruments. This is without prejudice to the right of the parties to ask the tribunal to decide *ex aequo et bono*, a possibility expressly provided for, for instance, in Article 42(3) ICSID[19] and Article 38(2) of the Statute of the ICJ.[20]

In contrast, governments do not usually consider MSENs from an exclusively legal perspective. In foreign affairs matters, legal questions are embedded in a politicized environment whereas tribunals are expected to be politically neutral. A legal counsel of a foreign affairs department may have a strong opinion on the proper interpretation and application of a rule, but his legal communication will not necessarily be followed when it is found politically undesirable or impracticable.[21]

An example of strong political involvedness is the treatment of so-called sovereign wealth funds (SWFs). Such funds aim at investing abroad and are controlled by a state or one of its subdivisions. SWFs may have market access under the General Agreement on Trade in Services (GATS) and

[17] See, in particular, *ibid*, R Higgins (Separate Opinion) 225, 235–38. See also H Thirlway, 'The Law and Procedure of the International Court of Justice 1960–1989, Supplement, 2006: Part Three' (2006) 77 *British Yearbook of International Law* 1, 73.

[18] In *European Communities – Approval and Marketing of Biotech Products*, Panel Report, WT/DS291/R, 29 September 2006 (unappealed) para 7.70, the Panel held that 'it makes sense to interpret Article 31(3)(c) as requiring consideration of those rules of international law which are applicable in the relations between all parties to the treaty which is being interpreted'. In literature, compare, for instance, J Pauwelyn, *Conflict of Norms in Public International Law. How WTO Law Relates to other Rules of International Law* (Cambridge, Cambridge University Press, 2003); see especially 460–61, with J Trachtman, 'The Domain of WTO Dispute Resolution' (1999) 40 *Harvard Journal of International Law* 333, especially 342.

[19] Available at: www.icsid.worldbank.org (entered into force 14 October 1966).

[20] Available at: www.icj-icj.org (entered into force 24 October 1945).

[21] On the political environment in which legal US State Department Legal Advisers have to operate, see MP Scharf, 'International Law in Crisis: A Qualitative Empirical Contribution to the Compliance Debate' (2009) 31 *Cardozo Law Review* 1, 45–96. In the Netherlands, a report of the Iraq Committee revealed that legal advice of foreign affairs legal counsels on the legitimacy of the armed attack on Iraq on 20 March 2003 was ignored. Contrary to the legal opinion the government argued that a material breach of UNSC Res 1441 would justify the use of force against Iraq. The report was published on 12 January 2010: www.onderzoekscommissie-irak.nl.

enjoy protection under bilateral investment treaties (BITs), but still be denied access under domestic laws because governments may disapprove of investments by a foreign sovereign investor.[22] Although legally disputable, there have so far been no cases where the refusal to admit SWFs has been challenged before international tribunals.[23]

In a politicized setting, there may also be some bias in favour of or against a particular interpretation of a MSEN. This may depend on the orientation of the government agency involved. For instance, a MSEN such as the requirement to prevent 'unjustifiable or arbitrary discrimination' when applying trade restrictive measures[24] deals with the relationship between trade and environment. An executive officer of the trade ministry might have a different view on the proper application of this MSEN than an officer from an environmental department.

In the application of MSENs, political considerations will often be accompanied by a cost-benefit analysis. In dealing with two or more MSENs, governments need to define their respective contents, examine to what extent they may diverge and figure out which kinds of remedies they provide for. This delicate analysis is particularly important in respect to the decision concerning compliance – or non-compliance – with some or all of the obligations imposed by MSENs.

The following example illustrates a typical situation governed by MSENs. A Swiss investment in the service sector in Croatia is protected by several legal instruments containing a variety of MSENs. [25] In particular, under Article VIII(2) of the Articles of Agreement of the International Monetary Fund (IMF Articles),[26] Article XI(1) of GATS, Article 5 of the

[22] Examples are the disputed acquisition of UNOCAL by the Chinese SWF Cnooc and P&O by Dubai Ports World. For a Chinese perspective see, 'US lawmakers meddle in CNOOC's Unocal bid' *China Daily* (6 July 2005): www.chinadaily.com.cn/english/doc/2005-07/06/content_457677.htm. For a discussion on SWFs see, *Generally Accepted Principles and Practices (GAPP) – Santiago Principles*, October 2008, adopted under the auspices of the IMF: www.iwg-swf.org/pubs/eng/santiagoprinciples.pdf.

[23] See Swiss Department of Foreign Affairs, 'Accords de promotion et protection des investissements. Qualité d'investisseur octroyée à un Etat et traitement à donner à ses investissements', Legal Opinion (20 November 2007) GAAC 2008.11, 183–88.

[24] This MSEN can be found in the chapeau of art XX, General Agreement on Tariffs and Trade (GATT); Preamble and art 5(5), Agreement on the Application of Sanitary and Phytosanitary Measures; art XIV, General Agreement on Trade in Services (GATS); art 4, Agreement on Trade-Related Aspects of Intellectual Property Rights (TRIPS). All these agreements are available at: www.wto.org and entered into force on 1 January 1995. See also, art 3(5) of the UN Framework Convention on Climate Change (1992) 31 ILM 851 (UNFCCC); and Principle 12 of the 1992 Rio Declaration on Environment and Development, UN Doc A/CONF. 151/26/Rev 1 (1992): www.unep.org/Documents.Multilingual/Default.asp?documentID=78&ArticleID=1163..

[25] For a critical assessment of the degree of consistency between BITs, FTAs and GATS, see F Ortino and A Sheppard, 'International Agreements Covering Foreign Investment in Services: Patterns and Linkages' in L Bartels and F Ortino (eds), *Regional Trade Agreements and the WTO Legal System* (Oxford, Oxford University Press, 2006) 201.

[26] Articles of Agreement of the International Monetary Fund (adopted 22 July 1944, entered into force 27 December 1945) 2 UNTS 39.

Bilateral Investment Treaty (BIT) between Switzerland and Croatia,[27] and Article 13 of the Free Trade Agreement between EFTA and Croatia (FTA EFTA – Croatia),[28] Croatia must refrain – subject to certain exceptions – from adopting measures restricting payments on current transactions.[29] If a dispute arises, World Trade Organization (WTO) adjudicatory bodies, investment arbitral tribunals and a tribunal established within the FTA may apply different MSENs or different combinations of MSENs depending on the respective rules governing applicable law.

In contrast, the governments of Croatia or Switzerland are expected to comply in good faith with *all* relevant MSENs. Governments are also aware that in case of violation of the relevant MSENs, different remedies would be available to different subjects. According to Article XXVI(2) of the IMF Articles, the IMF may declare the member that has failed to comply with any of the obligations imposed in the Articles, ineligible to use the general resources of the Fund. Under Article XXIII(1) GATS, all Members of the Organization could resort to the WTO dispute settlement system.[30] Under Article 8 of the Swiss-Croat BIT, in turn, a Swiss investor may file a case before the International Centre for Settlement of Investment Disputes (ICSID). Under both Article 9 of the Swiss-Croat BIT and Article 29 and Annex VIII of the Free Trade Agreement between EFTA and Croatia, finally, Switzerland may bring the case before an arbitral tribunal.

III IDENTICAL MSENS

Identical MSENs can be defined as MSENs imposing exactly the same obligations on the same addressees. Identical MSENs may be contained in two or more treaties, or co-exist in treaty law and customary international law. As held by the ICJ in the *Nicaragua* case,

> even if a treaty norm and a customary norm . . . were to have exactly the same content, this would not be a reason for the Court to take the view that the operation of the treaty process must necessarily deprive the customary norm of its separate applicability.[31]

[27] Bilateral Investment Treaty (BIT) between Switzerland and Croatia (adopted 30 October 1996, entered into force 17 June 1997): www.admin.ch/ch/f/as/2002/537.pdf.

[28] Free Trade Agreement between EFTA and Croatia (FTA EFTA – Croatia) (adopted 21 June 2001, entered into force 1 April 2002): www.efta.int/content/legal-texts/third-country-relations/croatia/HR-FTA.pdf.

[29] A payment for a current transaction means a payment due in connection with foreign trade, other current business, including services, and normal short-term banking and credit facilities. *Cf* art XXX IMF Articles of Agreement; art XXX: www.imf.org/external/pubs/ft/aa/aa30.htm.

[30] Croatia and Switzerland are both members of the IMF and WTO.

[31] *Nicaragua* (Merits), above (n 8) para 175.

The striking feature of the *Nicaragua* case is indeed the extent of the agreement on the essential correspondence between the rules of the Charter concerning the use of force and non-intervention, and the parallel rules to be found in customary international law.[32] This view was shared by some of the judges who wrote separate or dissenting opinions[33] and by both the parties.[34] The United States, in part, maintained without hesitation that the Charter '*is* the "customary and general international law" with respect to the questions concerning the lawfulness of the use of armed force'.[35]

The coexistence of identical MSENs embodied in different treaties may be due in the first place, to their identical text, although textually identical MSENs are less common than one may expect. Sometimes MSENs are modelled after each other and have virtually identical texts. This is the case, for instance, of the performance requirements prohibited under both Article 2 of the Agreement on Trade-Related Investment Measures (TRIMs)[36] and Article 5 of Energy Charter Treaty (ECT).

Under Article 2 TRIMs, WTO members must refrain from adopting any TRIM which is inconsistent with the obligation of national treatment or the obligation to eliminate quantitative restrictions, respectively, under Articles III and XI GATT. An annex to the treaty provides a non-exhaustive illustrative list of prohibited TRIMs. Article 5 ECT reproduces the content of Article 2 TRIMs, and the non-exhaustive list of TRIMs is directly included in the text.

However, identical texts do not necessarily amount to conclusive evidence as to their identical normative content. The same terms or expressions contained in provisions of different treaties – and even of the same treaty[37] – may bear different meanings. In the *Mox Plant* case, the International Tribunal

[32] In *Legal Consequences of the Construction of a Wall in the Occupied Palestinian Territory* (Advisory Opinion) [2004] ICJ Rep 1984 136, para 87, the ICJ relied on the *Nicaragua* case to affirm that 'the principles as to the use of force incorporated in the Charter reflect customary international law'.

[33] *Nicaragua* case, (Ago, Separate Opinion), *ibid*, 183, spoke of a 'virtual identity' of and 'close correspondence' between treaty and customary rules on the use of force. See also, Schwebel (Dissenting Opinion), *ibid*, 614.

[34] Nicaragua took the view that 'the principles contained in art 2(4) of the Charter form part of general international law'. *Case Concerning Military and Paramilitary Activities in and Against Nicaragua* (Memorial Pleadings) [1984] ICJ Rep 4, 118.

[35] *Case Concerning Military and Paramilitary Activities in and Against Nicaragua* (Counter-Memorial Pleadings) ICJ Rep 2, 91. It further observed that 'Article 2(4) of the Charter is customary and general international law', *ibid*, 94 (italics in the original).

[36] Agreement on Trade-Related Investment Measures (adopted 15 April 1994, entered into force 1 January 1995) 1868 UNTS 186 (TRIMs).

[37] See, for instance, the meaning of 'like product' across WTO law. In WTO, *Japan – Alcoholic Beverages* (4 October 1996) WT/DS8/AB/R at 21, the Appellate Body held that '[t]he concept of "likeness" is a relative one that evokes the image of an accordion. The accordion of "likeness" stretches and squeezes in different places as different provisions of the WTO Agreement are applied. The width of the accordion in any one of those places must be determined by the particular provision in which the term "like" is encountered as well as by the context and the circumstances that prevail in any given case to which that provision may apply'.

for the Law of the Sea (ITLOS) pointed out that 'the application of international law rules on interpretation of treaties to identical or similar provisions of different treaties may not yield the same results, having regard to, *inter alia*, differences in the respective contexts, objects and purposes, subsequent practice of parties and *travaux préparatoires*'.[38] The finding is undoubtedly correct. It must, nonetheless, be stressed that the tribunal referred to potential normative differences as a reason not to defer jurisdiction over a case that could have been brought elsewhere. Furthermore, nothing in the award undermines the very strong – yet still rebuttable – presumption on the convergent meaning of identical or similar provisions.[39]

Conversely, MSENs may have identical content in spite of differently formulated text. A state may be bound to admit a foreign investor in the service sector by virtue of both the GATS and of a BIT.[40] Although the former is based on the so-called positive listing approach and the later normally on the negative listing approach,[41] both treaties may provide for the admission of a certain category of foreign investors under the same conditions.

MSENs may also converge into identical norms due to their interaction or their interpretation and application. The prohibition on torture and inhuman treatment, for instance, is contained in a number of international treaties including the UN Convention against torture,[42] several regional and universal human rights treaties[43] and several humanitarian law treaties.[44] As held by the International Criminal Tribunal for former Yugoslavia in *Prosecutor v Furundžija*:

[38] *MOX Plant (Ireland v United Kingdom)* (Provisional Measures, Order of 3 December 2001) ITLOS Reports 2001, 51. The non-exhaustive list also includes, in accordance with art 31(3)(c) VCLT, above (n 6), any other rules applicable to the parties.

[39] As pointed out by Griffith in dissenting opinion in *Ireland v United Kingdom* ('OSPAR' Arbitration), above (n 14) para 23, 'ordinary principles of comity and interpretation may here be invoked to suggest that the same State Parties broadly may be assumed to understand similarly or identically worded obligations in the same way'.

[40] A significant number of BITs, including several concluded by the US, Canada and Japan, provide for the right to admission. See also, NAFTA above (n 12) art 1102 (1).

[41] A positive list approach in GATS means that WTO members must offer market access and national treatment only to the extent they have accepted obligations in a given service sector. GATT works the other way around. WTO members must accept market access and national treatment unless an exception can be invoked. *Cf* M Matsushita, TJ Schoenbaum and PC Mavroidis, *The World Trade Organization: Law, Practice and Policy* (Oxford, Oxford University Press, 2003) 240.

[42] Convention against Torture and Other Cruel, Inhuman or Degrading Treatment or Punishment, (adopted 10 December 1984, entered into force 26 June 1987) 1465 UNTS 85.

[43] International Covenant on Civil and Political Rights (adopted 16 December 1966, entered into force 23 March 1976) 999 UNTS 171 (ICPR) arts 7 and 10(1); Convention for the Protection of Human Rights and Fundamental Freedoms (adopted 4 November 1950, entered into force 3 September 1953) amended by Protocols nos 3, 5, 8 and 11 (entered into force 21 September 1970, 20 December 1971, 1 January 1990 and 1 November 1998 respectively) 213 UNTS 222 (ECHR) art 3; American Convention on Human Rights (adopted 21 November 1969, entered into force 18 July 1978) 1144 UNTS 123, art 5(2); African Charter on Human and Peoples' Rights (adopted 27 June 1981, entered into force 21 October 1986) 1520 UNTS 217, art 5.

[44] With regard to international armed conflicts, see Geneva Convention for the Amelioration of the Condition of the Wounded and Sick in Armed Forces in the Field (adopted 12 August

> [t]he broad convergence of the aforementioned international instruments and international jurisprudence demonstrates that there is now general acceptance of the main elements contained in the definition set out in Article 1 of the Torture Convention.[45]

In this case, the general adoption of the same definition of torture results from the interaction of the different treaties and of the cross-fertilization of the decisions of international tribunals and bodies. This is another confirmation of the consolidated tendency of international tribunals to take into account – without any formal kind of legal obligation – the decisions and experience of other tribunals. It is a common feature of all international tribunals to borrow legal reasoning from each other, even if they are mandated to settle disputes in distinct substantive areas or between different subjects.[46] Investment arbitral tribunals, for instance, have on several occasions referred to the jurisprudence of the ICJ, the Appellate Body of the WTO and the European Court of Human Rights (ECtHR).[47]

Another example of interaction is the prohibition of 'arbitrary or unjustifiable discrimination or a disguised restriction on international trade'. This phrase was originally conceived in the chapeau of Article XX GATT (1947) and was then used in other WTO texts.[48] This prohibition can also be found outside the WTO framework. The United Nations Framework Convention on Climate Change[49] (UNFCCC) reflects this in Article 3(5) in the context of combating climate change, by stating that '[m]easures taken to combat climate change, including unilateral ones, should not constitute a means of arbitrary or unjustifiable discrimination or a disguised

1949, entered into force 21 October 1950) 75 UNTS 31 (GCI) arts 12 and 50; Geneva Convention for the Amelioration of the Condition of Wounded, Sick and Shipwrecked Members of Armed Forces at Sea (adopted 12 August 1949, entered into force 21 October 1950) 75 UNTS 85, (GCII) arts 12 and 51; Geneva Convention Relative to the Treatment of Prisoners of War (adopted 12 August 1949, entered into force 21 October 1950) 75 UNTS 135 (GCIII) arts 17, 87 and 130; Geneva Convention Relative to the Protection of Civilian Persons in Time of War (adopted 12 August 1949, entered into force 21 October 1950) 75 UNTS 287 (GCIV) arts 32 and 147; Protocol Additional to the Geneva Conventions of 12 August 1949, and Relating to the Protection of Victims of International Armed Conflicts (Protocol I) (adopted 8 June 1977, entered into force 7 December 1978) 1125 UNTS 3, art 2. With regard to non-international armed conflicts, see Geneva Conventions, Common Article 3; Protocol Additional to the Geneva Conventions of 12 August 1949, and Relating to the Protection of Victims of Non-International Armed Conflicts (Protocol II) 1125 UNTS 609 (adopted 8 June 1977, entered into force 7 December 1978) art 4(2).

[45] International Criminal Tribunal for former Yugoslavia, Trial Chamber, *Prosecutor v Furundžija* (Judgment) IT-95-17/1 (10 December 1998) para 161. The tribunal further found that the prohibition not only exists also under customary international law, but has attained the status of *jus cogens*: see paras 134–64.

[46] R Higgins, 'A Babel of Judicial Voices? Ruminations from the Bench' (2006) 55 *International and Comparative Law Quarterly* 791; B Simma, 'Universality of International Law from the Perspective of a Practitioner' (2009) 20 *European Journal of International Law* 282, 282–83.

[47] Among many examples, see *ADC and ADC & ADMC v Hungary*, ICSID Case No ARB/03/16, Award (2 October 2006).

[48] Above, (n 24).

[49] *Ibid*.

In the above examples, similarity (or likeness) was related to tax treatment, situations related to developing countries, or products. In the case of MSENs, what may be similar is the normative content of two (or more) MSENs or the conducts they impose in the sense of 'pointing in the same direction'.

Similar MSENs must satisfy four elements. First, they stem from different equivalent sources and are applicable to the same addressees. Secondly, they have the same subject-matter, in accordance with the *ejusdem generis* principle[63] and therefore may simultaneously be applied to a particular situation. The *ejusdem generis* principle is well established with regard to the Most Favoured Nation Treatment, although its application by investment arbitral tribunals has been rather problematic and inconsistent.[64] Thirdly, it is possible to comply with some or all similar MSENs. In other terms, they do not cause any conflict in the sense of impossibility to comply simultaneously with all of them.[65] Fourthly, their content is similar. This is the most difficult element as it implies an assessment of the extent in which similar MSENs point in the same direction.

The rules on lawful expropriation contained in investment treaties and human rights conventions may offer a useful example of similar MSENs. Article 5 BIT between Ireland and the Czech Republic, for instance, reads in part:

> 1. Investment of investor of either Contracting Party shall not be nationalized, expropriated or subjected to measures having effect equivalent to nationalization or expropriation . . . except for a public purpose. The expropriation shall be carried out under due process of law, on a non discriminatory basis and shall be accompanied by provision for the payment of prompt, adequate and effective compensation.[66]

Article 1 of Protocol No 1 to ECHR, in turn, reads:

> Every natural or legal person is entitled to the peaceful enjoyment of his possessions. No one shall be deprived of his possessions except in the public interest and subject to the conditions provided for by law and by the general principles of international law.

[63] See *Ambatielos* case (*Greece v UK*), Commission of Arbitration (1963) 12 RIAA 107. BA Garner, *Black Law Dictionary* (St Paul, West Group, 1999) 535, describes the principle as 'A canon of construction that when a general word or phrase follows a list of specific persons or things, the general word or phrase will be interpreted to include only persons or things of the same type as those listed'.

[64] For a discussion on the *ejusdem generis* principle in respect of the Most Favoured Nation Treatment, see in particular, A Newcombe and L Paradell, *Law and Practice of Investment Treaties: Standards of Treatment* (The Hague, Kluwer, 2009) especially 204 ff.

[65] On the notion of conflict in international law, see Pauwelyn, *Conflict of Norms in Public International Law*, above (n 18) especially 184–88.

[66] Adopted 28 June 1996: www.unctad.org/sections/dite/iia/docs/-bits/czech_ireland.pdf.

Whereas Article 5 BIT clearly states the four conditions for lawful expropriation, Article 1 of Protocol No 1 ECHR expressly *incorporates*[67] two of them (public purpose and due process of law) and contains a *renvoi* to international law. The ECtHR has held on several occasions that the reference to the general principles of international law as stipulated in Article 1 Protocol 1 operates only with regard to acts of a state in relation to non-nationals.[68] The Committee of Ministers of the Council of Europe has also found that the expression 'general principles of international law' in Article 1 Protocol 1 entails the obligation to pay compensation, although limited to non-nationals.[69]

As a result, Article 5 BIT and Article 1 Protocol 1 are to be considered as similar MSENs since (a) they are both binding upon Ireland and the Czech Republic although they have been established through different equivalent international instruments; (b) they have the same subject matter; (c) they have a similar normative content; and (d) Ireland and the Czech Republic can comply with either or both of them in respect of the same act of expropriation.

It is submitted that at least for the time being investment arbitral tribunals and the ECtHR may assess in a similar but not necessarily identical manner whether each of the above-mentioned conditions for lawful expropriation are satisfied. The due process requirement, in particular, may assume different connotations due to textual and contextual differences, subsequent practice, not to mention the specificity of and degree of sophistication reached in the jurisprudence of the Strasbourg Court.

Similarly, the ECtHR may require in the case of lawful expropriation of a foreign investment a level of compensation lower than prompt, adequate and effective compensation as provided for in Article 5 BIT. This may occur if the ECtHR finds that prompt, adequate and effective compensation is not sufficiently well established in customary international, which it has to apply by virtue of the *renvoi* contained in Article 1 Protocol 1.[70] Even assuming that the Court accepts that customary international law requires prompt, adequate and effective compensation, it may still hold that certain

[67] See *Case of James and Others v United Kingdom* (App No 8793/79) ECHR 21 February 1986, para 61; *Case of Lithgow and Others v United Kingdom* (App No 9006/80) EHRR 8 July 1986, para 114.

[68] See in particular, *James v United Kingdom* and *Lithgow v United Kingdom*, *ibid*, respectively paras 58 ff and paras 118 ff.

[69] See Resolution (52) 1, adopted by the Committee of Ministers, 19 March 1952: wcd.coe.int/ViewDoc.jsp?id=720463&Site=COE&BackColorInternet=DBDCF2&BackColorIntranet=FDC864&BackColorLogged=FDC864.

[70] In literature compare R Dolzer and C Schreuer, *Principles of International Investment Law* (Oxford, Oxford University Press, 2008) 91; T Wälde and B Sabahi, 'Compensation, Damages and Valuation in International Investment Law' in P Muchlinski, F Ortino and C Schreuer (eds), *The Oxford Handbook of International Investment Law* (Oxford, Oxford University Press, 2008) 1049, 1069 with S Ripinsky and K Williams, *Damages in International Investment Law* (London, British Institute of International and Comparative Law, 2008) 71 ff.

special circumstances – such as historical political transformation or large economic reforms – or considerations of equity may justify a lower level of compensation.

So far, violations of Article 1 Protocol 1 concerning an act of expropriation of foreign investment were held to be due to disregard of the conditions provided by the law. As a matter of judicial economy, the Court refrained from determining whether the other conditions, including compensation, were satisfied.[71]

It can be expected that the Court, faced with the question of compensation for lawful expropriation, will apply the general principles of international law as required under Article 1 Protocol 1. It can only be speculated to what extent it will rely on the case law developed by investment arbitral tribunals.[72] This may imply a different treatment of non-nationals and nationals which the Court has already held to be consistent with Article 1 Protocol 1. Whereas the former are entitled to the protection provided for by international law, the latter

> must in principle obtain compensation 'reasonably related to its value', even though 'legitimate objectives of "public interest" may call for less than reimbursement of the full market value". . . . It follows that the balance mentioned above is generally achieved where the compensation paid to the person whose property has been taken is reasonably related to its 'market' value, as determined at the time of the expropriation.[73]

It is, nonetheless, worth noting that in quantifying compensation due to unlawful expropriation,[74] the Court has recognized that reparation should aim at putting the applicant in the position it would have been had the violation not occurred.[75] In so doing it relied on its own jurisprudence rather than on the classic decision in *Chorzow*.[76] In sharp contrast with investment arbitral tribunals, it has quantified compensation on the basis of equity.[77]

[71] See in particular, *Zlínsat, Spol. S R.O. v Bulgaria* (App No 57785/00) ECHR 15 June 2006; *Bimer S.A. v Moldova* (App No 15084/03) 10 July 2007.

[72] Another interesting question will be the extent to which the Court would resort to any investment treaty that may be applicable between the parties for the purpose of systemic interpretation under art 31(3) (c) VCLT, above (n 6). For some precedents on systemic interpretation by the EtCHR see *Golder v United Kingdom* (App No 4451/70) (1975) 1 EHRR 524, para 29; *Al-Adsani v United Kingdom* (App No 35763/97) (2001) 34 EHRR 273, para 55.

[73] *Pincová and Pinc v the Czech Republic* (App No 36548/9) ECHR 5 November 2002, para 52.

[74] On the distinction between lawful and unlawful expropriation for the purpose of compensation, see Ripinsky and Williams, *Damages in International Investment Law*, above (n 70) section 4.1.

[75] See in particular, *Zlínsat, Spol. S R.O. v Bulgaria* (App No 57785/00) Just Satisfaction, 10 January 2008, para 39; *Bimer S.A. vMoldova*, above (n 71) para 68.

[76] *Chorzów Factory* (*Germany v Poland*) (Merits) PCIJ Series A, No 17, 48.

[77] See in particular, *Zlínsat, Spol. S R.O. v Bulgaria*, above (n 75) paras 41 and 45; *Bimer S.A. v Moldova*, above (n 71) para 71.

V COMPLIANCE OR NON-COMPLIANCE WITH MSENS

The choice a state has to make with regard to compliance with *identical* MSENs is straightforward: either it complies with all of them or it violates all of them. A sort of exponential *pacta sunt servanda* principle will provide a formidable incentive for compliance, whereas non-compliance means exposure to all remedies available in respect to each MSEN.

Legal advisors will warn governments that the same action or omission in violation of two or more identical MSENs would expose them to the remedies, including judicial or arbitral proceedings if any, attached to each of them. They may be asked to identify, in relation to each MSEN, the injured parties and the different remedies they may resort to. With regard to judicial or arbitral proceedings, an additional exam may be requested on jurisdictional issues, applicable law, binding effect of decisions and awards, and possibly recognition and enforcement of decisions and awards.

The advice rendered by legal advisors may be completed by that of political and economic analysts on the extent injured parties may be expected to avail themselves of these remedies, the likeness of a friendly settlement of the dispute, the impact on the political relations between the concerned states and the potential economic consequences of these remedies.

In case of compliance, identical MSENs clearly contribute to the unity of international law by increasing its coherence and enhancing its effectiveness. The contribution is amplified when the MSENs impose *erga omnes* obligations as all contracting parties to the treaty (*erga omnes contractantes*) or all states are to be considered as injured states. As held in *Prosecutor v Furundžija, erga omnes* obligations are

> obligations owed towards all the other members of the international community . . . the violation of such obligation simultaneously constitutes a breach of the correlative right of all members of the international community and gives rise to a claim for compliance accruing to each and every member.[78]

Identical MSENs contribute to the unity of international law even if the concerned state decides not to comply with them and to face the consequences attached to their violation. Indeed, the violation of the MSENs is

[78] See above (n 45) para 151. See also, United Kingdom, *House of Lords, A (FC) and others (FC)* (Appellants) *v Secretary of State for the Home Department* (Respondent)*; A and others* (Appellants) *(FC) and others v Secretary of State for the Home Department* (Respondent) (Conjoined Appeals), 8 December 2005, Lord Bingham of Cornhill, [2005] UKHL 71: www.publications.parliament.uk/pa/ld200506/ldjudgmt/jd051208/aand.pdf; S Schwebel, *Justice in International Law* (Cambridge, Cambridge University Press, 1994) 164, observes that 'when a State protests that another is violating the basic human rights of the latter's own citizens, the former State is . . . seeking to vindicate international obligations which run towards it as well as all other States'. In literature, see in particular, C Tams, *Enforcing Obligations Erga Omnes in International Law* (Cambridge, Cambridge University Press, 2005).

not the end of the matter. Compliance may be induced through negotiations, protest, acts of retortion, counter-measures and judicial or arbitral proceedings. The reaction of one or more injured parties in response to a violation of one or more identical MSENs may incite the concerned state to abandon the unlawful conduct and consequently to comply with all MSENs.

The matter is more complicated in the case of *similar* MSENs where compliance with one (or more) similar MSEN(s) is compatible with non compliance with another (or other) similar MSEN(s). This could be the case where MSENs have a substantial overlap but are not entirely congruent. In the example above, both the BIT between Ireland and the Czech Republic and the ECHR contain partly equivalent conditions for a lawful expropriation. Either state may satisfy the conditions of the ECHR while failing to satisfy those of the BIT or the other way around.

Considering for the sake of simplicity two similar MSENs, governments have three options:

1. compliance with both (applies to both identical and similar MSENs)
2. non-compliance with both (applies to both identical and similar MSENs)
3. compliance only with one while disregarding the other one (applies to similar MSENs only).

Generally the choice between compliance or non-compliance depends on a number of factors, such as: the authoritativeness of legal opinion in foreign policy matters; the desire to be consistent in foreign policy; a cost-benefit analysis based primarily on the possible impact of non-compliance on the domestic economy; the political relations with the counter-part(s) and remedies available to the injured state(s) or party(ies).

Under the third option, selective compliance with similar MSENs is rather unlikely when the more onerous MSEN provides for the stronger remedies on behalf of the injured state or may cause more serious economic and political consequences than the less onerous MSEN. The additional effort needed to comply with both MSENs would be limited and is likely to be convenient as it would avoid exposure to any remedy. From this perspective, similar MSENs are highly beneficial for the respect, coherence and unity of international law.

Using again the example above, and assuming that the BIT between Ireland and the Czech Republic contains more onerous MSENs on compensation for expropriation than the ECHR, it is most probable that the concerned states will comply with all MSENs in order to avoid the stronger and more effective remedies available under the BIT.

The other scenario is more challenging. A government may consider complying with the less onerous MSEN but not with the more onerous one when the former provides for stronger remedy on behalf of the injured state or party, may bring about more serious economic and political consequences, or both. From a cost-benefit perspective, selective compliance may be appropriate when the additional cost of full compliance outweighs the detrimental effects that non-compliance with the more onerous MSEN may be expected to cause. As a result, the concerned government avoids exposing itself to the stronger remedies while accepting the risk that the injured party (or parties) resort(s) to the weaker remedies.

A government that has already decided to comply with the less onerous obligation, however, may find it convenient to comply with the more demanding obligation too. In economic terms, there may be a high marginal utility for compliance with the more onerous MSEN. In this case, the MSEN with the strongest remedy has a pulling effect towards full compliance.

This may be illustrated by the case of two similar MSENs contained in a foreign investment treaty and a human rights treaty, with the latter imposing more onerous obligations, for instance, with regard to due process, non discrimination or protection of property.[79] The strong remedies – including compensation, which is normally not available in human rights treaties – that are available under the first category of treaties provide an incentive for compliance with the MSEN embodied in the investment treaty. The decision to comply (or not to comply) also with the human rights MSEN is based on an assessment of the advantages of compliance (or disadvantages of non-compliance) against the additional costs related to full compliance (or benefits related to selective compliance).

VI STATE PRACTICE AND CONVERGING MSENS

In addition to the mutual beneficial effect that MSENs may have towards compliance, an important factor promoting the convergence of MSENs is the desire and expectation that governments are consistent (and thereby predictable) in their policies. Consistency requires that governments make the same judgements and take the same decisions in situations that are relevantly similar. This behaviour is likely to direct governments towards uniform interpretation of MSENs that are identical or similar.[80] Consistency does not mean that policy behaviour must be inflexible. Policies may change, but new policies must be announced and the reason for change must be explained.[81]

[79] As noted by M Hirsh, 'Interaction between Investment and Non-Investment Obligations' in Muchlinski, Ortino and Schreuer (eds), *The Oxford Handbook of International Investment Law*, above (n 70) 154, 156, however, 'the interrelationship between international investment and non-investment obligations are not necessarily contradictory. Legal rules deriving from these spheres often complement and reinforce each other'.

[80] According to VCLT, above (n 6) art 31, para. 3(b).

[81] Eg, the need to notify changes in policies is codified in art 7 of the WTO Agreement on the Application of Sanitary and Phytosanitary Measures (15 April 1994).

Consistency of policies follows from the principle of good governance[82] and is particularly important in international economic transaction where long-term financial commitments are made by traders and investors. Accordingly, the WTO frequently refers to good governance and requires WTO-members to apply law and regulations 'in a uniform and impartial and reasonable manner'. [83] In the field of international investment law, consistency and transparency are important elements of the fair and equitable treatment standard.[84]

A consistent approach in governmental administration treats subjects equitably and delivers certainty and reliability. Consistency may also be presumed as governments expect consistency from foreign governments as well. The desire to be consistent may even override other considerations such as the negative result of a cost-benefit analysis. Governments are likely to prefer a consistent application of similar MSENs, even if occasional non-compliance to one MSEN would give them a substantial benefit. Consistency may also contribute to lower transaction costs for all parties involved. An investor or trader that develops commercial activities in a predictable environment is likely to spend less on legal assistance and other transaction costs.

Consistency must be contrasted with opportunism, which can be defined as the practice of ignoring legal principles in order gain a one-time benefit. An example of disputed but consistent behaviour in the treatment of foreign investors is the US policy to treat 'fair and equitable treatment' and the 'international minimum standard' as equivalent norms. It is unlikely that the United States will deviate from this policy because it may benefit a US company in a particular case.

Another example may illustrate this. Investment treaties usually contain a standard clause requiring that expropriation is carried out in the 'public interest' (and additional conditions). Suppose a state is party to several investment treaties that include a 'public interest' clause. These clauses may be treated as MSENs. The state will interpret and apply 'public interest'[85] consistently, even if MSENs are stipulated in different legal instruments, drafted differently and couched in different contexts. Government will construe 'public interest' in such as way as to support a consistent policy and increased legal predictability. Rather than considering different

[82] For a discourse on good governance see F Weiss, 'Transparency as an Element of Good Governance in the Practice of the EU and the WTO: Overview and Comparison' (2007) 30 *Fordham International Law Journal* 1545.

[83] See art X GATT above (n 24). This provision is elaborated in *European Communities – Selected Customs Matters*, Appellate Body Report, adopted on 13 November 2006, WT/DS315/AB/R, para 224.

[84] See for instance, *Tecmed S.A. v Mexico*, ICSID Case No ARB (AF)00/2, Award, 29 May 2003, para 154.

[85] This is a typical MSEN in BITs. It refers to expropriation and stipulates that expropriation can only be done for the sake of public interest.

contexts or subsequent agreements and practice, that state will stick to its own policy which is consistent and therefore predictable. In the case of trade and investment agreements, most-favoured-nation clauses would also have a converging effect on MSENs as this would offer the identical treatment on the highest obtainable level for traders and investors that are protected by the MFN clause.

By seeking consistency there is convergence of MSENs through state practice: State A and State B each consistently interpret 'public interest' (even if stemming from different sources) but their interpretations may not be in harmony. The next step towards convergence would be synchronizing state practice to achieve uniform interpretation of 'public interest' across states. Courts and tribunals may contribute to the harmonization of state practice by developing a consistent jurisprudence on the scope of 'public interest'. Admittedly, consistent jurisprudence may be expected from permanent courts and tribunals, but may not always feasible in case of ICSID arbitrations and ad hoc arbitrations, because of the different composition of tribunals and their independence.[86]

VII CONCLUSIONS

Governments' perspective of MSENs is different from courts and tribunals. The latter are required to observe restrictions on jurisdiction and applicable law in the application of MSENs, whereas governments are not. Accordingly, government will be confronted with MSENs more likely than courts and tribunals. On the other hand, governments, when applying MSENs, may also consider political preferences, whereas courts are expected to be politically neutral. Therefore, the application of identical or similar MSENs may result in different responses from tribunals and governments.

The behaviour of governments when applying MSENs is determined by a number of factors that will contribute to the unity of international law. This is evident with regard to identical MSENs. Failure to comply with one norm will amount to the simultaneous violation of other identical norms and may trigger the remedies available for each of them thus amplifying the chances to induce compliance. A remedy which will be easily available to an aggrieved party (state or individual), therefore, drives towards compliance and unity.

The contribution to the unity of international law may be less evident – but nonetheless still plain – in the case of similar MSENs. Their normative similarity generally means a significant – although not necessarily

[86] See for instance, *AES Corp v Argentina*, ICSID Case No ARB/02/17, Decision on Jurisdiction, 26 April 2005, paras 30–31.

decisive – pulling effect towards full compliance. When the more onerous obligation provides for weak remedies, a normally high marginal utility still provides an important incentive for full compliance. However, governments may opt for selective compliance when the advantages expected from partial non-compliance outweigh its negative consequences. In case of non-compliance, moreover, similar MSENs mutually benefit from their respective remedies at least to the extent that their normative contents coincide.

Another factor that drives towards converging application of identical or similar MSENs is the desire of states to be consistent in their policies. Consistency and predictability of state behaviour are manifestations of good governance. This behaviour is likely to direct governments towards the uniform interpretation of MSENs even when context or legal intricacies would suggest otherwise.

The distinction between identical and similar MSENs, finally, is a relative one as similar MSENs tend to converge due to their interaction, interpretative principles and cross-contamination of international decisions. Equally important, the mutual interest in the consistency, coherence and legal predictability of the international legal order strongly encourages states to uniformly apply all MSENs even if they stem from different sources, may be phrased differently and placed in different contexts.

Part II

MSENs in Judicial Practice

5

*Interpreting Multi-Sourced Equivalent Norms: Judicial Borrowing in International Courts**

Benedikt Pirker

I INTRODUCTION

THE EXPANSION OF international treaty law and the proliferation of international courts and tribunals engaged in the interpretation of those norms does not only entail the potential for conflicting interpretations and disputes over jurisdiction and applicable law; courts and tribunals can also grasp the opportunity to inform themselves on how their counterparts tackle similar legal problems, arising from parallel, Multi-Sourced Equivalent Norms (MSENs). In domestic law, constitutional courts often refer comparatively to solutions found by courts in other countries to bolster and improve their legal reasoning on difficult questions of interpretation, sometimes with far reaching outcomes. In just one example, the *Du Plessis* case,[1] the South African Constitutional Court had to rule on the horizontal effect of constitutional rights. It embarked on an extensive analysis of how the topic is dealt with, for this purpose, in Irish, US, Canadian and German constitutional law. Finally, it bolstered its decision, which was similar to the one found in German constitutional law among other reasons with the similarity of the German legal system. As an additional argument, German legal thinking had played an important role in the drafting process of the South African Constitution according to the Court.[2] In international law, the emerging mass of case law in different fields allows for a similar comparative approach. Some studies

* The author would like to thank Thomas Burri for valuable comments on a first draft of this chapter and all the participants of the 'Concluding Conference on Multi-Sourced Equivalent Norms', held at the Leonard Davis Institute, The Hebrew University of Jerusalem for their comments, in particular Yuval Shany, Tomer Broude, Ralf Michaels, Lorand Bartels, Moshe Hirsch and Luís Miguel Poiares Maduro. All mistakes are exclusively mine.

[1] *Du Plessis* case 1996 (3) SA 850 (CC), 879.

[2] J Fedtke and B Markesinis, 'The Judge as Comparatist' (2005) 80 *Tulane Law Review* 11, 67.

show tendencies to converge and diverge between similar concepts. In the fields of multilateral and regional trade liberalization, similar norms exist in treaty regimes such as the World Trade Organization (WTO), the MERCOSUR, the European Community (EC) or the European Economic Area (EEA). At the same time, similar problems such as the definition of national treatment are approached in international trade law and international investment law in substantially different ways.[3] In recent case law, courts active in the interpretation of regional integration agreements have engaged in borrowing reasoning and legal arguments from one another – a practice that will be referred to as 'judicial borrowing'. The European Court of Justice (ECJ) became, thus, the source of inspiration for both the MERCOSUR Permanent Review Court (PRC)[4] and the European Free Trade Association Court (EFTA Court).The practice of borrowing goes beyond mere judicial dialogue, as effectively one jurisdiction 'transplants' part of the legal reasoning of a different jurisdiction to a case. The present chapter intends to shed some light on the motives for courts and tribunals to use borrowing as a tool and the problems linked to it. Section II links judicial borrowing to MSENs and discusses the views of comparative law on borrowing in the context of national courts. Some first elements of reflection on how to transpose these views to the level of international courts and tribunals are given. Section III embarks on a case study of the EFTA Court's *L'Oréal Norge* decision.[5] The Court used judicial borrowing under particular circumstances, both because the case required a very clear cut decision and because a treaty clause (the so-called 'homogeneity clause') imposed homogeneous interpretation on it. In section IV the second case study examines the MERCOSUR PRC's approach to judicial borrowing. In a comprehensive effort it reformed its case law on weighing trade and environmental concerns and drew for this purpose on principles and reasoning developed by the ECJ in earlier case law. Finally, some conclusions are drawn regarding the circumstances that can render judicial borrowing based on the normative equivalence of MSENs, either a successful technique or a danger for the independence and institutional position of an international court or tribunal.

II JUDICIAL BORROWING, MULTI-SOURCED EQUIVALENT NORMS AND INTERNATIONAL COURTS AND TRIBUNALS

MSENs can be understood in different ways. Some focus on the conflicts of norms that are inherent in MSENs, despite the existence of normative

[3] N DiMascio and J Pauwelyn, 'Nondiscrimination in Trade and Investment Treaties: Worlds Apart or Two Sides of the Same Coin?' (2008) 102 *American Journal of International Law* 48.
[4] The original Spanish designation is 'Tribunal Permanente de Revisión'.
[5] Cases E-9/07 and E-10/07 *L'Oréal Norge AS v Per Aarskog AS, Nille AS and Smart Club AS* (EFTA Court, Judgment of 8 July 2008, not yet reported).

equivalence; others' interest is raised by conflicts of jurisdictions and the consequences these entail. The present contribution focuses on the aspect of similar wording of norms, as an expression of normative equivalence. Building on the definition established by the study group at the beginning of the project, MSENs are defined as 'two or more norms which are (1) binding upon the same international legal subjects; (2) similar or identical in their normative content (in the words of the International Law Commission, 'point in the same direction'); and (3) have been established through different international instruments or 'legislative procedures or are applicable in different substantive areas of the law'.[6]

A The Playing Field for Judicial Borrowing and Comparative Law in International and Municipal Law

Since the focus here is on the judge as a potential 'comparatist',[7] the question of whether two particular norms are binding on the same international subject is less relevant for our purpose. In some cases this might be the case. A norm is binding on a state as a member of a regional trade agreement, while a similar or identical norm exists in a substantially equivalent phrasing at the WTO level and is, thus, binding on two levels. However, borrowing might also arise when the borrowed interpretation is of a similar or identical norm from a regime that is not binding on the state in question. Our interest here is more focused on this second category. Comparative law seems to emerge as a discipline gaining relevance also at the international level due to the emergence of more tribunals and increasingly common case law in contexts as diverse as international criminal law, trade law, investment law or human rights law. Judicial bodies at the international level are aware of the dangerous reproach of judicial activism threatening their legitimacy. As a remedy, some such as the WTO Appellate Body, tend to stay rather close to the text and words of the provision which they are called on to interpret. This seems true in particular for newly established judicial bodies.[8] In such a case, the existence of MSENs of the type examined in this chapter, ie, MSENs that are substantially equivalent in wording, although established by different instruments or procedures, eases the transfer of legal reasoning from one treaty regime to the other (even if they are not necessarily binding on the same parties).

[6] See in this volume, T Broude and Y Shany, 'The International Law and Policy of Multi-Sourced Equivalent Norms' in T Broude and Y Shany (eds), *Multi-Sourced Equivalent Norms in International Law* (Oxford, Hart Publishing, 2011) p 5.

[7] Fedtke and Markesinis, above (n 2) 11.

[8] See, eg, the Appellate Body's reading of art XX GATT in the early *US–Gasoline* case (WTO, *United States: Standards for Reformulated and Conventional Gasoline – Report of the Appellate Body* (adopted 29 April 1996) WT/DS2/AB/R).

For the given setting, one famous and much studied example of judicial *dialogue* that comes to mind is the relationship between the European Court of Human Rights (ECtHR) and the ECJ, often described as a classic example of judicial peer review.[9] To provide some new input into the debate, it appears fruitful to focus more specifically on the phenomenon of judicial *borrowing*, whereby one tribunal does not only discuss or refer to an interpretation given by another or reviews the peer's standards of protection, but virtually uses the concept developed in that interpretation to decide the case before it. Therefore, we focus on courts which pursue a similar rationale, as they are the most likely to engage in a fruitful manner in judicial borrowing. The ECJ, the EFTA Court, the MERCOSUR *Ad hoc* Tribunal and the PRC are all courts or tribunals established to interpret regional integration agreements and face similar legal problems brought before them. One might be tempted to speak of 'multi-sourced equivalent courts/tribunals'. Despite their dialogue, the ECJ and the ECtHR work in a different setting and their discussion sooner or later always returns to one topic: the respect for the fundamental rights standards of the latter in the case law or institutional structure of the former. Even if individuals before the ECJ invoke fundamental rights, it is in the context of the EC Treaty and the market freedoms that the latter are interpreted and applied by the ECJ.[10]

International courts in a similar treaty setting also face similar challenges. In the context of European integration as well as in the MERCOSUR, conflict on competing interests is bound to arise. Trade versus environmental protection is but one well-known example of such interests requiring conciliation. Comparative law as a discipline has so far focused on national courts which discuss and sometimes use legal solutions from courts of other countries in fields such as tort or contract law. By focusing on international courts and tribunals active in similar fields of international law, the ideas and arguments discussed in the field of comparative law as it stands can now be considered for transfer to the context of international law.[11]

[9] See S Douglas-Scott, 'A Tale of Two Courts: Luxembourg, Strasbourg and the Growing European Human Rights Acquis' (2006) 43 *Common Market Law Review* 629 or more recently G Harpaz, 'The European Court of Justice and its Relations with the European Court of Human Rights: The Quest for Enhanced Reliance, Coherence and Legitimacy' (2009) 46 *Common Market Law Review* 105.

[10] For but one of numerous examples, see the *Schmidberger* case (Case C-112/00 *Eugen Schmidberger, Internationale Transporte und Planzüge v Republik Österreich* [2003] ECR I-5659). The ECJ allowed here a restriction on the free movement of goods (protesters on a motorway) in order to respect the right to free expression, as long as proportionality of the restriction is granted and judicial review possible.

[11] It should be added as a caveat that the present contribution only focuses on international economic law and is, thus, far from exhaustive. Other potentially fruitful areas of study might be found in international criminal law or human rights law, where 'multi-sourced equivalent courts/tribunals' also exist.

B Comparative Law in a Municipal Context

Many studies in comparative law offer helpful insights. In most cases researchers focus on constitutional courts, probably because they perceive them as the highest authorities of a municipal legal system to decide on the introduction of foreign legal ideas and arguments. As an example, one might take the United States' Supreme Court decision in *Roper v Simmons*.[12] The Court abolished in this sentence the death penalty for juvenile delinquents and used for this purpose, as one of the weighty arguments among others, the international consensus that outlawed such punishment. Judges as well as commentators engaged during and after the case in a very lively debate on whether and how the views of foreign legal communities should influence the interpretation of the United States' Constitution. Not all aspects of the debate can be usefully transferred to a comparative study on different international tribunals. Justice Scalia, for example, raises the reproach in his Dissenting Opinion that 'the views of our own citizens are essentially irrelevant to the Court's decision today, [while] the views of other countries and the so-called international community take centre stage'[13] and questions the democratic legitimacy of such an approach. Such criticism could hardly arise in the context of intergovernmental dispute settlement before a court on rather technical matters.[14] While citizens' awareness of international adjudication could be described at best as limited, it would be the contracting parties of treaties that would raise the reproach of judicial activism against a court for using 'foreign' legal ideas.

What other arguments for judicial borrowing developed by comparative law in the context of municipal law can be relevant to the setting of international courts and tribunals? National courts use judicial borrowing influenced by the context in which they operate. Are foreign materials easily available both in terms of library resources and language barriers? Do time constraints hamper the use of such materials? How suitable is the subject matter of the dispute for a comparative approach? Certainly, a comparative approach on a particular problem of tort law is less value-laden and prone to cause rejection by the domestic legal community than a highly influential decision like *Roper v Simmons*. Additionally, judges are

[12] *Roper v Simmons*, 125 S. Ct. 1183 (2005).

[13] *Ibid*, 1225 (Scalia, Dissenting Opinion).

[14] On the other hand, undeniably the Supreme Court's approach of searching the constitutional traditions of other states for a common denominator reminds the spectator immediately of the ECJ's technique when it develops the general principles of community law (see, eg, Joined Cases 7/56, 3/57 to 7/57 *Algera v Common Assembly of the European Coal & Steel Community* [1957] ECR (English special edn) 39, paras 55–56). Arguably, the more dispute settlement moves towards a supranational paradigm and addresses issues of individuals, thus, the more similar the problems for the democratic legitimacy of judicial borrowing become. The development of fundamental rights as part of the general principles of Community law is, arguably, one expression of these concerns (See Case 11/70 *Internationale Handelsgesellschaft* [1970] ECR 1125, para 4).

human beings. Contact with a different system, be it during their initial training or later practical experience at conferences or even contacts established during practical cooperation, make it more likely that a national judge will decide to take inspiration from a legal order beyond the borders.

Sometimes, the law itself will provide support. The most straightforward solution in national law to encourage judges to look beyond their domestic legal horizon is an express reference. The South African Constitution contains such a provision and thereby invites judges to look to foreign case law while they interpret fundamental rights as enshrined in the Constitution.

Finally, the context in which a judge decides always also includes the socio-economic and political environment of the legal order. A judge cannot easily import foreign ideas without testing them for their compatibility with the cultural and social background of the country. In *Roper v Simmons* some argue that the Court should not have extended the denominator – ie, the basis for defining mainstream opinion – to the international level.[15] It should be entirely the decision of the people of a state to define what constitutes a disproportionate punishment.

C Taking it to the Next Level: Judicial Borrowing by International Courts and Tribunals

After these preliminary observations, what can we learn from these aspects of 'domestic judicial borrowing' for the context of international law? Case studies will allow a less abstract and more practical understanding. Some issues arise in similar terms, such as technical barriers.[16] The argument on democratic legitimacy of judges when they use foreign law, however, would follow a different logic. Judges at the WTO Appellate Body, for example, are not bound to a specific national constitution and the understanding of a certain group of people. They are, however, limited by the constraints of the treaty they are called to interpret and the contracting parties will watch them closely. Judicial activism is but a different name for a similar issue: a perceived imbalance between the legislator (here the contracting parties) and the interpreting judicial authority. Personal contacts between judges at the international level can play a similar role as in the domestic context, as the European experience has shown.[17]

[15] E Young, 'The Supreme Court, 2004 Term – Comment: Foreign Law and the Denominator Problem' (2005) 119 *Harvard Law Review* 148, 153–54.

[16] As a practical example, all MERCOSUR case law is only available in Spanish and Portuguese on the MERCOSUR website and had to be translated for the present contribution.

[17] Regular meetings take place between judges of the ECJ and the ECtHR. See C Romano, 'From the Consensual to the Compulsory Paradigm in International Adjudication: Elements for a Theory of Consent' (2006) *New York University Public Law & Legal Theory Research Paper* No 06-05, 48. Similarly, the ECJ judges and Advocates General at many occasions encounter

The two following case studies aim to clarify these thoughts. The EFTA Court, the main actor in the first case study, is closely modelled, both in its function and in the legal materials it has to interpret, on the ECJ. Due to a treaty clause, it even ought to aim for harmonious interpretation with the solutions found by the ECJ. However, a hard case brings up the limits of such interpretative homogeneity and arouses the question of judicial 'quasi-legislative' powers, when judges seem to nearly re-write a treaty by means of interpretation.[18]

In the second case study, the MERCOSUR Permanent Court of Review (PCR) decides on its own to follow an interpretation given by the ECJ to a provision, which is similarly drafted both in the EC Treaty as well as in the MERCOSUR Treaty of Montevideo. Again, some positive impacts of this approach can be weighed against more problematic features, and some conclusions on judicial borrowing are eventually drawn.

III THE EFTA COURT AND THE *L'ORÉAL NORGE* CASE

The EEA Agreement provides for a unique feature in international law which has lead to a substantial amount of research: a homogeneity clause. Before delving into the case law and the potential pitfalls of this clause as interpreted by the EFTA Court, some elements of the EEA Agreement's origins and legal framework deserve closer attention.

A The Origins and Legal Framework of the EEA

In the 1980s, unsatisfied with a process of bilateral association of individual states with the internal market of the European Economic Community, the Member States of the EFTA were looking for a closer participation in the internal market project, without, however, full accession and the loss of sovereignty associated with such a step.[19] The idea that emerged out of a complex negotiation process[20] was the EEA: an enhanced free trade

the EFTA Court judges; see C Baudenbacher, 'The EFTA Court, the ECJ, and the Latter's Advocates General – a Tale of Judicial Dialogue' in A Arnull, P Eeckhout and T Tridimas (eds), *Continuity and Change in EU Law – Essays in Honour of Sir Francis Jacobs* (Oxford, Oxford University Press, 2008) 122.

[18] For a good study on such judicial activism in the context of the WTO see, eg, L Bartels, 'The Separation of Powers in the WTO – How to Avoid Judicial Activism' (2004) 53 *International and Comparative Law Quarterly* 861.

[19] See generally, ch 1, 'Historical Background to the EEA Agreement' in S Norberg, K Hökborg, M Johansson, D Eliasson and L Dedichen (eds), *The European Economic Area – EEA Law – A Commentary on the EEA Agreement* (Stockholm, Fritzes, 1993) 35 ff.

[20] At some point one of the negotiators compared the task of the treaty drafters to 'mixing oil and vinegar', K Almestad, 'The Squaring of the Circle – The Internal Market and the EEA' in U Bernitz, M Johansson and N Wahl (eds), *A European for all Seasons – Liber amicorum in Honour of Sven Norberg* (Brussels, Bruylant, 2006) quoting Sven Norberg at 2.

area, which would transfer the legal *acquis communautaire* of the single market mainly in the fields of the four freedoms and competition policy by means of an international agreement to the EFTA members. Furthermore, the Joint Committee would keep track of the developments of the law of the internal market and continue to transfer legislation to the EFTA members.[21] The Surveillance Authority and the EEA Court should take care of the supervision of the respect and the interpretation of the EEA Agreement's provisions. The aim of the project was to create two parallel legal orders that would not be identical, but should follow a homogeneous development.[22] Any divergence should be remedied already at the stage of interpretation of the law by means of the (now notorious) homogeneity clauses inserted in different parts of the complex legal structure of the EEA Agreement, the best known being Article 6 EEA:

> Without prejudice to future developments of case law, the provisions of this Agreement, in so far as they are identical in substance to corresponding rules of the Treaty establishing the European Economic Community and the Treaty establishing the European Coal and Steel Community and to acts adopted in application of these two Treaties, shall in their implementation and application be interpreted in conformity with the relevant rulings of the Court of Justice of the European Communities given prior to the date of signature of this Agreement.

For future interpretive divergences, Article 111 EEA foresees additional mechanisms as a last resort of dispute settlement. The Joint Committee can discuss such problems and look for a solution, or one party can ask the ECJ for an opinion. Finally, safeguard measures such as the suspension of parts of the agreement can be taken by either party.

As an additional element, the EFTA members introduced a more dynamic notion of homogeneity in an agreement concluded among themselves in 1992, the Agreement on the Establishment of a Surveillance Authority and a Court of Justice (SCA Agreement). Article 3(2) of this Agreement provides:

> In the interpretation and application of the EEA Agreement and this Agreement, the EFTA Surveillance Authority and the EFTA Court shall pay due account to the principles laid down by the relevant rulings by the Court of Justice of the European Communities given after the date of signature of the EEA Agreement and which concern the interpretation of that Agreement or of such rules of the Treaty establishing the European Economic Community and the Treaty establishing the European Coal and Steel Community in so far as they are identical in substance to the provisions of the EEA Agreement or to the provisions of Protocols 1 to 4 and the provisions of the acts corresponding to those listed in Annexes I and II to the present Agreement.

[21] Art 7 of the Agreement on the European Economic Area, [1994] OJ L1/3.

[22] As art 1(1) EEA sets out: 'The aim of this Agreement of association is to promote a continuous and balanced strengthening of trade and economic relations between the Contracting Parties with equal conditions of competition, and the respect of the same rules with a view to creating a homogeneous European Economic Area, hereinafter referred to as the EEA'.

Before the entry into force of the EEA Agreement, the ECJ was asked for an opinion on several aspects of the Agreement, including the homogeneity clause. After some preliminary concerns issued by the ECJ, the Agreement was changed accordingly and could enter into force.[23] The newly established EFTA Court took up its position and according to several scholars a fruitful judicial dialogue has since then emerged between the two courts.[24] Still, the question to what extent the EFTA Court is *bound* to follow interpretations given by the ECJ in cases after the signature of the EEA Agreement remained open. Is the bridge built by the provisions on homogeneous interpretation voluntary and useful for judicial borrowing or can it become a burden for the EFTA Court's interpretative freedom? This question came to the fore in *L'Oréal Norge* and shall inform our evaluation of the use made of judicial borrowing by the EFTA Court.

B The Case law before *L'Oréal Norge*: Interpretive Divergence, but Justified?

The EC Trade Mark Directive,[25] intended to harmonize several aspects of national trade marks for the purpose of free circulation of goods in the internal market, provides in its Article 7 for exhaustion of trade marks within the single market.[26] Member States have to make sure, thus, that traders cannot erect trade barriers between them by invoking their trade marks to block imports. The provision, however, leaves a priori open the question whether EC Member States may provide in their national law for

[23] Opinion 1/91 [1991] ECR I-6079 and Opinion 1/92 [1992] ECR I-2821 *Draft agreement between the Community, on the one hand, and the countries of the European Free Trade Association, on the other, relating to the creation of the European Economic Area*. The ECJ expressed concerns on several issues, among which the fact that the same judges would sit on the bench of both courts and that in the interpretation of some provisions, EEA Court judges could reinterpret the limits of competences between EC Member States and the EC. In the second opinion, the ECJ accepted the agreement as the required amendments had been implemented and the role of the relabelled EFTA Court had been substantially reduced to interpret only EEA provisions.

[24] See, eg, C Timmermans 'Creative Homogeneity' in Bernitz, Johansson and Wahl (eds), *A European for all Seasons*, above (n 20) 482 ff or Baudenbacher, above (n 17) 96. The latter author shows that, eg, in the *Fidium Finanz* case (Case C-452/04 *Fidium Finanz AG v Bundesanstalt für Finanzdienstleistungsaufsicht* [2006] ECR I-9521) the ECJ referred to the earlier *State Management Debt Agency v Íslandsbanki-FBA* case (Case E-1/00 [2000] EFTA Ct Rep I-8) to establish the test to adopt in order to distinguish whether a certain restriction had to be examined under the provisions on free movement of services or on those on free movement of capital.

[25] First Council Directive (EEC) 89/104 of 21 December 1988 to approximate the laws of the Member States relating to trade marks [1989] OJ L40/1 (Trade Mark Directive).

[26] *Ibid*, art 7: '1. The trade mark shall not entitle the proprietor to prohibit its use in relation to goods which have been put on the market in the Community under that trade mark by the proprietor or with his consent. 2. Paragraph 1 shall not apply where there exist legitimate reasons for the proprietor to oppose further commercialization of the goods, especially where the condition of the goods is changed or impaired after they have been put on the market'.

international exhaustion for trade marks of goods originating from outside the internal market.

As a general comment, international exhaustion of trade marks is perceived as beneficial for consumers, as it encourages parallel imports and increases price competition. Traders are thereby prevented from invoking their trade mark to block imports of a product into the country of their trade mark if they have bought the product on the market in another country or it has been bought on the market there with their consent. The trade mark right is exhausted in such a case. The opposite solution, regional exhaustion, facilitates the free movement of goods within a region, as traders can invoke their national trade mark to prevent imports from outside a specific region (in the present case, the EC internal market or the EEA), while inside the region goods can move freely without any impediment from trade mark owners.

This slightly blurry legislation, having been transposed into the EEA context, resulted in both the ECJ and the EFTA Court being confronted with the same question relating to its Article 7. The EFTA Court answered first in *Maglite*:[27] it acknowledged that cases of the same question were pending before the ECJ; however, as no case law before or after the signature of the EEA Agreement had ruled out international exhaustion, it felt free to render judgment.[28] On the merits, the Court decided that Norway was allowed to provide for international exhaustion in its national law and emphasized the advantages for consumers which this principle entails.

Only six months later, the ECJ answered the same question differently in *Silhouette*.[29] The Court weighed and balanced elements of the wording, the legislative history and the objectives of the Trade Mark Directive in a different manner and gave precedence to the need to ensure the free movement of goods within the EC's internal market. It could not be admitted, according to the ECJ, that traders in some Member States could invoke their trade marks and would thereby cause a division of the internal market. The Member State at issue could therefore not provide for international exhaustion in its domestic law; Article 7 provided in this respect for full harmonization at EC level.[30] Only the Advocate General referred in his Opinion to the EFTA Court's *Maglite* ruling, but distinguished the two hypotheses: the EFTA Court did not rule on goods from within the EEA, for which also regional exhaustion must apply, and therefore no contradiction arose between the two judgments.[31] The Advocate General seemed to

[27] Case E-2/97 *Mag Instruments Inc. and California Trading Company Norway, Ulsteen* [1997] EFTA Ct Rep 129.

[28] *Ibid*, paras 18, 22.

[29] Case C-355/96 *Silhouette International Schmied GmbH&Co. KG v Hartlauer Handelsgesellschaft mbH* [1998] ECR I-4799.

[30] *Ibid*, paras 22–25.

[31] Case C-355/96 *Silhouette*, Advocate General Jacob's Opinion [1998] ECR I-4802, paras 43–44.

perceive the EEA as a free trade area, whereby elements of external competence such as the rules of exhaustion of international property rights of goods originating from outside the area of the Agreement are left to the individual EEA Member States. However, the ECJ did not take care to distinguish so carefully and its interpretation of Article 7 therefore seems to clash with the EFTA Court's view.

C *L'Oréal Norge*: A Revolutionary 'Presumption of Homogeneity'?

Finally, after 10 years of uncertainty, a case similar to *Maglite* was brought before the EFTA Court. This time, the Court took a very different approach: already in the part on the legal framework, Article 3(2) SCA about dynamic homogeneity was emphasized.[32] The goods in question originated from outside the EEA as in *Maglite*, but the EFTA Court only paid lip service to this fact.[33] Instead, it recalled the objective of the EEA Agreement, the establishment of a 'homogeneous EEA' as in Article 1(1) EEA and, as a consequence, stated that

> the principle of homogeneity therefore leads to a presumption that provisions framed in the same way in the EEA Agreement and EC law are to be construed in the same way. However, differences in scope and purpose may under specific circumstances lead to a difference in interpretation between EEA law and EC law.[34]

The EFTA Court clarified later that this presumption would arise as soon as ECJ case law was available[35] and would only be rebutted if 'compelling reasons' could be found.[36]

With this reading of the homogeneity clause, the Court decided to follow the interpretation given by the ECJ. The EEA Agreement had, thus, implicitly always foreseen the exclusion of international exhaustion of trade marks as a future development, even for goods originating from outside the EEA. The Court, however, did not go into detail on why there was no difference between the EEA as originally a free trade area and the EC internal market. There might have been arguments to that end, as Advocate Jacobs had shown in his Opinion in *Silhouette*. It seems, thus, that the EFTA Court had in the meantime fundamentally changed its vision of the EEA to overcome any potential conflict of interpretation, which becomes apparent at one point when it speaks of the 'internal market within the EEA'.[37]

[32] *L'Oréal Norge*, above (n 5) para 24.

[33] *Ibid*, para 26.

[34] *Ibid*, para 27. *Cf* Case 270/80 *Polydor a.o./Harlequin a.o* [1982] ECR 329, paras 15–18, where the ECJ had made clear that even identically phrased provisions of an agreement between the EC and a third country could and would be interpreted in a different manner because of the diverging objectives between the agreement in question and the EC Treaty.

[35] *L'Oréal Norge*, above (n 5) para 29.

[36] As required in *ibid*, para 31.

[37] *Ibid*, para 29.

D Evaluation of the Process of Judicial Borrowing in *L'Oréal Norge*: The Neglected Nature of the EEA

To start with the obvious reasons encouraging judicial borrowing, the views of the EFTA Court can certainly be understood in terms of the existence of such a clearly phrased clause as Article 3(2) SCA. It is an express reference with even some elements of interpretive hierarchy. The relationship between the SCA and the EEA Agreement, however, is not expressly regulated. Should one see it as an improvement on the vague homogeneity formulae laid down in the EEA? It is an agreement concluded later than the EEA Agreement between the EFTA members only. Did they thereby want to 'improve' on homogeneity as foreseen in the EEA Agreement? It can at least be upheld that the additional clause in the SCA supports judicial borrowing as an interpretative mechanism. Unfortunately, the EFTA Court did not discuss at all the legal position it adopted towards the relationship between the EEA and the SCA.

Ultimately, the reading adopted by the Court in L'Oréal Norge seems to go even beyond the wording of the clause in the SCA. The judicial creation of a presumption of homogeneity has to find a basis in additional elements of the setting. Certainly, the personal contact plays a role, as the judges of both the ECJ and the EFTA Court maintain close relationships and also certainly discuss each other's views outside the courtroom.[38]

Other factors discussed before are also rather favourable to judicial borrowing considering the circumstances of the case. There are no major technical difficulties to be found, and the cultural or socio-economic background is similar enough so as to enable a transfer of judicial reasoning. In terms of legal certainty, more concerns arise in L'Oréal Norge than in previous jurisprudence. The presumption of homogeneity constitutes quite a departure from what had been the approach until then in the EC context.[39]

Moreover, one might be led to question the independence of the EFTA Court when it fully relies on interpretations given by another court as a consequence. This is a question which could arise in a domestic context as well, but with less grave consequences. International courts such as the EFTA Court are not rooted in a national, constitutionally consolidated judicial system. States create them for a specific purpose, and a perceived severe lack of independence could eliminate just this very reason for their existence. The EEA is typically marked by a certain tension between its basic ideas of homogeneity and sovereignty.[40] However, the borrowing as done by the EFTA Court in the present case transforms dialogue with 'outside' judges

[38] Baudenbacher, above (n 17) 122.

[39] See the *Polydor* case, above (n 34).

[40] T-I Harbor, 'The European Economic Area Agreement: A Case of Legal Pluralism' (2009) 78 *Nordic Journal of International Law* 201, 222.

into subordination and automatic introduction of 'outside' legal reasoning. As an aggravating factor, the judgments of the EFTA Court, similar to the ECJ, do not provide for Dissenting Opinions of individual judges. The chamber, thus, has to come to a decision often leaving out contentious parts of legal reasoning which would possibly have made clearer why the Court decided to follow the ECJ's view on particular points.

Finally, in addition to the points already made, the outcome of the L'Oréal Norge case constitutes a full legal transplant of an EC solution. Such an outcome brings the EFTA Court close to a legislative function[41] and raises concerns of judicial activism. It is suggested that in particular this point makes the present decision of the EFTA Court to follow the ECJ's views a wrong one in terms of reasoning. The early Polydor case[42] by the ECJ had made this point clear: even if the words of an agreement are phrased after the relevant provisions of the EC Treaty, the interpretation can still be different if the objectives between the two treaties do not coincide. If the EFTA Court reads the provisions on homogeneity as overriding this rule, it will give interpretations which do not take into account the specificities of the EEA legal framework, at least in hard cases. The L'Oréal Norge case constituted such a hard case from two perspectives.

First, as discussed previously, because of the temporal dimension. While the EFTA Court had pronounced itself first on the particular problem of Article 7 of the Trade Mark Directive and had found that solution A (international exhaustion is possible), the ECJ contradicted this view shortly after by stating B (regional exhaustion is compulsory). Not only had the EFTA Court, thus, to consider whether to follow the ECJ, but it had to reverse its own case law for this purpose. This aspect weakened the reasoning in L'Oréal Norge additionally, since the EFTA Court could not find any other legal instrument to reverse its old views but the questionable interpretation of the SCA discussed above.

Secondly, also in terms of substance, the case put the EFTA Court between a rock and a hard place. The question of exhaustion of intellectual property rights such as trade marks only leaves two possibilities to answer: regional or international exhaustion. At the same time, the status of this question is unclear. Is the choice of the exhaustion doctrine part of the external commercial policy of a state to decide on which concept applies? Is it just a question of internal policy? At the end of the day, traders are the ones who actually 'implement' the exhaustion by invoking trade marks to block trade flows.[43] The EFTA members argued in L'Oréal Norge that the

[41] For a good discussion of this problem in the context of comparative municipal law, see Fedtke and Markesinis above (n 2) 29.

[42] See the *Polydor* case above (n 34).

[43] The contentious nature of the debate can be seen, eg, in the WTO context: art 7 of the TRIPs Agreement excludes the issue fully from being addressed by means of dispute settlement.

EFTA Court would harmonize aspects of their external commercial policy if it followed the solution found by the ECJ. Arguably, the Court should have discussed this point in more detail. As the judgment came out, the impression given is that the EFTA Court transformed the very nature of the EEA from an enhanced free trade area into something similar to a common market with features of a common external commercial policy. There is neither strong textual nor contextual support for the EFTA Court's solution. The EEA continues to be a quite unique construction, its EFTA members maintaining substantial freedom of action in areas not covered by the provisions of the EEA Agreement. The continuous process of transposition of the acquis communautaire in matters of the internal market and the competition policy is open ended and not aimed at full convergence or accession to the EC.

Next to pure legal reasoning, it should be added that politics and economic weight certainly play a major role in the EEA–EC relations. The EEA depends very much on the free access of its EFTA members to the single market of the EC. The EFTA Court, thus, had an important incentive to avoid all possible controversy with the ECJ on interpretation of provisions of 'common' legislation. Inter-institutional policy comes into play as well in international courts. The self-perception of the Court at issue has its bearing on the outcome in favour of extensive judicial borrowing. With its far-reaching reading of what one might call a duty to homogeneity, the EFTA Court has subordinated itself to the ultimate interpretative authority of the ECJ in a stronger manner than the EEA Agreement's provisions do. The EEA Agreement creates indeed a dispute settlement mechanism in its Article 111 for cases of diverging interpretations, and a predominant role is given to the ECJ which can be asked for opinions. Still, the reading of homogeneity in terms of virtually automatic precedence of ECJ interpretations is a creation of the L'Oréal Norge case. Additionally, it limits arguably the effet utile of Article 111 EEA on dispute settlement in cases of interpretative differences.

Thus, while technically the conditions for judicial borrowing in the L'Oréal Norge case were ideal, the outcome arguably represents a contestable solution. The nature and context of the EEA and the EEA Agreement should have played a more prominent role in the EFTA Court's reasoning, which is certain to face severe criticisms if applied in such a manner in the future.[44]

[44] As a caveat, it should be added that to the author's knowledge there is no further case law to date endorsing the *L'Oréal Norge* formula for homogeneous interpretation, as the EFTA Court only deals with a small number of cases per year.

IV THE MERCOSUR *RETREADED TYRES* DISPUTE

The second case study focuses on the MERCOSUR dispute settlement system,[45] which provides a more traditional setting for judicial borrowing. There is no express clause encouraging or mandating judicial borrowing, so by default the general rules of customary international law on interpretative methods as enshrined in Articles 31 and 32 of the Vienna Convention on the Law of Treaties (VCLT) apply for the ad hoc arbitral tribunals and the PRC. Since its beginnings in the 1991 Treaty of Asunción, MERCOSUR's dispute settlement system has evolved quite substantially. While in the treaty only negotiation was suggested as a means for settling disputes, the Protocol of Brasilia soon created judicial dispute settlement by establishing ad hoc arbitration tribunals. The real breakthrough was, however, the 2005 Protocol of Olivos which created the PRC as a permanent appellate instance of legal review.[46] The following analysis shows that such judicial reform has not only had a consolidating effect on the case law, but encourages the newly appointed appellate judges to engage in judicial borrowing.

A The Earlier Case Law on Retreaded Tyres

To understand the substantive controversies, the environmental problems caused by tyres as waste must be highlighted. Tyres, when discarded in waste dumps, provide a breeding place for mosquitos, in particular the ones capable of transferring the dangerous Dengue fever to humans. The Brazilian and Argentinian governments therefore decided to adopt a policy to encourage local retreading of used tyres, by which these tyres would receive a prolonged lifespan, and to discourage at the same time the importation of tyres that have already been retreaded, as these have a substantially shorter lifespan than new tyres. As part of this initiative, import bans for retreaded tyres were introduced. In a first case in 2002,[47] Uruguay took Brazil before an ad hoc arbitral tribunal to challenge its import ban. The arbitral tribunal developed its reasoning in terms of classic public international law, while striking down the Brazilian legislation as a new

[45] All MERCOSUR documents mentioned are available under www.mercosur.int/msweb.

[46] See generally, J Gama Sa Cabral and G Giovanna Lucarelli de Salvio, 'Considerations on the Mercosur Dispute Settlement Mechanism and the Impact of its Decisions in the WTO Dispute Resolution System' (2009) 42 *Journal of World Trade* 1013, 1016 ff.

[47] *Laudo del Tribunal arbitral ad hoc del MERCOSUR constituido para entender de la controversia presentada por la República oriental del Uruguay a la República federativa del Brasil sobre 'Prohibición de importación de neumáticos remoldeados (remolded) procedentes del Uruguay'*, 9 January 2002, [2002] *Boletín official del MERCOSUR* no 20 (available at: www.mercosur.int/msweb, all excerpts are translated from the original Spanish version by the author).

restriction on trade contrary to MERCOSUR law due to the principle of estoppel.[48] For reasons unknown,[49] Brazil did not invoke the environmental defence which would have been available under Article 50 of the earlier Treaty of Montevideo.[50] This provision rephrases Article XX(b) GATT and therefore allows proportionate restrictions to trade for the purpose of protecting the life and health of humans, animals and plants.

After this early pronouncement, in 2005 another ad hoc arbitral tribunal examined a challenge by Uruguay to a law introduced by Argentina in 2002 which extended an import ban on used tyres to retreaded tyres.[51] In a lengthy ruling, the tribunal spent several pages on identifying the principles of environmental protection which could limit the principle of economic integration,[52] then negated the applicability of the principle of estoppel to the present case in contradiction to the arbitral tribunal's award between Brazil and Uruguay in 2002.[53] It also briefly, but expressly, excluded the applicability of that award to the present situation, as there were extensive submissions on the environmental derogation of Article 50 Treaty of Montevideo in the present case, while the issue had not been brought up in the 2002 judgment.[54] The tribunal, thus, insisted that it could not ignore the environmental problems caused by the waste tyres[55] and came to the rather terse conclusion that the Argentinian law was compatible with MERCOSUR law.

As a brief comment, after stating that the 2002 award did not even mention Article 50 of the Treaty of Montevideo, the ad hoc arbitral tribunal

[48] The arbitral tribunal found that the obligations undertaken by the parties under MERCOSUR law imply a stand still obligation and a prohibition on new restrictions on trade flows, *ibid* at s II.B.2.c 'Los principios Generales de Derecho: el *estoppel*'.

[49] In a later dispute, the WTO Appellate Body was called to deal with this judgment and also expresses between the lines mild bewilderment at this omission by Brazil: 'It is not appropriate for us to second-guess Brazil's decision not to invoke Article 50(d), which serves a function similar to that of Article XX(b) GATT 1994. However, Article 50(d) of the Treaty of Montevideo, as well as the fact that Brazil might have raised this defence in the MERCOSUR arbitral proceedings . . ., show, in our view, that the discrimination associated with the MERCOSUR exemption does not necessarily result from a conflict between provisions under MERCOSUR and the GATT 1994[.]' WTO, *Brazil – Measures Affecting Imports of Retreaded Tyres – Report of the Appellate Body* (3 December 2007) WT/DS332/AB/R, para 246.

[50] This art forms part of the MERCOSUR *acquis* via a particular construction: the clause of art 8 of the Treaty of Asunción foresees that the rights and obligations of parties under earlier agreements such as the Treaty of Montevideo shall be preserved, while art 2 Annex I to the Treaty of Asunción removes from the ambit of the definition of a trade restriction 'measures adopted according to situations foreseen in article 50' (author's translation from Spanish original version).

[51] Controversia entre la República oriental de Uruguay y la República Argentina, Laudo Arbitral, 25 October 2005 [2005] Boletín official del MERCOSUR No 34.

[52] See especially, paras 57–61 and 68–70 of the Laudo Arbitral on art XX of the GATT, art 50(d) of the Treaty of Montevideo and the principles of environmental integrity ('integridad ambiental') as well as the precautionary principle.

[53] Arbitral on art XX of the GATT, *ibid*, para 103.

[54] *Ibid*, para 110.

[55] *Ibid*, para 111.

itself does not go into any more detail on any balancing between the interests of environmental protection and freedom to trade.[56] The mere invocation by Argentina of the aim of environmental protection pursued by its legislation is sufficient for the tribunal to uphold it. Although one might be satisfied that the public interest at stake is taken into account, the absence of a comprehensive legal reasoning or test is striking.

B Laudo No 1/2005: The PRC and the ECJ's Case Law on Balancing Trade and Environmental Interests

Uruguay filed an appeal against the tribunal's decision and the case went before the PRC. The latter rendered what might be called a pedagogic judgment.[57] The PRC revealed that the nature of the legal order of the MERCOSUR was not merely one of pure international law, but of integration law, aspiring to become supranational law.[58] The arbitral tribunal was found to have committed a severe mistake in not properly setting out and analyzing the criteria to be applied in the case of an environmental derogation being invoked by a party. The PRC identified the present dispute as a 'pilot case'[59] where a reference to well-established case law in a different context was permitted. The ECJ's case law in an infringement action of the European Commission against Austria[60] was then taken to show how a step-by-step analysis should be undertaken. Referring both to Advocate General Geelhoud's Opinion in the case and the ECJ's judgment, the PRC stated that first the trade restrictive effect, then its discriminatory or equally applicable character and finally its possible justification had to be examined.[61] As a fourth and crucial issue that the arbitral tribunal had neglected, the measure had to be scrutinized in light of the principle of proportionality as the ECJ had done it in the *Commission v Austria* case or the WTO Appellate Body in *Korea-Beef*.[62] As an interpretive guidance the PRC referred, arguably rather as an obiter dictum, to a guide on the application of Articles 28–30 EC Treaty issued by the European Commission.[63] In conclusion, the Court repealed the arbitral tribunal's conclusions and

[56] *Ibid*, para 110.

[57] *Laudo No 1/2005 del Tribunal Permanente de Revisión constituido para entender en el recurso de revisión presentado por la República Oriental del Uruguay contra el Laudo arbitral del Tribunal arbitral ad hoc de fecha 25 de octubre 2005 en la controversia 'Prohibición de importación de neumáticos* remoldeados procedentes del Uruguay' 20 December 2005 [2005] *Boletín official del MERCOSUR* No 34.

[58] *Ibid*, para 9.

[59] *Ibid*, para 14 (author's translation from Spanish original version 'caso piloto').

[60] Case C-320/03 *Commission v Austria* [2005] ECR I-9871.

[61] Laudo No 1/2005, above (n 57) paras 15–16.

[62] *Ibid*, para 17, referring to *Korea – Measures Affecting Imports of Fresh, Chilled and Frozen Beef – Report of the Appellate Body* (11 December 2000) WT/DS161/AB/R.

[63] Laudo No 1/2005, above (n 57) para 18.

ordered Argentina to review its measures in light of the principles which it had just laid down.

C Evaluation of the Process of Judicial Borrowing by the PRC

Has the PRC done the right thing in following so closely the ECJ's views on how to balance the conflicting interests of free trade and environmental protection? At first, the incentives to engage in judicial borrowing are less prominent than in *L'Oréal Norge*. There is no express reference or provision to other courts' or tribunals' case law as a guide to interpreting the provisions of MERCOSUR law in the latter's treaties. In terms of personal contacts among judges, there is no obvious link either. Still, technical obstacles at least pose few problems, as the relevant case law of the ECJ is easily available in many different languages. Additionally, there exists a vivid exchange between academic communities of MERCOSUR countries and the EC Member States.[64]

Should the socio-economic and cultural context have its bearing on judicial borrowing in the MERCOSUR context? There are certainly two valid arguments which can be made. First, the MERCOSUR is an integration project between developing and emerging countries. Tensions are likely to arise between the means available to developing countries to implement environmental policies and strict scrutiny of the proportionality of a trade restricting measure exercised by a judicial body.[65] Secondly, the institutional setting and process of integration follows a much more intergovernmental pattern in the MERCOSUR, as opposed to the supranational ethos followed in the EC. This criticism can, however, be countered with the result of the case: the introduction of a balancing test between the conflicting interests of environmental protection and trade still leaves some leeway.[66] The PRC only imposes the principle, without fleshing out its concrete application. There is, thus, still room in subsequent controversies for arbitral tribunals to find solutions with less strict judicial scrutiny and which respect more regulatory autonomy and the limited resources MERCOSUR members might have at their disposal.

[64] This exchange is mostly related to the ongoing negotiation process for an association agreement between MERCOSUR and the EU which would include the creation of a free trade area. For an overview on this process see the European Commission's website: ec.europa.eu/external_relations/mercosur/index_en.htm.

[65] See for an example of the strict scrutiny of the ECJ the well known *Danish Bottles* case (Case C-302/86 *Commission v Denmark* [1988] ECR 4607, paras 21–22).

[66] For a comprehensive overview on this point see, J Trachtman, 'Trade and . . . Problems, Cost-Benefit Analysis and Subsidiarity' (1997) 1/97 *Harvard Jean Monnet Working Paper* 1. The author establishes a comprehensive classification of trade-off devices, ranging from least trade-restrictive alternative tests via narrow proportionality to different methods of interest balancing tests, several of which can be applied by tribunals under the wide heading of proportionality.

Furthermore, legal certainty and predictability seems also better safeguarded with the application of legal principles rather than the virtually diplomatic language used in the ad hoc arbitral tribunal's award.[67] It remains to be seen whether MERCOSUR tribunals will understand the PRC's ruling as an invitation to base themselves in the future to a large extent on what the ECJ has established in relevant case law. Again, MERCOSUR countries could face difficulties 'digesting' the *acquis communautaire*[68] due to the mentioned differences between the EC and the MERCOSUR in terms of membership, objectives and progress of the integration project. The PRC, however, seems to indicate itself a future autonomous development of the jurisprudence in the MERCOSUR framework after the foundations have been laid with help 'from outside' when it speaks of the present case as a 'pilot case'.

One of the most prominent factors in the present case is the institutional perspective adopted by the judges sitting in the PRC. The PRC was a newly established court and had to bolster its position by introducing coherence into the inaccurate case law emerging from the prior *Retreaded Tyres* disputes. The Protocol of Olivos brought about a similar change as the creation of the Appellate Body in the WTO. The question is how far such a paradigm change influences the mindset of judges sitting on the bench of a newly established permanent appeal instance. There is likely to be a more responsive feeling to develop a coherent new legal order with sustainable legal solutions. It is suggested that there are two strategies by means of which these newly appointed 'judges' can leave behind the stage of being mere 'arbitrators'. Arbitrators tend to be more willing to use all available means to resolve the particular dispute they are called to decide on. Permanent judges can opt for adopting a more autonomous perspective of their respective treaty regime. The ECJ is, in several aspects certainly, an example for this approach.[69] As in the case of the PRC, however, judges can also lean on an already well established peer at an early stage. The new court thereby profits from the reputation the peer has already acquired. Judicial borrowing facilitates this approach, as the process is

[67] The diplomatic tone of the 2002 award even reminds of some of the case law established by panels in the pre-WTO phase of the GATT 1947. For a more intense discussion of this 'diplomatic' paradigm in international economic relations and the change towards a more rule of law based approach with the creation of the WTO, see JHH Weiler, 'The Rule of Lawyers and the Ethos of Diplomats: Reflections on the Internal and External Legitimacy of WTO Dispute Settlement' (2000) *Harvard Jean Monnet Working Paper* 9/00.

[68] One should additionally not forget that this body of case law of the ECJ itself is not free of inconsistencies. For a famous example see, Case C-379/98 *PreussenElektra AG v Schleswag AG* [2001] ECR I-2099, paras 79–81. In this case, the ECJ accepted that German legislation that should promote the production of renewable energies favoured locally produced electricity without explaining why renewable energies from other Member States would not receive the same favourable treatment.

[69] For a recent comprehensive study on this topic see M Bronckers, 'From "Direct Effect" to "Muted Dialogue" – Recent Developments in the European Court's Case Law on the WTO and Beyond' (2008) 11 *Journal of International Economic Law* 885.

informal and no hard questions arise for the applicable law. The PRC did not have to go beyond the law as it is written in the Treaty of Montevideo. The MSEN allowed it to borrow from the ECJ, but to interpret its own norm. Nonetheless, in the long term the PRC could face challenges due to its perceived lack of independence if it should continue to rely extensively on ECJ case law.

It is suggested that mainly with this idea of gaining authority by means of borrowing, the PRC turned towards the learned case law of the ECJ which the latter had developed in more than three decades on similar subjects. The introduction of this principle into MERCOSUR law allowed the PRC to give a push to the integration process. The PRC clarifies in the judgment that it perceives the MERCOSUR legal order as having moved forward, and that more autonomy from the international legal order would support the evolution from a 'integration law' towards an aspired-to supranational law.[70] Read in this light, the dynamic adaptation to the ECJ's case law seems more justified and coherent with the MERCOSUR legal framework as the principle of regional exhaustion of trade marks read into the EEA legal framework by the EFTA Court. It is, thus, neither revolution nor transformation, but a stage in a continuous process.

Finally, the PRC's decision arguably provides a sound legal reasoning and an acceptable outcome to the case. The process of judicial borrowing has given an impetus to the development of a more dynamic and properly reasoned legal approach to the topic of environmental protection and trade in the MERCOSUR. Nonetheless, as in the *L'Oreal Norge* case, significant doctrinal and theoretical questions on 'judicial borrowing' remain.

V CONCLUSION

This chapter has intended to outline some aspects of the development of judicial borrowing and the use of international comparative law by international courts. While some factors such as lower technical barriers and closer personal connections among the limited group of international judges can oil the mechanisms of judicial borrowing and dialogue, judges have to be careful of this practice in several other respects. In particular, the context and nature of the treaty they are interpreting sets limits to the transfer of legal reasoning. In *L'Oréal Norge* the EFTA Court adopted the full legal reasoning of the ECJ on the MSEN in question and thereby came close to rewriting the EEA Agreement, introducing quite a fundamental change in the functioning of this free trade area and the homogeneity clause's reading itself. In the *Tyres* cases, the PRC used a MSEN to import the legal reasoning on the principle of proportionality as the ECJ

[70] Laudo No 1/2005, above (n 57) para 9.

had developed it in EC law to balance restrictions of trade against legitimate measures to protect the environment.

Despite the risks, examined in this chapter, which judicial borrowing entails, it is suggested that international courts should not refrain too easily from broadening their horizons. Judicial borrowing does not mean slavish obedience to 'foreign' judges, but rather a discussion of the same case based on a broader range of legal arguments, none of which should and will automatically prevail. Judicial borrowing should not be seen as a loss of independence of courts and tribunals, but as a voluntary process of discussion.

In the context of international judicial bodies, concerns present in a domestic context are aggravated by the fact that judges are not embedded in a developed constitutional structure as in a state. Their function has not been carved out during the political process which created the division of powers. Therefore, the additionally discussed aspects gain importance. First, in the *L'Oréal* case, through judicial borrowing the EFTA Court avoided an interpretative conflict, but also changed its relationship with the ECJ and thereby endangered its position as an independent court. Secondly, in the *Tyres* case, the PRC used judicial borrowing to bolster its position within the changed system of institutions within the MERCOSUR and tried to rely on the 'borrowed' authority of the ECJ.

Courts such as the PRC and the EFTA Court have to justify their existence and the powers attributed to them much more by their action and output than domestic courts. Judicial borrowing offers here advantages such as the use of 'sophisticated' legal solutions from an old established court like the ECJ. At the same time pitfalls lurk. Courts might be tempted to neglect setting out a comprehensive legal reasoning or adapting the transplanted legal solution sufficiently to the particular legal context.

The context of international economic law, regional integration and the WTO is particularly encouraging for the emergence of comparative approaches for international tribunals. But evidence for example in international criminal law shows that judicial dialogue is certainly not limited to this field.[71] Markesinis states in a slightly different context that 'we live in a shrinking world, need to break down trade barriers, and have to learn to sacrifice sacred cows of all sorts in order to survive in (relative) harmony with one another in an overcrowded planet'.[72] Judicial borrowing is certainly only a first, but nonetheless crucial step towards the awareness

[71] In the *Tadić* case (IT-94-1-A, Judgment, 15 July 1999, paras 83–162) for example the International Criminal Court had to interpret the notion of control of a state over a group committing certain acts and discussed for this purpose views of the International Court of Justice, the International Law Commission's Draft on State Responsibility, the Iran-United States Claims Tribunal and the European Court of Human Rights.

[72] B Markesinis, 'Understanding American Law by Looking at it through Foreign Eyes: Towards a Wider Theory for the Study and Use of Foreign Law' (2006) 81 *Tulane Law Review* 123, 183.

of the challenges as well as chances the proliferation of international law and international judicial bodies entails. As far as MSENs are concerned, these can provide a useful interface for judicial borrowing due to their similar wording. It should, however, not be forgotten that homogeneous interpretation cannot be a goal in itself. The treaty in which a MSEN is embedded may render such borrowing a flawed approach with negative consequences for the authority of the tribunal or court in question.

6

*Jurisdiction and Applicable Law Clauses: Where does a Tribunal find the Principal Norms Applicable to the Case before it?**

Lorand Bartels

I INTRODUCTION

EVERY INTERNATIONAL TRIBUNAL must identify the principal norms which it is to apply in the case before it.[1] In many cases, these norms are identified in the specific jurisdictional instrument – for example, a Special Agreement, application, or terms of reference – instructing the tribunal on the determinations which it must make in that given case. A typical example would be a jurisdiction clause stating that a tribunal has jurisdiction with respect to disputes concerning the interpretation and application of a given instrument. But this is not always done. It is not uncommon, particularly in investment disputes, for a tribunal to be asked to resolve a 'dispute' without any further reference to the norms to be applied by the tribunal. In these cases, the principal norms applicable to the case will be found in a relevant applicable law clause, such as Article 38(1) of the International Court of Justice (ICJ) Statute[2] or Article 42(1) of the International Centre for Settlement of Investment Disputes

* I am grateful to the participants of the MSEN research group as well as Zachary Douglas, Holger Hestermeyer, Petros Mavroidis, Campbell McLachlan, Eric Vranes and Michael Wood for their comments and discussions on the matters covered in this chapter. Naturally the views represented here and any errors are my own. I gratefully acknowledge the generous support of the Alexander von Humboldt Foundation and the Arts and Humanities Research Council (AHRC).

[1] A tribunal that applies the wrong norms acts in excess of jurisdiction: *Industria Nacional de Alimentos (previously Lucchetti) v Peru* (ICSID Case No ARB/03/4) Annulment (5 September 2007) para 98; *Soufraki v UAE* (ICSID Case No ARB/02/7) Annulment (5 June 2007) para 85 (distinguishing this from 'an error in the application of the law, which is not a ground for annulment').

[2] Statute of the International Court of Justice (adopted 26 June 1945, entered into force 24 October 1945) 3 Bevans 1153, art 38(1).

(ICSID) Convention,[3] which purport to instruct tribunals on the norms which they are to apply in the exercise of their jurisdiction. But if applicable law clauses serve to identify the principal norms applicable in these cases, do applicable law clauses also serve to identify the principal norms applicable in cases in which a jurisdiction clause itself purports to set out the principal norms applicable to the case? What, in short, is the relationship between jurisdiction and applicable law clauses when both purport to set out the principal norms applicable to a given case?

This question, which has troubled tribunals over the years, theoretically arises even when the norms set out in jurisdiction and applicable law clauses are identical. But it presents itself with particular force when the norms in both clauses are not identical, either in form or in content, but nonetheless apply equally to the case at hand: that is to say, in the case of tribunals faced with the application of Multi-Sourced Equivalent Norms (MSENs).[4]

In treating this question, this chapter proceeds as follows. Section II draws a distinction, based on the powers of a tribunal, between norms that for any given question are principal and those that are incidental. Incidental norms, according to this taxonomy, include norms that determine the applicability of principal norms, which usually appear by way of a defence to a claim. Section III explains why, although jurisdiction and applicable law clauses have some functional distinctions, they have a common function when it comes to establishing the principal norms relevant to any given determination. This section goes on to argue that, precisely for this reason, when a jurisdiction clause instructs a tribunal on the principal norms to be applied in a case, this instruction operates to the exclusion of any references to 'applicable law' in an applicable law. For the same reason, a jurisdiction clause may establish principal norms that are to be applied even if they are not mentioned in an applicable law clause. Section IV proceeds to address the functions of applicable law clauses with respect to incidental norms. In particular, it discusses the function of applicable law clauses in authorizing a tribunal to make determinations about the validity and applicability of any given principal norm: in other words, how these clauses authorize tribunals to take into account norms cited as defences to claims.

[3] International Centre for Settlement of Investment Disputes Convention (adopted 18 March 1965, entered into force 14 October 1966) 575 UNTS 159 (ICSID) art 42(1).

[4] MSENs are norms which have an independent formal existence (or exist in independent substantive areas of law) but are identical *ratione personae, ratione temporae* and *ratione loci*, and identical or similar *ratione materiae*. In addition, to the extent that jurisdiction and applicable law clauses both purport to be equally applicable to the same situation they may be considered are MSENs in their own right, though MSENs involving powers rather than rights and obligations.

II PRINCIPAL AND INCIDENTAL NORMS

The argument presented in this chapter is based on a particular taxonomy of norms, namely one that is focused not on their *content*, but rather on their *function* in adjudicative proceedings. This, in turn, depends on the powers of a tribunal in any given case, and in particular its powers to determine any given question in any given case. This taxonomy distinguishes between principal norms and incidental norms. Principal norms are those norms used by a tribunal to make principal determinations. These are determinations that a tribunal is authorized to make by its relevant jurisdictional instruments. By contrast, incidental norms are norms used by a tribunal to make the additional determinations necessary for it to be able to make principal determinations. To identify whether a norm is principal or incidental, it is necessary to identify the precise question being asked of a tribunal in any given case. Furthermore, a norm that is principal for one purpose, in any given case, may be incidental for another, and vice versa.

This taxonomy resembles one relevant to the principle of *non ultra petita*. In *Arrest Warrant*, the ICJ said that '[w]hile the Court is thus not entitled to decide upon questions not asked of it, the *non ultra petita* rule nonetheless cannot preclude the Court from addressing certain legal points in its reasoning'.[5] According to the taxonomy suggested here, norms relevant to determinations made according to the *petitum* are principal, whereas norms relevant to the other 'legal points in [the Court's] reasoning' are incidental. There is also an analogy to be made with a taxonomy relevant to *res judicata*, though one that is perhaps a little looser. In *Genocide Convention* (Merits) the ICJ said, relevantly, that a distinction must be drawn between 'first, the issues which have been decided with the force of *res judicata*, or which are necessarily entailed in the decision of those issues; [and] secondly any peripheral or subsidiary matters, or *obiter dicta*'.[6] It decided in the end that the force of *res judicata* attached to 'a finding, whether it be regarded as one of jurisdiction *ratione personae*, or as one anterior to questions of jurisdiction, which was necessary as a matter of logical construction'.[7] The distinction in this case follows very closely the taxonomy suggested here, although the line is drawn in a different place. That is to say, for the purposes of *res judicata* the Court placed in one category primary issues, issues 'necessarily entailed in the decision of those [primary] issues' and findings that are 'anterior' to primary determinations; and in another category it placed 'peripheral or subsidiary matters, or *obiter dicta*'. By contrast, according to

[5] *Arrest Warrant (DRC/Belgium)* [2002] ICJ Rep 3, para 43.
[6] *Genocide Convention (Bosnia/Serbia)* (Merits) [2007] ICJ Rep 1, para 126.
[7] *Ibid*, para 136.

the distinction suggested here, all issues except primary issues would be treated as 'incidental', and would correspondingly be determined according to incidental norms.

The norms that can function as principal norms are limited only by the questions addressed to a tribunal.[8] If a tribunal is asked to interpret or apply a given instrument, it is the norms in that instrument that constitute the principal norms for the purposes of this question. If a tribunal is asked to resolve a 'dispute', it is the norms chosen by the tribunal to resolve that dispute, if none are specified by the parties, which constitute the principal norms for the purposes of this question. If a tribunal has to determine whether it has jurisdiction, it is the norms relevant to its jurisdiction which constitute the principal norms for the purposes of this question. If a tribunal is asked to order provisional measures, it is the norms governing its power to order such measures that constitute the principal norms for the purposes of this question. These examples are deliberately broad in order to make the point that, in each case, the nature of the question is irrelevant. What is important is that a tribunal is directly required to make a determination on a given matter, and the principal norms are those norms that are applied for this purpose.

Incidental determinations, and consequently incidental norms, appear in a variety of contexts. One involves the determination of a 'legal fact' for the purpose of making a principal determination.[9] An international tribunal needing to determine matters relating to municipal law, such as the nationality or property rights of individuals, may, for this purpose, need to interpret and apply municipal law.[10] An international tribunal needing

[8] In principle, a tribunal may be required to make any kind of determination, although by definition a judicial tribunal will (at least predominantly) make determinations involving legal norms. The identification of a tribunal as having a judicial character depends on an objective analysis of its functions. Such tribunals benefit from powers that are presumed to be inherent to the judicial function, as well as powers that are incidental to the actual functions that the tribunal has been given. Some tribunals, particularly those with an advisory or hierarchically superior function, have limited functions with respect to facts. The WTO Appellate Body is not able to make factual findings (*cf* Understanding on Rules and Procedures Governing the Settlement of Disputes, Marrakesh Agreement Establishing the World Trade Organization, Annex 2, art 17(6), 33 ILM 1226 (1994) (DSU), and the European Court of Justice, at least under the preliminary rulings procedure (Treaty on the Functioning of the European Union (TFEU) [2010] OJ C83/47, art 267), is neither able to make factual findings nor to apply the law to the facts. At the other extreme, the International Court of Justice may be authorized to make determinations *ex aequo et bono*, which is to say, without the application of law (art 38(2) ICJ Statute, above (n 2)).

[9] *Cf* N MacCormick, 'Law as Institutional Fact' (1974) 90 *Law Quarterly Review* 102; R Allen and M Pardo, 'The Myth of the Law-Fact Distinction' (2003) 97 *Northwestern University Law Review* 1769, 1792; K MacKinnon, 'Redefining the Facts – Marginalising the Claimant?' in R Creyke (ed), *Tribunals in the Common Law World* (Sydney, Federation Press, 2008) 130 ff.

[10] *Barcelona Traction, Light and Power Company, Limited* (New Application) (Second Phase) [1970] ICJ Rep 3, para 38. By contrast, the WTO Appellate Body refused to consider municipal law in determining whether standing timber amounts to 'goods' within the meaning of art 1.1(a)(1)(iii) of the WTO Agreement on Subsidies and Countervailing Measures: WTO Appellate Body Report, *US – Softwood Lumber IV*, WT/DS257/AB/R (adopted 17 February

to apply a treaty provision permitting measures that are 'necessary' to protect a country's national security interests may, for this purpose, need to interpret and apply international rules on the use of force.[11] The resulting findings on nationality, property rights or violations of the use of force are 'legal facts' used by the tribunal for the purpose of making its necessary primary determinations. But these legal facts are found by the interpretation and application of incidental norms to social 'facts'. As can be seen by these examples, incidental norms are potentially unlimited in scope and variety.

In addition, incidental norms can have a meta-normative function, in the sense that they determine the interpretation, validity and applicability of any given principal norms. That is to say, when a rule on interpretation is applied to another norm by a tribunal, the rule of interpretation is being applied as an incidental norm. Norms on validity and application are typically relevant in the context of defences to principal claims: norms on application would include norms setting out normative hierarchies, norms such as estoppel or the equitable principle of 'clean hands'.[12] In practice, these norms appear by way of defence to a given claim, but the crucial point is that they are separate from the principal norms applicable in the case, including any defences set out in those principal norms. Section IV considers in more detail the role of applicable law clauses as an authority for a tribunal to apply these incidental norms, and in particular norms used as defences to claims based on the principal norms in a given case.

A final point might be noted. It may, during the interpretive operation just described, be necessary also to make a determination about an entirely different norm, for example, a treaty concluded in connection with the main treaty, in which case that treaty would be incidental in the sense described in the previous paragraph, and therefore incidental to the incidental rule of interpretation. Incidental norms may form a chain of infinite regress. By contrast, principal norms are finite, determined by reference to the actual question before the tribunal at any given stage of proceedings.

There is of course more to be said about the way in which a tribunal manages principal and incidental norms, but this is sufficient for present purposes. What should also perhaps be said, however, is that because the

2004), para 56. For the argument in the context of private international law that treating foreign law as 'fact' is a mere fiction, see N Jansen and R Michaels, 'Die Auslegung und Fortbildung ausländischen Rechts' (2003) 116 *Zeitschrift für Zivilprozess* 3, 8–9. My thanks go to Ralf Michaels for the reference.

[11] Eg, *Case Concerning Oil Platforms (Iran/US)* (Merits) [2003] ICJ Rep 161.

[12] The status of the rules of state responsibility on circumstances precluding the wrongfulness of conduct in this context is complicated: *CMS Gas Transmission Co v Argentine Republic* (ICSID Case No ARB/01/8) Decision of the *Ad hoc* Committee on the Application for Annulment (25 September 2007) paras 133–34. The question turns on the basis on which a tribunal is able to determine the consequences of a violation of an obligation.

present taxonomy is neutral as to the content or type of norms at issue, it does not exactly match other common taxonomies. In particular, it does not exactly match the distinction between primary and secondary rules, as these concepts are used in the International Law Commission's (ILC) Articles on State Responsibility (hereinafter ILC Articles),[13] or the distinction between substantive and procedural norms, as these terms are used in certain dispute settlement contexts, or the distinction between merits and preliminary phases of an adjudicative hearing. A norm that is of primary relevance to one tribunal may be of incidental relevance to another; furthermore, a norm that is of primary relevance at one stage of proceedings before a tribunal may be of incidental relevance at another stage of the same proceedings. It all depends on how it is asked, which in turn depends on the rules and powers of the tribunal itself.[14]

III PRINCIPAL NORMS

A Default Functions of Applicable Law Clauses

As mentioned, there is a close connection between the jurisdiction of a tribunal and the notion of principal norms. In the vast majority of cases, the instrument setting out the jurisdiction of a tribunal specifies the principal norms that the tribunal must apply in making its determination. With some refinements (for example, counterclaims), that essentially resolves the identity of these norms. But in some cases a tribunal has jurisdiction without being instructed specifically as to the principal norms relevant to the proceedings. In these cases – but only in these cases – the tribunal must find a principal norm elsewhere. And in these cases, it is applicable law clauses that will function as default repositories of principal norms.[15]

Applicable law clauses only function as a default depository of norms in some cases. They do not have this function where there is a jurisdiction clause making reference to the 'interpretation and application' of a given instrument. Such jurisdiction clauses are found both in ordinary treaties and in treaties establishing specialized tribunals,[16] although even

[13] ILC, *Articles on Responsibility of States for Internationally Wrongful Acts with Commentaries* (2001) GAOR 56th Session Supp 10 UN Doc A/56/10, 20.

[14] *Cf Genocide Convention* (Merits), above (n 6) para 117.

[15] Statements to this effect are comparatively rare. One is K Simmonds, 'Remarks in Roundtable' (1987) 22 *Texas International Law Journal* 149, 161.

[16] See also J Verhoeven, 'Article 21 of the Rome Statute and the Ambiguities of Applicable Law' (2002) 33 *Netherlands Yearbook of International Law* 3, 15–19. I am grateful to André Nollkaemper for drawing my attention to this reference.

here there are exceptions.[17] But, empirically, resort to an applicable law clause for the principal norms relevant to a case is likely to occur in two cases: first, in ad hoc arbitrations, including investment arbitrations; and secondly, in institutional dispute settlement systems which are, in principle, open to cases of a general nature, such as the Permanent Court of Arbitration (PCA) and the ICJ. The following illustrates the point by reference to the contentious jurisdiction of the ICJ.[18]

There is, on its face, ample scope for the contentious jurisdiction of the ICJ to be invoked without reference to any principal norms. This is most apparent in terms of the ICJ's jurisdiction in 'all cases' (Article 36(1)) and 'all legal disputes' (Article 36(2).[19] But the same applies to its jurisdiction in respect of 'all matters specially provided for in the Charter of the United Nations or in treaties and conventions in force' (Article 36(1)), in that such 'matters' might exist without reference to principal norms. Examples of such 'matters' involving unspecified norms are the original application by the United Kingdom in *Corfu Channel* for a determination on a 'dispute . . . arising out of an incident',[20] and cases based on Article XXXI of the Pact of Bogotá, which provides for ICJ jurisdiction in respect of 'all juridical disputes' concerning the matters set out in Article 36(2) of the ICJ Statute.[21]

[17] The European Court of Justice has jurisdiction, inter alia, to determine 'the validity . . . of acts of the institutions of the Community and of the ECB' (art 267 TFEU above (n 8)), and the law to be applied in the making of such determinations is set out in a different provision – and now a separate agreement – entirely (Treaty on European Union (TEU) [2010] OJ C83/13), art 19. Art 19 has been described as a 'jurisdiction' clause, even though it does not itself establish any causes of action: Joined Cases C-402/05 P and C-415/05 P, *Kadi v Council* [2008] ECR I-6351, paras 282, 287.

[18] The same point cannot be made in relation to the Court's advisory jurisdiction because (a) under art 68 recourse to art 38(1) is not mandatory and (b) the Court has never said in this context that it is applying art 38(1). On the first of these assertions see the US Statement, in *Effect of UNAT Awards*, ICJ Pleadings 133; though *contra*, see *Legality of the Threat or Use of Nuclear Weapons* [1996] ICJ Rep 226 (Fleischhauer J, Separate Opinion) 308; (Koroma J, Dissenting Opinion) 557.

[19] Rosenne distinguishes between compromissory clauses in instruments under art 36(1) and under art 36(2) and states that '[w]here the jurisdiction is based on paragraph 1, the Court is empowered only to apply the specific treaty. Where it is based on paragraph 2, the Court's jurisdiction may allow it and even require it to have recourse to rules of customary international law which resemble the rules of a treaty but which exist independently of the treaty, if for any reason that treaty is excluded from the scope of the jurisdiction of the Court in that particular case'. This is not correct. What is important is simply whether the compromissory clause mentions principal norms. See S Rosenne, *The Law and Practice of the International Court 1920–2005, Vol II, Jurisdiction* 4th edn (Leiden, Martinus Nijhoff, 2006) 648–49.

[20] Letter dated 13 May 1947 and Annex 3, Application Instituting Proceedings, *Corfu Channel*, at: www.icj-cij.org/docket/files/1/1499.pdf. The original claim was founded on a UN Security Resolution under art 25 of the UN Charter. Albania was subsequently held to have consented to jurisdiction on the basis of *forum prorogatum*, and the case was eventually submitted on the basis of a Special Agreement.

[21] Although in *Border and Transborder Armed Actions (Nicaragua/Honduras)* (Jurisdiction and Admissibility) [1988] ICJ Rep 69, paras 32–34, the ICJ declined to decide whether this provision was a collective optional clause declaration or a treaty under art 36(1). See further, C Tomuschat, 'Article 36' in A Zimmermann et al (eds), *The Statute of the International Court of Justice: A Commentary* (Oxford, Oxford University Press, 2006) 618–19, para 47.

Nonetheless, it is comparatively rare that a contentious case before the ICJ is lodged without an express instruction as to the principal norms to be applied,[22] even when the instruction is as vague as a statement that a dispute is to be determined in accordance with 'international law'[23] or that '[t]he principles and rules of international law applicable to the dispute shall be those recognized in the provisions of Article 38, paragraph 1, of the Statute of the International Court of Justice'.[24]

The reason that it is rare for cases to be lodged before the ICJ without an instruction as to the applicable principal norms is because, for unconnected reasons,[25] the Court has encouraged claimants to specify the applicable norms, even in its Rules of Court.[26] But this encouragement need not be followed. While it is true that under Article 40(1) of the ICJ Statute the parties must indicate 'the subject of the dispute' when they bring a case to the Court,[27] this does not mean that a principal norm must be mentioned. After all, in a definition still often cited, the Permanent Court of International Justice (PCIJ) described a 'dispute' more broadly as 'a disagreement on a point of law *or fact*, a conflict of legal views or interests between two persons'.[28] But in practice the Court has frowned upon the bringing of cases that do not include reference to a principal norm.[29] It is not presently to the point whether the Court is correct to encourage litigants, even by these means, to cite the principal norms at issue when they institute proceedings. What is important is simply that in most cases they do so, with the result that in almost no cases has the Court applied

[22] An unusual case is *Frontier Dispute (Burkina Faso/Mali)* [1986] ICJ Rep 554, para 19 where the applicable principal norms were identified in the Preamble of the Special Agreement.

[23] Eg, paras 1 and 2 of the Special Agreement in *Corfu Channel (UK/Albania)* or the Application in *Territorial and Maritime Dispute (Nicaragua/ Honduras)*, below (n 30). References to decisions made 'in accordance with international law' may not have this effect.

[24] Eg, art 5 of the Special Agreement in *Sovereignty over Pedra Branca/Pulau Batu Puteh, Middle Rocks and South Ledge (Malaysia/Singapore)* [2008] ICJ Rep 130 or art 6 of the Special Agreement in *Frontier Dispute (Benin/Niger)* [2005] ICJ Rep 90. Although these provisions are entitled 'applicable law' they take effect under art 36(1) of the ICJ Statute, above (n 2).

[25] This is for legal security and the good administration of justice: *Fisheries Jurisdiction (Spain/Canada)* (Jurisdiction) [1998] ICJ Rep 432, para 29, but also to prevent vexatious claims: Tomuschat, 'Article 36', above (n 21) 598, para 10.

[26] Art 38(2) of the ICJ Rules states that: '[t]he application shall specify as far as possible the legal grounds upon which the jurisdiction of the Court is said to be based; it shall also specify the precise nature of the claim, together with a succinct statement of the facts and grounds on which the claim is based'. The rule is not mandatory: see *Legality of Use of Force (Serbia and Montenegro/Belgium)* (Kooijmans J, Separate Opinion) [2004] ICJ Rep 279, para 21 .

[27] In his Separate Opinion in the *South West Africa Cases* (Preliminary Objections) [1962] ICJ Rep 319, 423, Judge Jessup refined the *Mavrommatis* formula by saying that expressly that '"dispute" in the context of a compromissory clause is one which can be settled by the application of principles of law'. The 'dispute' is determined by the Court on an objective basis, taking into account the positions of the parties: *Fisheries Jurisdiction (Spain/Canada)* (Jurisdiction), above (n 25) paras 30–31.

[28] Emphasis added. *Mavrommatis (Greece/United Kingdom)* (Jurisdiction) PCIJ Rep Series A No 2, 6, 11.

[29] See generally Tomuschat, 'Article 36', above (n 21) 598, para 10.

Article 38(1), even by implication, as authority for establishing the principal norms applicable to a case. Nonetheless, for various reasons, some cases not mentioning principal norms have slipped through the net.

A number of these cases concern territories, where the Court is sometimes simply asked to determine sovereignty or boundaries,[30] or a territorial dispute *(Libya/Chad)*, in which the Special Agreement provided that '[i]n the absence of a political settlement of their territorial dispute, the two Parties undertake . . . to submit the dispute to the [ICJ]'.[31] Non-territorial disputes which fail to specify a principal norm are rarer. In addition, to the first phase of *Corfu Channel*, mentioned already, one example is *Fisheries Jurisdiction (Spain/Canada)*, where the Court was asked, *inter alia*, to declare Canadian legislation to be non-opposable to Spain and that Spain must refrain from various acts and make reparations.[32] Then there is a rather unusual case, namely, *North Sea Continental Shelf*, in which the Court was asked by a Special Agreement to determine '[w]hat principles and rules of international law are applicable' to a given situation.[33] It might be thought that in this case the ICJ was asked to apply these 'principles and rules', but in fact this was not the question: the Court was rather asked about the applicability of these 'principles and rules'. Consequently, the norms directly relevant to this question were norms on their validity and applicability; the 'principles and rules of international law' were for this purpose no more than 'legal facts'.[34] In none of these cases did the Court relevantly refer to Article 38(1) of the ICJ Statute. However, it is submitted that this must have been the authority for applying the relevant principal norms in these cases.

B Relationship between Jurisdiction and Applicable Law Clauses

If it is true that both jurisdiction and (in default) applicable law clauses can determine the principal norms applicable in any given case, then the question arises whether applicable law clauses should be restricted to these default situations, or whether they can also establish the principal norms

[30] Eg, *Territorial and Maritime Dispute (Nicaragua/Colombia)* (Application) [2001] ICJ Rep 2.

[31] The matter was complicated by the fact that, in their separate applications under art 40(1) of the ICJ Rules, both parties asked the Court to decide the matter in accordance with international law. See *Case Concerning Territorial Dispute (Libya / Chad)* [1994] ICJ Rep 6, 9.

[32] Application in *Fisheries Jurisdiction*, above (n 25).

[33] *North Sea Continental Shelf* [1969] ICJ Rep 3; *cf Continental Shelf (Tunisia/Libya)* [1982] ICJ Rep 18.

[34] On 'legal facts', see above (n 9). If the tribunal is then also asked to apply the norm to a fact situation, that norm will then function as an ordinary norm, but only at this stage and for this purpose. Thus, in the second part of the request in *Continental Shelf (Tunisia/Libya)*, *ibid*, the Court was asked to 'clarify the practical method for the application of these principles and rules in this specific situation'. It was at this stage that these norms were to be applied (though in an abstract sense, the concrete delimitation being reserved for the parties).

applicable to a case in other situations as well. The proposition advanced here is in the negative; in other words, it is submitted that whenever jurisdiction clauses set out the principal norms applicable to a case, no matter how vaguely, these norms will prevail over any norms set out in an applicable law clause.

The following illustrates this proposition by reference to the two situations in which, logically, this question can arise: (a) when there is a claim based on a norm included in an applicable law clause that is not included in a jurisdiction clause; and (b) when there is a claim based on a norm in a jurisdiction clause that is not included in an applicable law clause.[35] The explanation suggested is that in both cases the jurisdiction clause will prevail over the applicable law clause, not because of any functional distinction between the two types of clause, at least as far as the substantive law is concerned, but because of the application of the principle of *lex specialis*.

i Claims based on Norms set out only in an Applicable Law Clause

Sometimes tribunals are asked to apply, as principal norms, norms that are found in an applicable law clause but not found in a relevant jurisdiction clause. They have responded to these requests in a variety of ways.

a 'Cardinal' Distinction between Jurisdictional and Applicable Law Clauses?

The question arose in *MOX Plant* (UNCLOS),[36] a case involving the UN Convention on the Law of the Sea (UNCLOS).[37] Article 288(1) of UNCLOS, the relevant jurisdiction clause, states that:

> A court or tribunal referred to in article 287 shall have jurisdiction over any dispute concerning the interpretation or application of this Convention which is submitted to it in accordance with this Part.

Article 293(1) of UNCLOS, the relevant applicable law clause, states that:

> A court or tribunal having jurisdiction under this section shall apply this Convention and other rules of international law not incompatible with this Convention.

The respondent alleged that the claimant was seeking to base its claims on norms set out in Article 293(1) that did not involve the interpretation or

[35] As mentioned above, in both cases the norms can be considered MSENs, in the sense that they have a separate existence but simultaneously apply to the same situation.

[36] *MOX Plant* (UNCLOS), Suspension of Proceedings on Jurisdiction and Merits and Request for Further Provisional Measures, Order No 3, UNCLOS Annex VII Arbitration, Permanent Court of Arbitration, 24 June 2003.

[37] UN Convention on the Law of the Sea (adopted 10 December 1982, entered into force 16 November 1994) 1833 UNTS 396 (UNCLOS).

application of UNCLOS itself. The tribunal did not make a ruling on this point, but said, *arguendo*, and without further elaboration, that:

> [T]here is a cardinal distinction between the scope of [the Tribunal's] jurisdiction under article 288, paragraph 1, of the Convention, on the one hand, and the law to be applied by the Tribunal under Article 293 of the Convention, on the other hand. . . . [T]o the extent that any aspects of Ireland's claims arise directly under legal instruments other than the Convention, such claims may be inadmissible.[38]

This passage was later quoted, with approval, in the *Eurotunnel* arbitration.[39] This arbitration involved a jurisdiction clause stating, relevantly, that '[a]ny dispute between the [parties] relating to this Agreement shall be submitted to arbitration'.[40] There was also an applicable law clause stating that:

> [I]n order to resolve any disputes regarding the application of this Agreement, the relevant provisions of the Treaty and of this Agreement shall be applied. The rules of English law or the rules of the French law may, as appropriate, be applied when recourse to those rules is necessary for the implementation of particular obligations under English law or French law. In general [*En outre*], recourse may also be had to the relevant principles of international law and, if the parties in dispute agree, to the principles of equity.[41]

The claimant based its claims on various norms set out in this very broad applicable law clause but not forming part of the instruments described in the jurisdiction clause. The tribunal rejected this approach, quoting the *MOX Plant* (UNCLOS) passage, and explaining that the 'cardinal' distinction is between 'the scope of the rights and obligations which an international tribunal has jurisdiction to enforce and the law which it will have to apply in doing so'.[42] Consequently, it held 'the Tribunal's jurisdiction is limited to claims which implicate the rights and obligations of the Parties under the Concession Agreement'.[43]

But simply saying that there is a distinction between two types of clause does not say what the distinction is. Neither the *MOX Plant* tribunal nor the *Eurotunnel* tribunal were able to explain why, contrary to the claimants' submissions in each case, the applicable law clause should not be capable of establishing the principal norms applicable in the case. Perhaps it was this doctrinal vacancy that led the *Eurotunnel* award in its further reasoning to abandon the distinction between the jurisdiction and applicable law clauses, and to try a new tack instead. It referred to a governing law clause, which stated that:

[38] *MOX Plant*, above (n 36) para 19.
[39] *Eurotunnel*, Partial Award, Permanent Court of Arbitration, 30 January 2007, para 152.
[40] *Ibid*, para 77.
[41] *Ibid*, para 99.
[42] *Ibid*, para 152.
[43] *Ibid*, para 153.

> The relationship between the [parties] shall be governed by the provisions of the Treaty, as given effect to by this [Concession] Agreement, and by the provisions of this [Concession] Agreement.[44]

This was an important clause for the tribunal. The tribunal stated that, while the applicable law clause had some incidental functions, 'it is the relationship between the [parties] as defined in [the governing law clause] on which the Tribunal is called to pronounce'.[45] But quite how this helps is unclear. The question at issue had nothing to do with the principal norms that applied to the parties (which in any case, as the claimants said, extended beyond the instruments mentioned in this clause) but rather the principal norms that could be applied by the tribunal.[46] It was a question not of substance but of judicial power. And it follows that the answer to this question cannot be found in a provision on the principal norms binding the parties, but must be found in provisions on the powers of the tribunal: in other words, jurisdiction and applicable law clauses.

b *Lex Specialis*

After these two cases, one is still left wondering what the basis is for the 'cardinal distinction' between jurisdiction and applicable law clauses. And this is all the more so given that, as demonstrated above, in principle jurisdiction clauses and applicable law clauses can both set out the principal norms applicable to a principal determination to be made by a tribunal. So how can one justify giving priority to a jurisdiction clause in situations in which both this clause and an applicable law clause purport to set out the principal norms applicable to a determination?

It is suggested that the answer is obscured by the implication, fostered by the *MOX Plant* arbitration tribunal, that, as far as the identification and application of principal norms is concerned, though of course not in other respects, there is a functional difference between jurisdiction and applicable law clauses. Rather, it is submitted, the reason that a jurisdiction clause mentioning principal norms will prevail over an applicable law clause is not because of any functional distinction between the two but rather, at least to this extent, because of a functional identity. This, crucially, establishes the conditions for the operation of the principle of *lex specialis*.

To put it simply: a jurisdiction clause that *specifically* instructs a tribunal on the principal norms to be applied will prevail over an applicable law clause that *generally* instructs (or authorizes) a tribunal on the norms to be

[44] *Ibid*, para 98.

[45] *Ibid*, para 151.

[46] This governing law clause was in itself peculiar. Usually governing law clauses set out the law applicable to an instrument, not to a 'relationship between parties'. That could only have some meaning if it purported to set out exhaustively the norms governing relations between the parties. This it neither did nor could have done.

applied. The corollary is that where a jurisdiction clause does not set out any specific norms, the principle *lex specialis* has no application.

It is freely admitted that this proposition has not been put in so many words, perhaps because the point is implicitly understood, at least in most cases. But it explains, for example, the following passage in the *Genocide Convention Case*:

> The jurisdiction of the Court in this case is based solely on Article IX of the Convention . . . It has no power to rule on alleged breaches of other obligations under international law, not amounting to genocide, particularly those protecting human rights in armed conflict. That is so even if the alleged breaches are of obligations under peremptory norms, or of obligations which protect essential humanitarian values, and which may be owed *erga omnes*.[47]

This passage is undoubtedly correct, but the Court does not explain directly why it has no power to make determinations on 'other' obligations under international law. After all, Article 38(1) of the ICJ Statute seems on its face to require the Court to apply these rules of international law. It is suggested that the answer is that, despite Article 38(1), these norms could not constitute the principal norms in the case because they were ousted by the principal norms set out in the relevant jurisdiction clause.[48]

Further support for the proposition advanced in this chapter may be derived from cases involving a restricted jurisdiction clause carving out the application of certain principal norms. Functionally, such a clause is analogous to a jurisdiction clause limiting a priori the principal norms which can be applied to the case at hand.[49] This is illustrated by *Nicaragua*

[47] *Genocide Convention* (Merits), above (n 6) para 147. This does not mean that the substantive law is the only law that is relevant to a legal determination. Two paragraphs on, the ICJ explained that it had the power still to apply, for incidental purposes, 'the rules of general international law on treaty interpretation and on responsibility of States for internationally wrongful acts': *ibid*, para 149. This might be taken as a reference to art 38(1) of the ICJ Statute (above (n 2)). But it is not certain that resort to art 38(1) is necessary for the determination of incidental questions of interpretation or responsibility. On the latter point, see *Chorzów Factory* (Indemnity) (Jurisdiction) PCIJ Rep Series A No 9, 24, in which the PCIJ held that a jurisdiction clause included an authority to order reparations.

[48] In the *MOX Plant* (UNCLOS) proceedings Ireland said that 'there is no provision comparable to UNCLOS Article 293(1) and the other provisions of UNCLOS cited above. There was, therefore, no basis in the Genocide Convention upon which jurisdiction could be claimed for the application of other rules of international law. There is plainly such a basis in UNCLOS, Article 293(1)': *MOX Plant*, above (n 36), *Ireland Reply*, vol 1, para 5.17. This oddly overlooks art 38(1) of the ICJ Statute.

[49] Not all restricted jurisdiction clauses are of this type. In particular, jurisdiction clauses which carve out certain 'disputes' (Arbitral Tribunal Constituted Under Annex VII of the United Nations Convention on the Law of the Sea (UNCLOS) Permanent Court of Arbitration 4 August (2000); see also UNCLOS, Arbitral Tribunal (4 August 2000), *Southern Bluefin Tuna* (2000) 39 ILM 1359; *Territorial and Maritime Dispute (Nicaragua/Colombia)* (Preliminary Objections), above (n 30) or 'measures' *(Fisheries Jurisdiction (Spain/Canada)*, above (n 25)), do not directly limit the applicable principal norms; indeed, it is likely that those norms must be applied precisely in order to determine whether the 'legal facts' constituting these 'disputes' or 'measures' exist.

(Merits). Here, as a result of a reservation to the Court's jurisdiction, the principal norms applicable by the Court included all international law except for certain specified multilateral treaties.[50] It is significant that despite some references to the continuing application of Article 38(1) of the Statute,[51] the Court did not propose that this provision could serve as a basis for applying these multilateral treaties as the principal norms in the case. Again, one explanation for this approach is that the Court implicitly understood that a jurisdiction clause prevails over an applicable law clause in accordance with the principle of *lex specialis*.

c Failure to apply the *Lex Specialis* Principle

Some cases have recognized the functional identity of jurisdiction and applicable law clauses as potential sources of principal norms, but have failed to apply the *lex specialis* principle. There are four of note.

The first of these, *Saiga (No 2)*,[52] was a case heard by the International Tribunal for the Law of the Sea (ITLOS) involving UNCLOS. A jurisdiction clause gave the tribunal jurisdiction with respect to 'the interpretation or application of [UNCLOS]' and an applicable law clause stated, relevantly, that '[a] court or tribunal having jurisdiction under this section shall apply this Convention and other rules of international law not incompatible with this Convention'. The tribunal made an express finding, in the operative provisions of its award, that the respondent had violated rules on the use of force.[53] It justified this as follows:

> Although the Convention does not contain express provisions on the use of force in the arrest of ships, international law, which is applicable by virtue of article 293 of the Convention, requires that the use of force must be avoided as far as possible and, where force is unavoidable, it must not go beyond what is reasonable and necessary in the circumstances.[54]

On this point, *Saiga (No 2)* was entirely replicated in *Guyana/Surinam*,[55] an Annex VII UNCLOS arbitration involving the same provisions, in which a similar claim was made about a violation of a prohibition against the use of force. In this case, unlike the other, the respondent objected that the tribunal had no jurisdiction to make findings on the use of force.[56] But this was to no avail: the tribunal quoted the above passage from *Saiga (No 2)*

[50] *Nicaragua* (Merits) [1986] ICJ Rep 14, para 182; J Crawford, 'Multilateral Rights and Obligations in International Law' (2006) 319 *Recueil des Cours de l'Académie de Droit International* 325, 396, fn 160.

[51] *Nicaragua* (Merits), *ibid*, paras 56 and 172.

[52] *M/V 'Saiga' (No 2) (Saint Vincent and the Grenadines v Guinea)* (Provisional Measures, Order of 11 March 1998) ITLOS Reports 1998, 24.

[53] *Ibid*, para 183.

[54] *Saiga (No 2)*, above (n 52) para 155.

[55] *Guyana/Surinam*, Award, 17 September 2007, available at: www.pca-cpa.org, para 405.

[56] *Guyana/Surinam* (Surinam Rejoinder), available at: www.pca-cpa.org, para 4.7.

and in exactly the same way made a finding as to the use of force in the operative provisions in its award.[57]

It follows from the above analysis that a tribunal is not able to apply, as principal norms for purposes of making a principal determination, norms not included among norms expressly set out in a jurisdiction clause. Consequently, both of these tribunal decisions are wrong. The question is why this is the case. It is suggested that the reason is not, as the *MOX Plant* statement would have it, because Article 293 cannot furnish the principal norms in the case for functional reasons. Rather, it is suggested that these cases are wrong because, in face of an express jurisdiction clause setting out the principal norms applicable in the case, an otherwise relevant applicable law clause must yield due to the principle of *lex specialis*.

There are also cases which make a similar error, but despite this, reach the correct result. One is the *Abyei Award*.[58] Here the tribunal determined that a panel had committed an excess of jurisdiction. The question was whether, having made this determination, the tribunal had the power to annul the entire award or whether it had the power only to sever those parts that were beyond the jurisdiction of the first panel. The tribunal quite properly reached its decision on the basis of the relevant provision of the arbitration agreement, which it had the power to interpret and apply under the relevant jurisdiction clause. But then it said that the same result was 'require[d]' by '[t]he "general principles of law and practices" that the Tribunal must apply to these proceedings pursuant to [the applicable law clause] of the Arbitration Agreement'.[59] This was incorrect. These principles might support the tribunal's reasoning, and might even be a legitimate source of law for interpreting the arbitration agreement. But the applicable law clause setting out these principles do not *require* the tribunal to do anything. Only when a jurisdiction clause entirely fails to mention principal norms can an applicable law clause have this function.

A second example is *MOX Plant* (OSPAR).[60] Article 32(1) of the OSPAR Convention[61] gave the tribunal jurisdiction with respect to disputes relating to the interpretation or application of the OSPAR Convention. Article

[57] *Guyana/Surinam*, above (n 55) para 488. It should be emphasized that the question is not (for the present) whether the respective tribunals might have been able to make *incidental* determinations on the use of force; it is whether they were entitled to make *primary* findings, as expressed in the operative provisions of their awards, on this point: *cf Oil Platforms* (Merits) (Simma J, Separate Opinion), above (n 11) para 6. Whether or not a tribunal may apply incidental norms not included in a jurisdiction clause is a different matter, discussed below.

[58] *The Government of Sudan/The Sudan People's Liberation Movement/Army (Abyei Arbitration)* Final Award, 22 July 2009, available at: www.pca-cpa.org.

[59] *Ibid*, para 416.

[60] *MOX Plant* (OSPAR) Final Award, 2 July 2003, available at: www.pca-cpa.org.

[61] Convention for the Protection of the Marine Environment of the North-East Atlantic (opened for signature 22 September 1992, entered into force 25 March 1998) (1993) 32 ILM 1069 (OSPAR Convention).

32(6)(a) stated that '[t]he arbitral tribunal shall decide according to the rules of international law and, in particular, those of the Convention'.[62] The claimant made various claims based on other treaties. The tribunal rejected these claims. It began by stating that the parties were not relieved of their obligations beyond those set out in the OSPAR Convention and continued:

> However, [this] does mean that the competence of a tribunal established under the OSPAR Convention was not intended to extend to obligations the Parties might have under other instruments (unless, of course, parts of the OSPAR Convention included a direct *renvoi* to such other instruments).[63]

This was perfectly correct. However the tribunal then said that:

> Interpreting Article 32(6)(a) otherwise would transform it into an unqualified and comprehensive jurisdictional regime, in which there would be no limit ratione materiae to the jurisdiction of a tribunal established under the OSPAR Convention. Here, there is no indication that the Parties to the OSPAR Convention have, in their individual capacities, submitted themselves to such a comprehensive jurisdictional regime with respect to any other international tribunal. Nor is it reasonable to suppose that they would have accepted such a jurisdictional regime through the vehicle of the OSPAR Convention.[64]

This reference to the applicable law clause was misplaced. The reason that the tribunal had no power to apply principal norms other than those set out in the OSPAR Convention was very plainly because of its limited jurisdiction clause. It had nothing to do with the applicable law clause, or how this clause might be interpreted.[65] Still, the award does at least have two merits: it reached the correct conclusion, and it recognized, perhaps instinctively, that there was no functional distinction between jurisdiction and applicable law clauses.[66]

ii Claims based on Norms set out only in a Jurisdiction Clause

The second situation in which the *lex specialis* principle comes into play is when a jurisdictional clause requires a tribunal to apply a law that (by implication) it is prohibited from applying by virtue of an applicable law

[62] *Ibid*, art 32(1).

[63] *MOX Plant* (OSPAR), above (n 60) para 85.

[64] *Ibid*, para 85.

[65] R Churchill and J Scott, 'The MOX Plant Litigation: The First Half-Life' (2004) 53 *International and Comparative Law Quarterly* 643, 670–01. V Röben, 'The Order of the UNCLOS Annex VII Arbitral Tribunal to Suspend Proceedings in the Case of the MOX Plant at Sellafield: How Much Jurisdictional Subsidiarity?' (2004) 73 *Nordic Journal of International Law* 223, 235 entirely misses the point.

[66] For identical reasoning, quoting this passage, see *Methanex* (Final Award on Jurisdiction and Merits) 3 August 2005, Pt II, ch B, para 6, available at: www.state.gov/documents/organization/51052.pdf.

clause. This is a rare event, because it depends on the following cumulative conditions: (a) the existence of an exhaustive applicable law clause, (b) the existence of a jurisdiction clause that sets out a contradictory norm and (c) no established hierarchy between the two clauses. For various reasons it is unlikely that all three conditions will be fulfilled simultaneously.

The first condition is not fulfilled in those institutional dispute settlement systems in which a tribunal is authorized to decide 'on the basis of respect for law', such as the PCA,[67] the Iran–US Claims Tribunal,[68] or, for that matter, the advisory jurisdiction of the ICJ.[69] The second condition is not fulfilled in those systems in which the jurisdiction clause is necessarily a subset of the applicable law clause, for example, in the ITLOS Convention or the ICC Statute of Rome.[70] It is also only rarely fulfilled in ad hoc dispute settlement. It is unlikely, though not impossible, that the parties to an agreement would establish principal norms in a jurisdiction clause which are not included among those set out in an applicable law clause. And the third is not fulfilled in those systems in which there is a built-in priority for jurisdiction clauses, for example, under the ICSID Convention[71] or the PCA.[72] Nor does a conflict present itself in those rare situations in which there is no applicable law clause at all, of which the WTO dispute settlement system, and some regional systems modelled on the WTO, are the prime examples. What is left, then, is essentially the contentious jurisdiction of the ICJ.

a Article 36 prevails over Article 38(1)

As far as the ICJ is concerned, the question, put simply, is whether the applicable law clause in Article 38(1) of the ICJ Statute limits the principal norms set out in an instrument lodged under Article 36.[73] It is suggested here that it does not.

The text of the ICJ Statute affords no a priori reason why Article 36 should be constrained by Article 38(1), given that both provisions have

[67] Art 37 of the 1907 Convention for the Pacific Settlement of International Disputes, 1 Bevans 557.

[68] Art V of the Iran–US Claims Settlement Declaration, 19 January 1981, 20 ILM 230 (1981).

[69] ICJ Statute, above (n 2) art 68.

[70] Rome Statute of the International Criminal Court (adopted 17 July 1998, entered into force 1 July 2002) 2187 UNTS 90.

[71] Art 42(1) of the ICSID Convention, above (n 3).

[72] Art 33 of the PCA Optional Rules for Arbitrating Disputes between Two States, 20 October 1992, 32 ILM 572 (1993).

[73] It is clear from *Aegean Sea Continental Shelf (Greece/Turkey)* [1978] ICJ Rep 3 and *Maritime Delimination (Qatar/Bahrain)* [2001] ICJ Rep 40 that Special Agreements are ordinary treaties. For an earlier suggestion that they are merely 'formal' and to be distinguished from 'normal' treaties that create substantive law, see S Jacoby, 'Some Aspects of the Jurisdiction of the Permanent Court of International Justice' (1936) 30 *American Journal of International Law* 233, 240.

the same hierarchical status. It follows also that an agreement (or declaration) authorized by Article 36 need not be constrained by Article 38(1).[74]

There is also some jurisprudence to this effect. The most important case on this point is *Serbian Loans*, in which the Permanent Court of International Justice (PCIJ) asserted jurisdiction over a dispute which it acknowledged was 'exclusively concerned with relations between the borrowing State and private persons, that is to say, relations which are, in themselves, within the domain of municipal law'.[75] In holding that it had jurisdiction to determine such matters, the Court made one key point,[76] namely, that Article 38 was a non-exclusive mandate. It said:

> Article 38 of the Statute cannot be regarded as excluding the possibility of the Court's dealing with disputes which do not require the application of international law, seeing that the Statute itself expressly provides for this possibility. All that can be said is that cases in which the Court must apply international law will, no doubt, be the more frequent, for it is international law which governs relations between those who may be subject to the Court's jurisdiction.[77]

This is the fullest expression of the Court's power to apply principal norms not set out in Article 38(1) in the exercise of its contentious jurisdiction. Other cases in which the Court has to consider norms not included among those set out in Article 38(1) are rare, at least in cases involving both principal norms (as opposed to incidental norms) and the Court's contentious jurisdiction.[78] Indeed, the best that can be said is that the Court has considered this permissible in obiter dicta. One example is *Free Zones*, where the Court was asked to decide on one of two interpretations of a treaty. The Court said that:

> From a general point of view, it cannot lightly be admitted that the Court, whose function it is to declare the law, can be called upon to choose between two or more constructions determined beforehand by the Parties, none of which may

[74] The argument is strengthened if one sees art 38(2) as applicable to art 36. This would imply that art 36 cases need not be subject to art 38(1). On the other hand, art 38(2) might also be seen as an alternative to art 36.

[75] *Serbian Loans* [1929] PCIJ Rep Series A No 20, 18.

[76] It is sometimes said that the Court found that the matters at issue were facts which, if established, would lead to a breach of an international obligation within the meaning of art 36(2)(c): eg, *Serbian Loans, ibid* (Pessôa J, Dissenting Opinion) 64; Jacoby, above (n 73) 233, 236–43, 238. This misreads the Court's judgment: it was merely pointing out that, abstractly, its jurisdiction was not limited to decisions based on international law: *Serbian Loans, ibid*, 19.

[77] *Serbian Loans, ibid*, 19–20.

[78] These cases must be distinguished from those in which non-art 38(1) norms have been applied as *incidental norms*: this distinction is not made, eg, in CW Jenks, 'The Interpretation and Application of Municipal Law by the Permanent Court of International Justice' (1938) 19 *British Yearbook of International Law* 67, 67. Such norms include, inter alia, the unilateral declarations in *Nuclear Tests (Australia/France; New Zealand/France)* [1974] ICJ Rep 253, the UN decisions in *Lockerbie* (Preliminary Objections) *(Libya/UK)* [1998] ICJ Rep 9 and expired norms in cases involving the doctrine of intertemporality and related doctrines in other cases. Also to be distinguished are cases involving the Court's advisory jurisdiction, where, as mentioned above (n 18), art 38(1) is not mandatory.

> correspond to the opinion at which it may arrive. Unless otherwise expressly provided, it must be presumed that the Court enjoys the freedom which normally appertains to it, and that it is able, if such is its opinion, not only to accept one or other of the two propositions, but also to reject them both.[79]

The point in this passage is that despite its strong inclination against being able to interpret the treaty as it saw fit, the Court conceded that if it was expressly asked to make a determination based on a norm that, by definition, conflicted with a norm of international law (namely, a predetermined interpretation) that is what it would have to do.

A second, and somewhat similar, example is *Continental Shelf (Tunisia/Libya)*. Here the Court was asked, inter alia, the following question:

> What principles and rules of international law may be applied for the delimitation of the area of the continental shelf appertaining to the Socialist People's Libyan Arab Jamahiriya and to the area of the continental shelf appertaining to the Republic of Tunisia, and the Court shall take its decision according to *equitable principles, and the relevant circumstances which characterize the area, as well as the new accepted trends in the Third Conference on the Law of the Sea.* (emphasis added)

It was not clear whether the norms in the emphasized part of this passage were included among the norms set out in Article 38(1). In the end, the Court decided that they were. However, it still indicated, in an obiter dictum, that it would have applied such norms, had this been necessary:

> [i]t would no doubt have been possible for the Parties to have identified in the Special Agreement certain specific developments in the law of the sea of this kind, and to have declared that in their bilateral relations in the particular case such rules should be binding as *lex specialis*.[80]

Admittedly, in this passage, the Court only goes as far as stating that the parties may agree to be bound by a *lex specialis*; it did not specifically state that in such an event the Court would respect this *lex specialis* by applying it to the exclusion of otherwise applicable norms set out in an applicable law clause. But this is the inescapable inference to be drawn from this passage.[81]

[79] *Free Zones*, PCIJ Rep Series A/B, No 46, 138. But *cf Minquiers and Ecrehos (France/United Kingdom)* [1953] ICJ Rep 47, where the Court had no difficulty in having been asked not to declare the disputed islands *terra nullius* or *condominium*.

[80] *Continental Shelf (Tunisia/Libya)*, above (n 33) para 24.

[81] What is more problematic is that the Court sought to justify this proposition by reference to art 38(1). It said: '[w]hile the Court is, of course, bound to have regard to all the legal sources specified in Article 38, paragraph 1, of the Statute of the Court in determining the relevant principles and rules applicable to the delimitation, it is also bound, in accordance with paragraph 1(a), of that Article, to apply the provisions of the Special Agreement', *ibid*, para 23 (*cf Oscar Chinn* (van Eysinga J, Separate Opinion) PCIJ Rep Series A/B No 63, 135). This presents a problem: if the Court's authority to apply the norms in the Special Agreement stems from art 38(1), then this statement is either redundant or self-contradictory. It is redundant if the norms in the Special Agreement are included among the norms set out in art 38(1);

There is an undeniable paucity of contentious cases in which the ICJ has directly applied principal norms not included in Article 38(1). But what practice there is supports the proposition that Article 36 is a separate head of authority for applicable law under which the Court may be authorized to apply principal norms not found in Article 38(1).

Nonetheless, there are arguments that Article 38(1) takes priority. One of these is squarely directed at *Serbian Loans*. The argument is that, whatever the position might have been for the PCIJ, the situation has now changed as a result of an amendment to Article 38 (now Article 38(1) of the ICJ Statute) by the insertion of a statement that the function of the ICJ is to settle disputes in accordance with international law. The problem with this argument is that in *Serbian Loans* itself the PCIJ expressly acknowledged this principle. It is therefore difficult to see what change the codification of this point brings about.[82]

Two other arguments in favour of the priority of Article 38(1) were advanced by Judge Lauterpacht in his Separate Opinion in *Norwegian Loans*. The first was that the Court is obliged 'to function in accordance with the provisions of its Statute'.[83] But this is circular, given that the meaning of the Statute is precisely the question at issue. The second reason he expressed, rhetorically, as follows:

> What would be the position if the Declaration were to make it a condition that . . . contrary to what is said in Article 38 of its Statute, the Court shall apply only treaties and custom in the sense that it shall not be authorized to apply general principles of law as recognized by civilized States and that if it is unable to base its decision on treaty or custom it shall pronounce a *non liquet*? What would be the position in the case of any such reservation?[84]

The short answer to this question is 'yes', in such a situation a tribunal would have to pronounce a *non liquet*. The longer answer is that this situation cannot arise, because in the absence of a principal norm (as set out in the jurisdictional provisions underlying the dispute) there would be no legal dispute before the Court.

In sum, there is no good reason why Article 38(1) should be considered to take priority over Article 36.

and it is self-contradictory if they are not, as then art 38(1) would be an authority for applying norms which it does not itself recognize. But despite the implausibility of explanation the core point stands: that the principal norms applicable in a dispute need not be confined to those in art 38(1).

[82] See, *South West Africa Cases* (Jessup J, Separate Opinion) above (n 27) 423.

[83] *Norwegian Loans* (Lauterpacht J, Separate Opinion) [1957] ICJ Rep 9, 44. The obligations are set out in art 1 of the ICJ Statute, above (n 2) and art 92 of the UN Charter.

[84] *Norwegian Loans, ibid*, 45.

b Principal Norms cannot be Applied under Article 36 in Violation of International Law

As mentioned, in its obiter dictum in *Continental Shelf (Tunisia/Libya)* the ICJ hypothesized that parties to a dispute could, in a Special Agreement, establish a *lex specialis* which, one may infer, the Court would also apply to the exclusion of any otherwise applicable norms set out in an applicable law clause. It is suggested, however, that while a Special Agreement may establish a *lex specialis* as well as instructing the Court to apply this *lex specialis*, it should also be able to instruct the Court to apply a norm that is not binding on the parties, either as a *lex generalis* or as a *lex specialis*. There may be difficulties in linking the norm with the subject-matter of the case, and perhaps also with the parties to the case, should this be relevant; but these difficulties should be confronted on their own terms. There is no a priori requirement for limiting the norms that can be applied to a particular case to norms that are binding on the parties to that case. If this were not the case, it would be difficult to understand how in *Serbian Loans* the PCIJ applied domestic law, which by definition was not binding on the parties to the dispute in that case as a matter of international law.

However, this proposition is subject to a condition, which is that whatever the Court is asked to do, it may not act in violation of international law. The justification for this proposition is the principle, recognized by the PCIJ in *Serbian Loans*,[85] and now included in the opening sentence of Article 38(1) of the Statute, that the Court must act 'in accordance with international law'. Contrary to what is often asserted, it is suggested that this provision does not mean that the Court must always apply international law.[86] What it means, rather, is that the Court must not violate international law.[87] In consequence, the Court may apply any norms, including domestic norms and newly invented norms[88] except for norms that are void or otherwise in violation of international law.

[85] Above (n 75).

[86] See, *Legality of the Threat or Use of Nuclear Weapons* [1996] ICJ Rep 226 (Koroma J, Dissenting Opinion) 557; A Pellet, 'Article 38' in Zimmerman et al (eds), *The Statute of the International Court of Justice*, above (n 21) 700, para 72 ('According to the usual analysis . . . the Court applies exclusively public international law ([Article 38] para 1)').

[87] *South West Africa Cases*, above (n 27) (Jessup J, Separate Opinion) 423; Rosenne, above (n 19) 525, fn 48; HF van Panhuys, 'Relations and Interactions between International and National Scenes of Law' (1964) 112 *Recueil des Cours de l'Academie de Droit International de la Haye* 1, 18–19, 21; Jenks, 'The Interpretation and Application of Municipal Law', above (n 78) 67.

[88] It has been argued that under art 36(1) the Court is competent to decide non-legal questions: A Verdross, in ILC, 'Consideration of the Model Draft on Arbitral Procedure', 438th Meeting, 7 May 1958 (1958) I *YILC* 32, para 71. The question concerned a draft of art 6(2) of the 1958 Model Rules on Arbitral Procedure, which states that '[i]n the case of a sole arbitrator or of the president of the tribunal, the question of disqualification shall, in the absence of agreement between the parties, be decided by the International Court of Justice on the application of one of them'.

There are two obvious ways in which this could happen. One was mentioned by Judge Evensen in his Dissenting Opinion in *Continental Shelf (Tunisia/Libya)*, where he said that:

> I share the view of the Court that these provisions may have a bearing on the sources of law available to the Court in the present case; and likewise the observation by the Court that the reference to these factors in Article 1 may affect the legal relations of the Parties in the present case only, but cannot affect the position in law of other States.[89]

The Court did not in fact make this qualification in its relevant obiter dictum, athough it did make reference to the rights of third states in its actual decision (which was not based on any *lex specialis* set out in the Special Agreement). Hence, it is Judge Evensen's own comment which stands for the relevant – and, it is submitted correct – proposition. It is indeed an instance of the *pacta tertiis* rule,[90] applied in this case to a Special Agreement.

An example of how this might work may be seen in *Oscar Chinn*.[91] As viewed by the Separate Opinions of Judge van Eysinga and Judge Schücking, the question was whether the Court could, by agreement of the parties, apply an *inter se* treaty which was (on their reading) concluded in violation of a multilateral treaty, the Treaty of Berlin.[92] Both judges refused to apply the *inter se* treaty on the basis that it was invalid. It is of course no longer accepted that such an *inter se* treaty would be invalid,[93] but it is still possible that a tribunal might refuse to apply such a treaty on the basis that it would violate the *pacta tertiis* rule.

In addition, in this case Judge Schücking indirectly addressed another way in which the Court might violate international law by applying a given norm. This followed from three logically linked points. The first was that '[i]t is an essential principle of any court, whether national or international, that the judges may only recognize legal rules which they hold to be valid'. The second was that '[Article 38(a) of the PCIJ Statute] cannot be intended to mean that the Court is bound to apply conventions which it knows to be invalid'.[94] The third was that a treaty that violates *jus cogens* would be invalid and 'a tribunal finds itself in the same position if a convention adduced by the parties is in reality null and void . . . even when jurisdiction is conferred on the Court by virtue of a Special Agreement'.[95]

[89] *Continental Shelf (Tunisia/Libya)*, above (n 33) (Evensen J, Dissenting Opinion) 279.

[90] The principle of *pacta tertiis nec nocent nec prosunt* is reflected in arts 34–36 of the Vienna Convention on the Law of Treaties (adopted 23 May 1969, entered into force 27 January 1980) 1155 UNTS 331 (VCLT).

[91] *Oscar Chinn*, above (n 81).

[92] The case had the additional complication that the Special Agreement was silent on the law to be applied, and the parties' agreement on the application of the Convention arose in written and oral argument: *Oscar Chinn, ibid* (van Eysinga J, Separate Opinion) 135.

[93] The matter is now dealt with as a question of state responsibility: see VCLT, above (n 90) art 30(5).

[94] *Oscar Chinn*, above (n 81) (Schücking J, Separate Opinion) 149–50.

[95] *Ibid*, 150. This was before *jus cogens* gained general acceptance.

Some of this reasoning is imperfect. The reference to Article 38(1)(a), as the provision is now numbered, was irrelevant, as it was not on that basis that the Court was being asked to apply the allegedly void treaty. But, for the reasons given above, it is suggested that the central contention that the Court is not able to apply norms in violation of international law is correct. This would be the result of applying a norm in violation of *jus cogens*.[96]

IV INCIDENTAL NORMS

If jurisdictional clauses, when they set out the principal norms, override applicable law clauses on the basis of *lex specialis*, the next question is what remains of applicable law clauses. In *Eurotunnel*, *Nicaragua* and *Genocide Convention*, among other cases, tribunals have indicated that applicable law clauses have some function, though not the function of establishing the principal norms to be applied to the principal determinations to be made by the tribunal. It is suggested that these functions are exercised predominantly in the context of incidental determinations. The following are three of the most frequent of these determinations.

A Validity or Applicability of a Principal Norm

By far the most significant form of incidental determination is when a tribunal decides that a principal norm is not valid or applicable to the case before it. This typically arises in the context of a defence to a claim based on that norm. Nonetheless, a defence based on the invalidity or inapplicability of the norm must be distinguished from a defence based on principal norms (for example, express defences set out in a treaty). In this case, a tribunal derives its authority to disapply the primary norm from the primary norm set out in its jurisdictional instrument.[97] The former case is quite different. Here, the invalidity or inapplicability of the norm depends on the application of a meta-norm. The question is where the tribunal derives its authority to apply this meta-norm. It is suggested that this authority may spring from a relevant applicable law clause.

This may be illustrated by the Separate Opinion of Judge Hudson in the *River Meuse*. This was an Optional Clause case, but the complaints were framed in terms of violations of a treaty between the applicant and the respondent, and the Court treated the case essentially as one concerning that instrument. It said that:

96 *Cf* arts 40 and 41 of the ILC Articles on State Responsibility, above (n 13).

97 On the duty to disapply norms on the basis of a 'meta-norm', in this case a conflicts rule, see Case 106/77 *Simmenthal* [1978] ECR 629.

> In the course of the proceedings, both written and oral, occasional reference has been made to the application of the general rules of international law as regards rivers. In the opinion of the Court, the points submitted to it by the Parties in the present case do not entitle it to go outside the field covered by the Treaty of 1863. The points at issue must all be determined solely by the interpretation and application of that Treaty.[98]

This was true as far as the basic claims were concerned. However, Judge Hudson, unlike the Court, considered that Article 38 of the PCIJ Statute gave the Court the authority to apply equity (specifically, the doctrine of 'clean hands') 'as part of the international law which it must apply' for the purposes of determining the applicability of the treaty in the first place.[99] If one takes this rationale at face value, it means that an applicable law clause has relevance to sources of law beyond those mentioned in the jurisdictional title of a dispute, but with the specific function of determining their legal applicability.

Statements of this sort are rare. This may be explained on the basis that where there is a broad applicable law clause, tribunals do not often bother to refer to it. But this does not mean that applicable law clauses are not used for this purpose by implication. For example, the existence of an applicable law clause might be the justification for the argument in *Lockerbie* that UN Security Council resolutions overrode the treaty (the Montreal Convention)[100] on which the claim was founded.[101] This argument was not about the applicability of the Security Council resolutions, as such, but rather about the applicability of the Montreal Convention in light of the norms (the resolutions) which were hierarchically superior (because of the combined operation of Articles 25 and 103 of the UN Charter). Those norms were not adduced under Article 36(1); they must therefore have been based on Article 38(1).

There is, however, an alternative explanation for a tribunal's power to determine the applicability of a principal norm. This argument is that, as an inherent aspect of jurisdiction to apply a principal norm, a tribunal also has jurisdiction to determine the applicability of that norm. The leading authority on this is the *ICAO Case*.[102] This case concerned a jurisdiction clause giving the International Civil Aviation Organization (ICAO) Council jurisdiction with respect to disputes on the interpretation and application of two instruments. Neither of these instruments contained an applicable law clause. India argued that the Council's jurisdiction did not

[98] *Meuse*, PCIJ Rep Series A/B No 70, 16. See also, van Eysinga J (Separate Opinion) 53.
[99] *Meuse*, *ibid* (Hudson, Separate Opinion) 77.
[100] Convention for the Unification of Certain Rules Relating to International Carriage by Air (12 October 1929) 137 LNTS 13.
[101] *Lockerbie* (Preliminary Objections) above (n 78) para 37. The Court did not address the argument, disposing of the case on other grounds: *ibid*, paras 38 and 44.
[102] *ICAO Case (India/Pakistan)* [1972] ICJ Rep 46.

extend to the making of determinations about the suspension or termination of the relevant treaties. The Court held that it did. This was principally because the treaties themselves had clauses relevant to suspension and termination, but the Court also hinted strongly that such a ruling would have been within the Council's jurisdiction in any case.[103] Given the absence of any relevant applicable law clause, the implication therefore must be that the ICJ supported the proposition that an international tribunal with jurisdiction with respect to the application of a treaty is by implication entitled also to determine the *applicability* of that treaty.

The significance of this reasoning is perhaps only fully apparent when it is juxtaposed with the practice of WTO tribunals, which likewise operate without an applicable law clause. Unlike the *ICAO* Case, the ICJ in WTO tribunals have been reluctant to consider whether WTO norms might be inapplicable because of factors extraneous to the WTO covered agreements themselves.[104] A complete explanation of the Appellate Body's jurisprudence on this issue is beyond the narrow scope of this chapter, but it clearly has something to do with the absence of an express applicable law clause and, it is suggested, the requirement in Article 3.2 (and Article 19.2) of the DSU (Understanding on Rules and Procedures Governing the Settlement of Disputes) that it not add to or diminish the rights and obligations set out in the covered agreements. These rights and obligations remain valid, regardless of any subsequent practice or treaties concluded by WTO Members outside the WTO framework. The question is whether they are still applicable in light of such other activity and, most importantly, whether the WTO tribunals have the power to determine that they are not applicable in WTO disputes. As Article 3.2 and especially Article 19.2 DSU are expressly directed at the powers of the WTO tribunals, it is at least arguable to propose that these provisions direct these tribunals to assume that these rules are not only valid but also applicable, regardless of the situation under general international law.[105]

[103] *Ibid*, para 27. See E Cannizzaro and B Bonafé, 'Fragmenting International Law through Compromissory Clauses? Some Remarks on the Decision of the ICJ in the Oil Platforms Case' (2005) 16 *European Journal of International Law* 481, who initially express scepticism on whether a tribunal has the power, under a jurisdiction clause, to decline jurisdiction '[i]f the parties agree in principle on the applicability of the treaty, but disagree as to the effect on the treaty of a different legal rule' (486–87) but are convinced by the *ICAO Case*: '[o]nce it is ascertained that the Court's jurisdiction arising under a compromissory clause encompasses the jurisdiction to decide disputes on the applicability of a treaty to a given situation, the only step that remains to be accomplished is the identification of the law to be applied in order to settle the dispute' (488). This is true, but it does not explain the authority of the Court is able to apply that law.

[104] J Pauwelyn, *Conflict of Norms in Public International Law: How WTO Law Relates to Other Rules of International Law* (Cambridge, Cambridge University Press, 2003); L Bartels, 'Applicable Law in WTO Dispute Settlement Proceedings' (2001) 35 *Journal of World Trade* 499; E Vranes, 'Jurisdiction and Applicable Law in WTO Proceedings' (2005) 48 *German Yearbook of International Law* 265 and I Van Damme, 'Interpretation, Jurisdiction, and Applicable Law' in D Bethlehem, D McRae, R Neufeld and I van Damme (eds), *Oxford Handbook of International Trade Law* (Oxford, Oxford University Press, 2009).

[105] I referred to these provisions as functioning analogously to a conflicts rule in Bartels, *ibid*.

B Rules of Interpretation

There are also other ways in which applicable law clauses seem to be of relevance. One concerns the rules of interpretation of international norms. Without an applicable law clause, it is not entirely certain on what basis a tribunal would be able to apply rules of interpretation.

In most cases, a tribunal would claim that the power to apply these rules is part of its inherent jurisdiction. But at least one possible effect of stipulating that a determination is to be made by applying international law is that the tribunal is *obliged* to apply the ordinary rules on interpretation. In *Peace Treaties*, for example, Judge Read in his Dissenting Opinion said that he was 'bound, by the terms of Article 38 of the Statute and in accordance with the views of this Court, as set forth in the case cited above' to interpret a clause in a manner that would avoid an unreasonable result.[106] Admittedly, this was in the context of an Advisory Opinion, and so it is doubtful, as said above, that Article 38 could in fact have this binding effect. But despite this, the point is still valid for applicable law clauses. Even the WTO has seen the merit in this approach, including a specific obligation to apply these norms in Article 3.2 of the DSU.

C Legal Facts

A further possible function of applicable law clauses concerns their role in relation to the determination of legal facts.[107] It is often necessary to make a subsidiary determination about a legal fact involving a norm outside a tribunal's principal jurisdiction. Sometimes this has been uncontroversial. For example, in *EC–Bananas III* there was a waiver of a WTO obligation for action 'necessary . . . to provide preferential treatment . . . as required by the relevant provisions of the Fourth Lomé Convention'. Despite objections by the respondent, the Appellate Body, approving a statement by the Panel, permitted itself to examine the provisions of the Lomé Convention 'in so far as it [was] necessary to interpret the Lomé waiver'.[108] In fact, it went further than this, making express findings about whether various acts (such as 'the allocation of tariff quota shares to ACP States exporting non-traditional ACP bananas') were required under the Lomé Convention. Even this could be justified as an incidental matter in the course of its legal reasoning. However, it is notable that the Appellate Body included these findings in the operative parts of its report.[109]

[106] *Peace Treaties* [1950] ICJ Rep 65 (Read J, Dissenting Opinion) 245.

[107] See above (n 9).

[108] WTO Panel Report, *EC–Bananas III,* WT/DS27/R/USA (adopted 25 September 1997), para 7.98; WTO Appellate Body Report, *EC–Bananas III,* WT/DS27/AB/R (adopted 25 September 1997), para 167.

[109] WTO Appellate Body Report, *EC–Bananas III, ibid,* paras 255(g) and (h). *Cf* above (n 57).

In both respects, *EC–Bananas III* contrasts with *Mexico – Soft Drinks*, in which the WTO Appellate Body refused to consider the application of the principle that a party to judicial proceedings may not rely on its own illegal act. This was not because the principle was not applicable (a point which the Appellate Body accepted *arguendo*) but because the Appellate Body would have been obliged in applying the principle to determine whether the United States had acted illegally under non-WTO law. This was not possible, said the Appellate Body, because it had no jurisdiction 'to adjudicate non-WTO disputes'.[110] Quite what this means, and how it relates to the Appellate Body's findings about the Lomé Convention in *EC–Bananas III*, is not entirely clear. As this chapter is focused on tribunals' authority to apply principal norms, rather than their authority to apply incidental norms, it is not possible to enter into a discussion of the possible rationales for each of these cases.[111] But it could yet be suggested that the outcome of the second case may well have been different had the Appellate Body had the ability to draw on a relevant applicable law clause.

V CONCLUSION

This chapter has considered one specific aspect of MSENs, namely, how a tribunal should choose between two different clauses (a jurisdiction clause and an applicable law clause) when both purport to instruct the tribunal on the principal norms to be applied to the question before it. Its argument is as follows: jurisdiction clauses and applicable law clauses share the same function of establishing the principal norms to be applied by a tribunal in making its principal determinations. Applicable law clauses serve this function by default in the absence of this being done by a jurisdiction clause. Further, where a jurisdiction clause performs this function, it overrides any otherwise applicable law clause by virtue of the principle of *lex specialis*.

The chapter also recognizes that applicable law clauses have additional functions, namely, to authorize a tribunal to make incidental determinations involving norms not necessarily relevant to the principal jurisdiction of the tribunal. Chief among these are norms determining the validity and applicability of a principal norm, and those on interpretation and norms relevant in the determination of legal facts necessary for the application of principal or incidental norms. But these additional functions of applicable law clauses are entirely independent of their functions when it comes to establishing the principal norms applicable in a given case.

[110] WTO Appellate Body Report, *Mexico – Soft Drinks*, WT/DS308/AB/R (adopted 24 March 2006), para 56.

[111] A later study will take up these issues in more detail: L Bartels, *Applicable Law before International Courts and Tribunals* (Oxford University Press, forthcoming).

7

*The OSPAR Convention, the Aarhus Convention and EC Law: Normative and Institutional Fragmentation on the Right of Access to Environmental Information**

Nikolaos Lavranos

I INTRODUCTION

SINCE THE EARLY 1990s the access to information has quickly developed into an important tool for increasing transparency in the decision-making process of public authorities regarding projects that may have a negative impact on the environment. Indeed, the fast development of environmental law – at the international, European and national levels[1] – as well as the increasing awareness of citizens and non-governmental organizations (NGOs) of their potential to prevent or at least reduce environmental pollution, has been one of the most important reasons for the wide recognition received by the right to access to information. In fact, the right of access to information has been enshrined in numerous international and European instruments, so that it can serve as a prime example for analyzing this book's main topic of international Multi-Sourced Equivalent Norms (MSENs), which are defined 'as two or more norms which are: (1) binding upon the same international legal subjects; (2) similar or identical in their normative content (in the words of the ILC, "point in the same direction"); and (3) have been established

* The opinions in this contribution are expressed solely in personal capacity and cannot be attributed in any way to the Dutch Government.

[1] See, eg, D Bodansky, J Brunee and E Hey, *The Oxford Handbook of International Environmental Law* (Oxford, Oxford University Press, 2007); J Jans and H Vedder, *European Environmental Law* (The Netherlands, Europa Law Publishing, 2008); H Kranenborg and W Voermans, *Access to Information in the EU: A Comparative Analysis of EC and Member State Legislation* (The Netherlands, Europa Law Publishing, 2005).

through different international instruments or "legislative" procedures or are applicable to different substantive areas of the law'.[2]

This chapter will discuss the proceeding under the Convention for the Protection of the Marine Environment of the North-East Atlantic (OSPAR)[3], which formed part of the wider *MOX Plant* dispute,[4] as a case study for identifying the existence of MSENs concerning the right to access to environmental information. It will subsequently analyze the extent to which MSENs create divergent rights and obligations for states that could lead to divergent or conflicting outcomes and ultimately to fragmentation. Accordingly, section II will identify the MSENs involved in this case study and discuss the substantive aspects of the right to access to environmental information. Based on that, section III will examine how the OSPAR arbitral tribunal dealt with the MSEN issue. A few concluding remarks will wrap up this chapter.

II THE RELEVANT MSEN

As is well known, the *MOX Plant* dispute revolved around the longstanding complaint of Ireland against the UK that its MOX plant situated in Sellafield, UK, is radioactively contaminating the Irish Sea and thereby causing environmental (and health) damages. The dispute involved a host of different legal instruments and three separate proceedings[5]: (i) Law of the Sea Convention (UNCLOS) arbitral proceedings concerning the alleged violation of UNCLOS[6]; (ii) Proceedings initiated by the European Commission (the 'Commission') against Ireland before the European Court of Justice (ECJ) for alleged infringement of Article 292 EC Treaty, ie, the ECJ's exclusive jurisdiction provision[7], and (iii) OSPAR arbitral proceedings regarding

[2] See in this volume, T Broude and Y Shany, 'The International Law and Policy of Multi-Sourced Equivalent Norms' in T Broude and Y Shany (eds), *Multi-Sourced Equivalent Norms in International Law* (Oxford, Hart Publishing, 2011) p 5.

[3] Permanent Court of Arbitration (PCA), Dispute concerning Access to Information under art 9 OSPAR Convention (Convention for the Protection of the Marine Environment of the North East Atlantic adopted 22 September 1992, entered into force 25 March 1998); *Ireland v UK*, Final Award, 2 July 2003: www.pca-cpa.org/upload/files/OSPAR%20Award.pdf. See further M Fitzmaurice, 'Case-Note on the OSPAR Arbitral Tribunal Award' (2003) 18 *International Journal of Marine and Coastal Law* 541; T McDorman, 'Access to Information under Article 9 OSPAR Convention (Ireland v UK)' (2004) 98 *American Journal of International Law* 330.

[4] See further Y Shany, 'The First MOX Plant Award: The Need to Harmonize Competing Environmental Regimes and Dispute Settlement Procedures' (2004) 17 *Leiden Journal of International Law* 815.

[5] See for an overview, R Churchill and J Scott, 'The MOX Plant Litigation: The First Half-Life' (2004) 53 *International and Comparative Law Quarterly* 643.

[6] See for all documents relating to the dispute: PCA, UNCLOS Arbitral Tribunal, *Ireland v UK, MOX Plant*, available at: www.pca-cpa.org/showpage.asp?pag_id=1148.

[7] Case C-459/03 *Commission v Ireland* [2006] ECR I-4635; see further C Ramano, 'Case note on MOX Plant' (2007) 101 *American Journal of International Law* 171.

the alleged violation by the UK of Article 9 OSPAR Convention[8] which contains a right to access to information.

The subsequent analysis only focuses on the OSPAR proceeding, ie, the right of access to information concerning the operation of the MOX plant, which Ireland had been requesting from the UK for many years.[9] However, before proceeding with the analysis, it is appropriate to summarize the factual and legal background of the *MOX Plant* case as far as the OSPAR proceeding is concerned.

A The Factual Background

The Sellafield nuclear facility is located in north west England, on the Irish Sea, about 180 km from the coast of Ireland. Established in 1947 to produce plutonium and other nuclear materials for the British atomic bomb project, Sellafield was the site of the world's first civilian nuclear reactor and has, throughout its history, played a central role in Britain's nuclear programme – both military and civilian. The facility covers about 4 km^2, employs 10,000 workers and includes plutonium production facilities, reprocessing plants and nuclear power reactors.

In 1993, British Nuclear Fuels (BNFL), which operates the Sellafield facility (the facility was a wholly government-owned company until 2005), applied to the local authorities for permission to build a MOX plant in order to process spent nuclear fuels by retrieving and blending separated plutonium oxide and uranium oxide into pellets to be reused as fuel in nuclear reactors.

The approval of the planned MOX plant involved both domestic and international procedures. Pursuant to domestic UK law, BNFL prepared an environmental impact study as part of the permission procedure. The British authorities concluded that the radioactive discharges from the MOX plant would be minimal, at levels permissible under the existing authorization. Accordingly, domestic approval was granted in 1994 and the plant was erected in 1996.

However, the MOX plant also needed the approval of the Commission. According to Article 37 EURATOM (European Atomic Energy Community) and various EURATOM Directives, the MOX plant must meet two

[8] Above (n 3).

[9] See further regarding the various proceedings of the MOX plant, S Maljean-Dubois and J-C Martin, 'L'affaire de l'Usine MOX devant les tribunaux internationaux' (2007) 134 *Journal du Droit International* 437; S Adam, 'Het Europees Hof van Justitie en andere internationale rechtsprekende organen. Enkele opmerkingen naar aanleiding van het MOX-Fabriek arrest' (2007) *Revue Belge de Droit International* 113; N Lavranos, 'Protecting its Exclusive Jurisdiction: The MOX Plant Judgment of the ECJ' (2006) 5 *The Law and Practice of International Courts and Tribunals* 479; V Roeben, 'The Order of the UNCLOS Annex VII Arbitral Tribunal to Suspend Proceedings in the Case of the MOX Plant at Sellafield: How Much Jurisdictional Subsidiarity?' 73 (2004) *Nordic Journal of International Law* 223.

separate sets of conditions: (i) the absence of a serious harmful environmental impact and (ii) a clear economic justification for the operation of the MOX plant.

Regarding the first set of conditions, the UK had to provide the Commission with information regarding the plans to dispose of nuclear wastes, so that the Commission could determine whether, in line with Article 37 EURATOM, the plant is 'liable to result in the radioactive contamination of the water, soil or airspace of another Member State'. Following the submission of detailed information by the UK, the Commission concluded in February 1997 that the normal discharges from the MOX plant would have negligible effects on other Member States, and that even unplanned discharges resulting from an accident would not likely result in significant radioactive contamination.

Regarding the second set of conditions, Article 6 of EURATOM Directive 80/836[10] requires Member States to perform a cost-benefit analysis of every new activity that results in exposure of ionizing radiation in order to ensure that the activity is justified by the benefits which it produces. This Directive, which was later replaced by EURATOM Directive 96/29,[11] requires that an activity that is detrimental to health must be justified by its economic, social or other benefits. In this framework, the UK held five public consultation rounds between the years 1997–2000 on the economic justification of the MOX plant.

Ireland participated in the first round of public consultations as a respondent. On 4 April 1997 Ireland made a submission in which it strongly opposed the commissioning of the MOX plant on the grounds that it would perpetuate the nuclear fuel reprocessing industry in Britain. Ireland also stressed that the quality of available information gathered

[10] Council Directive (EC) 80/836/Euratom of 15 July 1980 amending the Directives laying down the basic safety standards for the health protection of the general public and workers against the dangers of ionizing radiation [1980] OJ L246/1. Art 6 reads as follows:The limitation of individual and collective doses resulting from controllable exposures shall be based on the following general principles:

(a) every activity resulting in an exposure to ionizing radiation *shall be justified by the advantages which it produces*;
(b) all exposures shall be kept as low as reasonably achievable; (emphasis added).

[11] Council Directive (EC) 96/29/Euratom of 13 May 1996 laying down basic safety standards for the protection of the health of workers and the general public against the dangers arising from ionizing radiation [1996] OJ L159/1. Art 6 reads as follows:

1. Member States shall ensure that all new classes or types of practice resulting in exposure to ionizing radiation are justified in advance of being first adopted or first approved by their economic, social or other benefits in relation to the health detriment they may cause.
2. Existing classes or types of practice may be reviewed as to justification whenever new and important evidence about their efficacy or consequences is acquired.
3. In addition each Member State shall ensure that:

   (a) in the context of optimization all exposures shall be kept as low as reasonably achievable, *economic* and social factors being taken into account; (emphasis added).

by the UK authorities was deficient. In order to provide additional information, BNFL hired PA Consulting Group to carry out a detailed cost-benefit assessment. In addition, PA was requested to identify if there were areas of the economic activities that were not commercially sensitive and therefore could be published in the public domain. However, the 'PA full report' submitted to BNFL, was considered partly as commercial confidential so that certain parts of the public version of the 'PA report' of 27 December 1997 were redacted under section 4(2) of the UK Environmental Information Regulations 1992.

In the second round of public consultation, Ireland submitted a statement which was critical of the PA report with regard to its alleged failure to fulfil the purpose of this further consultation, namely to provide in the public domain sufficient commercial information to justify the commissioning and operation of the MOX plant. On 30 July 1999, Ireland requested the full, unedited copy of the PA report, on the basis of EURATOM Directive 80/836 and EC Directive 90/313/EEC,[12] which provides for freedom of access to environmental information.

The OSPAR Convention was first raised by Ireland in connection with the redacted information from the PA report on 25 May 2000, when it wrote a letter to the Department for the Environment, Transport and the Regions (DETR) invoking a request for information redacted from the PA report, based on Article 9 OSPAR Convention. This request was refused by the DETR so as not to prejudice commercial interests of the enterprise by disclosing commercially confidential information. Ireland again requested full information on 22 May 2001 and added that absent such information it was going to pursue legal measures for the release of the information.

In the spring of 2001, BNFL prepared a new confidential document setting out the economic justification for the MOX plant and, further, it appointed the consulting firm Arthur D Little (ADL report), to analyze the business case and to report on the responses to the public consultation exercise on it. The redacted ADL report was made public in July 2001. During the fifth public consultation, Ireland again requested the full report.

Notwithstanding the concerns of Ireland, on 31 October 2001, a decision was adopted by the competent UK authority approving the manufacture of the MOX plant at Sellafield. Greenpeace also challenged the decision but its application for review was rejected and failed on appeal. Ireland's application to the International Law of the Sea Tribunal (ITLOS) for provisional measures against commissioning of the plant also failed.[13]

Following the events described above, Ireland contended that the UK was obliged to make the information concerning the economic justification

[12] Council Directive (EC) 90/313/EEC of 7 June 1990 on the freedom of access to information on the environment [1990] OJ L158/56.

[13] ITLOS, (MOX Plant) *Ireland v UK*, Request for Provisional Measures, Order of 3 December 2001: www.itlos.org/case_documents/2001/document_en_197.doc.

of the MOX plant redacted from the consultation reports available under Article 9 OSPAR Convention.

On 14 June 2001, it requested that an arbitral tribunal be constituted under Article 32 OSPAR Convention to determine its dispute with the UK concerning the UK's refusal to make available information redacted from both reports.

As is apparent from this summary of the facts, Ireland's claim of a right to access to information was primarily based on the OSPAR Convention and the EURATOM and EC Directives. Moreover, as will be explained below, the Convention on Access to Information, Public Participation in Decision-Making and Access to Justice in Environmental Matters (Aarhus Convention) which at the time when the dispute arose was signed but not yet ratified by the UK, Ireland and the EC, also came into play.[14] In other words, the OSPAR Convention, the Aarhus Convention as well as EC legislation form the framework for the subsequent analysis. All these instruments are – to varying degrees – binding on the UK and Ireland and have been established by different sources. However, in order to qualify for a true MSEN case study, it is also necessary that they should all have similar or identical normative content or at least point in the same direction. For our purposes, the normative content must point towards a right to access to *economic* information relevant to the protection of the environment.

Accordingly, it must be examined whether a similar or identical normative content can be identified in the relevant OSPAR, Aarhus and EC law provisions.

B Access to Information under the OSPAR Convention

The OSPAR Convention was adopted in 1992, combining and updating the 1972 Oslo and 1974 Paris Conventions, concerning the pollution of the north east Atlantic, in particular pollution from land-based sources, pollution by dumping and pollution by offshore sources.[15]

[14] Ireland signed the Aarhus Convention (Convention on Access to Information, Public Participation in Decision-Making and Access to Justice in Environmental Matters 2161 UNTS 447) on 25 June 1998 but has not yet ratified it. The UK signed the Aarhus Convention also on 25 June 1998 and ratified it on 23 February 2005. The EC signed the Aarhus Convention also on 25 June 1998 and ratified it on 17 February 2005. See on the status of signature and ratification of the Aarhus Convention: www.treaties.un.org/Pages/ViewDetails.aspx?src=TREATY&mtdsg_no=XXVII 13&chapter=27&lang=en. Meanwhile, it should be noted that the EC has adopted several measures for the purpose of implementing the Aarhus Convention into the Community legal order; see for an overview: ec.europa.eu/environment/aarhus/. Thus, even though Ireland has not yet ratified the Aarhus Convention it is nonetheless bound by it by virtue of Community law.

[15] See for an excellent overview on the OSPAR Convention, 'L de La Fayette, The OSPAR Convention Comes into Force: Continuity and Progress' (1999) 14 *International Journal of Marine and Coastal Law* 242. For further details on the OSPAR Convention see: www.ospar.org/.

Article 2 OSPAR Convention contains the three main obligations of the OSPAR Contracting Parties: (i) preventing and eliminating pollution, (ii) application of the precautionary and 'polluter pays' principles; and (iii) application of best available techniques and best environmental practices.

Regarding land-based pollution, Article 3 OSPAR Convention prescribes that Contracting Parties 'shall take, individually and jointly, all possible steps to prevent and eliminate pollution from land-based sources in accordance with the provisions of the Convention, in particular as provided for in Annex I'.

With regard specifically to the right to access to information, Article 9 OSPAR Convention states that:

> '1. The Contracting Parties shall ensure that their competent authorities are required to make *available the information* described in paragraph 2 of this Article to any natural or legal person, in response to any reasonable request, without that person's having to prove an interest, without unreasonable charges, as soon as possible and at the latest within two months.
> 2. The information referred to in paragraph 1 of this Article is any available information in written, visual, aural or data-base form on the state of the maritime area, on activities or measures adversely affecting or likely to affect it and on activities or measures introduced in accordance with the Convention.
> 3. The provisions of this Article shall not affect the right of Contracting Parties, in accordance with their national legal systems and applicable international regulations, to provide for a *request for such information to be refused* where it affects:
>
> (a) the confidentiality of the proceedings of public authorities, international relations and national defence;
> (b) public security;
> (c) matters which are, or have been, *sub judice*, or under enquiry (including disciplinary enquiries), or which are the subject of preliminary investigation proceedings;
> (d) commercial and industrial confidentiality, including intellectual property;
> (e) the confidentiality of personal data and/or files;
> (f) material supplied by a third party without that party being under a legal obligation to do so;
> (g) material, the disclosure of which would make it more likely that the environment to which such material related would be damaged.
>
> 4. The reasons for a refusal to provide the information requested must be given' (emphasis added).

In other words, Article 9 OSPAR Convention is specifically confined to information relating to the state of the maritime area or activities affecting that area. Thus, prima facie, it appears doubtful whether the information relating to the economic justification of the operation of the MOX plant requested by Ireland falls within the scope of Article 9 OSPAR Convention.

Indeed, as will be discussed below, this issue was highly disputed between the parties but also within the OSPAR arbitral tribunal. If Ireland could prove that the 'economic' information requested had environmental significance, the UK would, in principle, be obliged to make that information, ie, the redacted parts of the PA and ADL reports, available to Ireland, unless it could reasonably rely on the exception of protecting commercial confidentiality as provided for in Article 9(3)(d) OSPAR Convention.

In this context, it should be mentioned that despite the fact that Article 9 OSPAR Convention refers to requests of natural or legal persons, thereby seemingly excluding Ireland, the OSPAR arbitral tribunal circumvented this issue by accepting that this dispute concerned the interpretation and application of Article 9 OSPAR Convention: according to Article 32, any dispute between the Contracting Parties on the interpretation and application of the OSPAR Convention shall be resolved by arbitration; hence, this dispute could be brought under the heading of Article 32 OSPAR Convention.

C Access to Information under the Aarhus Convention

The Aarhus Convention on Access to Information, Public Participation in Decision-making and Access to Justice in Environmental Matters 1998 (in short, Aarhus Convention) which entered into force in October 2001 is a remarkable treaty in several respects.[16] In the first place, it gives individuals and NGOs a formal role in ensuring that the Contracting Parties to the Aarhus Convention comply with it. Secondly, the Aarhus Convention is arguably the first multilateral environmental treaty that focuses exclusively on obligations of the Contracting Parties vis à vis their citizens.

The environmental rights contained in the Aarhus Convention are divided into three so-called pillars:

- the right to access to environmental information;
- the right to participate in environmental decision-making;
- the right to access to justice in environmental matters.

Article 2(3) of the Aarhus Convention defines 'environmental information' as:

> 3. 'Environmental information' means any information in written, visual, aural, electronic or any other material form on:
>
> (a) The *state of elements of the environment*, such as air and atmosphere, water, soil, land, landscape and natural sites, biological diversity and its compo-

[16] See for an excellent overview on the Aarhus Convention, S Kravchenko, 'The Aarhus Convention and Innovations in Compliance with Multilateral Environmental Agreements' (2007) 7 *Yearbook of European Environmental Law* 1. For further details on the Aarhus Convention see www.unece.org/env/pp/.

nents, including genetically modified organisms, and the interaction among these elements;

(b) Factors, such as substances, energy, noise and radiation, and activities or measures, including administrative measures, environmental agreements, policies, legislation, plans and programmes, affecting or likely to affect the elements of the environment within the scope of subparagraph (a) above, and *cost-benefit and other economic analyses* and assumptions used in environmental decision-making;

(c) The state of human health and safety, conditions of human life, cultural sites and built structures, inasmuch as they are or may be affected by the state of the elements of the environment or, through these elements, by the factors, activities or measures referred to in subparagraph (b) above (emphasis added).

More specifically, Article 4 Aarhus Convention regulates the right to access to information as follows:

1. Each Party shall ensure that, subject to the following paragraphs of this article, public authorities, in response to a request for *environmental information*, make such information available to the public, within the framework of national legislation, including, where requested and subject to subparagraph (b) below, copies of the actual documentation containing or comprising such information:

(a) Without an interest having to be stated;
(b) In the form requested unless:

   (i) It is reasonable for the public authority to make it available in another form, in which case reasons shall be given for making it available in that form; or
   (ii) The information is already publicly available in another form.

. . .

4. A *request for environmental information may be refused if the disclosure would adversely affect*:

. . .

(d) The *confidentiality of commercial and industrial information*, where such confidentiality is protected by law in order to protect a legitimate economic interest. Within this framework, information on emissions which is relevant for the protection of the environment shall be disclosed (emphasis added).

Since information on cost-benefit analysis is explicitly included in the scope of Article 2(3)(b) Aarhus Convention, this provision would also have been a suitable legal basis for Ireland to request access to the original version of both reports. However, as mentioned above, Ireland and the UK had not ratified the Aarhus Convention at the time the dispute arose, so that it was not formally binding on both parties. But both parties had already signed the Aarhus Convention in 1998 and thereby indicated their willingness to ratify it in due course. Accordingly, both parties expressed their intention to be bound by the Aarhus Convention. This is even further supported by the fact that the EC had also signed the Aarhus Convention in 1998 and has subsequently adopted several Community law provisions for the purpose of implementing the Aarhus Convention into the Community legal order.[17]

Indeed, if one compares the OSPAR Convention with the Aarhus Convention, it becomes clear that the rights and obligations concerning the right to access to information related to activities that may adversely affect the environment and the reasons for its refusal are quite similar. However, there is one important difference regarding the terminology used in both conventions.

While the OSPAR Convention refers to 'any available information' specifically related to the state of the maritime area, on activities or measures adversely affecting or likely to affect it and on activities or measures introduced in accordance with the Convention, the Aarhus Convention refers to 'environmental information' in general.

Accordingly, Ireland would have to make it plausible that the operation of the MOX plant is detrimental to the maritime area, ie, the Irish Sea, so that the economic information requested by Ireland is directly relevant for determining the question whether or not the operation of the MOX plant is harmful to the environment. While the Commission as well as the UK authorities have concluded that the operation of the MOX plant does not pose any significant dangers for the environment, the OSPAR Contracting Parties (with the abstention of the UK) have repeatedly expressed their concern about the high level of radioactive emissions of the Sellafield MOX plant.[18] Accordingly, with some effort Ireland could argue that it

[17] See for an overview of relevant EC law measures: www.ec.europa.eu/environment/aarhus/index.htm.

[18] It should be noted that the OSPAR Contracting Parties adopted (with the abstention of the UK and France) OSPAR Decision 2000/1 on *Substantial Reductions and Elimination of Discharges, Emissions and Losses of Radioactive Substances with Special Emphasis on Nuclear Reprocessing* in Copenhagen in June 2000. In that Decision the OSPAR Contracting Parties explicitly stated their concern regarding the nuclear discharges that can be traced back in the Irish Sea among other maritime areas and they expressed their wish that the Contracting Parties should not authorize any new nuclear plants: www.ospar.org/documents/dbase/decrecs/decisions/od00-01e.doc). A year later the OSPAR Contracting Parties adopted in Valencia (again with the abstention of the UK and France) OSPAR Decision 2001/1 on the *Review of Authorisations for Discharges or Releases of Radioactive Substances from Nuclear Reprocessing Activities* in which they explicitly stated: 'Recognising that nuclear spent fuel reprocessing activities represent the dominant source of radioactive contamination of the marine environment of the North-East Atlantic': www.ospar.org/documents/dbase/decrecs/decisions/od01-01e.doc. Both Decisions were adopted while the approval of the Sellafield MOX plant took place. But it should also be noted that the 2007 *Report on Liquid Discharges from Nuclear installations of the OSPAR Commission on Radioactive Substances* has noted an overall reduction for the period between 1990–2007 of radioactive discharges of the Sellafield and La Hague MOX plants: www.ospar.org/documents/dbase/publications/p00456_Liquid%20Discharges%20data%20report%202007.pdf. See for a detailed discussion of this point: de La Fayette, above (n15) 275 ff.

cannot be ruled out that the operation of the MOX plant poses a danger to the maritime environment and therefore needs to have access to the cost-benefit analysis.

But, prima facie, it seems that this 'economic' information does not squarely fall into the scope of the OSPAR Convention, since OSPAR would seem to cover only 'operational' information regarding, for example, the level of radioactive emissions of the MOX plant which may affect the Irish Sea. Compared with this, the scope of information covered by the Aarhus Convention is much broader because it is not limited to information concerning the 'maritime area' nor to specific activities, but must merely relate to 'environmental information'. Indeed, Article 2(3)(b) explicitly includes cost-benefit analysis in the scope of 'environmental information' covered by the Aarhus Convention. Thus, the redacted information of both reports, which Ireland was requesting from the UK, clearly would fall within the scope of the Aarhus Convention, but arguably outside the scope of the OSPAR Convention.

D Access to Information under EC Law

i EC Directive 90/313 and Directive 2003/4

Within EC law, the right to access to information was introduced by EC Directive 90/313[19] on the Freedom of Access to Information on the Environment.[20] As Article 1 of this Directive states, its main objective is to ensure freedom of access to, and dissemination of, information on the environment held by public authorities of the Member States.

Article 2 of this Directive defines 'information relating to the environment' as

> any available information in written, visual, aural or data-base form on the state of water, air, soil, fauna, flora, land and natural sites, and on activities (including those which give rise to nuisances such as noise) or measures adversely affecting, or likely so to affect these, and on activities or measures designed to protect these, including administrative measures and environmental management programmes.

According to Article 3 of this Directive, all public authorities of the Member States are required to make available information relating to the environment to any natural or legal person at his request and without his having to prove an interest. At the same time, Article 3 provides for grounds for

[19] Council Directive (EC) 90/313/EEC of 7 June 1990 on the freedom of access to information on the environment [1990] OJ L158/56.

[20] See for an overview of recent developments, S de Abreu Ferreira, 'Passive Access to Environmental Information in the EU – An analysis of recent developments' (2008) 17 *European Energy and Environmental Law Review* 186.

refusal of such requests which, inter alia, includes 'commercial confidentiality'.

However, it should be noted that Directive 90/313 contained a review process, which obliged the Member States to report to the Commission their experiences with this Directive and required the Commission to draw up a report and, if necessary, a proposal for improvements. This has led to the adoption of Directive 2003/4,[21] which repealed Directive 90/313. This new Directive took account of the fact that the EC had signed the Aarhus Convention in 1998 and intended to clarify and harmonize various definitions, thereby further strengthening the exercise of the right to access to environmental information.

Accordingly, Article 2 of Directive 2003/4 defines 'environmental information' as

> any information in written, visual, aural, electronic or any other material form on:
>
> (a) the *state of the elements of the environment*, such as air and atmosphere, water, soil, land, landscape and natural sites including wetlands, coastal and marine areas, biological diversity and its components, including genetically modified organisms, and the interaction among these elements;
> (b) factors, such as substances, energy, noise, radiation or waste, including radioactive waste, emissions, discharges and other releases into the environment, affecting or likely to affect the elements of the environment referred to in (a);
> (c) measures (including administrative measures), such as policies, legislation, plans, programmes, environmental agreements, and activities affecting or likely to affect the elements and factors referred to in (a) and (b) as well as measures or activities designed to protect those elements;
> (d) reports on the implementation of environmental legislation;
> (e) *cost-benefit and other economic analyses* and assumptions used within the framework of the measures and activities referred to in (c); and
> (f) the state of human health and safety, including the contamination of the food chain, where relevant, conditions of human life, cultural sites and built structures inasmuch as they are or may be affected by the state of the elements of the environment referred to in (a) or, through those elements, by any of the matters referred to in (b) and (c) (emphasis added).

It is interesting to note that the definition of 'environmental information' is broader here than in the old Directive and that information concerning cost-benefit analysis is now explicitly enumerated. Thus, both of the contested reports clearly fall within the scope of this Directive. Also, the grounds for refusal have been further specified in Directive 2003/4, com-

[21] Council Directive (EC) 2003/4/EC of the European Parliament and of the Council of 28 January 2003 on public access to environmental information and repealing Council Directive (EC) 90/313/EEC [2003] OJ L41/26.

pared with the old Directive: According to Article 4(2) of Directive 2003/4, Member States can refuse the request for access to information on the grounds that a disclosure of the information would adversely affect:

> . . .
>
> (d) the *confidentiality of commercial or industrial information* where such confidentiality is provided for by national or Community law to protect a legitimate economic interest, including the public interest in maintaining statistical confidentiality and tax secrecy;
>
> . . .
>
> The grounds for refusal mentioned in paragraphs 1 and 2 shall be interpreted in a restrictive way, taking into account for the particular case the public interest served by disclosure. In every particular case, the public interest served by disclosure shall be weighed against the interest served by the refusal. Member States may not, by virtue of paragraph 2(a), (d), (f), (g) and (h), provide for a request to be refused where the request relates to information on emissions into the environment (emphasis added).

Consequently, the confidentiality of commercial information exception must be applied more restrictively under the new Directive.

Still, it should be noted that both EC Directives grant the right to access to information specifically to legal and natural persons, a formulation which raises the question whether Ireland would be able to rely on these Directives. In principle, Ireland could either rely on the Directives before the relevant UK authorities or start an infringement procedure against the UK before the ECJ on the basis of Article 227 EC arguing that the refusal of the UK authorities to publish the redacted parts of the reports constitutes a violation of the various EC Directives.[22]

[22] Art 259 Treaty on the Functioning of the EU ([2008] OJ C115/47) (ex art 227 TEC) reads as follows:

> A Member State which considers that another Member State has failed to fulfil an obligation under the Treaties may bring the matter before the Court of Justice of the European Union.
>
> Before a Member State brings an action against another Member State for an alleged infringement of an obligation under the Treaties, it shall bring the matter before the Commission.
>
> The Commission shall deliver a reasoned opinion after each of the States concerned has been given the opportunity to submit its own case and its observations on the other party's case both orally and in writing.
>
> If the Commission has not delivered an opinion within three months of the date on which the matter was brought before it, the absence of such opinion shall not prevent the matter from being brought before the Court.

ii Regulation 1049/2001 and Regulation 1367/2006

For the sake of completeness, EC Regulations 1049/2001 and 1367/2006 should also be mentioned. Regulation 1049/2001[23] is the general provision regulating public access to documents held by the European Parliament, Council and Commission. According to Article 1 of this Regulation, its purpose is to define the principles, conditions and limits concerning the right of access to documents held by the European Parliament, Council and Commission in such a way as to ensure the widest possible access to these documents. The Regulation applies to all documents held by a Community institution, ie, documents drawn up or received by it and in its possession, in all areas of activity of the European Union (EU). Moreover, any citizen of the EU, and any natural or legal person residing or having its registered office in a Member State, has a right of access to documents of the institutions, subject to the principles, conditions and limits defined in this Regulation. Article 4 (2) of this Regulation provides the grounds for the refusal of a request of information which includes, inter alia, commercial interests of a natural or legal person.

While Regulation 1049/2001 is the general legal basis for access to information, Regulation 1367/2006[24] is the *lex specialis,* which was specifically adopted in order to apply the Aarhus Convention to environmental information held by the Community institutions.[25] Article 2(1)(d) of Regulation 1367/2006 defines 'environmental information' as

> (d) any information in written, visual, aural, electronic or any other material form on:
>
> (i) the *state of the elements of the environment*, such as air and atmosphere, water, soil, land, landscape and natural sites including wetlands, coastal and marine areas, biological diversity and its components, including genetically modified organisms, and the interaction among these elements;
> (ii) factors, such as substances, energy, noise, *radiation or waste, including radioactive waste, emissions, discharges and other releases into the environment*, affecting or likely to affect the elements of the environment referred to in point (i);

[23] Reg (EC) No 1049/2001 of the European Parliament and of the Council of 30 May 2001 regarding public access to European Parliament, Council and Commission documents, [2001] OJ L145/43.

[24] Reg (EC) No 1367/2006 of the European Parliament and of the Council of 6 September 2006 on the application of the provisions of the Aarhus Convention on Access to Information, Public Participation in Decision-making and Access to Justice in Environmental Matters to Community institutions and bodies, [2006] OJ L264/13.

[25] It should be noted that the adoption of EC Reg 1367/2006 made it necessary to align Reg 1049/2001 with Reg 1367/2006. Accordingly, a proposal for recasting Reg 1049/2001 is currently discussed in the European institutions. See Proposal for a Regulation of the European Parliament and the Council Regarding Public Access to European Parliament, Council and Commission documents (recast), 10859/1/09 REV 1, 22 July 2009: www.register.consilium.europa.eu/pdf/en/09/st10/st10859-re01.en09.pdf. See further I Harden, 'The Revision of Regulation 1049/2001 on Public Access to Documents' (2009) 15 *European Public Law* 239.

(iii) measures (including administrative measures), such as policies, legislation, plans, programmes, environmental agreements, and activities affecting or likely to affect the elements and factors referred to in points (i) and (ii) as well as measures or activities designed to protect those elements;

(iv) reports on the implementation of environmental legislation;

(v) *cost-benefit and other economic analyses* and assumptions used within the framework of the measures and activities referred to in point (iii);

(vi) the state of human health and safety, including the contamination of the food chain, where relevant, conditions of human life, cultural sites and built structures in as much as they are or may be affected by the state of the elements of the environment referred to in point (i) or, through those elements, by any of the matters referred to in points (ii) and (iii); (emphasis added).

As is apparent from the previous sections, this definition has been aligned with the definition adopted in Directive 2003/4 and in the Aarhus Convention.

With regard to the addressee of the right to access to information Regulation 1367/2006 refers to

> any request by an applicant for access to environmental information held by Community institutions and bodies without discrimination as to citizenship, nationality or domicile and, in the case of a legal person, without discrimination as to where it has its registered seat or an effective centre of its activities.

So, in principle this Regulation could be applicable in our case, if the Commission has a copy of the redacted parts of both reports. The writer is not aware of this, but it cannot be excluded, in particular in view of the fact that the Commission plays such a prominent role under the EURATOM provisions. Indeed, since generally the relevant national authorities are working closely with the Commission, it could very well be that the Commission also has a copy of the information requested by Ireland. But this remains speculative. Another question is whether Ireland as a Member State would be able to rely on this Regulation, if it would be applicable in terms of *ratione materiae*. In this regard what has been stated above concerning EC Directives applies also for EC Regulations.

Thus, the application of the various EC law provisions cannot be ruled out. In any case, considering the fact that all these EC law provisions state the law regarding the right to access to (environmental) information at the European level and the fact that the ECJ jurisprudence is very influential also at the national level, it is important to keep them in mind – even if only as a source of inspiration.

In sum, it can be concluded that the various pieces of EC legislation discussed above illustrate that the right to access to (environmental) information is firmly grounded and accepted in the Community legal order and consequently in the domestic legal systems of the Member States.

In fact, the right to access to information has been elevated to a true fundamental right by Article 42 of the European Charter of Fundamental Rights, which has become legally binding with the entering into force of the Lisbon Treaty on 1December 2009.[26]

E Summary

In general, it appears that the various sources discussed above have one similar general aim of providing a right to access to (environmental) information. Accordingly, the norms governing the dispute meet all the criteria for a MSEN case study. Nonetheless, it is also clear that there are subtle differences between the various sources.

The main issue is, of course, the definition of the terms 'information' and 'environmental information'. While the OSPAR Convention uses a rather limited definition of the term 'information', the Aarhus Convention and the various EC law measures use a much more broadly defined term of 'environmental information', which, moreover, have been aligned with each other. In this context, it is interesting to note that with the exception of the OSPAR Convention, all other sources explicitly include 'economic' information such as cost-benefit analysis in the scope of the right to access to information.

Another difference concerns the varying binding effects of the various sources. For example, while the OSPAR Convention and the relevant EC law measures are legally binding on both the UK and Ireland, the binding effect of the Aarhus Convention is questionable since it was not ratified by the parties at the time the dispute arose.

Finally, one must also consider the different dispute settlement forums that are offered by the various MSENs. Whereas the OSPAR and Aarhus Conventions provide the Contracting Parties with the possibility to settle any disputes on the application and interpretation of both treaties before an arbitral tribunal or the ICJ, the various pieces of EC legislation must be enforced before the national courts and, ultimately, before the ECJ.

III ANALYSIS

After having established in the previous section *in abstracto* that a MSEN situation exists, it is now time to analyze how in practice the OSPAR arbitral tribunal dealt with the MSEN issue.

[26] Art 42 Charter of Fundamental Rights reads as follows: 'Right of access to documents: 'Any citizen of the Union, and any natural or legal person residing or having its registered office in a Member State, has a right of access to European Parliament, Council and Commission documents'. See also Case C-64/05 P *Sweden v Commission* (Opinion of AG Maduro, [2007] ECR I-11389, para 40): www.curia.europa.eu/jurisp/cgi-bin/form.pl?lang=en.

As will be apparent from the following analysis of the OSPAR award, the three arbitrators (Professor Reisman, Dr Griffith and Lord Mustill) were very much aware of the MSEN issue. Indeed, the three arbitrators' views on how to deal with the MSEN issue displayed great divergence. This was particularly reflected in the Dissenting Opinion of Dr Griffith.

Essentially, the MSEN issue was approached in two diametrically opposed ways.

The majority of the OSPAR arbitral tribunal (Reisman, Mustill) chose the 'clinical isolation' approach by solving the dispute exclusively on the basis of the OSPAR Convention. In contrast, Griffith preferred to apply a much more holistic, contextual and dynamic approach by looking also at the various other relevant sources such as the Aarhus Convention and EC law provisions.

The starting point for both approaches is Article 32(6) OSPAR Convention, which prescribes that the arbitral tribunal 'shall decide according to the rules of international law, and, in particular, the OSPAR Convention'. Thus, on the basis of Article 9 OSPAR Convention, Ireland requested

> full disclosure of the two reports commissioned by the UK Government in the context of the authorisation of a new facility . . . in order to be in a better position to consider the impacts which the commissioning of the MOX plant will or might have on the marine environment . . . and to be able to assess the extent of the compliance by the UK with its obligations under . . . the *OSPAR Convention, the 1982 UNCLOS and various provisions of European Community law, including in particular Council Directive 96/29 EURATOM* (emphasis added).

Already the formulation of the Irish request brings the MSEN issue to the centre of attention of the OSPAR arbitral tribunal by emphasizing the linkages between various sources. Indeed, it is interesting to note that the Aarhus Convention was not included in this paragraph, although, as will be discussed below, it plays an important role. This can probably be explained by the fact that at the time the dispute was brought before the OSPAR arbitral neither Ireland nor the UK had ratified the Aarhus Convention. It is also interesting to note that UNCLOS is mentioned, whereas both parties were in the process of establishing an UNCLOS arbitral tribunal for determining the question whether or not the operation of the MOX plant violates UNCLOS obligations of the UK.[27]

[27] In fact, the UNCLOS *Ad hoc* Arbitral Tribunal was established on 25 October 2001, that is four months after the OSPAR *Ad hoc* Arbitral Tribunal had been established on 15 June 2001. Moreover, it should be noted that the UNCLOS Arbitral Tribunal first stayed the proceedings in order to await the decision of the ECJ regarding the scope of its jurisdiction. In its judgment, the ECJ claimed exclusive jurisdiction vis-à-vis the jurisdiction of the UNCLOS Arbitral Tribunal. As a consequence thereof, the UNCLOS arbitral Tribunal terminated the proceedings in 2008. See for a detailed analysis, N Lavranos, 'The Epilogue in the MOX Plant Dispute: An End without a Finding' (2009) 18 *European Energy and Environmental Law Review* 180.

In any case, on the basis of the request of Ireland and the response by the UK, the OSPAR arbitral tribunal formulated and subdivided the issues it had to decide as follows:

1. Does Article 9(1) OSPAR Convention require a Contracting Party to disclose, or to set up a procedure to disclose, 'information' within the meaning of Article 9(2) OSPAR Convention?
2. If so, does the material the disclosure of which Ireland has requested constitute 'information' for the purposes of Article 9 OSPAR Convention?
   If so, has the UK redacted and withheld any and what information requested by Ireland contrary to Article 9(3)(2) OSPAR Convention?

The OSPAR arbitral tribunal dealt with these questions under two different headings: (i) the applicable law and (ii) the definition of the term 'information'.

A The Applicable Law

The majority on the tribunal, consisting of Reisman and Mustill, started off its analysis by stating the obvious, ie, that the dispute is governed by the OSPAR Convention and that the Vienna Convention on the Law of Treaties (VCLT)[28] governs the construction of the provisions of the OSPAR Convention.[29] Moreover, referring to Article 32(6) OSPAR Convention, the OSPAR arbitral tribunal considered it to be its first duty to apply the OSPAR Convention, while it would also apply customary international law and general principles, unless and to the extent that the Parties have created a *lex specialis*.[30]

On that basis, the OSPAR arbitral tribunal, perhaps unsurprisingly, rejected Ireland's MSEN approach by arguing that if other sources of international law were to be taken into account, Article 32(6)(a) OSPAR Convention would be transformed into 'an unqualified and comprehensive jurisdictional regime, in which there would be no limit *ratione materiae* to the jurisdiction of a tribunal established under the OSPAR Convention'.[31] Similarly, Ireland's broad interpretation of the term 'applicable international regulations' contained in Article 9(3) OSPAR Convention, which according to Ireland means that the OSPAR arbitral tribunal should take the Aarhus Convention and EC Directive 90/313 into account, was for the same reasons also rejected by the OSPAR arbitral tribunal.[32]

[28] Vienna Convention on the Law of Treaties (VCLT) (adopted 23 May 1969, entered into force 27 January 1980) 1155 UNTS 331.
[29] OSPAR, Arbitral Award (MOX plant) para 81.
[30] *Ibid*, para 84.
[31] *Ibid*, para 85.
[32] *Ibid*, para 104.

Thus, the majority of the OSPAR arbitral tribunal avoided the MSEN issue by interpreting the OSPAR Convention in 'clinical isolation' from all other related international or European law sources.

In contrast, in his Dissenting Opinion, Griffith offered a different approach by dealing with MSENs in a truly holistic way. More specifically, Griffith rejected the majority's view that the mandate of the OSPAR arbitral tribunal is solely confined to the OSPAR Convention.[33] Instead, he pointed out that the term 'rules of international law' contained in Article 32(6)(a) OSPAR Convention must be interpreted broadly by taking into account other sources of international law that have a direct relevance to the OSPAR Convention and the specific dispute.[34]

In particular, Griffith, noted that the OSPAR Convention

> stands as a *lex specialis* between the Parties to be interpreted within the general context of other relevant rules and principles of international law. Its drafters plainly perceived the OSPAR Convention as an *integral part of a matrix of international instruments directed to environmental protection*[35] (emphasis added).

As a result, Griffith argued that it is the explicit mandate of the arbitral tribunal to interpret Article 9 OSPAR Convention as a *lex specialis* between the parties consistently with 'international law' broadly defined.[36] Quite clearly, Griffith was concerned that a deviating interpretation of 'environmental information' for the purpose of Article 9 OSPAR Convention could undermine the common understanding of the concept of 'environmental information' as expressed in the various sourced discussed above, and which have been accepted by both Ireland and the UK. In other words, interpreting Article 9 OSPAR Convention in a deviating way could reduce the effectiveness of the right to access to information, which in turn could lower the level of environmental protection in general. In order to avoid such a development and instead achieve consistency with the other similar source, Griffith considered it necessary and appropriate to explain the relevance of the Aarhus Convention and the various EC law measures. Regarding the Aarhus Convention, he concluded that despite the fact that both parties had signed but not yet ratified it at the material time, the Aarhus Convention 'does have a relevant normative and evidentiary value'.[37] Indeed, Griffith accepted that the Aarhus Convention may be invoked by Ireland to inform the proper construction of Article 9(2) OSPAR Convention, in particular regarding the scope of the definition of 'environmental information'.[38] Since the UK accepted to be bound

[33] *Ibid* (Dissenting Opinion) para 2.
[34] *Ibid*, para 2.
[35] *Ibid*, para 4.
[36] *Ibid*, para 5.
[37] *Ibid*, para 10.
[38] *Ibid*, para 16.

by the Aarhus Convention, it falls within the definition of applicable law and therefore is a source to be taken into account for the interpretation of Article 9(2) OSPAR Convention.[39]

Accordingly, Griffith not only used the other MSENs as interpretative tools that inform the proper interpretation of Article 9 OSPAR Convention, but as sources of additional obligations that both parties have entered into within different legal frameworks. Thus, Griffith considered the OSPAR Convention as *lex sprecialis* in the sense that the dispute about the interpretation and application of Article 9 OSPAR Convention is fully but not exclusively regulated by the OSPAR Convention. In other words, while the OSPAR Convention is the first and foremost instrument to consider for resolving the present dispute, it is also necessary and appropriate to take cognizance of the other relevant MSENs.

Regarding the EC law measures, Griffith pointed out the very close relationship between the OSPAR Convention and EC Directive 90/313, both in terms of their substance and the fact that much the same people had drafted both instruments.[40] Referring to 'ordinary principles of comity and interpretation', Griffith argued that 'the same State parties broadly may be assumed to understand similarly or identically worded obligations in the same way'.[41] In addition, Griffith emphasized the fact that the EU is a principle party to OSPAR.[42] In short, he concluded that EC Directive 90/313 informs the interpretation of Article 9(2) OSPAR Convention.

In the same vein, Griffith considered EC Directive 2003/4 as representing a 'significant development in EU environmental law'[43] that should be taken into account even though it was promulgated after the oral hearings of the OSPAR arbitral tribunal. Indeed, according to Griffith, EC Directive 2003/4 'now independently constitutes a relevant international regulation that provides for a broad definition of information consistent with the meaning of Article 9(2) OSPAR Convention'.[44] Indeed, he went one step further by stating that:

> On its face Directive 2003/4 favours Ireland's interpretation of the definition of Article 9(2) OSPAR Convention as including commercial data and economic analyses, and it explicitly applies like definitions to those of the Aarhus Convention as relevantly binding on both the UK and Ireland.[45]

For these reasons, he criticized the 'impermissibly restrictive' view of the majority by failing to take account of the other relevant sources.[46]

[39] *Ibid*, para 19.
[40] *Ibid*, para 23. The close relationship between OSPAR and EC law is also pointed out by de La Fayette, above (n 15) 261 et seq.
[41] *Ibid*, para 23.
[42] *Ibid*, para 24.
[43] *Ibid*, para 26.
[44] *Ibid*, para 28.
[45] *Ibid*, para 29.
[46] *Ibid*, para 32.

This far-reaching embracement of EC law provisions by Griffith is not only remarkable from the point of view of the OSPAR Convention, but arguably even more so from the point of view of Community law. If EC law is so clearly at issue in this dispute, the general question arises whether the dispute should not have been brought before the ECJ in accordance with Article 292 EC, which prescribes that all disputes between EC Member States that touch on Community law must be brought exclusively before the ECJ.[47]

Indeed, in the proceeding before the ECJ regarding the UNCLOS arbitration, the ECJ unequivocally found that Ireland violated Article 292 EC when it brought the MOX plant dispute before the UNCLOS arbitral tribunal.[48] More specifically, the ECJ argued that considering the fact that UNCLOS has become integral part of the Community legal order, no tribunal other than ECJ is competent to interpret the UNCLOS obligations of the EC Member States. Otherwise, the ECJ claimed, its exclusive jurisdiction to interpret and apply Community law, and thereby the consistency and uniformity of Community law within the EC would be endangered. Clearly, the ECJ would put forward the same arguments regarding the OSPAR arbitral tribunal if it had had the chance to pronounce itself on this proceeding. Accordingly, the restrictive approach of the majority of the OSPAR arbitral tribunal regarding the interpretation of the term 'environmental information' does not contribute to the consistency and uniformity of Community law.

Of course, it could be argued that it is not the task of the OSPAR arbitral tribunal to be concerned with Community law. However, as Griffith rightly argued, one simply cannot ignore the fact that this dispute involves two EC Member States, which means that existing Community law is binding on both parties and therefore is somehow relevant to this dispute. Moreover, by applying and interpreting Community law in line with the ECJ's jurisprudence in the context of the OSPAR dispute, Griffith showed comity towards the ECJ and thereby avoided any divergence or conflict with Community law.[49]

Arguably, this approach strengthens the level of environmental protection, which after all is the overarching aim of the various MSENs involved.

[47] See further on art 292 EC, B Hofstötter, 'Can She Excuse My Wrongs'? The ECJ and International Courts and Tribunals' (2007) 3 *Croatian Yearbook of European Law and Policy* 391; Lavranos, 'Protecting its Exclusive Jurisdiction', above (n 9) 479.

[48] Case C-459/03 *MOX Plant* [2006] ECR I-4635. See further N Lavranos, 'The Scope of the Exclusive Jurisdiction of the Court of Justice' (2007) 32 *European Law Review* 83.

[49] See, eg, N Lavranos, 'The Solange-Method as a Tool for Regulating Competing Jurisdictions Among International Courts and Tribunals' (2008) 30 *Loyola Los Angeles International & Comparative Law Review* 275.

B The Definition of the term 'Information'

With regard to the second question, Ireland again adopted a broad interpretation of the term 'information' arguing that the cost-benefit analysis information is part of the overall information regarding the possibly dangerous activities related to the operation of the MOX plant.[50]

However, the majority of the arbitrators, consisting again of Reisman and Mustill, used a more restrictive approach by classifying the information sought by Ireland in accordance with Article 9(2) OSPAR Convention into three categories, ie: information on the state of the maritime environment; (ii) information on activities or measures likely to affect the maritime area; and (iii) information on activities or measures introduced in accordance with the Convention.

As a starting point, the OSPAR arbitral tribunal stated that Article 9(2) OSPAR Convention 'is not a general freedom of information statute'.[51]

Besides, the majority of the OSPAR arbitral tribunal argued that the information sought by Ireland could only fall within the scope of the second and third categories mentioned above. After a careful analysis, the majority of the OSPAR arbitral tribunal concluded that Ireland failed to establish that the redacted information from the PA and ADL reports falls within the scope of the second category of Article 9(2) OSPAR Convention.[52] For this reason, the majority of the OSPAR arbitral tribunal concluded that there was also no need to examine whether or not the information sought could fall within the scope of the third category. Thus, the OSPAR arbitral tribunal concluded that Ireland's claim did not arise.

Again, Griffith dissented by using a much broader definition of the term 'information', which is informed by and consistent with the relevant other sources, in particular the EC Directives and ECJ jurisprudence. In particular, Griffith deviated from the majority's approach, which confined its analysis only to the redacted parts of the report, applying instead an inclusive approach regarding the two reports. According to Griffith, the main question is whether *both reports as a whole* fall, in principle, within the scope of Article 9(2) OSPAR Convention, rather than determining whether or not specific parts of the redacted sections of the reports fall within this scope.[53] Interestingly, Griffith supported his approach by referring to the ECJ's *Mecklenburg*[54] judgment.

In this important ruling regarding the right to access to environmental information, the ECJ gave the following broad definition:

[50] See above (n 18).
[51] OSPAR, Arbitral Tribunal Award, para 170.
[52] *Ibid*, para 182.
[53] *Ibid* (Dissenting Opinion) paras 44–45.
[54] Case C-321/96 *Mecklenburg* [1998] ECR I-3809.

> 19. It must be noted in the first place that Article 2(a) of the directive includes under 'information relating to the environment' any information on the state of the various aspects of the environment mentioned therein as well as on activities or measures which may adversely affect or protect those aspects, 'including administrative measures and environmental management programmes'. The wording of the provision makes it clear that the *Community legislature intended to make that concept a broad one, embracing both information and activities relating to the state of those aspects.*
>
> 20. Secondly, the use in Article 2(a) of the directive of the term 'including' indicates that 'administrative measures' is merely an example of the 'activities' or 'measures' covered by the directive. As the Advocate General pointed out in paragraph 15 of his Opinion, *the Community legislature purposely avoided giving any definition of 'information relating to the environment' which could lead to the exclusion of any of the activities engaged in by the public authorities,* the term 'measures' serving merely to make it clear that the acts governed by the directive included all forms of administrative activity.
>
> 21. In order to constitute 'information relating to the environment for the purposes of the directive', it is sufficient for the statement of views put forward by an authority, such as the statement concerned in the main proceedings, to be an act capable of adversely affecting or protecting the state of one of the sectors of the environment covered by the directive. That is the case, as the referring court mentioned, where the statement of views is capable of influencing the outcome of the development consent proceedings as regards interests pertaining to the protection of the environment[55] (emphases added).

Indeed, the broad definition of 'information relating to the environment' in Community law was particularly emphasized by Advocate General La Pargola in this case when he stated that:

> 13. There can be *no doubt* that the Community legislature intended to include within the concept of 'information relating to the environment' *all conduct* on the part of public authorities, as defined in the Directive, subject only to the exceptions specially provided for in that regard. The *concept of information* relating to the environment is, by the express intention of the Community legislature, *all-embracing.*
>
> . . .
>
> For the definition in the Directive to be satisfied, the data or other information in point must be produced or collected or processed with the principal aim of protecting the environment or must at least be related to the environment[56] (emphasis added).

Griffith did not see a 'basis for a different approach' regarding Article 9 OSPAR Convention.[57] In fact, in the remaining part of his analysis, Griffith

[55] *Ibid.*
[56] Case C-321/96 *Mecklenburg* (Opinion of AG La Pergola) in [1998] ECR I-3809.
[57] See above (n 53) para 48.

continued to draw inspiration from EC law for the proper construction of Article 9 OSPAR Convention. In particular, he accepted Ireland's contention that the Aarhus Convention and the various EC law provisions

> confirm regional trends exposing the intention of States and the EU itself to include economic analyses in the definition of the environmental information. At the least, these trends appear to broaden the content of the definition of environmental information so as explicitly to include cost-benefit and other economic analyses.[58]

Again, Griffith found support for his approach by referring to EC Directive 2003/4 as a clarification of Article 9 OSPAR Convention.[59]

In conclusion, Griffith was of the opinion that the majority of the OSPAR arbitral tribunal erred by applying a narrow interpretation of 'information' and thereby concluding that the redacted parts of both reports would not fall within the scope of Article 9 OSPAR Convention. Instead, Griffith convincingly showed that a broader interpretation of Article 9 that would have been fully in line with other relevant MSENs would probably have led to a different conclusion; namely, that the UK was indeed obliged to make the requested information available to Ireland, unless, of course, the conditions for 'commercial confidentiality' were met.

IV CONCLUDING REMARKS

This case study has illustrated that the OSPAR *MOX Plant* dispute is truly a MSEN case, which has been approached in two different ways, reflecting two different attitudes on the task and responsibility of international judges and arbitrators.

Essentially, the majority of the OSPAR arbitral tribunal opted for avoiding the MSEN issue by applying the very restrictive 'clinical isolation' approach. Apparently, this approach is informed by a presumed intent by the OSPAR drafters not to invoke MSENs in proceedings brought on the basis of one parallel norm. Whether or not that is a correct assumption remains speculative. In any case, the advantage of this approach is that the majority of the OSPAR arbitral tribunal was able to dispose of the case in a clean and simple way, without having to indulge in an extensive analysis regarding other relevant sources, their content and their interpretative potential for solving the dispute. Indeed, the OSPAR arbitral tribunal avoided giving a clear answer to the question whether or not the UK was required to grant Ireland access to the redacted parts of the reports under instruments other than the OSPAR Convention. Interestingly, much

[58] *Ibid* (Dissenting Opinion) para 117.
[59] *Ibid*, paras 120–23.

the same can be said regarding the UNCLOS arbitral tribunal proceedings, which were eventually terminated without an examination of the substance of the case.[60] Similarly, also the ECJ confined itself by deciding only the jurisdictional issue.[61] Thus, after a litigation of several years before three different courts and tribunals, it still has not been adjudicated whether or not the operation of the MOX plant endangers the environment and the health of human beings.

More generally, the disadvantage of the restrictive, 'in clinical isolation' approach is that it leads to unsatisfactory results, which in turn cause both substantive norm and authority fragmentation.[62] Indeed, as Tomer Broude has explained, there is a clear correlation between substantive norm fragmentation and authority fragmentation, which in fact are two sides of the same coin.[63]

With regard to substantive norm fragmentation, the narrow interpretation of the term 'information' of Article 9 OSPAR Convention as applied by the majority of the OSPAR arbitral tribunal not only reduced its effectiveness concerning the protection of the environment, but potentially challenges the broader interpretation used for the other sources. In other words, if the narrow interpretation becomes the standard for OSPAR, Contracting Parties to, for example, the Aarhus Convention could claim that the narrow approach is generally accepted and thus should also be used to inform the Aarhus Convention. So, the establishment of a restrictive approach not only undermines the very purpose of the OSPAR Convention, which is after all the effective protection of the marine environment, but may weaken the effectiveness of other related environmental law instruments. This OSPAR decision has created a precedent that is diametrically opposite to the common understanding of the right to access to information as established by the other MSENs. In fact, this norm fragmentation is particularly disturbing considering the fact that all the MSENs are closely related in terms of substance and affect the same parties, ie, Ireland, UK and the EC.

In relation to authority fragmentation, the OSPAR arbitral tribunal's restrictive 'clinical isolation' approach is an invitation for Contracting Parties to select the dispute settlement forum that provides for the lowest common denominator regarding the level of environmental protection. Moreover, by not taking into account the ECJ's jurisprudence and the Aarhus Convention, the OSPAR arbitral tribunal contributed to authority

[60] See further Lavranos, 'The Epilogue in the MOX Plant Dispute', above (n 27).

[61] See further N Lavranos, 'The MOX Plant-Judgment of the ECJ: How Exclusive is the Jurisdiction of the ECJ?' (2006) 15 *European Environmental Law Review* 291.

[62] See for a detailed analysis, T Broude, 'Fragmentation(s) of International Law: On Normative Integration as Authority Allocation' in T Broude and Y Shany (eds), *The Shifting Allocation of Authority in International Law: Considering Sovereignty, Supremacy and Subsidiarity* (Oxford, Hart Publishing, 2008) 99.

[63] *Ibid*, 104 et seq.

fragmentation rather than opting for joining the ECJ, thereby contributing to the unification or at least strengthening of the authority of the dispute settlement forums that have been empowered to define the right of access to information.

In light of these considerations, the question arises: how to avoid those negative effects associated with the restrictive approach to the MSEN issue. One answer is to be found in the application of the comity principle.[64]

As I have explained above,[65] in disputes which involve MSENs and therefore by their nature involve multiple dispute settlement bodies, the comity principle is one of the important tools that can be applied in order to avoid the fragmentary effects described in this contribution. In short, comity means that judges and arbitrators are first of all aware of other sources and judicial decisions relevant to a specific dispute. Secondly, after having identified the existence of relevant sources and judicial decisions, judges and arbitrators should consider whether another court or tribunal is better placed to adjudicate the dispute *in fine*. If they come to this conclusion, they should relinquish their jurisdiction in favour of the better placed forum. If, however, it has been decided to proceed with the case, then the case should be decided as much as possible in light of the other relevant sources and judicial decisions. In this way, maximum consistency and uniformity between MSENs is ensured, which in turn enhances the overall effectiveness of the MSENs as a whole. This is particularly important with regard to the protection of the environment.

Indeed, if, as Griffith had suggested, comity had been applied by the majority OSPAR arbitral tribunal, the following options would have presented themselves.

First, in view of the possible application of Community law provisions, the OSPAR arbitral tribunal could have relinquished its jurisdiction in favour of the ECJ. The ECJ would most likely have applied its broad interpretation of the term 'environmental information', thus coming to the conclusion that the UK must give access to the redacted reports.

Secondly, the OSPAR arbitral tribunal could have followed the UNCLOS arbitral tribunal's decision to stay the proceedings and request the parties to first find out whether or not the exclusive jurisdiction of the ECJ is established. If that were to be the case, the OSPAR arbitral tribunal would have to terminate the proceedings or decide the case – preferably in light of the ECJ's jurisprudence. Again, the result would have been that the UK would be required to publish the redacted parts of the reports.

Thirdly, the OSPAR arbitral tribunal could have decided the case by taking the holistic approach of Griffith, ie, taking all relevant MSENs

[64] See further, Y Shany, *The Competing Jurisdictions of International Courts and Tribunals* (Oxford, Oxford University Press, 2003).

[65] N Lavranos, 'Regulating Competing Jurisdictions among International Courts and Tribunals' (2008) *Zeitschrift für ausländisches öffentliches Recht und Völkerrecht* 575.

into account for the proper construction of Article 9 OSPAR Convention. Again, the result would have been the same as with the previous options.

In other words, had the majority of the OSPAR arbitral tribunal applied the comity principle, it would not only have served the protection of the environment, but would have delivered justice, which is after all the fundamental task and obligation of each court and tribunal.[66]

Unfortunately, the application of the comity principle currently entirely depends on the willingness of the individual judge or arbitrator. As this contribution and other case studies by the present author have shown, the comity principle has not yet been fully internalized by all judges and arbitrators.[67] Therefore, it is necessary that all international arbitrators and judges start recognizing that they have an inherent responsibility towards the system of international law as a whole.[68] Of course, it could be argued that each court or tribunal is first and foremost competent to resolve a dispute on the basis of the founding instrument and within the framework of its jurisdiction as determined by the Contracting Parties. While this is certainly true, it at the same time does not exclude the possibility to add the application of the comity principle to the general inherent obligations of every judge and arbitrator. Indeed, it is suggested here that the obligation of every judge and arbitrator consists of two elements: (i) a specific obligation to adjudicate the dispute before it on the basis of all relevant sources, including MSENs, and (ii) a general obligation to protect and, where possible, enhance the international legal system by contributing to the consistency, uniformity and maximum effectiveness of international law as a whole.

In conclusion, it is argued that only if this systemic responsibility is taken seriously, will it be possible to avoid or at least reduce the negative effects associated with the MSEN issue.

[66] See on the aspect of delivering justice, E-U Petersmann, 'Do Judges meet their Constitutional Obligation to Settle Disputes in Conformity with the "Principles of Justice and International Law"?' (2007) 2 *European Journal of Legal Studies* 1: www.ejls.eu/2/22UK.pdf.

[67] See N Lavranos, *Jurisdictional Competition* (The Netherlands, Europa Law Publishing, 2009).

[68] Petersmann, above (n 66).

8

*EU Review of UN Anti-Terror Sanctions: Judicial Juggling in a Four-Layer, Multi-Sourced, Equivalent-Norms Scenario**

Guy Harpaz

I INTRODUCTION

IN RECENT YEARS, international legal scholarship has been focused on the process of fragmentation of international law[1] under which a variety of forms of decision-making, law-making, policy-making,

* An earlier version of this chapter was presented in an international conference, 'Multi-Sourced Equivalent Norms', held on 24–25 May 2009 at the Hebrew University of Jerusalem. This chapter furthermore draws on two previous articles: G Harpaz, 'The European Court of Justice and its Relations with the European Court of Human Rights: the Quest for Enhanced Reliance, Coherence and Legitimacy' (2009) 46 *Common Market Law Review* 105; G Harpaz, 'Judicial Review by the European Court of Justice of UN "Smart Sanctions" Against Terror in the Kadi Dispute' (2009) 14 *European Foreign Affairs Review* 65. I would like to express my gratitude for the remarks of the participants of that conference and those of Nikos Lavranos, Iris Canor, Eve C Landau, Michael Schäfer, Arie Reich, Lior Herman, Yaël Ronen, Yuval Shany and Tomer Broude, for the first-rate research assistance of Noa Aviram and Ari Lazarus and for the generous support given by the Leonard Davis Institute for International Relations, the Hebrew University of Jerusalem. The usual *caveat* applies. The analysis in this chapter pertains to the pre-Lisbon Treaty legal order, unless otherwise stated.

[1] For selective literature on this theme, see J Pauwelyn, *Conflict of Norms in Public International Law: How WTO Law Relates to Other Rules of International Law* (Cambridge, Cambridge University Press 2003); B Simma and D Pulkowski, 'Of Planets and the Universe: Self-contained Regimes in International Law' (2006) 17 *European Journal of International Law* 483; T Broude, 'Fragmentation(s) of International Law: On Normative Integration as Authority Allocation Law' in T Broude and Y Shany (eds), *The Shifting Allocation of Authority in International Law: Considering Sovereignty, Supremacy and Subsidiarity* (Oxford, Hart Publishing, 2008); E Benvenisti and G Downs, 'The Empire's New Clothes: Political Economy and the Fragmentation of International Law' (2007) 60 *Stanford Law Review* 101; A Fischer-Lescano and G Teubner, 'Regime Collisions: The Vain Search for Legal Unity in the Fragmentation of Global Law' (2004) 25 *Michigan Journal of International Law* 999; E Vranes, 'The Definition of "Norm Conflict" in International Law and Legal Theory' (2006) 17 *European Journal of International Law* 395; R Wessel and J Wouters, 'The Phenomenon of Multilevel Regulation: Interactions between Global, EU and National Regulatory Spheres: Towards a Research Agenda' in R Wessel and J Wouters (eds), *Multilevel Regulation: Interactions and the EU* (Leiden, MNP, 2008) 13.

regulation and dispute-settlement forums are engaged at local, national, regional and global levels.[2] This phenomenon, which may be seen as 'an ephemeral reflection of a more fundamental, multi-dimensional fragmentation of global society itself',[3] has reached an unprecedented level of normative density and intensity.[4]
This state of affairs, which may result in 'the loss of an overall perspective on the law',[5] requires affirmation of international law's systemic building blocks.[6] The problem remains, however, that as stated by the ILC Report on Fragmentation of International Law,[7] there is no 'homogeneous, hierarchical, meta-system' available to address this state of affairs and therefore 'increasing attention will have to be given to the collision of norms and regimes and the rules, methods and techniques for dealing with such collisions'.[8]

This is precisely the objective of this book, which discusses Multi-Sourced Equivalent Norms (MSENs). MSEN situations were defined in the preparatory work leading to the publication of this book as those in which two or more distinct international legal rules (i) bind the same international legal subjects; (ii) are similar or identical in their normative content; (iii) have been established through different international instruments or procedures; and (iv) are applicable to different substantive areas of the law.[9] This chapter examines the MSENs phenomenon as it pertains to the European Community's (EC) implementation of United Nations anti-terror sanctions. The legal struggle against international terror is pursued at multilateral, regional and national levels, thereby creating the risk of overlapping and inconsistent regulatory regimes. This risk has materialized in the European Union (EU) context in relation to EC measures implementing UN Security Council (SC) Resolutions that had called for the imposition of financial sanctions against certain persons and entities associated with Osama Bin Laden, the al-Qaeda network and the Taliban. The EC implementing regime (just like its umbrella, UN regime) provided very limited human rights guarantees to those targeted by it, and as such it laid itself open to the charge that it contradicts international law (including human rights and *jus cogens* norms), EU law, the constitutions of the

[2] Wessel and Wouters, *ibid*, 11.

[3] Fischer-Lescano and Teubner, above (n 1) 1004.

[4] See in this volume, T Broude and Y Shany, 'The International Law and Policy of Multi-Sourced Equivalent Norms' in T Broude and Y Shany (eds), *Multi-Sourced Equivalent Norms in International Law* (Oxford, Hart Publishing, 2011) p 1.

[5] ILC, 'Report of the Study Group of the ILC, Fragmentation of International Law: Difficulties arising from the Diversification and Expansion of International Law' (2006) UN Doc A/CN.4/L.682, para 11.

[6] Simma and Pulkowski, above (n 1) 529.

[7] ILC Report, above (n 5).

[8] *Ibid*, para 493.

[9] Shany and Broude, 'The International Law and Policy of Multi-Sourced Equivalent Norms', above (n 4) p 5.

EU Member States, as well as the European Convention on Human Rights (ECHR).

The legality of the EC measures was brought before the EU judiciary, and in September 2008 the European Court of Justice (ECJ), after obtaining the Opinion of Advocate General Maduro (the Opinion),[10] held these measures to be illegal under EC law (*Kadi* judgment),[11] thereby overruling the verdict of the Court of First Instance (CFI and CFI verdict, respectively).[12]

In a judgment considered to be the most important one ever delivered by the ECJ with regard to the interface between EC law and international law,[13] the ECJ had to juggle four normative regimes that appear to overlap and to be potentially in conflict, namely the EC legal order, international law (including UN law) the ECHR and the laws of the EU Member States, operating in four different institutional and socio-political contexts, namely the EU, the international community, the Council of Europe and the EU/ECHR Member States. This dense, normative, institutional and socio-political environment falls within the ambit of this monograph, namely the exercise of judicial discretion in respect of distinct international, regional and national legal regimes which are governed by MSENs.

This chapter is designed to contribute to our appreciation of the phenomenon of MSENs as manifested in the EU context with respect to the struggle

[10] Case C-402/05 P *Yassin Abdullah Kadi v Council of the European Union and Commission of the European Communities* (Opinion of AG Maduro, 16 January 2008).

[11] Joined Cases C-402/05 and C-415/05 P *Kadi and Al Barakaat International Foundation v Council and Commission*, Judgment 3 September 2008 (*Kadi* judgment). For analysis, see T Tridimas and J Gutierrez-Fons, 'EU Law, International Law and Economic Sanctions against Terrorism: The Judiciary in Distress?' (2009) 32 *Fordham International Law Journal* 1083; G Harpaz, 'Judicial Review by the European Court of Justice of UN "Smart Sanctions" Against Terror in the Kadi Dispute' (2009) 14 *European Foreign Affairs Review* 65.

[12] Case T-315/01 *Yassin Abdullah Kadi v Council and Commission* [2005] ECR II-3649 (CFI) and Case T-306 *Yusuf and Al Barakaat International Foundation v Council and Commission* [2005] ECR II-3533 (CFI verdict). For analysis, see N Lavranos, 'Judicial Review of UN Sanctions by the Court of First Instance' (2006) 11 *European Foreign Affairs Review* 471; M Bulterman, 'Fundamental Rights and the United Nations Financial Sanction Regime: The Kadi and Yusuf Judgments of the Court of First Instance of the European Communities' (2006) 19 *Leiden Journal of International Law* 753; C Tomuschat, 'Case Law' (2006) 43 *Common Market Law Review* 537; EF Defeis, 'Targeted Sanctions, Human Rights, and the Court of First Instance of the European Community' (2006) 30 *Fordham International Law Journal* 1449; C Eckes, 'Judicial Review of European Anti Terrorism Measures – The Yusuf and Kadi Judgments of the Court of First Instance' (2008) 14 *European Law Journal* 74; E Guild, 'The Uses and Abuses of Counter-Terrorism Policies in Europe: The Case of the "Terrorist Lists"' (2008) 46 *Journal of Common Market Studies* 173; I Cameron, 'The European Convention on Human Rights Due Process and United Nations Security Council Counter-Terrorism Sanctions', *Report to the Council of Europe* (2006): www.coe.int; A Bianchi, 'Human Rights and the Magic of *Jus Cogens*' (2008) 19 *European Journal of International Law* 491; A Bianchi, 'Assessing the Effectiveness of the UN Security Council's Anti-Terrorism Measures: The Quest for Legitimacy and Cohesion' (2007) 17 *European Journal of International Law* 881; W Vleck, 'Acts to Combat the Financing of Terrorism: Common Foreign and Security Policy at the European Court of Justice' (2006) 11 *European Foreign Affairs Review* 491; A Reinisch, 'Introductory Note' (2006) 45 *International Legal Materials* 77; M Nettesheim, 'UN Sanctions against Individuals – A Challenge to the Architecture of European Union Governance' (2007) 44 *Common Market Law Review* 567.

[13] Tridimas and Gutierrez-Fons, above (n 11).

against international terror. Such a goal would be attained by addressing, in particular, the following questions and themes: (i) what were the source-parallelisms with which the ECJ was faced *vis-à-vis* its anti-terror sanctions regime?; (ii) what was the model chosen by the ECJ to regulate each MSENs situation with which it was faced?; (iii) what were the various considerations that led the ECJ to adopt the particular model in each MSENs situation?; (iv) what were the distinct normative regimes, constituencies, institutional contexts and political agendas that surrounded the proceedings and how did they affect the aforesaid choices?; (v) what was the set of secondary and background rules that the ECJ employed in order to alleviate the normative and institutional tensions?; (vi) what are the implications and repercussions of the ECJ's choices?; and (viii) can one distil from the judgment unifying features that are common to the various regulatory models?

II ANTI-TERROR SANCTIONS: THE MULTILATERAL, REGIONAL AND NATIONAL CONTEXTS

The UN is entrusted with primary responsibility for maintaining international peace and security.[14] In order to enable it to discharge its duties, its Members have charged the SC with 'primary responsibility' for the maintenance of international peace and security,[15] and have agreed to carry out its decisions in accordance with the UN Charter.[16] The SC is empowered under Chapter VII of the UN Charter (Chapter VII) to adopt non-military and military sanctions,[17] and such sanctions impose on the UN Members a legal duty to implement them.[18] Moreover, according to Article 103 of the UN Charter, these UN obligations enjoy legal supremacy: 'In the event of a conflict between the obligations of the Members of the United Nations under the present Charter and their obligations under any other international agreement, their obligations under the present Charter shall prevail'. It is under this legal framework that the SC is pursuing the multilateral struggle against international terrorism.[19]

In pursuit of that aim, the SC adopted Resolutions 1267 (1999)[20] and 1333 (2000)[21] in which it condemned the Taliban regime, which ruled

[14] Art 1(1) and (3) UN Charter.

[15] Art 24(2) UN Charter. For the limits imposed on that authority, see LMH Martinez, 'The Legislative Role of The Security Council in its Fight against Terrorism: Legal, Political and Practical Limits' (2008) 57 *International and Comparative Law Quarterly* 333.

[16] Art 25 UN Charter.

[17] Art 41 UN Charter.

[18] Art 48(2) UN Charter.

[19] For analysis, see Bulterman, above (n 12) 754 ff, Vleck, above (n 12) 494; J Almqvist, 'A Human Rights Critique of European Judicial Review: Counter-Terrorism Sanctions' (2008) 57 *International and Comparative Law Quarterly* 303, at 305 ff.

[20] UNSC Res 1267 (15 October 1999) UN Doc S/RES/1267.

[21] UNSC Res 1333 (19 December 2000) UN Doc S/RES/1333.

Afghanistan at that time, for allowing the use of the Afghan territory by Osama Bin Laden and others as a base for international terrorist operations. The Resolutions called on the UN Members to freeze funds held by the Taliban and by individuals and corporations suspected of being associated with it.[22] Following the fall of the Taliban regime in 2001, the SC adopted Resolution 1390 which renewed and extended these sanctions and which did not require for the purpose of imposition of sanctions any territorial nexus between the targeted entities and any particular territory or state. Due to their focus on individuals rather than on states, these sanctions are termed 'smart sanctions'. The SC Resolutions were subsequently reinforced and technically modified.[23]

The SC sanctions regime is supported by an intergovernmental, diplomatic UN organ entrusted with the task of listing and de-listing those individuals and entities subject to sanctions (Sanctions Committee).[24] On 8 March 2001 the Sanctions Committee published its first Consolidated List of those persons and entities whose funds were to be frozen. Since then the list has been amended several times to include applicants in the proceedings before the EC courts.

All EU Member States are UN Members and are therefore under a legal duty to implement the UN sanction regime. It was, however, the EU, which although not a formal Member of the UN, took upon itself to formulate on behalf of its Member States the sanctions regime that would be applied within the EU.

The EU's implementing regime includes financial sanctions adopted by Community Regulations under the First Pillar (the EC Treaty) in the form of Regulation (EC) No 337/2000, Regulation (EC) No 467/2001, Regulation (EC) No 2062/2001, Regulation (EC) No 881/2002 and Regulation (EC) No 561/2003.[25]

Annex I to EC Regulation 467/2001 contains the list of those affected by the freezing of funds. Under Article 10(1) of that Regulation, the EC Commission was empowered to amend or supplement the list on the basis of determinations made by either the SC or the Sanctions Committee. These EC Regulations apply to those designated by the UN, and in each instance in which the UN modifies its Consolidated List, the EC Regulation is amended accordingly.[26] The EC sanctions regime and its list of suspected terrorists thus constitute a carbon copy of the UN's Consolidated List.[27]

The EC Regulations form an integral part of the municipal laws of the EU Member States and as such any sanction they impose is in force in the

[22] See UNSC Res 1267, above (n 20) para 4(b).

[23] For analysis, see Bianchi, 'Human Rights and the Magic of *Jus Cogens*', above (n 12) 497.

[24] See Bianchi, 'Assessing the Effectiveness of the UN Security Council's Anti-Terrorism Measures', above (n 12) 882 and Cameron, above (n 12) 4.

[25] For detailed account of the legal regime, see Bulterman, above (n 12).

[26] *Ibid.*

[27] Eckes, above (n 12) 91.

EU Member States from the moment that the EC implementing Regulation enters into force.[28] Thus, the various failures of the UN sanctions regime to provide adequate constitutional guarantees to those suspected of being linked with terrorism were imported to the EU sanctions regime and then incorporated, through the direct applicability of these Regulations, into the legal orders of the EU Member States. The role of the Member States under the EU legal order is reduced to supervising compliance with and penalizing violation of the EC sanctions Regulation.[29]

The applicants before the CFI – Kadi, an international businessman holding a Saudi Arabian passport; Yusuf, a Swedish national and Al Barakaat, a Swedish organization associated with the largest money-transfer entity in Somalia – were added to Annex I by Commission Regulation (EC) 2062/2001 and by Commission Regulation (EC) 2199/2001, respectively, without any prior notice being given to them.[30] The applicants, who denied any association with terror, brought legal proceedings before the CFI, contesting the legality of Regulation (EC) 801/2002 (contested Regulation). They argued, inter alia, that the contested Regulation breached their fundamental rights (the right to be heard, the right to respect for property and the right to effective judicial review).

III THE MSENs SCENARIO

In implementing the UN sanctions regime, the EU was faced with normative (and, by implication, also a potential jurisdictional) overlap between the UN legal order, its own legal order and the legal orders of the ECHR and of its Member States. More specifically, the case in hand involved two sets of MSENs which clash with each other. The first set is the 'sanctions MSENs', including the anti-terror sanctions regime of the UN, EU and EU/ECHR Member States. The second set is the 'Due Process MSENs', including procedural guarantees to those suspected of being associated with terror, under the aegis of public international law, General Principles of EC Law, the ECHR and the constitutional order of the EU/ECHR Member States. These two sets of prima facie conflicting MSENs pose significant legal challenges for the EU.

The first set of two sets of MSENs is the anti-terror one. The EC is bound, according to the *Kadi* judgment, by UN law (SC Resolutions and determinations of the Sanctions Committee) by virtue of the EC Treaty itself.[31] Thus, in implementing its own sanctions regime the EC had to comply with the UN sanctions regime. In the same vein, all EU Member States are also UN

[28] Bulterman, above (n 12).

[29] *Ibid.*

[30] For analysis, see Eckes, above (n 12) 75.

[31] See below, section IV.

Members. They must implement the UN/EU sanctions regime in a manner which is compatible with their UN obligations. By virtue of its obligation to comply with the UN Charter, the Community must not act in a manner that would force its Member States to infringe their UN obligations. Thus, the EU/UN Member States are bound to comply with the UN sanctions regime due to their UN membership, while complying with the EU sanctions regime due to their EU membership. It must be emphasized that this three-layer MSENs scenario does not create meaningful legal obstacles because of the fact that the substantive contents of the sanctions regimes of the UN, EU and the Member States are, normatively, virtually identical.

The second set of MSENs is the due process one. The EU must comply with international law, in general, and with *jus cogens* norms, in particular, including with due process guarantees under public international law. Thus, the procedural guarantees offered under the EU sanctions regime to those suspected of being associated with terror must comply with procedural human rights under public international law.

Moreover, in implementing the UN sanctions regime, the EC is bound by its legal regime including its own General Principles of Law. This concept, which was first developed by the EU judiciary,[32] includes, in particular, the General Principle of Human Rights protection which is enshrined in Article 6 of the Treaty of the European Union (TEU):[33]

> 1. The Union is founded on the principles of liberty, democracy, respect for human rights and fundamental freedoms, and the rule of law, principles which are common to the Member States. 2. The Union shall respect fundamental rights . . . as general principles of community law.

Thus, the procedural guarantees offered under the EU sanctions regime to those suspected of being associated with terror must not run counter to the general principle of human rights protection. Prima facie, EC implementing measures with their inadequate human rights protection conflict with the EU human rights regime.[34]

Yet another challenge relates to the ECHR. As will be demonstrated below, the EU is still not a Contracting Party to the ECHR and yet, pursuant to the ECJ jurisprudence, it is under a quasi-obligation to follow the ECHR. That obligation is reinforced by Article 6(2) of the EU Treaty.[35]

[32] Case T-29/69 *Stauder v Ulm* [1969] ECR 419, para 7; Case T-11-70 *Internationale Handelsgesellschaft mbH v Einfuhr- und Vorratsstelle für Getreide und Futtermittel* [1970] ECR 1125, para 4.

[33] Treaty of the European Union (Maastricht) art 6.

[34] Almqvist, above (n 19) especially 310 ff; Cameron, above (n 12) 6; Guild, above (n 12); Bianchi, 'Assessing the Effectiveness of the UN Security Council's Anti-Terrorism Measures', above (n 12) 903 ff; P Hoffman, 'Human Rights and Terrorism' (2004) 26 *Human Rights Quarterly* 932; Defeis, above (n 12).

[35] For analysis, see JR Wetzel, 'Improving Fundamental Rights Protection in the European Union: Resolving the Conflict and Confusion between the Luxembourg and Strasbourg Courts' (2003) 71 *Fordham International Law Journal* 2823 at 2839.

Therefore, and as analyzed below, in formulating the anti-terror sanctions regime, the EU should back that regime with such human rights guarantees as would correspond to the protection granted to those rights under the ECHR. However, the UN sanctions regime (and therefore the EU implementing legislation) is prima facie in conflict with the ECHR human rights regime. These human rights infringements may include, substantively,[36] the infringement of the right to property,[37] the right to private and family life[38] and the right of freedom of movement,[39] and procedurally,[40] the right to access to court,[41] the right embodied in *nullum crimen*,[42] the right to be heard[43] and the right to effective judicial protection.[44]

An additional challenge with which the EU is faced pertains to its Member States. The few human rights protections embodied in the relevant EC Regulations permeate the legal orders of the EU Member States due to the direct applicability of the EC contested Regulation. The EC anti-terror regime with its inadequate human rights protection might therefore be in conflict with human rights guarantees enshrined in the respective Member States' constitutional orders.

Moreover, all EU Member States are also Contracting Parties to the ECHR. The implementation by them of the UN/EU sanction regimes must therefore be conducted in accordance with their ECHR human rights obligations. The Strasbourg Court indicated in the *Bosphorus* case that ECHR Members who are also EU Member States may be held accountable for violating their ECHR obligations when implementing their EC obligations in cases where the protection of ECHR rights under the implemented EC legal order is found to be 'manifestly deficient'.[45] Thus, the EU must within its legal order provide human rights protection equivalent to that enshrined in the ECHR, so as not to cause its Member States to breach their ECHR obligations. However, and as indicated above, the EU implementing measures and the domestic legal orders which incorporate the

[36] L van den Herik, 'The Security Council's Targeted Sanctions Regimes: In Need of Better Protection of the Individual' (2007) 20 *Leiden Journal of International Law* 797.

[37] Cameron, above (n 12) 5; Bianchi, 'Assessing the Effectiveness of the UN Security Council's Anti-Terrorism Measures', above (n 12) 908.

[38] Cameron, above (n 12) 5.

[39] *Ibid.*

[40] 'Strengthening Targeted Sanctions through Fair and Clear Procedures'.White Paper prepared by the Watson Institute commissioned by the governments of Germany, Sweden and Switzerland, UN Doc A/60/887–S/2006/331 (2006); Cameron (n 12).

[41] Cameron, *ibid.*

[42] Bianchi, 'Assessing the Effectiveness of the UN Security Council's Anti-Terrorism Measures', above (n 12) 907.

[43] *Ibid.*

[44] *Ibid.*

[45] See, *Bosphorus Hava Yollari Turizm Ve Ticaret Anonim Sirketi v Ireland* [2006] 42 EHRR 1, as analyzed by C Costello, 'The Bosphorus Ruling of the ECrtHR: Fundamental Rights and Blurred Boundaries in Europe' (2006) 6 *Human Rights Law Review* 87. For further analysis, see S Douglas-Scott, 'A Tale of Two Courts: Luxembourg, Strasbourg and the Growing European Human Rights *Acquis*' (2006) 43 *Common Market Law Review* 629, at 630 and 637–39.

EC measures fail to so do. EC measures, when applied by the EU Member States, may therefore expose the EU Member States to liability under the ECHR.[46]

In conclusion, the EU anti-terror legal regime interacts with international law and the laws of its Member States (with respect to the anti-terror provisions), as well as with international law, its own legal order and the legal orders of the ECHR and that of the EU/ECHR Member States (as they pertain to procedural guarantees). It thus emerges from the foregoing analysis that the EU is implementing the UN sanctions regime in multifaceted, four-layer, two-dimensional MSENs legal scenarios which interact within each other and between each other. The EU must implement that regime in a manner which would be faithful to: (i) the UN Charter and international law; (ii) its own General Principles of human rights protection; (iii) the ECHR; and, while doing so (iv) must not cause its Member States to breach their UN and ECHR obligations.

How could the EU judiciary have dealt with this MSENs scenario? Broude and Shany identify four models to address such a scenario[47]: (i) the dominant norm/regime model, under which the competing relevant instruments are compared by the relevant judicial organ, which will then select and apply, pursuant to rules of precedence, the most influential norm; (ii) the cumulative (or disintegrative) model, under which multi-sourced obligations are viewed as simultaneously applicable; (iii) the integrative model, under which all relevant norms are construed in light of the parallel norms, thereby seeking to harmonize, through interpretative means, all relevant norms/regimes; and (iv) the contesting model, under which the relevant judicial organ denies the very existence of the MSENs situation by adopting an interpretation that dismisses the similar attributes of the various applicable norms. The following section outlines the CFI verdict and the ECJ judgment, while the remainder of the chapter analyzes the verdict and the judgment according to this MSENs typology, focusing on the manner in which the EU judiciary adjudicated the interface between the two sets of MSENs.

IV THE CFI VERDICT AND THE ECJ JUDGMENT

The CFI dismissed the plea of illegality of the contested Regulation along the following line of reasoning[48]: (i) the EU is neither a UN Member, nor an addressee of SC Resolutions, nor the successor of its Member States' UN rights and obligations under public international law, and as such it is

[46] For analysis of the specific infringements, see Cameron, above (n 12) 5.

[47] Broude and Shany, 'The International Law and Policy of Multi-Sourced Equivalent Norms', above (n 4) p 13–14.

[48] For analysis, see above (n 12).

not bound by UN obligations under the UN Charter; (ii) the EC is bound by UN law by virtue of the EC Treaty itself; (iii) under customary international law, UN law enjoys legal supremacy over any domestic, bilateral, regional or multilateral treaty law; (iv) such supremacy is confirmed and reinforced by Article 297 of the EC Treaty:

> Member States shall consult each other with a view to taking together the steps needed to prevent the functioning of the Common Market being affected by measures which a Member State may be called upon to take . . . in order to carry out obligations it has accepted for the purpose of maintaining peace and international security

and by Article 307 of the EC Treaty:

> The rights and obligations arising from agreements concluded before 1 January 1958 or, for acceding States, before the date of their accession, between one or more Member States on the one hand, and one or more third countries on the other, shall not be affected by the provisions of the Treaty.[49]

(v) as such, EU Member States are bound, by virtue of EC law, to disregard any of their EC obligations which run counter to their UN obligations, even if the EC provision is classified as primary law or as General Principles of EC Law; (vi) such UN supremacy binds the EC, *mutatis mutandis*; (vii) the EC was bound to execute these UN obligations as they stood, and was prohibited from amending their content; (viii) this UN supremacy over EC law imposes structural limits on the ability of the EC judiciary to conduct judicial review. The EC contested Regulation falls outside the ambit of judicial review, the EC judiciary has no authority to call in question, directly or indirectly, its lawfulness under international or Community law, and it is bound instead to interpret and apply it in a manner compatible with these obligations under the UN Charter; (ix) such immunity from judicial review is subject to one proviso. The EC Court will review these measures against the benchmark of *jus cogens* norms, ie, those international norms accepted and recognized by the international community as those from which no derogation is permitted and which can be modified only by a subsequent norm of general international law having the same character; (x) the EC implementing measures did not infringe *jus cogens* norms vis-à-vis the applicants and these measures were therefore valid.

The CFI judgment, which evoked much academic concern,[50] was overruled by the ECJ in its judgment delivered after obtaining the Opinion of Advocate General Maduro. The ECJ confirmed the CFI's findings with regard to the binding force of UN law on the EU Member States and the EU itself. It differed from it, however, on the fundamental issue of the

[49] For further analysis, see Tomuschat, above (n 12) 541.

[50] See Defeis, above (n 12); Eckes, above (n 12); Guild, above (n 12); Cameron, above (n 12); Nettesheim, above (n 12); Bianchi, 'Assessing the Effectiveness of the UN Security Council's Anti-Terrorism Measures', above (n 12). But compare with Reinisch, above (n 12).

normative interface between the international law/UN legal order and the EC legal order. In essence, the CFI established the supremacy of the UN norms over EC norms (and hence the unavailability of judicial review of EC implementing measures), whereas the ECJ held a contrary position. The ECJ paid much lip service to the importance of international law, including, in particular, the UN Charter, within the EC legal order,[51] attaching 'special importance' to the fact that SC Chapter VII Resolutions constitute an exercise of 'primary responsibility' under the UN Charter.[52] It nevertheless concluded that the primacy of international agreements over acts of secondary Community law would not apply to primary EC law.[53] Such primary EC norms trump international law/UN law and that precedence extends to the General Principles of EC law, including, in particular, fundamental human rights.[54]

This EU primacy, affects, in turn, the scope of judicial review. Supreme, fundamental rights form an integral part of the General Principles of EC law whose observance the EC Court guarantees.[55] Such respect for human rights is a condition of the lawfulness of Community measures; hence measures that are incompatible with human rights are amenable to judicial review and are illegal under EC law.[56] An international agreement cannot affect the allocation of powers fixed by the EC/EU Treaties[57] and the obligations imposed by an international agreement (in our case the SC Resolutions) cannot prejudice these constitutional principles, the respect for which the EC courts must guarantee.[58] Nor does EC law provide the basis for immunity from judicial review.[59]

The ECJ therefore concluded, in accordance with the Opinion of Attorney General (AG) Maduro, that the EC courts must go beyond the limited *jus cogens* review offered by the CFI and conduct a full review of the lawfulness of all EC Acts including those designed to give effect to SC

[51] The ECJ reiterated in paras 291–97 the following observations: (i) The EC must respect international law and that EC measure must be interpreted, and its scope limited, in the light of the relevant rules of international law; (ii) Observance of the undertakings granted in the UN context is required when the Community gives effect, by adopting implementing measures, to SC Chapter VII resolutions (iii) In the exercise of that power the Community must attach special importance to the fact that such SC resolutions constitute the exercise of the primary responsibility with which the UN is entrusted for the maintenance of global peace and security (iv) When the EC's object is to implement SC resolutions, it must draw up its measures taking due account of the terms and objectives of the resolution concerned and of the relevant obligations under the Charter; (v) In interpreting the contested EC regulation, account must be taken of the wording and purpose of SC Resolution 1390 (2002) which that EC regulation is designed to implement.

[52] *Kadi* judgment, above (n 11) para 294.

[53] *Ibid*, paras 305–08.

[54] *Ibid*, para 283.

[55] *Ibid*, para 283.

[56] *Ibid*, para 284.

[57] *Ibid*, para 282.

[58] *Ibid*, para 285.

[59] *Ibid*, para 300.

Resolutions.[60] Such judicial review, which should be pursued according to fundamental rights forming an integral part of the General Principles of Community law, must, however, be conducted indirectly and not directly. The EC judiciary needs to examine the legality of the EC measures purporting to implement UN obligations but not the lawfulness of the UN Resolutions themselves.[61]

The ECJ concluded, after pursuing a full and comprehensive review of these measures, that the EC rights of defence, in particular the right to be heard and the right to effective judicial review of those rights were breached by the EU sanctions regime.

The EC infringed the applicants' rights of defence by not providing for a procedure for communicating the evidence that would justify the inclusion of their names in the anti-terror list and for hearing them, either at the time of inclusion or later. These infringements prevented the EC courts from undertaking a judicial review, thereby infringing the applicants' right to an effective legal remedy.[62] In addition, with respect to the right of property, the contested Regulation was adopted without furnishing any guarantees that enabled Kadi to put his case to the competent authorities, in a situation in which the restriction of his property rights was significant, and as such, it constituted an unjustified restriction of that right.[63]

In light of these human rights infringements, the contested Regulation was annulled, insofar as it pertained to the applicants. Such unqualified annulment would, however, be capable of seriously and irreversibly prejudicing the effectiveness of the restrictive measures, because the interval preceding its replacement with a valid Regulation would allow the applicants to take steps to prevent the sanctions from being applied to them again.[64] The ECJ therefore maintained the effects of the contested Regulation, so far as it concerned the appellants, for a period of up to three months, thereby allowing the Council to remedy the infringements found.[65]

The remainder of the chapter is devoted to an analysis of some of the central aspects of the CFI verdict and of the ECJ judgment as they pertain to judicial discretion in a MSENs scenario, focusing on the various models adopted by the EU judiciary to regulate the two sets of MSENs.

[60] *Ibid*, para 326.
[61] *Ibid*, paras 286–87. This approach can find support in the work Eckes, above (n 12) 84.
[62] *Ibid*, paras 345–53.
[63] *Ibid*, paras 369–70.
[64] *Ibid*, paras 373–76.
[65] *Ibid*.

V EU LAW VIS-À-VIS INTERNATIONAL LAW/UN LAW: THE DOMINANT REGIME MODEL?

A The ECJ's Traditional Approach

It may be argued from the perspective of international law that the EC and EU treaties are ordinary international treaties and hence that the EU legal order itself is but another sub-system of international law.[66] Numerous EU specialists, however, argue that that order bears strong characteristics of self-containment,[67] and hence that it is of a *sui generis* character.[68]

The latter approach was adopted by the EU judiciary. From its very early days, the ECJ has refused to treat the EU legal order as a sub-system of international law and it has declined to treat the European legal order as a mere international treaty operating solely under traditional public international law. The ECJ was determined instead to establish and safeguard the *sui generis* and autonomous nature of the EC legal order, holding in the seminal judgment of *Van Gend en Loos* that the Community constitutes 'a new legal order of international law' and that the EEC Treaty 'is more than an agreement which merely creates mutual obligations between the Contracting States'.[69] In another path-breaking ruling, the ECJ established that 'the law stemming from the Treaty' is 'an independent source of law' of 'special and original nature' and that 'by contrast with ordinary international treaties, the EEC Treaty has created its own legal system which, on the entry into force of the treaty, became an integral part of the legal systems of the member states and which their courts are bound to apply'.[70] The ECJ has thus regarded itself as serving a 'constitutional role',[71] transforming the constituting treaties into the EC's 'Constitutional charter' of a *sui generis* international entity.[72] Consequently, European integration has been undergoing a continuous and unprecedented process of constitutionalization, whereby

[66] Simma and Pulkowski, above (n 1) 516; G Arangio-Ruiz, 'Summary Records of the Meetings of the Forty-fourth Session' (1992) 1 *ILC Yearbook* 76.

[67] Simma and Pulkowski, *ibid*, 516.

[68] Arangio-Ruiz, above (n 66). The term 'self-contained' was referred to by the PCIJ in SS Wimbeldon, PCIJ Rep Series A No 1, at 23; for analysis, see Simma and Pulkowski, *ibid*.

[69] Case 26/62 *Van Gend en Loos* [1963] ECR 1.

[70] Case 6/64 *Costa v ENEL* [1964] ECR 685.

[71] Report of the Court of Justice on Certain Aspects of the Application of the Treaty on European Union, submitted to the European Council in preparation for the IGC (May 1995) at 4. See also B de Witte, 'The Past and Future Role of the European Court of Justice in the Protection of Human Rights' in P Alston (ed), *The European Union and Human Rights* (Oxford, Oxford University Press, 1999) 878, at 869.

[72] Opinion 1/91, Draft Agreement between the Community, on the one hand, and the countries of the European Free Trade Association, on the other, relating to the creation of the European Economic Area, ECR [1991] I-06079 (Opinion 1/91), as analyzed by LR Helfer and A-M Slaughter, 'Towards a Theory of Effective Supranational Adjudication' (1997–98) 107 *Yale Law Journal* 273, at 293

its legal order has been elevated from a set of traditional, horizontal legal arrangements binding sovereign states into a vertically integrated, quasi-federal, autonomous and *sui generis* legal regime, conferring enforceable rights on legal entities.[73]

The preference for a *sui generis*, autonomous, self-contained, constitutional model has been the defining maxim in ECJ jurisprudence, with the ECJ serving as the guardian of these features, by examining whether an international norm should have legal effect within its own legal boundaries and what that effect might be.[74] This preference has led the ECJ to employ a presumption in favour of a complete and exhaustive regulation, preferring to fill lacunas by recourse to the EC General Principles instead of relying on international law.[75]

This approach displayed by the ECJ towards the EU legal order, which can be classified as 'dualist', facilitated the advancement of the dominant regime model, under which EU norms are to be granted legal supremacy in MSENs scenarios. Indeed, as early as 1964 the ECJ established and safeguarded the normative supremacy of Community law over conflicting norms:

> [T]he law stemming from the Treaty, an independent source of law, could not, because of its special and original nature, be overridden by domestic legal provisions, however framed, without being deprived of its character as Community law and without the legal basis of the Community itself being called into question. The transfer by the states from their domestic legal system to the Community legal system of the rights and obligations arising under the Treaty carries with it a permanent limitation of their sovereign rights, over which a subsequent unilateral act incompatible with the concept of the Community cannot prevail.[76]

Since then, the ECJ has been labouring to safeguard and buttress that EC normative superiority.

That approach displayed towards the legal orders of the Member States was later extended to the inter-Community context and was applied in relation to the normative overlaps between EU primary norms and international law norms. According to the ECJ's settled jurisprudence, the hierarchy of norms in the Community legal order is as follows: highest norms include primary EC law (EC Treaty and General Principles, drawing on the ECHR), then come international agreements and decisions of international organizations, followed by secondary EC law, while the lowest norms are national law.[77] The traditional preference for a self-contained,

[73] U Haltern, 'Pathos and Patina: The Failure and Promise of Constitutionalism in the European Imagination' (2003) 9 *European Law Journal* 14.
[74] Nettesheim, above (n 12) 581–82.
[75] Simma and Pulkowski, above (n 1) 505.
[76] *Costa v ENEL*, above (n 70).
[77] Lavranos, 'Judicial Review of UN Sanctions by the Court of First Instance', above

constitutional order also assisted the ECJ in advancing the rule of (EU) law, supported by a complete set of judicial remedies,[78] the two principles which were enshrined in *Les Verts v European Parliament*.[79] The CFI chose in the *Kadi* proceedings to depart from the traditional, constitutional, self-contained approach in favour of a more pluralistic, integrative approach towards international law.

B The CFI Verdict

The CFI treated the EC legal order like any other ordinary 'domestic' law, subject to ordinary international rules of law pertaining to the interface between international law and municipal law.[80] The CFI ruling thus represents a monist, internationalist paradigm that runs counter to the above constitutional paradigm that advanced the model of closed entity.[81]

That approach allowed the CFI to subject the EU legal order (including its substantive sanctions provisions and its procedural guarantees) to the UN (substantive anti-terror provisions) legal order, utilizing Article 103 of the UN Charter as a strong background (conflicts) rule.[82]

Based on that Article, the CFI turned the EC's traditional hierarchy of norms upsidedown, providing the following hierarchy[83]: highest norms include *jus cogens*, then come international agreements and decisions of international organizations, secondary EC law (ie, EC Regulations implementing UN obligations) and only then primary EC law, including the ECHR, while lowest norms are national law.[84]

This approach also diverged from the traditional perception of (EU) rule of law, judicial review and judicial remedies. The CFI did refer to the above judgment of *Les Verts v Parliament* but this did not prevent it from holding that there is a lacuna in the EC system of legal remedies, that the rule of law will not regulate EC measures implementing UN sanctions, that such measures escape judicial review and that no remedy will be afforded in cases where such measures infringe EC fundamental human rights (subject to the jus cogens proviso).

The adoption of a dominant model may result in overriding the background rules which would have been otherwise applied.[85] That is what

(n 12) 478.

[78] K Lenaerts, 'The Rule of Law and the Coherence of the Judicial System of the European Union' (2007) 44 *Common Market Law Review* 1625.

[79] Case 294/83 *Les Verts v Parliament* [1986] ECR 1339, para 23.

[80] Nettesheim, above (n 12).

[81] *Ibid*, 587–88.

[82] For analysis, see Cameron, above (n 12) 27.

[83] Lavranos, 'Judicial Review of UN Sanctions by the Court of First Instance', above (n 12) 478.

[84] *Ibid*.

[85] Broude and Shany, 'The International Law and Policy of Multi-Sourced Equivalent

happened in our case. The CFI's choice of the (UN) dominant model relieved it of the need to rely on any background principles and rules such as lex specialis and lex posterior.

The only background rules that were employed by the CFI were certain EC Treaty provisions and the principle of *jus cogens* according to which EC implementing measures were reviewed. As to the EC Treaty, the CFI referred to the above-cited Articles 297 and 307 to substantiate the supremacy of UN law on EC foundations[86] and to support the findings regarding the unavailability of indirect judicial review.[87] The choice of the jus cogens background principle enabled the CFI to moderate the supremacy of UN law over EU law, thereby providing for a somewhat mitigated (UN) dominant model.

C The ECJ's Judgment

The ECJ judgment has brought us back to basics, restoring the *sui generis*, constitutional, closed and autonomous model. The ECJ reiterated that it is EC law which will determine the manner in which the UN obligations will be incorporated into the EC legal order and it is the EC judicature which will determine the precise force of UN obligations (or implementing EC measures) within the EC hierarchy of norms: 'The question of the Court's jurisdiction arises in the context of the internal and autonomous legal order of the Community'.[88] Such determination will be conducted according to the EC Treaty and not merely on the basis of Article 103 of the UN Charter. The ECJ thus refused to follow the CFI treatment of Article 103 as a strong background rule.

An international agreement (such as the UN Charter) cannot have the effect of prejudicing the EU's constitutional principles of supremacy, rule of law and effective judicial remedies, the respect for which the EC courts must guarantee.[89] Nor can such an agreement affect the allocation of powers fixed by the EC and EU Treaties or, consequently, the autonomy of the Community legal system.[90]

The CFI findings with regard to the superiority of UN law over EU law were therefore found to be wrong. Under this restored, self-contained regime, primary EC law takes precedence over international law, including the UN Charter. As a corollary, the ECJ also dismissed the CFI's findings with respect to the rule of law and judicial review. It found instead that the EC institutions can never escape the rule of law nor the corollary judicial review conducted by the EC judicature, that the EC system of remedies is

Norms', above (n 4) p 13–14.

[86] CFI verdict, above (n 12) paras 185–89.

[87] *Ibid*, paras 223–24.

[88] *Kadi* judgment, above (n 11) 298 and 317.

[89] *Ibid*, para 285.

[90] *Ibid*, para 282.

complete, that no lacuna exists in it and that a legal remedy will be provided to those whose human rights have been infringed by EC measures, even when such measures were intended to implement Chapter VII Resolutions.

The findings of the ECJ with regard to the rule of law are in line with its established case law and the Opinions of various Advocates General,[91] while subjecting EC implementing measures to judicial review is in line with the ECJ findings in the *Bosphorus* case.[92] As AG Maduro noted in his Opinion, the fact that the UN/EC sanctions regime raises highly sensitive political issues does not mandate the Community to 'turn its back' on its 'fundamental values'.[93] Thus, in the course of going to the core of the legal dispute, the ECJ reverted to time-honoured constitutional truisms.

D Analysis

When examining the EU-UN MSENs scenario, the CFI treated the EU legal order as an open and pluralistic order that intensively interacts with the international legal order under new rules of supremacy according to which UN (anti-terror, substantive) law takes precedent over primary (procedural guarantees) EU norms.

According to de Búrca, this approach represents a 'deferential engagement', the CFI being unwilling to subject the SC 'to review for compliance with the full gamut of EU standards', 'but insisting nonetheless on considering the legality of its action under minimum norms of non-derogable international law'.[94] This approach, which resembles that of the ECtHR towards international law,[95] displayed moderate jurisdictional deference towards the UN, thereby advancing the unity between the international legal order and the regional, European order. As Nettesheim explains, in opting for that model, the CFI safeguarded the integrity of the UN collective security system at the price of opening its legal order to the uncontrolled and unlimited influx of external acts, forcing the EC to implement system-wide measures over which it had little influence and in which only a small minority of its Member States are involved.[96]

[91] See C-355/04 P *Segi et al v Council*, judgments of 27 February 2007, at para 51 and the Opinion of AG Maduro in Case C-160/03 *Spain v Eurojust* [2005] ECR I-2077, para 17.

[92] In that judgment the ECJ refused to hold that the judicial review of the contested Regulation was restricted due to the fact that the Regulation was designed to implement the UN sanctions regime against the FRY, see Case C-84/95 *Bosphorus Hava Yollari Turizm ve Ticaret v The Minister for Transport et al* (Bosphorus) [1996] ECR I-3953, paras 22–23, as analyzed by Bulterman, above (n 12) 767 and Eckes, above (n 12) 85.

[93] Opinion of AG Maduro, above (n 10) para 44.

[94] G de Búrca 'The European Court of Justice and the International Legal Order after Kadi' (2010) 51 *Harvard International Law Journal* 1.

[95] According to de Búrca's analysis, the ECHR Court demonstrated in the past strong substantive deference towards the UN Security Council by denying its own jurisdiction on both formal and substantive grounds. See de Búrca, *ibid*, 15–17.

[96] *Ibid*.

By granting precedence to external legitimacy (effectively cooperating with its non-EU counterparts in the UN and treating them as its constituency) at the expense of internal legitimacy (advancing its own core values for the benefit of its own constituency, namely the EU nationals), the CFI promoted 'a systematic vision of international law as a coherent legal order at the expense of denying the Community its own enclosed constitutional universe'.[97] Such a move, which finds no support in the ECJ settled case law and which advances what AG Maduro termed in the discussions leading to the publication of this book 'external constitutional plurality',[98] could mitigate the fragmentation of international law at the expense of the integrity of the EC legal order.

AG Maduro adopted in his Opinion a different line of reasoning. Although the Community legal order and the international legal order do not 'pass by each other like ships in the night',[99] the EC judicature must still 'first and foremost' preserve the EC 'constitutional framework'[100] established by the EC Treaty and ensure that international law will permeate the Community legal order 'only under the conditions set by the constitutional principles of the Community'.[101]

The CFI's approach was also dismissed by the ECJ. In reinforcing the autonomous and supreme nature of the EC legal order, as analyzed above, the ECJ was erecting high walls between itself and the UN/international legal order. Drawing on the works of Shany and Nettesheim, one may categorize such judicial course of action as a closed and self-contained model.[102] Under this model, which is considered by Simma and Pulkowski as a particular category of sub-systems that embrace a full, exhaustive and definitive set of secondary rules,[103] the EC safeguards its self-containment by determining whether and in what manner to accept the internal applicability and effectiveness of an outsider's act (in our case the UN/international law).[104] This (EU) dominant model, which grew out of structures enshrined in the classic nation state, grants full expression to the principles of (EU's) autonomy, democratic self-determination and subsidiarity, thereby reflecting the structural, cultural and ethical differences that exist between itself and other entities.[105]

This approach presented the EU as a separate, self-contained and supreme system that determines its relationship to the international order

[97] Tridimas and Gutierrez-Fons, above (n 11).

[98] Luís Miguel Poiares Maduro, 'Foreword' in Broude and Shany (eds), *Multi-Sourced Equivalent Norms in International Law*, above (n 4) p vii.

[99] Opinion of AG Maduro, above (n 10) para 22.

[100] *Ibid*, para 27.

[101] *Ibid*.

[102] Nettesheim, above (n 12) 579, 591–92.

[103] Simma and Pulkowski, above (n 1) 492–93.

[104] Nettesheim, above (n 12) 579, 591–92.

[105] *Ibid*.

in accordance with its own internal values and priorities rather than in accordance with international law.[106] According to that approach, no meaningful engagement is pursued with international law, its nature, rules and sources. Similarly, little if no deference is displayed towards the SC, the ECJ treating international law, including UN Charter and SC Resolutions, as a separate and parallel order which exists 'on a separate plane' and whose normative demands do not penetrate the domestic (EC) legal order and cannot call into question or affect the nature, meaning or primacy of fundamental EC principles.

In pursuing this approach, the ECJ may be seen as striving to insulate the EC order from external influences of international law that might undermine the internal coherence of its legal order and disrupt the attainment of its specific goals, while promoting the integrity of an entity's own human rights standards.[107] It thus gave precedence to the concept of internal legitimacy (advancing its own core values for the benefit of its own constituency, namely the EU nationals) at the expense of external legitimacy (effectively cooperating with its non-EU counterparts in the UN) and over the systemic welfare of the international legal system. In doing so the ECJ accepts and promotes the fragmentation of international law into self-contained regimes.[108]

In setting the parameters of the conference leading to the publication of this book, Broude and Shany postulated that the dominant norm model may be utilized as an appropriate instrument to refer jurisdiction to the most appropriate normative framework.[109] This is precisely what the ECJ did, referring to its own legal order as the most appropriate one. Moreover, the ECJ's regulatory choice enabled it to avoid the use of any background principles and rules, such as *lex specialis* and *lex posterior*. The dominance of the EU primary legal order also enabled the ECJ to depart from the CFI findings and not employ the background principle of *jus cogens*.

In the same vein, such normative dominance enabled the ECJ to refuse to treat reservation clauses, enshrined in above-analyzed Articles 297 and 307 of the EC Treaty, as a source of UN supremacy,[110] as they cannot permit

[106] For a robust analysis of such approaches to international law and governance, see de Búrca, above (n 94) 26–40.

[107] *Ibid*.

[108] Y Shany, *The Competing Jurisdictions of International Courts and Tribunals* (Oxford, Oxford University Press, 2003) 108–21.

[109] Broude and Shany, 'The International Law and Policy of Multi-Sourced Equivalent Norms', above (n 4) p 13–14.

[110] See *Kadi* judgment, above (n 11) paras 301–04: The ECJ acknowledged that art 307 EC allows derogations from primary EC law, while art 297 EC implicitly permits obstacles to the operation of the Common Market when they are caused by measures taken by a Member State to carry out the international obligations it has accepted for the purpose of maintaining international peace and security. Yet the Court stressed that these provisions cannot authorize derogations from the principles of liberty, democracy and respect for human rights enshrined in art 6(1) TEU as a foundation of the Union, nor do they restrict the review by the Community judicature of the lawfulness of Community measures as regards their consistency with those fundamental rights.

derogations from the 'very foundations' of the EC legal order, which are enshrined in Article 6 of the EU Treaty, including human rights protection.[111]

Is this judicial choice defendable? It is submitted that it is. First, it is consistent with the ECJ's traditional approach, according to which internal coherence is perceived as a fundamental (albeit not absolute) value.[112] The ECJ has always seen itself as the 'gate-keeper' of the essentially dualist EU legal order,[113] determining in each legal scenario and according to internal EC norms whether and to what extent international and regional law should be permitted to enter through its gates. That self-proclaimed role was epitomised by leading cases such as Opinion 1/91[114] (legality of the original EEA Agreement) and C-149//96 *Portugal v Council*[115] (in the GATT/WTO context). In these cases and others, the 'gate-keeper' was willing to declare the importance of complying with international law and to display a welcoming approach towards effective multilateralism and external sources of law, including international law, as long as this was consistent with what it perceived to be in the EU interest.[116] However, when the external source of law was suspected of being detrimental to EU paramount interests, be they strategic, trade or economic, the ECJ has proved to be determined in keeping the external norm out. It must be stressed that the promotion of coherence carries with it an inherent value.[117]

Such a judicial approach, as Bertea demonstrates, may assist the judiciary in presenting the law as a meaningful whole, whose components are mutually supportive and independent rather than merely the result of the claims of an authority.[118] Legal reasoning based on coherence may assist the EU judiciary to make sense of the diversity of EU law,[119] serving as a regulative criterion of judicial argumentation.[120]

[111] *Kadi* judgment, *ibid*, 301–04.

[112] S Bertea, 'Looking for Coherence within the European Community' (2005) 11 *European Law Journal* 154, at 164–70: The ECJ advances constitutive and normative coherence, using coherence as a criterion of correctness (a standard for assessing possible alternative solutions).

[113] For dualism under international law, see G de Búrca and O Gerstenberg, 'The Decentralization of International Law' (2005) 47 *Harvard International Law Journal* 243.

[114] Opinion 1/91, above (n 72).

[115] C-149/96 *Portugal v Council* [1999] ECR I-8395.

[116] For analysis, see C Kaddous 'Effects of International Agreements in the EU Legal Order' in M Cremona and B de Witte (eds), *EU Foreign Relations Law: Constitutional Fundamentals* (Oxford, Hart Publishing, 2008) 291.

[117] For a critical analysis of the role of coherence, see J Raz, 'The Relevance of Coherence' in J Raz, *Ethics in the Public Domain, Essays in the Morality of Law and Politics* (Oxford, Clarendon Press, 1994) 277.

[118] Bertea, above (n 112) 157.

[119] LM Soriano, 'A Modest Notion of Coherence in Legal Reasoning: A Model for the European Court of Justice' (2003) 16 *Ratio Juris* 296, at 302, as quoted in Bertea, *ibid*, 158. But see Raz, above (n 117): The law does not make up a 'coherent rational system' but rather a 'higgledy-piggledy assemblage of the remains of contradictory past political ambitions and beliefs'.

[120] Bertea, *ibid*, 154–55.

A third explanation for the ECJ's choice relates to the fact that the coherence advanced by the ECJ carries with it a special value within the specific EU context. As analyzed by Bertea, the EC normative order is viewed as an outgrowth of national systems, while the Community is a network of local, national and supranational systems with a plurality of sovereign powers that coexist and interact with each other.[121] Internal coherence may promote internal integrity and such enhanced integrity can be instrumental, in turn, in promoting European unity and integration: 'Coherence and integration therefore get connected by way of integrity: to the extent that we bring coherence into operation in Community law, we promote a full-fledged integration . . . within the Community system'.[122]

Fourthly, the promotion of internal, European coherence at the expense of external, global coherence may be accounted for by the fact that the EU and the UN have different *raisons d'être*, constituencies and political agendas. According to Simma and Pulkowski, a particularistic approach focuses on the particular political purposes, the tailor-made character of the legal rules and the legal culture corresponding to the particular politics of the system.[123] This perception is applicable to this MSENs scenario. The EU is a regional entity, aimed at promoting high standards of European socio-political and economic integration, while the UN is a global entity focused on the maintenance of international peace and security. The EU is based on civic and democratic values, while the UN is based on a security ethos. The EU serves a European democratic constituency, while the UN serves a global, partially non-democratic constituency. In this state of affairs, it may be argued that it is only natural that the ECJ would prefer internal rather than external coherence, thereby reflecting the structural, cultural and ethical differences between the EU regime and the UN regime. As AG Maduro postulated in his Opinion, 'Respect for other institutions is meaningful only if it can be built on a shared understanding of these [fundamental] values and on a mutual commitment to protect them'.[124]

This perception is supported by sociological analysis of international law.[125] As argued by Hirsch,[126] the degree of socio-cultural distance (or proximity) between two legal orders may determine the willingness (or unwillingness) of the two to interact with each other in a mutually complementary manner. Hirsch's work focuses on the interface between international investment

[121] *Ibid*, 155.
[122] *Ibid*, 170.
[123] Simma and Pulkowski, above (n 1) 504–05.
[124] Opinion of AG Maduro, above (n 10) para 44.
[125] M Hirsch, 'The Sociology of International Law' (2005) 55 *University of Toronto Law Journal* 891.
[126] M Hirsch,'The Interaction between International Investment Law and Human Rights Treaties: A Sociological Perspective' in Broude and Shany (eds), *Multi-Sourced Equivalent Norms in International Law*, above (n 4) p 211.

law and international human rights,[127] but his findings are relevant, even *a fortiori*, to the interface between the EU and the UN.

The fifth justification for the ECJ's preference for a self-contained, dominant model relates to the process of constitutionalization of external relations. The phenomenon of multilevel governance might undermine the ability of the nation state to guarantee human rights.[128] That risk increases the need for heavier reliance, in the international context, on numerous constitutional criteria, including transparency, democratic control, legitimacy, rule of law and judicial protection of human rights.[129]

The need for constitutional restraints is especially relevant with respect to the UN SC. Traditionally the SC has dealt with classical intergovernmental, diplomatic-political issues pertaining to peace enforcement and war prevention, being expected to 'keep the peace and not to change the world order'.[130] As of the early 1990s, the SC's role has been expanding, as manifested in a significant increase in its activity and in the visionary manner in which its powers have been employed.[131] The move from pursuing measures against states to adopting smart sanctions is one manifestation of such a change.[132] By adopting smart sanctions, the SC is in fact acting as a quasi-legislature, judiciary and executive,[133] in a legal environment that does not have a comprehensive system of separation of powers and checks and balances.[134] This state of affairs places the SC in a position in which it may impinge on individuals' human rights, and contrary to the sanctions aimed at states, the targeted individuals are not adequately represented in the process.[135]

Admittedly, the SC reiterated its commitment to preserve international law, in general, and international human rights, in particular, in the adoption and implementation of its sanctions regime.[136] The problem remains

[127] M Hirsch, 'Interactions between Investment and Non-Investment Obligations in International Investment Law' in P Muchlinski, F Ortino and C Schreuer (eds), *The Oxford Handbook of International Law on Foreign Investment* (Oxford, Oxford University Press, 2008) 262.

[128] Wessel and Wouters, above (n 1) 32–35.

[129] *Ibid*, 47.

[130] ICJ's Advisory Opinion on the *Legal Consequences for States of the Continued Presence of South Africa in Namibia* (South West Africa), [1971] ICJ Rep 291 at 294, para 115 (Fitzmaurice, Dissenting Opinion).

[131] Martinez, above (n 15) 333–44.

[132] For general analysis, see *ibid*, 340–44, for the legislative nature of some of the Security Council Resolutions.

[133] Bianchi, 'Assessing the Effectiveness of the UN Security Council's Anti-Terrorism Measures', above (n 12) 883 and 906; Cameron, above (n 12) 8; Martinez, above (n 15) 344.

[134] See the Appeals Chamber of the ICTY in *Prosecutor v Tadić* (Jurisdiction) ICTY-94-1, 2 October 1995 at para 43, as analyzed by Bianchi, 'Assessing the Effectiveness of the UN Security Council's Anti-Terrorism Measures', *ibid*, 910.

[135] See MG Ketvel, 'The Jurisdiction of the European Court of Justice in Respect of the Common Foreign and Security Policy' (2006) 55 *International and Comparative Law Quarterly* 77, 108.

[136] For analysis, see Eckes, above (n 12) 89 and Bianchi, 'Assessing the Effectiveness of the UN Security Council's Anti-Terrorism Measures', above (n 12) 904.

that the UN sanctions regime is highly injurious to the human rights of those appearing in the Consolidated List,[137] and that that regime does not provide for any meaningful venue for (administrative or judicial) review.[138] This is particularly problematic given the fact that the Sanctions Committee is an intergovernmental, diplomatic-political body. Nor can applicants expect to obtain comprehensive review in the ECHR legal order[139] or in their national courts, in particular in the courts of the EU Member States.[140] Consequently, judicial scrutiny of the EC-UN sanctions regime, which could have served as a powerful, mitigating instrument of the SC's expanding role, remains 'episodic'.[141]

This state of affairs is highly problematic when examined through the prism of the rule of law.[142] Neither the UN Sanctions Committee nor the EC should be seen as *legibus solutus*. As Judge Jennings of the ICJ noted:

> [A]ll discretionary powers of lawful decision-making are necessarily derived from the law, and are therefore governed and qualified by the law . . . It is not logically possible to claim to represent the power and authority of the law, and at the same time, claim to be above the law.[143]

The CFI attempted to ameliorate the situation by providing indirect judicial review according to the benchmark of *jus cogens* norms. Yet, this solution is 'devoid of any actual substance',[144] because there are very few *jus cogens* rules and their content and scope are ambiguous and narrow.[145] This state of affairs is all the more peculiar in light of the Treaty of Lisbon[146] and given the fact that it was the EU which was the first international organization to treat international relations and international organizations with advanced

[137] Almqvist, above (n 19) especially 310 ff; Cameron, above (n 12) 6; Guild, above (n 12); Bianchi, *ibid*, 903 ff; Defeis, above (n 12).

[138] For extensive analysis, see van den Herik, above (n 36) 799 ff; Tomuschat, above (n 12) 538; Almqvist, *ibid*, 309; Nettesheim, above (n 12) 568.

[139] For analysis, see Lavranos, 'Judicial Review of UN Sanctions by the Court of First Instance', above (n 12) 484.

[140] For extensive analysis, see Bianchi, 'Assessing the Effectiveness of the UN Security Council's Anti-Terrorism Measures', above (n 12) 913–14; Vleck, above (n 12) 498; Eckes, above (n 12) 87; Ketvel, above (n 135) 112–13; Lavranos, *ibid*, 476 and 489.

[141] For analysis, see Bianchi, *ibid*.

[142] Bianchi, *ibid*, 885; P Eeckhout, *External Relations of the European Union: Legal and Constitutional Foundations* (Oxford, Oxford University Press, 2004) 464.

[143] In Questions of Interpretation and Application of the 1971 Montreal Convention arising from the Aerial Incident at Lockerbie *Libyan Arab Jamahiriya v United Kingdom* [1998] ICJ Rep 99, at 110 (Jennings, Dissenting Opinion).

[144] Tomuschat, above (n 12) 551.

[145] For analysis, see Tomuschat, *ibid*, 551; Cameron, above (n 12) 25; Almqvist, above (n 19) 321.

[146] The Lisbon Treaty (Treaty of Lisbon amending the Treaty on European Union and the Treaty establishing the European Community, 13 December 2007 [2007] OJ C306/50) subjects 'pure' second pillar CFSP actions to judiciary review, while ascribing legal force to the EU Charter of Fundamental Rights and providing the legal basis for the accession of the EU to the ECHR.

constitutional tools.[147] The comprehensive judicial review offered by the ECJ, based on a constitutional criterion, ameliorates that state of affairs, thereby addressing in a more satisfactory manner the expansion of SC competencies and the corollary risk for human rights.

In sum, the ECJ's choice of a self-contained, dominant model is well founded for the five reasons analyzed above. However, such a choice has some important drawbacks. First, some argue that the European integration has not yet reached such an advanced stage as to warrant its classification as a self-contained regime.[148]

Secondly, and as argued by Simma and Pulkowski, the notion of self-contained regimes cannot justify the existence of entirely autonomous sub-systems.[149] The perception of sub-systems of international law co-existing in isolation from the remaining bulk of international law is inconceivable.[150] In the words of the chairman of the ILC's Study Group on Fragmentation of International Law, 'no treaty, however special its subject-matter or limited the number of its parties, applies in a normative vacuum'.[151] The dominant model adopted by the ECJ towards the UN is likely, however, to minimize the interaction of the norm-applying body (in our case the EU) with external sources of law and law-making institutions (in our case UN law, international law and the UN itself),[152] thereby promoting global mistrust and suspicion and creating a 'mosaic' of different legal standards. This outcome is especially problematic in relation to the UN SC, given the veto power held by two EU countries in the SC.

Moreover, it may be argued that the dominant model required the pursuance of an indirect review of UN SC Resolutions, and such review may result in inconsistent interpretations of SC norms and in conflicting normative findings. Such a result might carry negative implications for the UN order in terms of legitimacy, coherency, uniformity and unity,[153] thereby undermining its primary authority to safeguard international peace and security.[154] If this is so, then it may be argued that the integrative model would have been a better choice than that of the dominant model chosen

[147] Wessel and Wouters, above (n 1) 33.

[148] Simma and Pulkowski, above (n 1) 519.

[149] *Ibid*, 492.

[150] *Ibid*.

[151] M Koskenniemi, quoted in Simma and Pulkowski, above (n 1) 492. See also Special Rapporteur James Crawford who took cognizance of the 'presumption against the creation of wholly self-contained regimes' in the field of reparation, J Crawford, 'Third Report on State Responsibility' (2000) UN Doc A/CN.4/507, para 147.

[152] Broude and Shany, 'The International Law and Policy of Multi-Sourced Equivalent Norms', above (n 4) p 13–14.

[153] For analysis, see Bianchi, 'Assessing the Effectiveness of the UN Security Council's Anti-Terrorism Measures', above (n 12) 914.

[154] Bulterman, above (n 12) 768. For analysis and rebuttal of this argument, see Bianchi, *ibid*, 896. See also the Third Report of the Analytical Support and Sanctions Monitoring Team Appointed Pursuant to Resolution 1526 (2004) 'Concerning Al Qaida and the Taliban and Associated Individuals and Entities' (9 September 2005) UN Doc S/2005/572, para 48.

by the ECJ. According to Bianchi, rather than focusing on the hierarchical superiority of the rule and its mechanical application, attention should be paid to implementing effectively its underlying values, duly taking context into account

> [a] presumption of consistency . . . with human rights obligations, and . . . all the more so with regard to peremptory norms, seems a perfectly viable interpretive tool to guarantee the required degree of consistency of SC resolutions with the international legal order. States therefore, should interpret their obligations under relevant SC resolutions consistently with their other obligations under international law, particularly those that are concerned with fundamental human rights.[155]

Fourthly, and as demonstrated by Broude,[156] the choice of the regulatory model may carry important implications for the allocation of jurisdictional-authority. According to him, normative integration and authority integration, like norm fragmentation and authority fragmentation, are two sides of the same coin, the two maintaining correlative relationship, each one producing and feeding on the other.[157] Greater normative coherence might therefore produce enhanced centralization and harmonization of authority and vice versa.[158] In our case, the normative choice of the ECJ may lead to a shift from a potential (albeit unlikely) judicial treatment of SC Resolutions by the ICJ or, more likely, by the UN Sanctions Committee,[159] to judicial review to be conducted in the ECJ and to the domestic courts of the EU Member States.

The fifth drawback of the ECJ's choice is that the dominant model cannot be perfectly reconciled with the EU's attempts, analyzed elsewhere, to enhance its external political actorness in international security matters, in general, and its role in the UN arena, in particular.[160] de Búrca went as far as to argue that such an approach would adversely affect the EU's ability to serve as a Normative Power.[161] Finally, the self-contained approach displayed by the ECJ towards the UN legal order is not consistent with its treatment of the ECHR human rights order, a theme to be explored below.

[155] Bianchi, 'Human Rights and the Magic of Jus Cogens', above (n 12) 504 and Bianchi, 'Assessing the Effectiveness of the UN Security Council's Anti-Terrorism Measure', above (n 12) 916–17.

[156] Broude, 'Fragmentation(s) of International Law' above (n 1).

[157] *Ibid*, 104–10.

[158] *Ibid*.

[159] CFI rulings in *Kadi*, above (n 11) para 289.

[160] See C Beyer, 'The European Union as a Security Policy Actor: The Case of Counterterrorism' (2008) 13 *European Foreign Affairs Review* 293.

[161] See de Búrca, above (n 94) 3.

VI EU LAW VIS-À-VIS THE ECHR: THE INTEGRATIVE MODEL?

As analyzed above, a normative overlap and conflict exist between the EU substantive legal provisions (ie, the anti-terror provisions) and the procedural guarantees offered by these provisions, and the procedural, due process guarantees enshrined in the ECHR. How was this legal state of affairs regulated by the EU judiciary?

A The Traditional Approach

The interface between the ECJ and the ECHR is complex.[162] Suffice to note the following: since the first specific references by the ECJ to the ECHR (*Nold* (1973)),[163] the ECJ has referred to the ECHR and to the jurisprudence of the ECHR Court in a growing number of cases,[164] ascribing to it 'special significance'.[165] Such reliance has proved to be more extensive, quantitatively and qualitatively, than its reliance on the case law of any other national or international (human rights or any other) legal regime or tribunal,[166] including that of the ICJ and the WTO Appellate Body.[167] Such reliance is characterized by a deferential approach, with which the ECJ follows the judgments of the Strasbourg Court in most relevant cases.[168] Yet, this relationship is by no means one-directional. The EC and the ECHR judicatures have in recent years displayed a growing interest in and reliance on each other's jurisprudence, leading prominent scholars to refer to their relations as 'cross-fertilization',[169] and 'mutual comity at the level of persuasion, if not at the level of authority'.[170]

The ECJ has always been resolute, however, in dismissing the argument that the ECHR may impose duties on the EC institutions, or that the inter-

[162] For analysis, see Douglas-Scott, above n 45; G Harpaz, 'The European Court of Justice and its Relations with the European Court of Human Rights: the Quest for Enhanced Reliance, Coherence and Legitimacy' (2009) 46 *Common Market Law Review* 105.

[163] Case 4/73 *Nold v Commission* [1974] ECR 491.

[164] For extensive analysis of the ECJ references to the Strasbourg jurisprudence and references to these cases, see Douglas-Scott, above (n 45).

[165] See, eg, Cases 46/87 and 222/88 *Hoechst AG v Commission of the European Communities* [1989] ECR 2859, para 13. For analysis of the chronology of the ECJ's 'gradual rapprochement' towards the Strasbourg Court, see A Rosas, 'Fundamental Rights in the Luxembourg and Strasbourg Courts' in C Baudenbacher, P Tresselt and T Orlygsson (eds), *The EFTA Court: Ten Years On* (Oxford, Hart Publishing, 2005) 163, 168–69.

[166] See Douglas-Scott, above (n 45) 650.

[167] G Jacobs, 'Judicial Dialogue and the Cross-Fertilization of Legal Systems: The European Court of Justice' (2003) 38 *Texas International Law Journal* 547, at 556.

[168] Douglas-Scott, above (n 45).

[169] Jacobs, above (n 167) 556.

[170] See, eg, C Lebeck, 'The European Court of Human Rights on the Relation between ECHR and EC law: The Limits of Constitutionalisation of Public International Law' (2007) 62 *ZÖR* 195, at 213; Costello, above (n 45).

pretations offered by the Strasbourg Court to the ECHR are binding on it.[171] Instead, it insists that it is free to offer its own, divergent jurisprudence of EU law,[172] and there are indeed a few cases in which the ECJ has departed from the verdicts of the Strasbourg Court.[173] This state of affairs led Weiler to conclude that it is unlikely that the ECJ will in substance allow a Community measure to violate a provision of the ECHR, yet at the same time it insists, for jurisdictional purposes, on interpreting the various human rights provisions in its own way.[174]

The precise formal legal force of the ECHR within the EU remains therefore not entirely unequivocal.[175] It would still be safe to argue that the EU is under a quasi-obligation to follow the ECHR and that that obligation is reinforced by the above-cited Article 6(2) TEU.

B The CFI Verdict and the ECJ Judgment

The proceedings before the CFI and the ECJ in the *Kadi* dispute serve as a vivid example of the traditional approach towards the ECHR. The parties,[176] Maduro,[177] the CFI[178] and the ECJ all relied extensively on the ECHR and its case law. The ECJ, in particular, referred to it to substantiate its findings regarding the appropriate scope of judicial review of UN sanctions and of domestic implementing measures.[179] It also held that in protecting human rights it draws inspiration from guidelines supplied by the ECHR, which has 'special significance' within the EC legal order.[180] The ECJ referred to the ECHR and to the Strasbourg case law in order to address allegations of infringements of the right to effective judicial protection[181] and of the right to property,[182] and in order to determine the legitimate limitations that can be placed on the right of effective judicial

[171] For support, see, eg, Lebeck, *ibid*, 207.

[172] Wetzel, above (n 35) 2839.

[173] See D Spielmann, 'Human Rights Case Law in the Strasbourg and Luxembourg Courts – Conflicts, Inconsistencies, and Complementarities' in *The EU and Human Rights*, above (n 71) 757, 764–66 for an analysis of cases in which the ECJ has either ignored human rights issues, ignored the Strasbourg Regime and/or the jurisprudence of the Strasbourg Court or ruled differently or even in conflict with that jurisprudence.

[174] For analysis, see JHH Weiler, 'Eurocracy and Distrust: Some Questions Concerning the Role of the European Court of Justice in the Protection of Fundamental Human Rights within the Legal Order of the European Communities' (1986) 61 *Washington Law Review* 1103, at 1126.

[175] For analysis see, eg, Lebeck, above (n 170) 207.

[176] See, eg, the arguments of *Kadi* according to which the re-examination procedure before the UN Sanctions Committee, based on diplomatic protection, does not afford protection of human rights equivalent to that guaranteed by the ECHR as construed by the case law cited.

[177] See the Opinion of AG Maduro, above (n 10) especially paras 36–37.

[178] See in particular the CFI ruling in *Kadi*, above (n 11) paras 210, 234 and 287.

[179] *Kadi* judgment, above (n 11) paras 310–14.

[180] *Ibid*, para 283.

[181] *Ibid*, para 335.

[182] *Ibid*, para 356.

protection[183] and on the right of property.[184] In the latter context it explicitly relied on the ECHR jurisprudence and on its principle of margin of appreciation in holding that the EC has wide discretion in choosing the means by which it would limit the right of property for the sake of advancing public interest.[185] Thus, the *Kadi* proceedings illustrate the ECJ's deferential approach, by which the EU judiciary relies on ECHR provisions and follows the judgments of the Strasbourg Court.[186] Nonetheless, the ECJ stressed that it is not bound by an interpretation offered by the Strasbourg Court to the ECHR, but that is free to offer its own, divergent jurisprudence of EU law, and it reiterated the fundamental, inherent differences between the two regimes.[187]

C Analysis

The overall, albeit non-unqualified, openness to the ECHR in the *Kadi* proceedings, may be characterized as a pluralistic approach, which views the EC legal order as forming part of a broader model of open networks that cooperate *inter se* in the mutual application and execution of their respective legal acts.[188] How should we then categorize that approach according to the MSENs typology identified above? That approach cannot be classified as belonging to the dominant regime model, as neither the CFI nor the ECJ asserted that the EU legal order carries more weight than that of the ECHR or vice versa. Nor can that approach be regarded as opting for the cumulative model because the EC courts did not find, at least explicitly, the EU human rights norms and the norms of the ECHR to be simultaneously binding and applicable.

Instead, and at face value, the approach can be classified as belonging to the contesting model. This is so because the EC judiciary did not recognize the legal issues in hand to be governed by overlapping norms of both the EU and the ECHR. Put differently, the EC judiciary contested the very existence of a MSENs scenario. It therefore did not explicitly refer to the possibility that it would act inconsistently with the ECHR and that the explicit conduct would be in breach of the above-quoted Article 6 TEU. Likewise, it did not refer to the possibility recognized by the ECHR Court

[183] *Ibid*, para 344.

[184] *Ibid*, paras 360, 363 and 368.

[185] *Ibid*.

[186] See Douglas-Scott, above (n 45) 650.

[187] *Kadi* judgment, above (n 11) paras 315–16: 'the question of the Court's jurisdiction to rule on the lawfulness of the contested regulation has arisen in fundamentally different circumstances . . . the review by the Court of the validity of any Community measure in the light of fundamental rights must be considered to be the expression, in a community based on the rule of law, of a constitutional guarantee stemming from the EC Treaty as an autonomous legal system which is not to be prejudiced by an international agreement'.

[188] Nettesheim, above (n 12) 580–81.

in the *Bosphorus* case that the EU's failure to provide adequate judicial protection might expose EU Member States to an ECHR infringement *qua* ECHR Contracting Parties. Instead, it reviewed the EC sanctions regime according to one legal benchmark, namely its own General Principles.

However, a more careful examination of the CFI verdict and the ECJ judgment might reveal that, de facto, the approach adopted by the EC courts towards the EU-ECHR interface resembles the integrative model more than that of the contesting model. As stated above, the integrative model construes the relevant MSENs in light of the parallel norms emanating from other branches of international law, seeking to harmonize, through interpretative means, the relevant norms (in our case EU's General Principle of human rights protection and the relevant provisions of the ECHR) and the relevant human rights regimes (in our case the EU and the ECHR regimes). It may be argued that this is precisely what the EC courts did when they placed heavy reliance on the ECHR and the Strasbourg Court's jurisprudence.

How can one explain the ECJ's choice with regard to the interface between the EU legal order and the ECHR order, as evident in the *Kadi* judgment? The first explanation is that such an approach is consistent with the above-analyzed traditional, deferential approach towards the ECHR. The second explanation relates to the intrinsic value of coherence. An attempt was made supra to analyze that value in the internal EU context. That value is also applicable in the inter-Community context. The EU legal order would benefit if it were generally consistent with international law, a verity that is acknowledged by the ECJ itself,[189] and is advanced by Teitel and Howse, according to which tribunals have always resisted 'collapse into or subordination to the outside, but always maintaining a dynamic engagement through interpretation'.[190]

The third explanation for the welcoming approach towards the ECHR relates to the degree of commonality between the distinct normative regimes, constituencies, institutional contexts and political agendas that surrounded the EU-ECHR MSENs scenario. Thus, the contrast between the approach displayed by the ECJ towards the UN and its approach towards the ECHR can be explained by the lack of normative commonality between the EU's advanced human rights protection and the embryonic protection granted to human rights within the global, UN legal order and the normative human rights commonality between the EU and the ECHR.

Contrary to the first interface which is characterized by different raisons d'être, different constituencies and different political agendas, the EU and the ECHR share a non-insignificant degree of normative, social and

[189] Bertea, above (n 112) 168.

[190] R Teitel and R Howse, 'Cross Judging: Tribunalization in a Fragmented but Interconnected Global Order', (2009) 41 *New York University Journal of International Law and Politics* 959, 968.

constitutional commonality and similarities regarding their constituencies.[191] These similarities manifest, according to Weiler, a considerable common cultural affinity among the European peoples, one which supports further supranational adjudication in the field of human rights.[192]

That commonality which I analyzed elsewhere[193] should (and actually did) influence the ECJ in *Kadi*, treating the Treaty-based EU-ECHR interface not along self-contained lines, but rather in a mutually complementary manner.[194] As Helfer and Slaughter concluded in their seminal work on effective supranational adjudication:

> The nations of Western Europe that form the core of the European Union and the Council of Europe are established liberal democracies with strong domestic traditions of the rule of law. They also share a common core of social, political, and legal values . . .. the collective European experience of supranational adjudication is greater than the sum of its parts. The ECJ and the ECHR have become part of a larger European 'community of law': a network of legal actors self-consciously interacting with one another on the basis of both self-interest and shared values in a nominally apolitical context.[195]

This is precisely what the ECJ did in *the Kadi* judgment and should be applauded for doing so. The dialogue conducted with the ECHR regime may assist the EU in building bridges between itself and the ECHR human rights order, thereby bolstering their normative-constitutional commonality, contributing to pan-European normative, socio-political integration based on such societal consensus of Europe's 'community of values'.

It must be added that this approach is consistent with the manner in which the EU and the European Free Trade Association (EFTA) interact under the aegis of the European Economic Area.[196] Thus, European normative commonality (be it in the sphere of trade or human rights) promotes an integrative, pluralistic approach on the part of the ECJ.[197]

It must, however, be stressed that the EU and the ECHR share common but not identical normative apparatuses and features, a fact that

[191] For analysis, see Harpaz, 'The European Court of Justice and its Relations with the European Court of Human Rights', above (n 162).

[192] See JHH Weiler, 'Fundamental Rights and Fundamental Boundaries: On Standards and Values in the Protection of Human Rights' in P Alston (ed), *The European Union and Human Rights*, above (n 71) 51, 74.

[193] For analysis, see Harpaz, 'The European Court of Justice and its Relations with the European Court of Human Rights', above (n 162).

[194] Costello, above (n 45).

[195] Helfer and Slaughter, above (n 72) 276, 298.

[196] As demonstrated by Pirker in his contribution to this monograph, the very high degree of (economic) commonality between the two may accommodate similar if not identical judicial interpretation, based on meaningful dialogue and mutual reliance between the ECJ and the EFTA Court: B Pirker, 'Interpreting Multi-Sourced Equivalent Norms: Judicial Borrowing in International Courts' in Broude and Shany (eds), *Multi-Sourced Equivalent Norms in International Law*, above (n 4) p 93.

[197] For support, see Jacobs, above (n 167) 552. It must be remembered, however, that the EEA was designed to provide for a common EU-EFTA homogeneous economic regime.

was acknowledged by the ECJ judgment itself.[198] Yet such differences should not be (and were not) used to shield the EU from the influence of the ECHR. After all, the spirit of human rights may transcend different regional instruments.[199] In placing heavy reliance on the ECHR while basing the judgment on internal Community norms, the ECJ was successful in advancing a more pluralistic regime, while safeguarding its own autonomous nature, thereby meeting the challenge described by Craven in *Unity, Diversity and the Fragmentation of International Law* as being 'simultaneously homogeneous and heterogeneous, unified but multi-polar'.[200]

The fourth explanation for the ECJ's choice of the integrative model relates to human rights protection. As I demonstrated elsewhere in greater detail,[201] such a choice may bolster human rights protection within the EU.[202] The EU (pre-Lisbon Treaty) human rights regime was criticised for lack of comprehensiveness, specificity, visibility and sophistication,[203] and for being founded in most instances on lower standards of protection than those of the ECHR and of some of the EU Member States' constitutions.[204] The ECHR regime may provide the EU with an advanced regime with which it can address the weaknesses of its own human rights policy and jurisprudence. It may improve the specificity,[205] visibility,[206] clarity and comprehensiveness[207] of EU human rights protection, thereby advancing the integrity of a European human rights regime.[208] The fifth explanation for the choice of the integrative model is that such a choice may assist EU Member States in not infringing the ECHR obligations *qua* EU members.[209]

The sixth explanation relates to the future of the European integration project. This project is the focus of a soul-searching exercise, seeking its own *raison d'être*, vision, inspiration, cohesive identity and legitimacy,

[198] The *Kadi* judgment, above (n 11) paras 315–16.

[199] Simma and Pulkowski, above (n 1) 524.

[200] M Craven, 'Unity, Diversity and the Fragmentation of International Law' (2003) XIV *Finnish Yearbook of International Law* 3, at 12.

[201] Harpaz, 'The European Court of Justice and its Relations with the European Court of Human Rights', above (n 162).

[202] See Wetzel, above (n 35) 2846.

[203] For support, see Douglas-Scott, above (n 45) 630.

[204] See de Witte, above (n 71) 878.

[205] For support, see Lebeck, above (n 170) 233.

[206] For support, see A von Bogdandy, 'The European Union as a Human Rights Organisation? Human Rights and the Core of the European Union' (2000) 37 *Common Market Law Review* 1307, at 1331.

[207] Alston and Weiler, 'An "Ever Closer Union" in Need of a Human Rights Policy' in P Alston (ed), *The EU and Human Rights*, above (n 71).

[208] Wetzel, above (n 35) 2846. Yet, the ECHR does not always provide higher standards of human rights protection than the standards afforded by the EU legal order, see Case C-145/04 *Spain v United Kingdom* [2006] ECR I-917 judgment of the Grand Chamber of 12 September 2006 and Case C-300/04 *Eman and Sevinger* [2006] ECR I-8055 judgment of the Grand Chamber of 12 September 2006 as analyzed by LFM Besselink in (2008) 45 *Common Market Law Review* 787.

[209] See below, section VII.

both internal and external. The sphere of human rights might be helpful in that respect. The search conducted by the EU's political organs for common values, for a normative, civilian force and for a cohesive identity may be supported by formulating common European human rights standards, and such standards may be best attained by extensive reciprocal judicial reliance by the EU and ECHR regimes.[210] The *Kadi* judgment must be seen in this context as a modest step in the right direction.

VII EU LAW VIS-À-VIS THE LEGAL ORDERS OF MEMBER STATES: THE CONTESTING MODEL?

As stated above, the inadequate human rights protection provided by the EC might have been in conflict with human rights guarantees provided by the Member States' respective constitutions. Moreover, all EU Member States are UN Members as well as Contracting Parties to the ECHR. They must therefore comply with their UN obligations and do so in accordance with their human rights and ECHR obligations. The EC Anti-Terror Regulation, which is directly applicable in their domestic legal orders, might therefore expose them to breaches under both UN law and the ECHR. The ECJ did not refer to the possibility, nor to the eventuality that the EU's sanctions regime, with its inadequate human rights protection, might be in conflict with the Member States' constitutional orders (as they pertain to due process guarantees).

In ignoring these potential conflicts the ECJ adopted, albeit implicitly, the contesting model, not acknowledging the very existence of a MSENs scenario between EU regime/norms and its Member States' regimes/norms. This regulatory choice can be explained by the ECJ's traditional and well-entrenched dominant model pertaining to MSENs situation between the EU and its Member States. Put differently, the concern that the Member States might breach their EU obligations takes precedence over the concern that they might breach their UN/ECHR obligations. Thus, the former concern negated the potential ECJ debate about the latter.

A reservation is in order, however, regarding that proposed regulatory classification. The pursuance of judicial review of the EC implementing measures and their interpretation in light of ECHR jurisprudence can assist the EU Members in meeting their ECHR obligations. Such judicial approach provides an ECHR-equivalent protection of human rights, thereby reducing the likelihood of their being held responsible for infringing ECHR obligations in their capacity as EU/ECHR Member States. It may be argued that the ECJ's attempt to reconcile EU norms with ECHR norms (the integrative model analyzed in the previous section) was designed to

[210] For support see Weiler, above (n 174) 1108.

reconcile the legal orders of the Member States with the ECHR. In such a case the treatment of the MSENs scenario between the EU and the Member States should in fact be classified as an integrative model and not as a contesting model.

VIII COMMON UNIFYING FEATURES

The analysis conducted above reveals that the ECJ adopted three different regulatory models, adopting a dominant model towards international law/UN law, a more deferential, integrative model towards the ECHR and a contesting model towards the legal orders of the Member States. This section attempts to distil from these three regulatory choices unifying features.

A Internalizing the MSENs Conflicts

The first common feature relates to the ECJ's attempt to avoid any direct conflict between EU norms and non-EU norms, internalizing (or 'communalizing') the MSENs scenario in hand. With respect to the EU-UN law normative overlap, the CFI subjected the former to the latter, placing heavy emphasis on public international law. The ECJ could have followed the same judicial approach. It could have dealt with this situation as a conflict between EU (due process) law and UN (anti-terror) law, it could have addressed the issue as an overlap between EU (anti-terror) law and international (due process) law and it could, as did the CFI, treat it as a potential conflict between EU (substantive, anti-terror) law and *jus cogens* (substantive and procedural human rights) norms. Yet, the ECJ chose a different judicial path. By and large, it dealt with the situation as if it were an internal, EU normative conflict between the EC anti-terror regime and the EU General Principle of Human Rights, due process, protection.[211]

The reasons for the ECJ's classification are evident. By internalizing the normative conflict, the ECJ avoided any direct confrontation between the EU and UN legal orders, pre-empting any criticism that its judicial review amounts to EU normative and jurisdictional imperialism or disrespect for the SC's prerogatives. In the words of the ECJ 'any judgment given by the Community judicature deciding that a Community measure intended to give effect to such a resolution is contrary to a higher rule of law in the Community legal order would not entail any challenge to the primacy of that resolution in international law'.[212]

[211] *Kadi* judgment, above (n 11) paras 327–29.
[212] *Ibid*, para 288.

The fact remains, however, that, in substance, the conflict was between the UN sanctions regime and EU General Principle of Human Rights protection, given the fact that the EC contested Regulation was a 'cut and paste' version of the UN sanctions regime. Thus, by conducting full and comprehensive review of the EC contested Regulation, the ECJ de facto pursued, albeit indirectly, a review of Chapter VII SC Resolutions, dismissing its supremacy in regard to a creature of international law, namely the EC.

With respect to the EU-ECHR MSENs scenario, the ECJ could have dealt with this situation as an overlap between its anti-terror sanctions regime and the ECHR, due process provisions. As stated above, such an overlap reveals a prima facie conflict between those two and that conflict is legally problematic given the fact that Article 6(2) TEU provides that 'The Union shall respect fundamental rights, as guaranteed by the European Convention for the Protection of Human Rights and Fundamental Freedoms'. The ECJ could have been expected to address that issue. It did not. It simply ignored it and adopted instead a different judicial strategy, treating the ECHR as a significant, inspirational interpretive instrument aimed at assisting it to construe the EC sanctions regime. In pursuing that course of action the ECJ avoided a direct conflict between its own legal order and that of the ECHR.

In the same vein, the ECJ could have been expected to address the conflict between the EC implementing, anti-terror regime and the ECHR, due process obligations of the EU/ECHR Member States. As stated above, according to the ECHR Court's jurisprudence, ECHR Members who are also EU Member States may be held accountable for violating their ECHR obligation in implementing their EC obligations when the protection of ECHR rights under the implemented EC legal order is 'manifestly deficient'. Such an eventuality has in the past caught the attention of the EC judiciary.[213] Scholarship indicates that the EC sanctions regime is precisely the case of such a risk. The ECJ once again ignored, at least demonstrably, that possibility, avoiding yet again any external conflict between the EU legal order (and the orders of the Member States) with an external regional instrument, namely the ECHR.

B One 'Offensive' and Two 'Defensive' Solange Instruments

It may be argued that in adopting the three regulatory regimes analyzed above, the ECJ utilized, albeit implicitly, one 'offensive' and two 'defensive' Solange (or as-long-as) instruments. As to the offensive use, for the

[213] Opinion of AG Mengozzi, of 26 October, 2006 in Case C-354/04 *P Gestoras Pro Amnistía v Council and others*: www.eulaw.soton.ac.uk/elforum/Gestoras%20Pro%20Amnistia_Segi_Opinion_Mengozzi_26Oct06_355_04_damages_JHA_terrorism.pdf.

sake of coherence, legitimacy and effectiveness of the system, the optimal level at which the balance should be struck between effectively combating international terrorism and between the need to refrain from imposing disproportionate restrictions on the human rights of those suspected of supporting terrorism, is the multilateral, UN level.[214] As long, however, as the UN sanctions regime embodies a 'legal protection limbo' of human rights,[215] as it does to a large extent,[216] the second-best option, in the EU context, would be for the EC judicature to strike and safeguard that balance.[217] The CFI failed in that regard, ascribing excessive pride of place to the internationalist, security-laden approach.[218] The ECJ rectified that failure by subjecting the EC implementing measures of the UN sanctions regime to judicial review, albeit indirect.

That choice could be read as conveying an implicit message to the UN. As long as the UN would not satisfactorily address the issue of human rights, the EC judiciary would be forced to do so. If that assumption, which finds no explicit basis in the judgment, but is explicitly raised by the appellant himself,[219] is correct, then the ECJ would refrain from conducting indirect review of SC Resolutions, once the UN has reached that satisfactory level of human rights protection.

As to the first defensive use of the Solange instrument, while rendering its judgment, the ECJ was aware of the ECHR Court's jurisprudence under which the latter would (i) refrain from conducting indirect review of EC measures, as long as the EC afforded within its regime ECHR-equivalent human rights protection (such equivalence constituting a rebuttable presumption of conformity of the national measures designed to implement EC law with the ECHR), but would (ii) conduct such review if that protection is not afforded, leading to a 'manifestly deficient' EU protection.

Thus, in conducting judicial review of the EC sanctions regime with the solid backing of the ECHR jurisprudence, the ECJ could be seen as reassuring the ECHR Court that the EU accords ECHR-equivalent level of human rights protection and that the ECHR Court should therefore not conduct an indirect review of EC measures.

As to the second defensive use of the Solange instrument, according to the jurisprudence of the German Federal Constitutional Court, the respect for the EC General Principle of EC supremacy is conditioned on the EC's ability to provide within its legal order adequate protection to

[214] For support, see Cameron, above (n 12) 28; S Peers, 'Salvation Outside the Church: Judicial Protection in the Third Pillar after the Pupino and Segi Judgments' (2007) 44 *Common Market Law Review* 883, at 929; Tomuschat, above (n 12) 551–54.

[215] RA Wessel, 'Editorial – The UN, the EU and Jus Cogens' (2006) 3 *International Organizations Law Review* 5–6.

[216] Tomuschat, above (n 12) 551; Nettesheim, above (n 12) 592.

[217] For UN reform, see Martinez, above (n 15) 359.

[218] For support, see Tridimas and Gutierrez-Fons, above (n 11).

[219] As described in para 256 of the *Kadi* judgment, above (n 11).

human rights, equivalent to that granted under German constitutional law. Thus, the German legal order would be willing to accord EU human rights protection supremacy over and above the protection afforded by the German legal order, as long as the level of protection afforded by the EU is equivalent to that granted under German constitutional law but such supremacy will not be recognized if the EC fails to meet that standard.[220] Thus, by refraining from conducting judicial review of the EC implementing regime, the ECJ might have made 'kosher', in German eyes, a deficient EU human rights standard, exposing the EU legal order to normative and jurisdictional intrusion from Germany (and possibly from other Members in revolt). In conducting a 'full' judicial review of the EC implementing measures according to the EU General Principle of Human Rights, the ECJ was responding to the threat embodied in the German Solange doctrine. It was in other words defending its own legal order from revolts that could potentially be sparked in Germany and other EU Member States which might not be willing to accept the legal supremacy of an EU sanctions regime when it fails to provide appropriate human rights guarantees.

These assumptions regarding the manner in which the ECJ perceives the ECHR and the EU Member States do not find an explicit expression in the judgment. Yet if they are well founded, then it may be deduced that in the pursuit of the two 'defensive' Solange instruments, the ECJ was not solely concerned with human rights protection, but also with the protection of the integrity, autonomy and supremacy of its own legal order and with its own exclusive jurisdiction to safeguard these characteristics, thereby protecting itself from normative and jurisdictional intrusions.

As demonstrated by Broude, the interconnection between normative integration and authority integration implies that (i) to integrate the norms of another system is to acknowledge the authority of that system to produce pertinent norms and to assert authority over these norms, while (ii) creating a problem of overlapping authority and raising the corollary need to resolve that overlap through authority-integrating means.[221] Yet, the ECJ's judicial course of action was intended to produce the converse results, namely authority fragmentation between itself and the ECHR Court.

IX SUMMARY AND CONCLUSIONS

The legal struggle against international terror is pursued at multilateral, regional and national levels, thereby creating the risk of overlapping

[220] For analysis see N Lavranos, 'Towards a Solange Method between International Courts and Tribunals?' in Broude and Shany (eds), *The Shifting Allocation of Authority in International Law: Considering Sovereignty, Supremacy and Subsidiarity*, above (n 1) 217.

[221] Broude, 'Fragmentation(s) of International Law', above (n 1) 111–14.

and inconsistent regulatory regimes. This risk has materialized in relation to EC measures implementing UN Security Council Resolutions that had called for the imposition of financial sanctions against the Taliban, Osama Bin Laden and persons and entities associated with them. The legal proceedings before the EU judiciary regarding the lawfulness of these EC implementing measures raised a multifaceted, four-layer, two-dimensional MSENs scenarios in which a normative (and, by implication, potential jurisdictional) overlap exists between the international and UN legal order, the EU's own legal order and the legal orders of the ECHR and of the EU/ECHR Member States. The ECJ conducted an indirect review of the SC Resolutions according to the benchmark of EU General Principles of law. In doing so, the Court adopted a robust, Euro-laden, human rights-oriented, constitution-based approach to the protection of human rights, thereby safeguarding the autonomous and supreme nature of the EC legal order.[222] In doing so, the ECJ appears to have adopted a dominant model pertaining to international law/UN law, a more deferential, integrative model regarding the ECHR and a contesting model pertaining to the legal orders of the Member States. The differences between these regulatory models are narrowed by two judicial unifying threads which were identified in this chapter as common to all three regulatory models. This chapter analyzed and contextualized the exercise of judicial discretion in the various MSENs scenarios and concluded that notwithstanding the drawbacks of that ECJ's approach, including, in particular, the promotion of the fragmentation of international law, that approach is nevertheless warranted. The ECJ, in relying heavily, but not exclusively, on its own internal values and norms, was able to attain the appropriate equilibrium between multilateralism and regionalism, between safeguarding uniform compliance with international law and enshrining the coherence of the EC legal order and between human rights protection and effective struggle against international terrorism.

[222] *Ibid.*

Part III

MSENs in Specific Normative and Institutional Contexts

9

*The Interaction between International Investment Law and Human Rights Treaties: A Sociological Perspective**

Moshe Hirsch

I INTRODUCTION

THE CHAPTER FOCUSES on the sociological dimension of the interaction between Multi-Sourced Equivalent Norms obligations (MSENs) deriving from investment and human rights treaties (MSENs are defined in this book as two or more norms which are (i) binding on the same international legal subjects; (ii) similar or identical in their normative content; and (iii) have been established through different international instruments or 'legislative' procedures or are applicable in different substantive areas of the law).[1] Sociologists of law have long emphasized that law is 'always rooted in communities'; laws have always been considered by these scholars as expressive types of these communities.[2] From this perspective, international law is a social phenomenon that reflects and aims to guide a variety of interactions in the international arena. Sociological analysis casts new light on a significant dimension of

* I am grateful to Ohad Abrahami for excellent research assistance.

1 See T Broude and Y Shany,'The International Law and Policy of Multi-Sourced Equivalent Norms' in T Broude and Y Shany (eds), *Multi-Sourced Equivalent Norms in International Law* (Oxford, Hart Publishing, 2011) p 5. The legal interactions between these branches of international law constitute a clear example of 'multi-sourced obligations' (MSEN) as two or more international norms deriving from investment and human rights treaties bind the same subject of international law (eg, the host state). In addition, the relevant norms have been established through different international instruments.

2 R Cotterrell, *Law, Culture and Society: Legal Ideas in the Perspective of Social Theory* (Aldershot, Ashgate, 2006) 117, 161. The link between societal processes and normative behaviour has long been recognized in sociological literature, and the founders of sociology appreciated the central role of law (together with economy, politics, and cultural institutions) in the modern world. R Banakar and M Traverse, 'Classical Sociology and Law' in R Banakar and M Travers (eds), *An Introduction to Law and Social Theory* (Oxford, Hart Publishing, 2002) 9, 10; WM Evan, 'Law and Society' in EF Borgatta and ML Borgatta (eds), *Encyclopedia of Sociology* vol 3 (New York, Macmillan, 1992) 1075.

the relationships among MSENs and enriches our understanding of social factors involved in the creation, interpretation and implementation of international rules.

The small number of publications addressing the sociology of international law[3] is conspicuous in light of the noticeable contribution of sociological theories to the disciplines of law[4] and international relations theory.[5] While sociological analysis provides a valuable tool for the analysis of various international legal topics, it does not aim to substitute rational or political analysis. This chapter aims to analyze a particular interaction of MSENs (human rights and investment treaties) from a socio-cultural perspective. The basic argument of this chapter is that legal interactions between various branches of international law may also be analyzed as *social interactions* between the relevant communities.

Sociological analysis of international law begins from the premise that individuals' behaviour and normative choices are significantly affected by their social context and socio-cultural factors.[6] Since international law reflects and aims to influence patterns of social interactions, Emile Durkheim's famous statement is of vital importance for international law scholars: society is more than the individuals who compose it; society has

[3] See, eg, M Hirsch, 'The Sociology of International Law' (2005) 55 *University of Toronto Law Journal* 891; AT Lang, 'Some Sociological Perspectives on International Institutions and the Trading System' in CB Picker, ID Bunn and D Arner (eds), *International Economic Law: The State and Future of the Discipline* (Portland, Hart Publishing, 2008) 73; R Goodman and D Jinks, 'How to Influence States: Socialization and International Human Rights Law' (2004) 54 *Duke Law Journal* 621; R Goodman and D Jinks, 'Incomplete Internationalization and Compliance with Human Rights Law' (2008) 19 *European Journal of International Law* 725.

[4] On the sociology of law see, eg, Cotterrell, *Culture and Society*, above (n 2); D Milovanovic, *An Introduction to the Sociology of Law* 3rd edn (New York, Criminal Justice Press, 2003); R Cotterrell, *The Sociology of Law*, 2nd edn (London, Butterworths, 1992); G Gurvitch, *Sociology of Law, Law and Society Series* (New Brunswick, Transaction Publishers, 2001); WM Evan, *The Sociology of Law* (New York, The Free Press, 1980) 1; Banakar and Travers, *An Introduction to Law and Social Theory*, above (n 2).

[5] On the constructivist approach in international relations theory see, eg, M Barnett, 'Social Constructivism' in J Baylis and S Smith (eds), *The Globalization of World Politics* 3rd edn (Oxford, Oxford University Press, 2006) 251; A Wendt, *Social Theory of International Politics* (Cambridge, Cambridge University Press, 1999); E Adler, 'Cognitive Evolution: A Dynamic Approach for the Study of International Relations and Their Progress' in E Adler and B Crawford (eds), *Progress in Postwar International Relations* (New York, Columbia University Press, 1991) 43; JG Ruggie, *Constructing the World Polity* (London, Routledge, 1998) 11–14; M Finnemore, 'Construction of Norms of Humanitarian Intervention' in PJ Katzenstein (ed), *The Culture of National Security: Norms and Identity in World Politics* (New York, Columbia University Press, 1996) 153; E Adler, 'Seizing the Middle Ground: Constructivism in World Politics' (1997) 3 *European Journal of International Relations* 319; E Adler, 'Constructivism and International Relations' in W Carlsnaes, T Risse and BA Simmons (eds), *Handbook of International Relations* (London, Sage Publications, 2001) 95.

[6] On this presumption in sociology see, eg, A Giddens, *Sociology* 5th edn (Cambridge, Polity Press, 2006) 7–8; M Hollis, *The Philosophy of Social Science* (Cambridge, Cambridge University Press, 1994) 112–13; SH Heap, M Hollis, B Lyons, R Sugden and A Weale (eds), *The Theory of Choice: A Critical Guide* (Oxford, Blackwell, 1992) 63–64; J Scott, *Sociological Theory* (Aldershot, Elgar, 1995) 1.

a life of its own that stretches beyond our personal experience.[7] The sociological core assumptions regarding the influential role of social factors on individual behaviour are extended to the economic realm by *economic sociology*. Sociologists who explore economic behaviour attack the 'under-socialized' concept of persons that characterizes the economists' analysis.[8] Under this concept, international economic activity does not constitute an exception, and trade, for instance, is conceived as one of various types of social interaction.[9] Existing literature demonstrates that socio-cultural factors influence international economic relations among states and individuals.

Empirical studies show that after accounting for economic factors, public attitudes are statistically correlated with trade and capital inflows, and that these attitudes are in turn correlated with indices of cultural affinity (ie, ethnic and religious similarity) and political ideologies.[10] Similarly, empirical evidence indicates that cultural distance on egalitarianism is a robust and economically significant obstacle to foreign investment flows.[11]

International economic relations are not only *affected by* socio-cultural factors, they often *influence* the socio-cultural features of the involved communities. Thus, for instance, international trade and foreign investments are considered a source of knowledge spillovers.[12] International trade spreads knowledge, norms and values, through traders who often cross boundaries and settle in new communities, and by the content of the products or services purchased by the members of different communities.

In light of the mutual interrelationships between international economics and socio-cultural factors, it is not surprising that international economic *rules* often reflect and affect societal factors (such as values and norms) and processes (such as socialization, conformity and social

[7] E Durkheim, *Sociology and Philosophy* (Glencoe, Ill, Free Press, 1953) 54–55.

[8] M Granovetter, 'Economic Action and Social Structure: The Problem of Embeddedness' in R Swedberg (ed), *Economic Sociology* (Cheltenham, Elgar, 1996) 239, 245. See also, F Dobbin, 'The Sociological View of the Economy' in F Dobbin (ed), *The New Economic Sociology: A Reader* (Princeton, Princeton University Press, 2004) 5.

[9] See, eg, MD Irwin and JD Kasarda, 'Trade, Transportation, and Spatial Distribution' in NJ Smelser and R Swedberg (eds), *The Handbook of Economic Sociology* (Princeton, Princeton University Press, 1994) 342.

[10] M Noland, 'Affinity and International Trade', Institute for International Economics Working Paper No WP 05-3 3, 8 (June 2005) and see the references therein. See also, A Cheptea, 'Trade and Cultural Affinity' paper presented at the 2007 RES Conference (23 February 2007): www.editorialexpress.com/cgi-bin/conference/download.cgi?db_name=res2007&paper_id=643; J Frankel, 'Regional Trading Blocks in the World Economic System' (Washington DC, Institute for International Economics, 1997) 45–46.

[11] JI Siegel, AN Licht and SH Schwartz, 'Egalitarianism, Cultural Distance, and FDI: A New Approach' (2 January 2008): www.ssrn.com/abstract=957306. See also, M Grinblatt and M Keloharju, 'Distance, Language, and Culture Bias: The Role of Investor Sophistication', Yale ICF Working Paper No 00-04 (February 2000); Yale SOM Working Paper No ICF 00-04: www. ssrn.com/abstract=222169.

[12] R Falvey, N Foster and D Greenaway, 'North-South Trade, Knowledge Spillovers and Growth' (2002) 17 *Journal of Economic Integration* 650.

exclusion). Different legal rules regulating international economic activities reflect different socio-cultural values and affect social processes. The link between international economic law and socio-cultural factors is evident in special rules for trade in cultural goods and services (publications, films, sound recordings and television programmes) which 'are seen as vehicles for transmitting intangibles that are the essence of a society: ideas, values, identity and a sense of shared experience and community'.[13] This relationship between international trade and culture is also discernable with regard to trade in other products and services. Similarly, the impact of sociological factors on the formation, content and implementation of Regional Trade Agreements (RTAs) is well-documented in economic and legal literature. From a sociological perspective, it is clear that these agreements are embedded in socio-cultural relations among state societies. Thus, the formation of RTAs is influenced by socio-cultural factors, and RTAs' provisions often reflect different socio-cultural values prevailing in the involved societies and the particular region.[14]

Analysis of sociological factors involved in various international economic activities is likely to affect legal policy regarding the interpretation of various legal rules, including the relationships between MSENs deriving from international investment law and human rights treaties.

II INVESTMENT TRIBUNALS AND HUMAN RIGHTS TREATIES

The relationship between foreign investment and human rights protection are mixed: foreign investment may promote human rights in some cases, and decrease their protection in others.[15] Thus, for instance, where foreign investors establish basic services that allow poor populations access to water or electricity, such investments may further the protection of social

[13] A McCaskill, 'Culture and the International Trade Rules: Issues and Outlook': www.cdc-ccd.org/First_Conference_en/McCaskill_en.doc.

[14] For a sociological analysis of regional trade agreements, see M Hirsch, 'The Sociology of International Economic Law: Sociological Analysis of the Regulation of Regional Agreements in the World Trading System' (2008) 19 *European Journal of International Law* 277.

[15] On the diverse links between human rights and investments see, eg, UNHCR, Report of the High Commissioner for Human Rights: 'Human Rights, Trade and Investment' (2 July 2003) UN Doc E/CN.4/Sub.2/2003/9, 8–13; K Kolben, 'Foreign Investment and Human Rights Link' (2006) *Human Rights, Trade and Investment Matters* 50–51; DL Richards, RD Gelleny and DH Sacko, 'Money with a Mean Streak? Foreign Economic Penetration and Government Respect for Human Rights in Developing Countries' (2001) 45 *International Studies Quarterly* 219; D Spar, 'Foreign Investment and Human Rights – International Lessons' *Challenge*' (January–February 1999): www.findarticles.com/p/articles/mi_m1093/is_1_42/ai_53697782/pg_1; LE Peterson and KR Gray, International Human Rights in Bilateral Investment Treaties and in Investment Treaty Arbitration (Winnipeg, IISD, 2003) 16–17; T Weiler, 'Balancing Human Rights and Investor Protection: A New Approach for a Different Legal Order' (2004) 27 *Boston College International and Comparative Law Review* 429.

and economic rights.[16] In contrast, the implementation of some projects by foreign investors may involve human rights violations. This may be the case, for example, where foreign investors breach their employees' basic worker rights in the host state (and in absence of host governmental intervention to protect the workers).[17] In other cases, the execution of an investment contract may involve a breach of rights of the local population residing in the relevant area. An argument of that sort was raised during the North American Free Trade Agreement (NAFTA) litigation between Glamis and the United States. The Quechan people contended that their indigenous rights – which were threatened by approval of the *Glamis* claim – were protected, inter alia, by the International Covenant on Civil and Political Rights (ICCPR), the ILO Convention concerning Indigenous and Tribal Peoples and the Inter-American Convention on Human Rights.[18]

The relationship between various binding norms established through different international instruments has recently attracted considerable attention from international law scholars.[19] Questions relating to the interactions between investment law and other spheres of international law have scarcely been discussed in international legal literature.[20] The ongoing proliferation of international investment agreements, the increasing number of treaties in other branches of international law and the considerable growth of investor-state arbitration[21] are all likely to enhance the prospects for overlaps between obligations included in investment and non-investment instruments. As a

[16] See, eg, U Kriebaum, 'Privatizing Human Rights' (2006) 3 *Transnational Dispute Management* 1.

[17] See, eg, S Polaski, 'Linking Trade and Investment Agreements to Improvements in Labor Rights' in (Amnesty International, May 2006) *Human Rights, Trade and Investment Matters* 36

[18] US Department of State, Non-Party Submission, *Glamis Gold Ltd v United States of America, Submission of the Quechan Indian Nation, Nature of the Cultural Resources and Sacred Places at Issue in Claim*, at 8–9: www.naftaclaims.com/Disputes/USA/Glamis/Glamis-Amicus-Quechan-01--19-08-05.pdf. The tribunal award did not directly address these arguments (though they were explicitly mentioned in the ward), *Glamis v USA*, Award of May 2009, para 8: www.naftaclaims.com/Disputes/USA/Glamis/Glamis-USA-Award.pdf. On this dispute, see J Wallace, 'Corporate Nationality, Investment Protection Agreements, and Challenges to Domestic Natural Resources Law: The Implications of Glamis Gold's NAFTA Chapter 11 Claim' (2005) 17 *Georgetown International Environmental Law Review* 365.

[19] See ILC, 'Conclusions of the Work of the Study Group on the Fragmentation of International Law: Difficulties arising from the Diversification and Expansion of International Law, Report of the 58th Session: Conclusion 2' (2006) GAOR 61st Session Supp 10 UN Doc A/61/10, para 251. See also the special issue of the *Michigan Journal of International Law* on 'Diversity or Cacophony?: New Sources of Norms in International Law Symposium' (2004) 25 *Michigan Journal of International Law*.

[20] See M Hirsch, 'Interactions between Investment and Non-Investment Obligations in International Investment Law' in P Muchlinski, F Ortino and CH Schreuer (eds), *The Oxford Handbook of International Law on Foreign Investment* (Oxford, Oxford University Press, 2008) 262; A van Aaken, 'Fragmentation of International Law: The Case of International Investment Protection' (2008) *Finnish Yearbook of International Law*, University of St. Gallen Law & Economics Working Paper No 2008-1: www.ssrn.com/abstract=1097529.

[21] For quantitative data on investors-state cases, see UNCTAD, 'Recent Developments in International Investment Agreements' (June 2008–09), IIA Monitor No 3 (2009): www.unctad.org/en/docs/webdiaeia20098_en.pdf.

result, arguments regarding the relationship between MSENs arising from investment and non-investment instruments (either consistent or inconsistent rules) are brought by different parties (host states, foreign investors and NGOs) and arise at different stages of international litigation, ie, during discussions over liability (for example, *SPP v Egypt*)[22] and over remedies (for example, *Santa Elena v Costa Rica*).[23]

In certain cases, investment tribunals were ready to interpret investment treaty provisions according to legal rules developed in other branches of international law and apply them to investment disputes. In fact, investment tribunals very often resorted to international rules regarding state responsibility or treaty law.[24] Similarly, investment tribunals were ready to apply some 'general principles of law' with regard to investments that involved corruptive or fraudulent practices. In the *World Duty Free* case (2006), an ICSID (International Centre for Settlement of Investment Disputes) tribunal found that a payment made by a foreign investor to a former Kenyan president to obtain a contract was in fact, a bribe.[25] Consequently, the tribunal ruled that bribery is contrary to the trans–national public policy,[26] and held that 'claims based on contracts of corruption or on contracts obtained by corruption cannot be upheld by this Arbitral Tribunal'.[27] Likewise, the tribunal in the *Inceysa Vallisoletana* case found that the claimant's investment had been fraudulently made. The tribunal stated that international public policy bars the parties from benefiting from their own fraud. Consequentially the tribunal ruled that the dispute was not arbitrable under the El-Salvador-Spain treaty.[28]

[22] 'SPP (ME) v Egypt' (1994) 19 *Yearbook Commercial Arbitration* 51, para 78 (regarding the relationship between the UNESCO World Heritage Convention and investment obligations).

[23] 'Santa Elena v Costa Rica' (2000) 15 *ICSID Review – Foreign Investment Law Journal* 169, para 71 (regarding the relationship between international environmental treaty and investment obligations).

[24] On the application of the 1969 Vienna Convention on the Law of Treaties (adopted 22 May 1969, entered into force 27 January 1980) 1155 UNTS 331 (VCLT) by investment tribunals, see CH Schreuer 'Diversity and Harmonization of Treaty Interpretation in Investment Arbitration' (April 2006) 3 *Transnational Dispute Management*: www.transnational-dispute-management.com. On the application of rules of state responsibility by investment tribunals see, eg, K Hober, 'State Responsibility and Attribution' in Muchlinski, Ortino and Schreuer (eds), *The Oxford Handbook of International Law*, above (n 20) 549.

[25] *World Duty Free Company Limited v Republic of Kenya* (ICSID Case No ARB/00/7) Award (4 October 2006) para 136: www.ita.law.uvic.ca/documents/WDFv.KenyaAward.pdf.

[26] *Ibid*, para 157. See also paras 138–56.

[27] *Ibid*, para 157. The tribunal held that the agreement was voidable and that Kenya 'was legally entitled to avoid and did avoid legally', and that '[t]he Claimant is not legally entitled to maintain any of its pleaded claims in these proceedings as a matter of *ordre public international* and public policy under the contract's applicable laws'. (*Ibid*, para 188). As to the impact of bribery on poor states and their inhabitants, the tribunal explained: 'The answer, as regards public policy, is that the law protects not the litigating parties but the public; or in this case, the mass of tax-payers and other citizens making up one of the poorest countries in the world'. *World Duty Free v Kenya*, above (n 25) para 181.

[28] *Inceysa Vallisoletana S.L. v Republic of El Salvador* (ICSID Case No ARB/03/26) Award (2 August 2006) para 242.

When encountering *inconsistent* rules derived from international investment and human rights laws, investment tribunals may draw on secondary rules developed in the sphere of public international law for the purpose of ordering the hierarchy between rules; rules such as Article 53 of the Vienna Convention on the Law of Treaties (VCLT) (regarding *jus cogens)* and Article 30 of VCLT (regarding the *lex posteriori* rules). While investment tribunals frequently resort to interpretative provisions of the VCLT, they have not invoked the above regulatory rules included in Articles 30 or 53 of this Convention. This practical disregard may appear even more puzzling in light of the fact that contemporary international investment law does not include a coherent body of rules in this sphere.

Analysis of investment tribunals' decisions relating to human rights instruments[29] reveals that while these tribunals often incorporate rules of general international law (particularly on state responsibility and treaty law), they adopt a quite consistent approach *opposing* the incorporation of international human rights law in investment disputes. [30] With the exception of the *Mondev* award (from 2002),[31] investment tribunals have declined to examine thoroughly the specific provisions of international human rights instruments invoked by the parties, notwithstanding the various arguments that were raised during different stages of litigation by various parties.

Investment tribunals that encountered such arguments presented diverse explanations for their *un*enthusiastic attitude towards resorting to human rights instruments.[32] Those reasons included lack of sufficiently elaborated arguments by the parties (the *Azurix*[33] and *Siemens*[34] cases), lack of jurisdiction (the *Biloune*[35] and *Euro-Tunnel*[36] cases) and the difference

[29] On the links between human rights and investment see, eg, UNCTAD, 'Selected Recent Developments in IIA Arbitration and Human Rights: International Investment Agreements' (2009) 2 *International Investment Agreements Monitor*; Peterson and Gray, above (n 15) 16–17; Weiler, above (n 15) 429; L Davarnejad, 'Strengthening the Social Dimension of International Investment Agreements by Integrating Codes of Conduct for Multinational Enterprises' (OECD Global Forum on Forum Investment VII, March 2008): www.oecd.org/dataoecd/10/5/40352144.pdf; UNHCR, 'Human Rights, Trade and Investment', above (n 15) 8–13; Kolben, above (n 15) 50–51.

[30] See, eg, M Hirsch, 'Investment Tribunals and Human Rights: Divergent Paths' in PM Dupuy, F Francioni and E-U Petersmann (eds), *Human Rights, International Investment Law and Investor-State Arbitration* (Oxford, Oxford University Press, 2009).

[31] *Mondev International Ltd v United States of America* (ICSID Case No ARB(AF)/99/2) Award (11 October 2002) para 1: iwww.state.gov/documents/organization/14442.pdf.

[32] For a detailed analysis of these investment tribunals' awards, see Hirsch, 'Investment Tribunals and Human Rights', above (n 30).

[33] *Azurix Corp. v Argentine Republic* (ICSID Case No ARB/01/12) Award (14 July 2006) para 3: ita.law.uvic.ca/documents/AzurixAwardJuly2006.pdf.

[34] *Siemens A.G. v Argentine Republic* (ICSID Case No ARB/02/8) Award (6 February 2007): ita.law.uvic.ca/documents/Siemens-Argentina-Award.pdf.

[35] *Biloune v Ghana* (1993) 95 ILR 184.

[36] *Channel Tunnel Group v Governments of the United Kingdom and France* Partial Award (30 January 2007).

between the two branches of international law (the *Siemens* case).[37] The *Sempra* award[38] did not elaborate the reasons for its decision to disregard human rights law. Three investment tribunals were ready to examine the impact of European human rights law on investment disputes (the *Mondev, Tecmed*[39] and *Azurix* awards). Two of them cited the case law of the European Court of Human Rights (ECtHR) (the *James* case)[40] in order to emphasize the vulnerability of investors in foreign countries (the *Tecmed* and *Azurix* cases). A later attempt by Argentina to apply the same ECtHR judgment was dismissed by the *Siemens* tribunal, emphasizing the inconsistency between the European Convention of Human Rights' (ECHR) rules regarding the 'margin of appreciation' and international investment law.[41] A more balanced analysis of the case law of the ECtHR was undertaken by the *Mondev* tribunal.[42]

So far, no investment tribunal has absolved a party that has encountered inconsistent human rights and investment obligations from its investment obligations, or reduced the amount of compensation due to be paid to the injured party in such cases. It should be noted that investment tribunals have not sought to develop a consistent body of rules regarding the relationships between human rights and investment instruments, and that their jurisprudence is still in a formative period.

III SOCIO-CULTURAL DISTANCE AND MSENS

As discussed above, while investment tribunals very often resort to international rules regarding state responsibility or treaty law, they are generally reluctant to accord significant weight to human rights treaties in international investment law. The generally negative approach of investment tribunals towards the application of human rights treaties may be explained by various factors[43]. This chapter focuses on socio-cultural factors relating to the social settings in which these rules of international law are formed, interpreted and implemented.

[37] *Siemens v Argentine Republic,* above (n 34) para 354.

[38] *Sempra v Argentina,* at paras 4, 93, available at www.investmentclaims.com/decisions/Sempra_Energy-Award.pdf.

[39] *Tecmed v Mexico* (2004) 43 ILM 133, para 122.

[40] *Young, James and Others v The United Kingdom* (App Nos 7601/76; 7806/77) 2 ECHR 21 February 1986, para 50.

[41] *Siemens v Argentine Republic,* above (n 34) para 354. On this part of the award, see L Liberti, 'The Relevance of Non-Investment Treaty obligations in the Assessment of Compensation' (2007) 4 *Transnational Dispute Management* No 6.

[42] See below, section II B.

[43] See, eg, M Hirsch, 'Conflicting Obligations in International Investment Law: Investment Tribunals' Perspective' in T Broude and Y Shany (eds), *The Shifting Allocation of Authority in International Law: Considering Sovereignty, Supremacy and Subsidiarity* (Oxford, Hart Publishing, 2008) 323.

The basic argument of this chapter is that legal interactions among MSENs (either integration or fragmentation) may also be analyzed as *social interactions* between the relevant communities. These legal interactions are affected by the particular features of relevant social settings. They are also affected by the mutual relationships between the relevant social groups. More specifically, the *socio-cultural distance* between the particular international legal settings affects the inclination of relevant decision-makers to incorporate or reject legal rules developed in other branch of international law. Generally, greater socio-cultural 'distance' between the involved social settings and groups decreases the prospects for mutual incorporation of legal rules developed in the other legal sphere. Thus, the propensity of investment tribunals to accord a significant role to human rights treaties is influenced by the cultural distance between these two branches of international law.[44]

The element of cultural distance in predicting *trade* between countries is often included in the famous 'gravity model'. International economic empirical studies employ different versions of this factor.[45] Generally, national cultural distance can be defined as the degree to which the shared norms and values in one country differ from those in another. Various studies suggest that an increasing cultural distance (manifested, for example, by language, religious beliefs, colonial past) reduces the amount of trade between countries.[46] This chapter does not aim to develop a sophisticated scale for measuring *socio-cultural distance* between various branches of international law but rather to assess the distance between international investment and human rights laws and discuss its implications.

IV THE SOCIO-CULTURAL DISTANCE BETWEEN INVESTMENT AND HUMAN RIGHTS LAWS

The social settings in which international investment[47] and human rights laws emerge and are interpreted are very different. The members of the

[44] This contention does not aim to downplay other factors influencing interactions among various branches of international law.

[45] See, eg, S Beugelsdijk, H de Groot, GJ Linders and A Slangen, *Cultural Distance, Institutional Distance and International Trade*: www-sre.wu-wien.ac.at/ersa/ersaconfs/ersa04/PDF/265.pdf; B Tadesse and R White, 'Does Cultural Distance Hinder Trade in Goods? A Comparative Study of Nine OECD Member Nations' (2010) *Open Economics Review* 237; B Tadesse and R White, 'Cultural Distance as a Determinant of Bilateral Trade Flows: Do Immigrants Counter the Effect of Cultural Distance?' (Applied Economics Letters, forthcoming): www.papers.ssrn.com/sol3/papers.cfm?abstract_id=1078045.

[46] See, eg, Beugelsdijk et al, *ibid*, 3–5; A Cheptea, 'Trade and Cultural Affinity', paper presented at the 2007 RES Conference (23 February 2007): www.editorialexpress.com/cgi-bin/conference/download.cgi?db_name=res2007&paper_id=643; G Hofstede, *Culture's Consequences: Comparing Values, Behaviors, Institutions, and Organizations across Nations* (London, Sage Publications, 2001).

[47] On other cultural aspects of some investment agreements and decisions, see A Froehlich, 'Cultural Matters in Investment Agreements and Decisions' in A Reinisch and C Knahr (eds), *International Investment Law in Context* (Utrecht, Eleven International Publishing, 2007) 141

two communities[48] pursue extremely different career paths. While most human rights lawyers work in legal divisions of NGOs or academia, foreign investment lawyers (and arbitrators) are predominantly senior lawyers-practitioners, legal scholars or former judges affiliated with major international law firms.[49] A brief survey of the background of arbitrators that rendered investment awards in 2008 (and which are publicly available) reveals that out of the 73 arbitrators, an overwhelming majority (75.34 per cent) are affiliated with commercial law firms. Similarly, most arbitrators (60.27 per cent) are members of commercial arbitration associations. On the other hand, only 35.62 per cent of these arbitrators had significant experience with international governmental organizations (INGOs) or international legal establishment not connected to commercial arbitration; and only 20.55 per cent of them had human rights related experience. As to governmental background, 36.99 per cent of these arbitrators fulfilled some sort of government capacity.[50]

While human rights lawyers are often linked to a certain social movement and are determined to take sides in political or moral struggles,[51] most investment lawyers are anxious to maintain a professional and neutral position.[52] These divergent career paths mean that the members of

[48] On community of international lawyers and judges see, R Teitel and R Howse, 'Cross-Judging: Tribunalization in a Fragmented but Interconnected Global Order' (2009) 41 *New York University Journal of International Law and Politics* 959.

[49] On 'mixing of roles' of arbitrators and lawyers, see Y Dezalay and B Garth, *Dealing in Virtue: International Commercial Arbitration and the Construction of a Transnational Legal Order* (Chicago, University of Chicago Press, 1996) 49–51. See also, CA Rogers, 'Regulating International Arbitrators: A Functional Approach to Developing Standards of Conduct' (2005) 41 *Stanford Journal of International Law* 53, 56–57. On the important role of large law firms in international arbitration, see Dezalay and Garth, *ibid*, 8, 37–38, 48, 53.

[50] I am grateful to Ohad Abrahami for undertaking this brief survey of the background of arbitrators. The survey examined the backgrounds of 73 arbitrators involved in 35 different arbitral investment proceedings – undertaken or concluded – and reported throughout 2008 in the Investment Treaty Arbitration: www.ita.law.uvic.ca/chronological_list.htm. The only two cases not reviewed were *Pren Nerka v Czech Republic* (UNCITRAL) and *Tembec Inc. v USA*, as they were unavailable to the public at the time of the survey (February 2009). The findings of the survey are as follows: out of the 73 arbitrators, an overwhelming majority of 55 arbitrators (75.34%) belonged to or were affiliated with some sort of law firm; 27 arbitrators (36.99%) served in some sort of government capacity; 26 arbitrators (35.62%) had significant experience with an INGO or international legal establishment not connected with commercial arbitration. Out of the 26 arbitrators who had INGO experience, 15 (20.55%) had human rights related experience. Twenty-seven arbitrators (36.99%) were career academics; 15 arbitrators (20.55%) noted in their CV a non-career teaching position or lecture given; 44 arbitrators (60.27%) are members of commercial arbitration associations; 12 arbitrators had other kinds of experience, such as military experience, membership in boards of directors, consulting or membership in arbitration periodicals editorial boards (a percentage is not given here due to the varied nature of that experience).

[51] On 'cause' (or 'public interest') lawyers and their determination to take sides in political and moral struggles, see CS Shdaimah, 'What's in a Name?: Cause Lawyers as Conceptual Category' (2006) Bepress Legal Series Paper No 903: www.law.bepress.com/cgi/viewcontent.cgi?article=4436&context=expresso.

[52] On the importance of neutrality as an element of the 'virtue' of arbitrators, see Dezalay and Garth, above (n 49) 8, 83. On the significance of being distant from politics, see Dezalay and Garth, above (n 49) 45, 98.

the two communities undergo starkly different socialization processes.[53] Thus, for instance, while investment lawyers are inclined to emphasize the importance of the unimpeded flow of capital, legal predictability and stability, as well as a market economy ideology; human rights lawyers are more concerned with universal values and underline the primacy of human rights over other international legal rules (including international economic treaties).

Each community has distinct heritage and narratives. For example, while 'the great petroleum arbitrations' during the 1960s and 1970s 'occupy a quasi-mythical position' in international investment law;[54] the adoption of the Universal Declaration of Human Rights and the Tiananmen Square Massacre constitute central collective narratives for human rights lawyers. The members of the two communities employ different terminologies. Thus, for example, while human rights lawyers frequently refer to 'the Covenants' or Committee on the Elimination of Racial Discrimination (CERD), many of them hardly understand terms like Most Favoured Nations (MFN), New International Economic Order (NIEO), or 'umbrella clauses'. These different vocabularies point to the fundamental conceptual differences between these spheres of international law.

On the significance of language of law, shared tradition and 'kind of brotherhood' of lawyers, Lawrence Friedman noted:

> Any occupational group will make use of verbal shorthand: indeed, any group with shared experiences will do so. Lawyers share a common training, in law schools and universities, This gives them a common culture . . . Words, phrases, and memories, drilled into lawyers' heads during training, unite the profession, link it to a shared tradition, mark it as a kind of brotherhood, separated from the layman's world.[55]

This difference between human rights and investment languages and concepts became clear, for instance, when the *Siemens* tribunal flatly rejected the doctrine of 'margin of appreciation'[56] afforded to states by the ECtHR.[57]

[53] Socialization refers to lifelong social experience by which individuals develop their human potential and learn patterns of their culture. Socialization is an ongoing process by which the society transmits norms and values to new members of the social group. The principal 'agents of socialization' are the family, school, peer group and the mass media. M Renzetti and DJ Curran, *Living Sociology* 2nd edn (Boston, Allyn & Bacon, 2000) 106–09; RJ Brym and J Lie, *Sociology* (Belmont, CA, Wadsworth, 2003) 92–105.

[54] See, eg, Dezalay and Garth, above (n 49) 74.

[55] LM Friedman, *Law and Society: An Introduction* (New Jersey, Prentice-Hall, 1977) 89.

[56] On the margin of appreciation doctrine under international law and the European Convention on Human Rights, see A Mowbray, *European Convention on Human Rights* (Oxford, Oxford University Press, 2007) 629–33; Y Shany, 'Toward a General Margin of Appreciation Doctrine in International Law?' (2006) 16 *European Journal of International Law* 907; E Benvenisti, 'Margin of Appreciation, Consensus, and Universal Standards' (1999) 31 *New York University Journal of International Law and Politics* 843.

[57] *Siemens v Argentine Republic*, above (n 34) para 354.

International investment and human rights laws have dissimilar 'legal cultures'[58] and the members of each community hold different views regarding the role of law[59] and tribunals.[60] On the substantive level, these two settings diverge along the private–public divide. Generally, international human rights law has evolved within the public law sphere,[61] as various freedoms, rights, authorities and obligations were assigned to individuals and states. Keeping in mind the original inferior position of individuals, human rights law has established an impressive list of individual rights and freedoms to protect weaker parties in their relations with sovereign states.

Aiming to cope with a parallel problem of asymmetric relations,[62] international investment law followed a distinctive route and focused on the private law aspects of the relations between host governments and foreign investors. Investment tribunals are predisposed to attach considerable weight to reciprocal promise-based obligations (arising, for example,

[58] As Nelken explains, legal culture is one way of describing relatively stable patterns of legally oriented social behaviour and attitudes. The identifying elements of legal culture range from facts about institutions, such as the number and role of lawyers or the ways judges are appointed, to various forms of behaviour such as litigation and aspects of ideas, values, aspirations and mentalities. Though numerous studies identify legal culture with the nation state, patterns of legal culture can and must also be sought both at the sub-national as well as at the transnational level. D Nelken, 'Using the Concept of Legal Culture' (2004) 29 *The Australian Journal of Legal Philosophy* 1, 3. On the concept of legal culture, see also, Cotterrell, above (n 2) 81–96. On the elements of legal culture, see D Nelken, 'Towards a Sociology of Legal Adaptation' in D Nelken and J Feest (eds), *Adapting Legal Cultures* (Oxford, Hart Publishing, 2001) 3, 25–26.

[59] On legal cultures and international law, see TM Franck, 'The Legal Culture and Culture Culture', *Proceedings of the Annual Meeting: American Society of International Law* (January 1999): www.asil.org/files/legalculture.pdf; E Jouannet, 'French and American Perspectives on International Law: Legal Cultures and International Law' (2006) 58 *Maine Law Review* 292: www.cerdin.univ-paris1.fr/IMG/pdf/French_and_American_Perspectives-version_CERDIN.pdf.

[60] On the economic role in creating the culture of international commercial arbitration, see T Ginsburg, 'The Culture of Arbitration' (2003) 36 *Vanderbilt Journal of Transnational Law* 1335. On legal traditions in international commercial arbitration, see L Trakman, 'Legal Traditions and International Commercial Arbitration' (Spring 2007) *American Review of International Arbitration*. UNSW Law Research Paper No 2007-29: www.papers.ssrn.com/sol3/papers.cfm?abstract_id=986507. See also P Martinez-Fraga, 'The Convergence of Legal Cultures in Arbitration and Amendments to the New York Convention: If it is Not Broken, Why Fix it, but if it is Good, Make it Better', Jean Monnet/ Robert Schuman Paper Series, vol 6, No 20 (October, 2006): www6.miami.edu/eucenter/EU_Long%20Paper20_fall06_MartinezFraga.pdf.

[61] For an insightful analysis of the history of the public–private divide, see MJ Horwitz, 'The History of the Public/Private Distinction' (1982) 130 *University of Pennsylvania Law Review* 1423. See also T Rowland, 'Private Law' in *The Philosophy of Law: An Encyclopedia* vol II (New York, Garland Publishing, 1999) 687.

[62] During the negotiations towards an investment contract and the 'entry stage', the gap between the parties' legal capacities is relatively smaller. Following this stage, and during most stages of the implementation of the investment, the superior position of the host state regarding its influence on the content of both domestic and international law is evident. See, eg, M Hirsch, *The Arbitration Mechanism of the International Center for the Settlement of Investment Disputes* (The Hague, Kluwer-Nijhoff Publishers, 1993) 133–34.

from the investment contract) and reliance-based obligations (arising, for example, from the host state's regulatory framework) that are primarily formed during the negotiations and the 'entry stage'.

The focus on private law aspects of investment relations constitutes a *de-politicizing* strategy that enables investment tribunals to avoid highly controversial issues regarding human rights. This tendency may be explained by investment tribunals' concerns that rulings on divisive issues may impair their legitimacy and apparent neutrality.[63]

Most international investment rules are included in bilateral treaties. The lack of dense global rules in this field is explained by various factors – prominently disagreements between developing and developed countries, as well as the opposition of NGOs.[64] Legal–ideological controversies are even more conspicuous in the sphere of international human rights, and particularly with regard to the human rights of foreign investors. Fundamental disputes regarding the content and implementation of international human rights law have often evolved along political and ideological lines (for example, East–West states, developing–developed states, Christian–Islamic states).[65] Questions regarding the human rights of foreign investors have had particularly divisive effects among states. Disagreements between Western and socialist countries regarding compensation for expropriations precluded the inclusion of the right of property in the 1966 Human Rights Covenants.[66]

[63] On some indicators of legitimacy in investment arbitration see, S Frank, 'The Legitimacy Crisis in Investment Treaty Arbitration: Privatizing Public International Law through Inconsistent Decisions' (2005) 73 *Fordham International Law Review* 1521, 1584–87; N Grossman, 'Legitimacy and International Adjudicative Bodies' (2009) 41 *George Washington International Law Review* 107. On various sources of legitimacy of the judiciary, see JLM Gribnau, 'The Legitimacy of the Judiciary' (2002) 6(4) *Electronic Journal of Comparative Law*: www.ejcl.org/64/art64-3.html

[64] See, eg, MJ Trebilcock and R Howse, *The Regulation of International Trade* 3rd edn (New York, Routledge, 2005) 457–61; M Matsushita, TJ Schoenbaum and PC Mavoroidis, *The World Trade Organization: Law, Practice And Policy* 2nd edn (Oxford, Oxford University Press, 2006) 836–38; AB Zampetti and P Sauve, 'International Investment' in AT Guzman and AO Sykes (eds), *Research Handbook in International Economic Law* (Massachusetts, Elgar, 2007) 211, 249–51

[65] J Gordon, 'The Concept of Human Rights: The History and Meaning of its Politicization' (1998) 23 *Brooklyn Journal of International Law* 691; MW Mutua, 'Politics and Human Rights: An Essential Symbiosis' in M Byers (ed), *The Role of International Law in Politics* (Oxford, Oxford University Press, 2000) 149; HJ Steiner and P Alston, *International Human Rights in Context: Law, Politics and Morals* (Oxford, Clarendon Press, 1996) 226; A Cassese, *International Law* 2nd edn (Oxford, Oxford University Press, 2005) 378–81. On Islamic-Christian disputes regarding the scope of the freedom of religion, see M Hirsch, 'Freedom of Proselytism under the Fundamental Agreement and International Law' (1998) 47 *Catholic University Law Review* 407.

[66] Cassese, *ibid*, 382–83; LF Damrosch, L Henkin, RC Pugh, O Schachter and H Smit, *International Law Cases and Materials* 4th edn (St Paul Minn, West Group, 2001) 601, 663, 672, 676. On the controversy regarding the right to property, see also, M Sornarajah, *The International Law on Foreign Investment* 2nd edn (Cambridge, Cambridge University Press, 2004) 367–71; FF Martin, SJ Schnably, RJ Wilson, JS Simon and MV Tushnet, *International Human Rights and Humanitarian Law* (Cambridge, Cambridge University Press, 2006) 911–37.

An examination of the *institutional* traits[67] of human rights and investment laws also reveals the public–private split between these two spheres. Investors' rights are primarily protected by arbitral tribunals that are mainly established by bilateral investment treaties. Investment arbitral tribunals are regularly established on an ad hoc basis, and tend to adopt the *inter-partes* model that characterizes international commercial arbitration.[68] This inclination to follow the private mode of adjudicating disputes[69] is illustrated, inter alia, by the prevalent confidential features of most investment arbitral proceedings.[70] In contrast to ad hoc investment arbitration, human rights tribunals (like the ECtHR, European and the Inter-American Court of Human Rights) present clear public features: they are permanent courts and their proceedings are regularly open to the public.[71] Unlike the enforcement of investment obligations, exposure of human rights violations to the public is a major instrument for inducing states to respect their international obligations ('the politics of shame').[72]

International tribunals fulfil two principal functions in the international legal system: settling disputes between the particular rival parties and developing legal norms to guide future behaviour.[73] Different tribunals

[67] On the importance of the institutional context for application and interpretation of international investment law, see S Ratner, 'Regulatory Taking in Institutional Context: Beyond the Fear of Fragmented International Law' (2008) 102 *American Journal of International Law* 475. For an institutional analysis of international commercial arbitration, see W Mattli, 'Private Justice in a Global Economy: From Litigation to Arbitration' (2001) 55 *International Organization* 919–47.

[68] See, eg, TW Wälde, 'The Present State of Research Carried Out by the English-Speaking Section of the Centre for Studies and Research' (2007) *Hague Academy Report on International Investment Law* 75–76; G Van Harten, *Investment Treaty Arbitration and Public Law* (Oxford, Oxford University Press, 2007) 5–6, 58; G Van Harten and M Loughlin, 'Investment Treaty Arbitration as a Species of Global Administrative Law' (2006) 17 *The European Journal of International Law* 121, 126–45. On the dominant private features of international arbitration, see also, CA Rogers, 'The Vocation of International Arbitrators' (2005) 20 *American University International Law Review* 944, 957, 993–94.

[69] On the commercial arbitration and public international law approaches in international investment law (and the dominant position of the first approach), see TW Wälde, 'Remedies and Compensation in International Investment Law' (July 2005) paper submitted to ILA Committee on International Law of Foreign Investment, 8–12.

[70] For an analysis of transparency clauses in the arbitration rules of UNCITRAL, ICSID and NAFTA, see C Knahr and A Reinisch, 'Transparency versus Confidentiality in International Investment Arbitration' (2007) 6 *International Courts and Tribunals* 97, 98–103; J Delaney and DB Magraw, 'Procedural Transparency' in Muchlinski, Ortino and Schreuer (eds), *The Oxford Handbook of International Law*, above (n 20) 721.

[71] On the difference between international commercial arbitration and international courts, see ML Movsesian, 'International Commercial Arbitration and International Courts' (2008) 18 *Duke Journal of Comparative and International Law* 423, 425–27, 437 ff.

[72] See, eg, JH Lebovic and E Voeten, 'The Politics of Shame: The Condemnation of Country Human Rights Practices in the UNCHR' (2006) 50 *International Studies Quarterly* 861.

[73] On the law-making function of international courts, see DT Ceasare, PR Romano and L Swigart, *The International Judge* (Oxford, Oxford University Press, 2007) 114–17, 127–28.

emphasize different roles, and the perception regarding their social role[74] often influences the content of their decisions.[75] Generally, tribunals that give significant weight to their law-making role are more likely to take into account wider public policy considerations (such as human rights) and seek a due balance between the competing principles. On the other hand, tribunals that perceive their role in settling the specific dispute between the particular parties (the '*inter-partes* model') are less likely to grant significant weight to broader policy issues that are reflected in such general treaties. Most investment tribunals (established by bilateral or trilateral treaties) incline to adopt the '*inter partes* model' (which is prevalent in commercial arbitration) and grant precedence to their role as settlers of disputes between the particular litigants.[76]

The statement of the *Glamis* tribunal reflects this perception of investment tribunals:

> 3. This Tribunal was constituted to address a particular dispute between Glamis and the United States of America. In this sense, *the Tribunal sees its mandate under Chapter 11 of the NAFTA as similar to the case-specific mandate ordinarily found in international commercial arbitration. In the normal contractual setting, a tribunal is a creature of contract, tasked with resolving a* ***particular dispute*** *arising under a particular contract. In all likelihood, a particular contract gives rises to only one arbitration.*
>
> 7. Therefore, this Tribunal, in undertaking its primary mandate of resolving this particular dispute, does so with an awareness of the context within which it operates. The Tribunal emphasizes that it in no way views its awareness of the context in which it operates as justifying (or indeed requiring) a departure from its duty to focus on the specific case before it[77] (emphasis added).

In light of this prevalent conception, most investment adjudicators are inclined to focus on the particular facts of the dispute and on the particular legal instruments governing the relationship between the particular parties (mainly contracts and the investment treaty).

[74] On the impact of judicial role perception and judges' voting in the International Court of Justice, see TR Hensley, 'Block Voting on the International Court of Justice' (1978) 22 *Journal of Conflict Resolution* 39.

[75] On the relationship between social support and the European Court of Justice tendency to adopt far-reaching judgments, see KJ Alter, 'The European Court's Political Power Across Time and Space' (2009) 59 *Revue Française de Science Politique*; Northwestern Law and Economics Research Paper No 09-03: www.ssrn.com/abstract=1334328.

[76] See, eg, Wälde, 'Remedies and Compensation' above (n 69) 75–76; Van Harten, Investment *Treaty Arbitration*, above (n 68) 5–6, 58.

[77] *Glamis Gold v United States of America*, Award, 8 June 2009, paras 3 and 7: www.naftalaw.org/Disputes/USA/Glamis/Glamis-USA-Award.pdf. The tribunal also noted in its award that '[t]he reality is that Chapter 11 of the NAFTA contains a significant public system of private investment protection. The ultimate integrity of the protections given to the many individual investments made under Chapter 11 is ensured by reference to a multitude of arbitral panels occupied by persons who are only occasionally reappointed. The ultimate integrity of the Chapter 11 system as a whole requires a modicum of awareness of each of these tribunals for each other and the system as a whole'. *Ibid*, para 7.

The relationship between these communities is often characterized by mistrust and antagonism. These hostile relationships were prominent during the attempts to establish the comprehensive Multilateral Agreement on Investment (MAI) that failed in 1998,[78] as well as during the failed negotiations to formulate an additional World Trade Organization (WTO) agreement on investment (1996–2004). Indeed, one of the significant factors leading to these negotiation failures relates to the opposition of human rights and environmental NGOs.[79]

In light of the considerable *socio-cultural distance* between investment and human rights laws, and the deep-rooted tensions between the relevant communities, it is not surprising that investment tribunals are generally reluctant to accord significant weight to human rights treaties in international investment law. Thus, the substantial socio-cultural distance between these socio-cultural settings parallels the normative distance between these branches of international law. When a *non*-investment tribunal encountered legal issues involving investment and human rights rules, it did not hesitate to grant significant weight to human rights treaties. The Southern African Development Community Tribunal discussed international legal rules applicable to expropriations undertaken by the government of Zimbabwe. It did not hesitate to apply human rights treaties.[80] In contrast to investment tribunals, however, this is a permanent tribunal (established in 1992) and its members are appointed for a term of five years (and may be reappointed for an additional term of five years).[81]

[78] On the MAI, see MJ Trebilcock and R Howse, *The Regulation of International Trade* 2nd edn (New York, Routledge, 2005) 459–60; Matsushita, Schoenbaum and Mavoroidis, above (n 64) 833–35; Zampetti and Sauve, above (n 64) 211, 249–51

[79] See, eg, Trebilcok and Howse, *ibid*, 457–61; Matsushita, Schoenbaum and Mavoroidis, above (n 64) 836–38; Zampetti and Sauve, *ibid*, 249–51; 'WTO: Members Decide On Way Forward In Doha Round' 7(43) (2003) *Bridges Weekly Trade News Digest*.

[80] *Campbell v Zimbabwe* (2008), Southern African Development Community Tribunal, 19–21, 47–51: www.zwnews.com/Ruling281108.pdf.

[81] The tribunal was established in 1992 as part of the SADC Treaty (South African Development Community) (art 9(g) SADC Treaty) and became operational in 2005 (www.sadc.int/tribunal). Its jurisprudence is based on the SADC treaty, along with other treaties, general rules of public international law and principles of the Law of States (art 21 of the tribunal's Protocol). The tribunal is comprised of five regular members, along with a pool of five replacement members selected by the president in case a regular member is ill or unavailable (art 3(2) of the Protocol). Sessions are administered by a panel of three members unless the tribunal decides on a full bench of five (art 3(3) of the Protocol). The sessions are held in public unless the tribunal or one of the parties requests otherwise (Rule 45 of the tribunal's Rules of Procedure). Members are appointed for a period of five years with the option of being appointed for another five (art 6(1) of the Protocol). On the SADC Tribunal see also, eg, the tribunal website: www.sadc.int/tribunal; OC Ruppel and FX Bangamwabo, 'Chapter 8 – The SADC Tribunal: A Legal Analysis of its Mandate and Role in Regional Integration' (2008) 1 *Monitoring Regional Integration in Africa Yearbook*; J Pauwelyn, 'Going Global, Regional or Both? Dispute Settlement in the Southern African Development Community (SADC) and Overlaps with the WTO and Other Jurisdictions' (2004) 13 *Minnesota Journal of International Law* 231, 239–40.

V DYNAMIC ASPECTS AND FUTURE NORMATIVE DISTANCE

The above discussion on the socio-cultural distance between investment and human rights laws and the corresponding social distance does not necessarily mean that these relationships are not likely to change in the future. Past experience shows that the relationship between MSENs is often dynamic (for example, the interaction between the laws of war and human rights or between the GATT/WTO law and environmental protection). Generally, the normative distance between these legal fields is likely to be affected by various socio-cultural factors and processes. Changes within each of the relevant communities (for example, population composition, change of social structure or changing values), their mutual interactions, as well as external factors may all affect the approach of investment tribunals to human rights treaties. Obviously, the relationships between these communities are not likely to be transformed within a short period, but rather gradually and over time.

The position of investment tribunals vis-à-vis human rights treaties may change, for instance, following increasing direct interpersonal interactions between the members of the two communities; or in the case of enhanced dissemination of information regarding one community among the members of the other community. Similarly, the employment of a more common language in the two communities may also narrow the socio-cultural distance between them. For example, investment literature may assess the injurious consequences of human rights violations in economic terms.[82] Similarly, investment scholars may discuss the negative implications of widespread breaches of human rights for economic development. They may also underline the significance of human rights protection for long-term economic development (measured by GNP per capita) and international investment relations. Existing empirical studies reveal that generally, rule of law promotes economic development.[83]

In addition, it seems that normative isolation is somewhat linked to isolation from the public. Thus, changes regarding the extent of investment

[82] As to the link between economics and environmental protection, some studies assess the economic costs of climate change. See, eg, S Agrawala and S Fankhause (eds), *Economic Aspects of Adaptation to Climate Change: Costs, Benefits and Policy Instruments* (OECD, Paris, 2008).

[83] R Daniels and M Trebilcock, 'The Political Economy of Rule of Law Reform in Developing Countries' (2004) 26 *Michigan Journal of International Law* 99, 15–21: D Rodrik, A Subramanian and F Trebbi, 'Institutions Rule, The Primacy of Institutions over Geography and Integration in Economic Development' (2004) 9 *Journal of Economic Growth* 131. Some scholars underline the significance of public and constitutional rules for long-lasting economic growth. Under the latter approach, democracy (including separation of powers and freedom of the press) is generally conducive to development. On the positive relationship between democracies and long-run growth rates, see D Rodrick, *One Economics Many Recipes: Globalization, Institutions and Economic Growth* (Princeton, Princeton University Press, 2007) 169–83.

tribunals' exposure to the public may entail a change in investment tribunals' approach to public interest issues, including human rights protection. The prevailing atmosphere of confidentiality in most investment arbitral proceedings tends to intensify the adjudicators' perception that their principal role is settling the particular dispute between the specific parties; and diminish the weight given by the tribunals to broader human rights that are occasionally involved in investment disputes. The current trend to enhance the transparency of investment tribunal proceedings to the public[84] may change these perceptions ('social role') of investment arbitrators, and encourage them to accord a greater weight to human right protection.

VI CONCLUDING REMARKS

The preceding sections analyze a particular case of MSENs derived from human rights and investment treaties from a socio-cultural perspective. As discussed above, investment tribunals did not hesitate to apply rules derived from certain non-investment branches of international law (state responsibility, treaty law and general principles of law regarding corruptions). Despite that, they are generally reluctant to accord significant weight to human rights treaties in international investment law.

This chapter argues that legal interactions between various MSENs, including investment law and other branches of international law (either integration or fragmentation) may be analyzed as social interactions between the relevant communities. These legal interactions are affected by the particular features of relevant *social settings*, as well as the mutual relationships between the relevant social groups. More specifically, it is argued that the *socio-cultural distance* between the particular international legal settings affects the inclination of relevant decision-makers to incorporate or reject parallel legal rules developed in other branches of international law. Consequently, greater socio-cultural 'distance' between the involved social settings and groups is likely to decrease the prospects for mutual incorporation of legal rules developed in the other legal sphere. As to the relationship between international investment and human rights laws, the likelihood of investment tribunals to accord a significant role to human rights treaties is influenced by the cultural distance between these two branches of international law.

An analysis of the relationships between the social settings involved in international human rights and investment laws reveals a considerable

[84] On this trend, see, eg, *Biwater Gauff v United Republic of Tanzania* (ICSID Case No ARB/05/22) Procedural Order (29 September 2006) para 114: www. icsid.worldbank. org/ICSID/FrontServlet?requestType=CasesRH&actionVal=showDoc&docId=DC531_En&caseId=C67; Knahr and Reinisch, above (n 70) 97; WW Park, *Arbitration of International Business Disputes* (Oxford, Oxford University Press, 2006) 42–43; JE Vinuales, 'Amicus Intervention in Investor-State Arbitration' (2007) 61 *Dispute Settlement Journal* 72.

socio-cultural distance between these branches of international law. In light of this and the deep-rooted tensions between the relevant communities, it is not surprising that investment tribunals are generally reluctant to accord significant weight to human rights treaties in international investment law. Thus, the considerable socio-cultural distance between these socio-cultural settings parallels the normative distance between these branches of international law.

The existing social and normative gaps between investment and human rights laws may change in the future. Past experience shows that the relationship between various branches of international law is often dynamic. Future socio-cultural changes within each community – or changes in the social interactions between the relevant communities – may narrow the normative distance between international human rights and investment laws.

10

*Delineating Primary and Secondary Rules on Necessity at International Law**

Jürgen Kurtz

I INTRODUCTION

THIS CHAPTER EXAMINES a specific embodiment of the phenomenon of Multi-Sourced Equivalent Norms (MSENs) at international law: the legal defence of 'necessity' which can, under select conditions, excuse state liability for breach of customary and treaty obligations at international law. This starting definition requires further refinement, especially given that this general category of defence can apply across a wide variety of sources of international law. Necessity as a ground for modification of state behaviour and liability finds reflection in human rights law, international humanitarian law, trade treaties (including the World Trade Organization agreements), bilateral and regional investment treaties and the customary law of state responsibility.

I focus my analysis on the specific question of the intersection between the legal defence of necessity as constructed across international investment law and the customary plea of necessity under general international law (as developed in Article 25 of the International Law Commission's (ILC) Articles on State Responsibility).[1] Recent and controversial effect has been given to the intersection between investment treaty defences of this sort and the customary plea in adjudication by investor-state arbitral tribunals. Foreign investors have invoked their rights under select Argentine investment treaties to challenge regulatory measures implemented by Argentina in the aftermath of its 2001–02 financial crisis. Argentina has received the highest number of claims of any state party in the system of investment treaty arbitration with most of these claims relating to that

* I would like to thank Tomer Broude and Yuval Shany for their helpful comments on an earlier draft.

[1] ILC, '2001 Draft Articles on Responsibility of States for Internationally Wrongful Acts with Commentaries' (2001) GAOR, 56th Session Supp 10 UN Doc A/56/10, 20 (hereinafter ILC Articles).

country's financial crisis.[2] In defence, Argentina has invoked a treaty exception entitling it to pass emergency measures 'necessary' for the maintenance of 'public order' or the protection of 'essential security interests'.[3] A range of arbitral tribunals have considered that defence and almost all of them have rejected it. Critically, those tribunals opposed to Argentina's invocation of the treaty exception have done so by using the stringent conditions in ILC Article 25 to inform their reading of the treaty exception.[4] This then raises an important question of the sufficiency of the interpretative methods and devices being used by those tribunals when navigating between these similar but not identical legal norms.

The next part of the chapter, section II, introduces the subjects of my inquiry: the customary plea of necessity in ILC Article 25 and Article XI of the 1991 US-Argentina Bilateral Investment Treaty. I plan here to explore not only these legal devices, but the history and context of their emergence. This, I hope, will give both an understanding of the relationship between these legal norms and a benchmark to assess the manner in which investor-state arbitral tribunals have in fact approached the relationship between them. My underlying claim here is a specification of one of the general statements made in the introduction to this book; context matters and any position on the connection between apparently similar legal norms requires careful assessment of their distinct historical backgrounds, normative goals and institutional environments.[5]

Section III then draws on these factors in constructing two readings of the relationship between the customary plea and treaty defence of necessity, defined respectively as 'separating primary-secondary applications' and 'the treaty exception as *lex specialis*'. Section IV then compares these readings against the actual interpretative approaches adopted in the arbitral case law to date in which a troubling set of pathologies is found at odds with these two robust and justifiable candidates for the intersection between the customary and treaty norms. Section V concludes by putting forward the reading that, in my opinion, is best equipped to guide future adjudicators faced with invocations of both customary pleas and treaty exceptions of this sort.

[2] UNCTAD, *Latest Developments in Investor-State Dispute Settlement* (IIA Monitor No 1, 2008) 1–2.

[3] Treaty Between the United States of America and the Argentine Republic Concerning the Reciprocal Encouragement and Protection of Investment, signed at Washington DC (14 November 1991, entered into force 20 October 1994) (1992) 31 ILM 124, art XI (hereinafter US-Argentina BIT].

[4] *CMS Gas Transmission Company v Argentine Republic* (ICSID Case No ARB/01/8) Award (12 May 2005); *Enron Corporation and Ponderosa Assets L.P. v Argentine Republic* (ICSID Case No ARB/01/3) Award (22 May 2007); *Sempra Energy International v Argentine Republic* (ICSID Case No ARB/02/16) Award (28 September 2007).

[5] See in this volume, T Broude and Y Shany, 'The International Law and Policy of Multi-Sourced Equivalent Norms' in T Broude and Y Shany (eds), *Multi-Sourced Equivalent Norms in International Law* (Oxford, Hart Publishing, 2011) p 1.

II THE LEGAL STANDARDS ON NECESSITY IN INTERNATIONAL LAW

A The Plea of 'Necessity' under Customary International Law

The first legal standard drawn on in the Argentine cases is Article 25 of the ILC's Articles on State Responsibility. Article 25 enables a state to rely on a plea of necessity to preclude the wrongfulness of an act which would be otherwise wrongful under international law. Before examining the constituent parts of Article 25, there is an important preliminary question: does Article 25 represent customary international law in this area? As discussed in section IV, investor-state arbitral tribunals have uniformly accepted that the ILC Articles are reflective of existing custom. But there remain important questions of whether this is an accurate and desirable account of the work of the ILC, at least in this particular area of the law.

On first view, the preparedness of arbitral tribunals to equate the ILC Articles with custom is perhaps justifiable. The ILC was established in 1947 by the United Nations General Assembly (UNGA) with the explicit objective of contributing to the progressive development of international law *and* its codification.[6] The topic of state responsibility was selected as an early candidate in the work of the ILC, and it has produced multiple reports on this difficult subject under the auspices of different rapporteurs. Moreover, that work has itself been accepted as codifying custom by a range of international tribunals including the International Court of Justice (ICJ).[7]

There remains though a legitimate question of whether the work of the ILC *should* be taken as a final expression of customary law, at least in this area. For one thing, there has been no attempt to transform the ILC Articles into a treaty through a diplomatic law-making conference.[8] David Caron has argued that several of the broad and often controversial ILC Articles are better viewed as part of the ILC's separate mission of the 'progressive development' of international law, rather than as part of its mandate of codification.[9] This approach would view them as 'an authoritative scholarly statement of

[6] UNGA Res 174 (II) (21 November 1947).

[7] See, eg, *Legal Consequences of the Construction of a Wall in the Occupied Palestinian Territory* (Advisory Opinion) [2004] ICJ Rep 131 (July 9) paras 140–42 (drawing on ILC art 25 in its discussion of the state of necessity at customary international law); *United Parcel Service of America Inc v Government of Canada* Award on the Merits (24 May 2007) paras 45–76 (identifying the rules on attribution in ILC arts 4 and 5 as representing customary international law).

[8] The articles were forwarded to the United Nations General Assembly by the ILC after its 2001 session. In Resolution 56/83, the General Assembly 'takes note of the articles' and then 'commends them to the attention of Governments without prejudice to the question of their future adoption or other appropriate action'. UNGA Res 56/83 (12 December 2001).

[9] D Caron, 'The ILC Articles on State Responsibility: The Paradoxical Relationship Between Form and Authority' (2002) 96 *American Journal of International Law* 857, 858.

the law that would provide some guidance and clarity, yet also grow and change as it confronted the tests that the world presents'.[10] Investing the ILC Articles with the status of a formal source of law, on the other hand, may obviate this flexibility as adjudicators could confer excessive authority to the ILC Articles. Caron's concern, expressed in 2002, is prescient given the inflexible application of the ILC Articles in the methodologies adopted in many of the Argentine investor-state cases.

If we accept that the work of the ILC codifies customary international law, then Article 25 is our first legal standard on necessity as a type of defence at international law. Article 25 provides:

1. Necessity may not be invoked by a State as a ground for precluding the wrongfulness of an act not in conformity with an international obligation of that State unless the act:

    (a) is the only way for the State to safeguard an essential interest against a grave and imminent peril; and
    (b) does not seriously impair an essential interest of the State or States towards which the obligation exists, or of the international community as a whole.

2. In any case, necessity may not be invoked by a State as a ground for precluding wrongfulness if:

    (a) the international obligation in question excludes the possibility of invoking necessity; or
    (b) the State has contributed to the situation of necessity.[11]

It is important to give careful consideration to the precise scope of operation of this provision. Along with a number of other provisions in Chapter V of the ILC Articles, Article 25 sets out particular circumstances that will *preclude* a wrongful act at international law.[12] Those clauses are thus logically predicated on the initial finding of a wrongful act at international law.

The current ILC Articles do not themselves define what constitutes a wrongful act. This is not accidental but instead represents an intentional departure from earlier ILC efforts to codify substantive principles of state responsibility. ILC Rapporteur García Amador produced a series of six reports from 1956 to 1961 that attempted the ambitious and difficult task of codifying the primary, substantive rules that would trigger state responsibility for injuries to aliens.[13] These included the politically charged issue

[10] *Ibid*, 861.

[11] ILC Articles, above (n 1) art 25.

[12] The six circumstances precluding wrongfulness comprise: (i) consent; (ii) self-defence; (iii) countermeasures; (iv) force majeure; (v) distress; and (vi) necessity. *Ibid*, ch V.

[13] See, eg, FV García Amador, Special Rapporteur, 'Responsibility of the State for Injuries Caused in its Territory to the Person or Property of the Alien, Part II: The International Claim,

of whether states were required to compensate foreign actors for nationalization of private property even when linked to decolonization processes. The difficulty of reaching agreement in this highly contested area drove a distinct shift in perspective and strategy in the operation of the ILC in the early 1960s. A new ILC Rapporteur, Roberto Ago, began work on *secondary* rules of state responsibility that would only apply on the prior finding of a wrongful act at international law.[14] These rules did not themselves identify what would constitute the wrongful act in the sense of operative rights and obligations. They instead provide the framework for determining whether primary obligations have been breached (such as the key issue of attribution of conduct to a state) together with the consequences that will flow at international law generally from a wrongful act (including the use of countermeasures to induce compliance).[15]

The current ILC rules – finalized by Rapporteur James Crawford in 2001 – also adopt this taxonomy. The question of wrongfulness is assessed by the primary rules of international law applied to a given fact-set, an essential precondition to the invocation of the ILC rules.[16] It is also exclusively a question for the substantive legal regime at issue, whether customary or conventional in origin. A breach of these primary obligations constitutes a wrongful act that, in turn, triggers the operation of the Articles in ILC Chapter 5.[17] Those Articles, including Article 25 on 'necessity', offer the *secondary* possibility of precluding wrongfulness as a matter of international law. ILC Article 25 then acts as a general defence that can, in principle, apply to *any* international legal obligation, whether customary or conventional in origin. Given this potentially expansive operation, it is entirely understandable that ILC Article 25 sets out a range of highly stringent conditions for the secondary plea of necessity to apply. This is also driven by the concern of potential abuse common to any form of general derogation.[18]

Third Report on State Responsibility' (1958) UN Doc A/CN.4/111.

[14] See A Cassese, *International Law* 2nd edn (Oxford, Oxford University Press, 2005) 244; R Rosentock, 'The ILC and State Responsibility' (2002) 96 *American Journal of International Law* 792 (linking Roberto Ago's focus on secondary rules to a desire to avoid 'the bigger fights over nationalization').

[15] On this distinction between 'primary' and 'secondary' rules, see generally, J Combacau and D Alland, 'Primary and Secondary Rules in the Law of State Responsibility: Categorizing International Obligations' (1995) 16 *Netherlands Yearbook of International Law* 81.

[16] In the General Commentary to the ILC Articles, the following is made abundantly clear: '[I]t is not the function of the articles to specify the content of the obligations laid down by particular primary rules, or their interpretation . . . The articles take the existence and content of the primary rules of international law as they are at the relevant time'. ILC Articles, above (n 1) 31.

[17] See J Crawford (ed), *The International Law Commission's Articles on State Responsibility: Introduction, Text and Commentaries* (Cambridge, Cambridge University Press, 2002) 185 (affirming that 'as embodied in article 25, the plea of necessity is not intended to cover conduct which is in principle regulated by the primary obligations').

[18] *Ibid*, 178 (noting that the special features of the plea mean that 'necessity will only rarely be available to excuse non-performance of an obligation and that it is subject to strict limitations to safeguard against potential abuse').

The constriction of the scope of the customary plea is especially evident in ILC Article 25(1)(a) which requires that the chosen governmental measure ('act') be the 'only way' for a state to safeguard an essential interest. There is no inherent, context-independent definition for when a particular measure will be 'necessary' to achieve a given end. By contrast, let us consider the jurisprudence on a similar sort of exception in the law of the World Trade Organization (WTO). Articles XX(a), (b) and (d) of the General Agreement on Tariffs and Trade (GATT) all require an otherwise GATT-inconsistent measure to be 'necessary' for certain ends in order for a WTO member to successfully invoke a particular treaty defence.[19] The WTO Appellate Body in the *Korea-Beef* case presented the interpretative options on the term 'necessary' in GATT Article XX(d) across a spectrum:

> We believe that, as used in the context of Article XX(d), the reach of the word 'necessary' is not limited to that which is 'indispensable' or 'of absolute necessity' or 'inevitable'. Measures which are indispensable or of absolute necessity or inevitable to secure compliance certainly fulfil the requirements of Article XX(d). But other measures, too, may fall within the ambit of this exception. As used in Article XX(d), the term 'necessary' refers, in our view, to a range of degrees of necessity. At one end of this continuum lies 'necessary' understood as 'indispensable'; at the other end, is 'necessary' taken to a mean as 'making a contribution to'.[20]

The Appellate Body was then free to choose a reading from this spectrum of degrees of closeness between chosen means and the ends pursued.[21] Unlike GATT Article XX(d), there is no continuum of meanings for an adjudicator to choose from when applying the customary plea of 'necessity'.[22] Instead, ILC Article 25(1)(a) supplies the strict and operative test; the chosen means must be indispensable as the 'only way' for the state to safeguard its essential interests. Where a state has multiple options open to it to safeguard an 'essential interest', the customary defence is simply not available. On the few occasions where the customary plea has been raised at international law, it is this highly restrictive test of means-end scrutiny that has been applied to defeat invocation of the plea.[23]

[19] General Agreement on Tariffs and Trade (30 October 1947) TIAS No 1700, 55 UNTS 194, art XX (hereinafter GATT)

[20] *Korea: Measures Affecting Imports of Fresh, Chilled and Frozen Beef – Report of the Appellate Body* (11 December 2000) WT/DS161/AB/R, WT/DS169/AB/R, para 161.

[21] The Appellate Body went on to rule that '[w]e consider that a "necessary" measure is, in this continuum, located significantly closer to the pole of "indispensable" than to the opposite pole of simply "making a contribution to"'. *Ibid*, para 161.

[22] Of course, as a primary legal norm, GATT art XX exists on a different legal plane from the secondary customary plea of necessity as formalized in ILC art 25. I am not here concerned with exploring that dimension which stands at the level of construction of the norm itself. My only point is to draw out the difference in strictness of operation when it comes to how we understand and define the specific term 'necessary' across these different legal spheres. The customary plea *supplies* a very strict test for necessity driven by its broad scope of operation. In contrast, the term 'necessary' is left undefined in GATT art XX, leaving it up to the adjudicator to develop her own understanding of that term.

[23] See, eg, *Libyan Arab Foreign Investment Company v Republic of Burundi* (*Ad hoc* Arbitration)

B The Treaty Exception: Article XI of the US-Argentine Bilateral Investment Treaty

The arbitral cases examined in section IV below all engage the same treaty exception: Article XI of the 1991 US-Argentina Bilateral Investment Treaty (BIT), which is nested within an overall treaty regime that imposes significant obligations on a state party in its dealings with foreign investors of the other signatory state. The treaty as a whole then prescribes the sort of primary rules whose application might lead to a finding of a wrongful act at international law. This, as we have seen, is a predicate for the invocation of the customary plea of necessity in the taxonomy of the ILC. Article XI of the US-Argentina BIT itself is remarkably brief and simply states:

> This Treaty shall not preclude the application by either Party of measures necessary for the maintenance of public order, the fulfilment of its obligations with respect to the maintenance or restoration of international peace or security, or the protection of its own essential security interests.[24]

The treaty provision thus encompasses three permitted regulatory objectives: (i) public order; (ii) obligations with respect to the maintenance or restoration of international peace or security; and (iii) essential security interests. A chosen measure of a signatory state must also be 'necessary' to achieve those goals, in order to fall within the scope of the exception.

There are various formulations of this sort of necessity exception in different treaty instruments. GATT Articles XXI(b) and (c) offer a useful site of comparison to the BIT exception. These Articles are firstly useful because they offer us some understanding of what *shared* key terms might mean (especially the notion of 'maintenance or restoration of public security') and how these treaty provisions relate (if at all) to customary law. GATT Article XXI(b) and (c) are also helpful in a subsidiary sense because *differences* in language with the BIT exception may be critical in delineating the overall scope of the BIT exception (which becomes, after all, an important interpretative exercise if we take the position the treaty exception is separate from the customary plea). These Articles provide:

> Nothing in this Agreement shall be construed:
>
> . . .
>
> (b) to prevent any contracting party from taking any action which it considers necessary for the protection of its essential security interests
>
> (i) relating to fissionable materials or the materials from which they are derived;

(4 March 1991) 96 ILR 279, 319; *Case Concerning the Gabčíkovo-Nagymaros Project (Hung. v. Slov.)* [1997] ICJ Rep 7 (Sep. 25) para 56; *Case M/V Saiga (No 2) (Saint Vincent and the Grenadines v Guinea)* (Merits) ITLOS Reports 1999, (1999) 38 ILM 1323, para 135.

[24] US-Argentina BIT, above (n 3) art XI.

(ii) relating to the traffic in arms, ammunition and implements of war and to such traffic in other goods and materials as is carried on directly or indirectly for the purpose of supplying a military establishment;
(iii) taken in time of war or other emergency in international relations; or

(c) to prevent any contracting party from taking any action in pursuance of its obligations under the United Nations Charter for the maintenance of international peace and security.[25]

Three key points can be drawn from a comparison between GATT Article XXI and the US-Argentina BIT exception. First, the text of GATT Article XXI(b) expressly reserves authority for a signatory state to determine what 'it considers necessary' for the protection of its essential security interests. Yuval Shany has described GATT Article XXI(b) as a type of a 'discretionary norm' whose application depends on the exercise of discretion by an invoking state.[26] There is no equivalent language within the BIT exception to suggest it reserves the same quality or level of discretion to the state as that of GATT Article XXI(b). This critical absence in the text makes it difficult to convincingly claim that the BIT exception is of an *entirely* self-judging nature.[27] I raise this point because Argentina's defence (as described in the awards) places enormous emphasis on the marginal claim that the BIT exception is self-judging.[28] Such a claim is especially marginal given the ruling of the ICJ denying auto-interpretation on an almost identical treaty provision to that of the BIT exception in the *Nicaragua* case.[29] This is not to deny that there are serious competence concerns surrounding the capacity of an arbitral tribunal to resolve particular questions especially the scope of a state's 'essential security interests'. It appears clear though that the BIT exception contemplates *some* role for an adjudicator in the application of the exception.[30]

[25] GATT, above (n 19) art XXI(b), (c).

[26] Y Shany, 'Towards a General Margin of Appreciation Doctrine in International Law?' (2005) 16 *European Journal of International Law* 907, 916.

[27] For an extended and convincing analysis along these lines, see JE Alvarez and K Khamsi, 'The Argentine Crisis and Foreign Investors: A Glimpse into the Heart of the Investment Regime' IILJ Working Paper 2008/5, 34–42: www.iilj.org/publications/2008-5alvarez-khamsi.asp.

[28] This is clearly evident throughout the awards; see *CMS Award*, above (n 4) paras 366–73; *Enron Award*, above (n 4) paras 335–39; *Sempra Award*, above (n 4) paras 279–388. The later *CMS* Annulment Committee appears puzzled by the insistence on litigating this marginal point. See *CMS Gas Transmission Company v Argentine Republic* (ICSID Case No ARB/01/08) Decision of the *Ad hoc* Committee on the Application for Annulment (25 September 2007) para 122 ('Then [the CMS Tribunal] addressed *the debate which the parties had chosen to engage in* as to whether Article XI is self-judging' (emphasis added)).

[29] *Military and Paramilitary Activities in and against Nicaragua* (*Nicaragua v US*) [1986] ICJ Rep 14, para 222.

[30] The difficulty of accepting supra-national adjudication on these delicate questions while appreciating the need for some level of oversight is incisively touched on in the individual opinion of Judge Anzilotti in the *Oscar Chinn* case. *See Oscar Chinn* (Anzilotti, Separate Opinion) PCIJ Series A/B No 61, 113–14.

Secondly, unlike the BIT exception, GATT Article XXI(c) identifies the source of the obligations 'for the maintenance of international peace and security' as located within the United Nations Charter. This would be a logical candidate for triggering the BIT exception even in the absence of such express wording. Under Chapter VII of the Charter, the Security Council has express authority 'to maintain or restore international peace and security'.[31] The implications of this branch of the BIT exception are often under-appreciated.[32] Like GATT Article XXI(c), it deals with an objective that falls outside the customary arena and offers crucial textual evidence that the state parties did not simply seek to displace or incorporate custom where this would result *only* in higher standards of investment protection. The multiple branches of the exception show that they also contemplated the priority of state action and even supranational action (such as the institutional operation of Chapter VII of the UN Charter) in defined settings.

The third key difference between the BIT exception and GATT Article XXI goes to the delineation of 'essential security interests' and the inclusion of 'public order' (in the former but not the latter). The GATT provision expressly limits the notion of security to traditional, interstate security objectives including military and defence matters. Although the BIT exception also speaks of 'essential *security* interests', there is no indicative list of examples of that concept. This then leaves open the possibility that an investment treaty adjudicator might interpret the notion of 'security interests' in dynamic rather than static terms, to extend it beyond classic embodiments of interstate security concerns. The BIT exception also offers a new ground of exemption for the 'maintenance of public order' that is entirely absent from ILC Article 25 (and as it happens, GATT Article XXI). As with the branch of the BIT exception for 'maintenance of international peace and security', this is again important evidence of contemplation of priority of state action over and above the permissible limits at customary law.[33] Finally, there is the charged question of when a given measure

[31] United Nations Charter 1945, art 39. Chapter VII of the United Nations Charter sets out a series of pre-conditions to the eventual possibility of authorization of use of force by the Security Council. These include, most notably, measures not involving use of force including 'complete or partial interruption of economic relations' under art 41. This can encompass a call by the Security Council for states to impound or otherwise restrict the assets of private nationals of the state subject to a Chapter VII process. Such an obligation would normally breach the guarantees of protection in a typical BIT. For an example of Security Council invocation of art 41 against the Federal Republic of Yugoslavia, see UNSC Res 757 (1992).

[32] See *Continental Casualty Company v Argentine Republic* (ICSID Case No ARB/03/9) Award (5 September 2008) para 163 and fn 234 (characterizing this branch as 'irrelevant in the context of the present arbitration').

[33] In contrast, Alvarez and Khamsi seem to suggest that the inclusion of 'public order' in art XI of the US-Argentina BIT was intended to clarify that the customary defence of distress would apply. See Alvarez and Khamsi, above (n 27) 47 and 66. Aside from the obvious naming point, their suggestion seems unlikely given that, as the ILC has documented, 'cases of distress have mostly involved aircraft or ships entering State territory under stress of weather or following mechanical or navigational failure'. ILC Articles, above (n 1) 78.

will be 'necessary' to achieve the permissible objectives listed in the BIT exception. As we have seen, there is no supplied test of means-end inquiry in the BIT exception, an important departure from the secondary plea of necessity in ILC Article 25.

III UNDERSTANDING THE RELATIONSHIP BETWEEN THE CUSTOMARY PLEA AND TREATY EXCEPTION: ENGAGING TEXT, CONTEXT AND HISTORY

In taking a position on the relationship between these legal norms, we could – as a first possibility – examine them in isolation and focus purely on similarities and differences in wording. At a superficial level, there is base textual commonality across the treaty exception and the customary plea which might suggest they share a common legal space. The treaty exception exempts measures necessary for the protection of a state's 'own *essential security interests*' while the customary plea is also directed at enabling a state to 'safeguard an *essential interest* against a grave and imminent peril'. But there are critical differences that also fall at the level of the textual formulation of these standards. In particular, the ILC Articles are framed purely and expressly as a means of 'precluding the wrongfulness of an act not in conformity with an international obligation' of the state concerned. The ILC Articles do not themselves specify what constitutes a wrongful act; this is a province of the primary legal standard whether customary or conventional in origin. Yet even this apparent distinction between primary (treaty) and secondary (customary) norms is not one driven simply by the text of the ILC Articles. That text is but a reflection of the unique history and context of the ILC's work and strategic election to focus on systemizing secondary rather than primary norms at international law. With this background in mind, we might favour an approach which separates the treaty exception from the customary plea as faithful to the ILC's own understanding of Article 25. But if we are to take a position on the important question of the relationship between these standards, we will need to consider the entire context of their emergence. I have so far only assessed one side of the emergence of these two standards, being the work of the ILC. I now turn to the historical background of the formation of investment treaties to assess what it might tell us about the relationship between these two standards.

The history of the shift from customary to treaty protections for foreign investors is complex and nuanced. There are multiple factors that led state parties to build a network of investment treaties in the decades following the Second World War. The most fundamental of these – especially from the perspective of capital exporting states – was a conviction that custom was increasingly ill equipped to deal with particular challenges faced by foreign economic actors.[34] The immediate decades following the Second World War witnessed a dramatic rise in expropriation of private property by capital importing states.[35] Although customary international law had devised protections for certain forms of governmental expropriation,[36] capital-importing states began to invoke justifications for newer forms of taking.[37] The most notable of these was the practice of nationalization where particular industries were targeted as part of a state-led development programme. This gave rise to an open question in the period as to whether nationalization would comprise a novel category of taking distinct from the existing customary rules on expropriation.[38] Custom, as an inherently evolutionary device, began to slowly shift in a direction favourable to capital importing states on these questions.[39] The treaty provisions to emerge from this period counter this development and mitigate the new risk faced by foreign economic actors; nationalization along with expropriation is expressly included as a category of taking that requires full compensation by a signatory state.[40]

The strategic concern as to the limitations of customary law in the contemporary period is also borne out when we consider the changes to

[34] Customary protections were not aimed solely at foreign investors nor were they concerned explicitly with an investor's competitive position in a host state. The customary standard was instead directed at 'aliens' and largely designed to counter risks specific to *individuals* present in another state. The typical complaint of the late nineteenth century in this field concerned the unlawful arrest and detention of individual aliens rather than the later strategic concern surrounding the competitive opportunities and treatment of foreign economic actors. See generally, F Dunn, *The Protection of Nationals: A Study in the Application of International Law* (Baltimore, The Johns Hopkins Press, 1932) 54.

[35] T Brewer and S Young, *The Multilateral Investment System and Multinational Enterprises* (Oxford University Press, USA, 1998) 53. Table 2.3 of this reference summarizes trends in expropriation from 1960 to 1992. The mean number of expropriations in this period was as follows: 1960–64: 11; 1965–69: 16; 1970–74: 51; 1975–79: 34; 1980–84: 3; 1985–89: 0.4 and 1990–92: 0.

[36] *Case Concerning the Factory at Chorzów (Germany v Poland)* (Merits) PCIJ Series A No 17 (Sep. 13) 47.

[37] See, eg, SN Guha Roy, 'Is the Law of Responsibility of States for Injuries to Aliens a Part of Universal International Law?' (1961) 55 *American Journal of International Law* 863, 866–86 (detailing the attempts to characterize the law of state responsibility as an instrument of imperialism and criticizing its application to newly independent states in the post-colonial period).

[38] CF Amerasinghe, *State Responsibility for Injuries to Aliens* (Oxford, Clarendon Press, 1967) 128–29 (describing nationalization as a species of expropriation but subject to special rules 'differentiated from the rules relating to other cases of expropriation').

[39] The narrative of newly-independent states advancing claims to changes in customary rules on expropriation through the 1960s (including the critical General Assembly Resolution 1803) and 1970s is well known. It is important also to recognize that by the mid-1970s, a range of lump sum settlement tribunals had begun to identify some of those resolutions (particularly 1803) as reflecting 'the state of customary law in the field'. *See TOPCO v Libya* (1974) 17 ILM 3, 27–31. Similar methodologies and findings were adopted in the 1983 *AMINOIL* award (involving the 1977 nationalization of Kuwait's oil industry) and the 1994 *Ebrahimi* award (of the Iran-US Claims tribunal).

[40] See generally, R Dolzer and CH Schreuer, *Principles of International Investment Law* (Oxford, Oxford University Press, 2008) 89–115.

dispute settlement processes. The customary rules on diplomatic protection entitle a state of an injured national to bring action against another state for injuries caused to that national by an internationally wrongful act.[41] Where the injured national is an artificial legal person such as a corporation, there is the added question of whether the ability to initiate diplomatic protection is limited to the state of the corporation or may in certain situations, extend to the state of individual shareholders (where these differ). This issue arose before the ICJ in the *Barcelona Traction* case which ruled that it is only the state of incorporation of the corporate entity, rather than the state of its controlling shareholders, that can invoke a claim for diplomatic protection.[42] The modern treaty provisions again counter this gap in customary international law and offer the possibility of direct investor-to-state dispute settlement and as such, are distinct from the state-to-state dynamic of customary international law. The ability to initiate this new form of dispute settlement extends beyond the foreign company that is operating in a signatory state. The typical broad, BIT definition of 'investment' gives shareholders in a company the ability to bring a claim on their own behalf.[43]

We have then two key examples of a desire not simply to displace customary norms, but to tailor the resultant treaty protections to specific concerns surrounding the entry and operation of foreign investors in host states. This is not to say that *all* the background elements of custom are displaced in the newer treaty instruments. Certain treaty instruments expressly link the obligation to accord fair and equitable treatment to the broader corpus of international law.[44] This textual link evidences an intention to incorporate, at the very least, customary international law (on the minimum standard of treatment to be afforded to aliens) in the treaty obligation. State parties though are adopting a pick and choose strategy when it comes to incorporating customary law into the new treaty protections. The choice to do so appears to be largely an express one. Absent this express link, other treaty components (such as expropriation and dispute settlement rules) clearly oppose customary law and offer tailored standards of operation.

What then does the above tell us, when it comes to a treaty exception such as Article XI of the US-Argentina BIT? One can, I think, make a sensible claim that the treaty exception *also* offers a tailored defence distinct

[41] ILC, '2001 Draft Articles on Diplomatic Protection with Commentaries' (2001) GAOR, 56th Session Supp 10 UN Doc A/61/10, art 1. See also *Case Concerning Ahmadou Sadio Diallo (Guinea v Congo)* (Preliminary Objections) [2007] ICJ Rep 103, para 39.

[42] *Barcelona Traction, Light and Power Company, Limited* [1970] ICJ Rep 3, paras 41–47.

[43] US-Argentina BIT, above (n 3) arts 1(a) (definition of 'investment'); VII (investor-state dispute resolution).

[44] US-Argentina BIT, above (n 3) art II(2)(a) ('Investment shall at all times be accorded fair and equitable treatment, shall enjoy full protection and security and shall in no case be accorded treatment less than that required by international law'.)

from the customary plea of necessity. To put this differently, the process of tailoring distinct treaty standards was not only designed to offer stronger commitments to restrain state conduct but, in certain limited circumstances, to allow for newer flexibilities on the part of the state.[45] There seem to me to be two key factors to support this claim. First, there is no clear textual link to customary law in the treaty exception. Where state parties had intended for such a linkage to occur they had proven themselves perfectly capable of doing so expressly in *other* parts of the treaty. More fundamentally, the structure of the new treaty exception contemplates the priority of the postwar institutional structure of the UN Charter. The state parties envisioned a new ground for excuse that falls entirely outside the scope of the customary defence. Similarly, the treaty exception includes a 'public order' component, which does not find direct reflection in customary law. These factors are strongly probative of an objective desire to expand the scope of the treaty exception over and above the customary plea. Perhaps most tellingly, the customary provision supplies an operative test for when a measure will be 'necessary' while the treaty standard is silent on the choice of means-end inquiry. This precise difference between a customary and treaty standard was relied on by the ICJ in *Nicaragua* in finding that the two sources of law in that case did not overlap and continued to exist alongside each other.[46]

At this stage, the only firm conclusion we can make is that the treaty exception is a tailored defence that, at some level, is separate from the customary plea of necessity. There is still a need to come up with a plausible account of the precise relationship and the degree of separation between those standards so as to guide future adjudicators. There are at least two possible readings that we can put forward consistent with the analysis so far.

First, there is the approach implicit in the ILC's taxonomy. The ILC Articles distinctly present the customary defence of necessity as applicable to the issue of state responsibility. The elements of that defence only become operative if we have first identified a wrongful act at international law. The test for wrongfulness, in turn, is purely a question for the substantive

[45] This perspective – which I base on my method of analysis of objective factors (text, context and history) – is *also* reflected in the account of Kenneth Vandevelde, who had advised on US BIT negotiations in the early to mid 1980s. See K Vandevelde, *United States Investment Treaties, Policy and Practice* (Boston, Kluwer, 1992) 222.

[46] In Nicaragua, the US had argued that the provisions on use of force in the United Nations Charter had subsumed similar rules of customary international law. See *Nicaragua*, above (n 29) paras 173–74. The ICJ rejected this argument and found pertinent differences between the two sources of law that meant custom continued to exist alongside the treaty provision of the Charter. The Court particularly noted that the Charter provision does not regulate *all* aspects of the content of the use of force in self-defence. In particular, art 51 of the Charter 'does not contain any specific rule whereby self-defence would warrant only measures which are proportional to the armed attack and necessary to respond to it, *a rule well established in customary international law*' (emphasis added). *Nicaragua, ibid*, para 176.

international legal regime at issue. This would involve an assessment of (i) whether there is a breach of the legal obligations of the investment treaty, and then (ii) whether the treaty exception applies to save that breach. It is only if we have an answer to 'yes' to (i) 'no' to (ii) that we have wrongful act at international law that would entitle an adjudicator to consider the customary defence. In short, the treaty and customary defences operate on a vertical plane in a cumulative fashion; the treaty defence is part of the set of primary legal rules that must be adjudicated upon first *before* possibly attracting the secondary, customary defence. This approach is not without precedent in the system. Select investor-state tribunals have identified key differences between primary and secondary rules in the ILC taxonomy.[47]

A second account would begin from the premise that the customary standard (formalized in ILC Article 25) is a *primary* legal rule that goes to the determination of breach, operating on the same legal plane as the treaty exception. But the treaty exception would be regarded as an expression of *lex specialis*, constituting a specific elaboration or updating the general customary norm.[48] The difference with our first account is that the norms now exist not on a vertical but a horizontal plane. The *lex specialis* principle finds general reflection in the ILC Articles[49] and seems to be the favoured approach of a number of commentators in the field.[50] For it to apply, however, it is not enough that the same subject matter is covered by the treaty and customary standards. There must be some actual inconsistency, the identification of which remains a question of interpretation.[51] If we accept the premise of the customary standard as primary legal rule, there are key differences between the two norms, especially the inclusion of the public order exception in the treaty provision. We have then the sort of inconsistency that might allow for the application of the *lex specialis* principle. But the identification of the treaty defence as *lex specialis* is only a start point. There is still the question of the scope of priority to be accorded to the

[47] See *Biwater Gauff (Tanzania) Ltd v United Republic of Tanzania* Award (ICSID Case No ARB/05/22) Award (24 July 2008) paras 461–67.

[48] There is an alternative. One might be tempted to claim that the treaty exception is a specific secondary norm that operates on the same level as the customary plea. This approach has some merit in that it does not force us, contrary to the ILC's strong assertion, to assume that ILC art 25 is a primary norm. The problem is, of course, that we relegate the treaty exception to the secondary plane, and there is nothing in the treaty to justify this move.

[49] ILC art 55 provides: 'These articles do not apply where and to the extent that the condition for the existence of an internationally wrongful act or the content or implementation of the international responsibility of a State are governed by special rules of international law'. ILC Articles, above (n 1) art 55.

[50] See, eg, W Burke-White and A von Staden, 'Investment Protection in Extraordinary Times: The Interpretation and Application of Non-Precluded Measures in Bilateral Investment Treaties' (2008) 48 *Virginia Journal of International Law* 307, 322; C McLachlan, 'Investment Treaties and General International Law' (2008) 57 *International and Comparative Law Quarterly* 361, 390.

[51] Crawford, above (n 17) 307.

treaty defence, a critical issue largely ignored by those sympathetic to this reading.[52] Here, two alternative approaches may be taken, with vastly different implications for the operation of the treaty exception.[53]

The first is that endorsed by the ILC Articles, which provide that the customary or general norm will continue to operate in a residual fashion.[54] This would see the general norm displaced *only* to the extent of any inconsistency, leaving other aspects of the general law still applicable.[55]The ILC Study Group on the Fragmentation of International Law presents the interpretative link in the following terms:

> [T]he point of the lex specialis rule is to indicate which rule should be applied . . . [T]he special, as it were, steps in to become applicable instead of the general. Such replacement remains, however, always only partial. The more general rule remains in the background providing interpretative direction to the special one.[56]

This approach was adopted by the ICJ in the *Oil Platforms* case[57] and has important implications for arbitral tribunals constituted to cases involving financial crisis. The extent of inconsistency between the customary and treaty standards at issue here goes to the articulation of permissible ends ('public order' and 'essential security interest' in the treaty exception against 'essential interest' in ILC Article 25). There is, however, a degree of overlap between the standards that cuts across this difference; both endorse 'necessity' as the legal standard for when a measure should be taken to have achieved a particular end. With this overlap in mind, the stringent customary test of 'necessity' – that a measure is the 'only way' to effect a given end – could apply in a residual fashion to give content

[52] McLachlan comes closest to addressing this issue but does so only tangentially: 'Where, as here, the customary rule lays down a stricter test than the treaty language, it is unlikely that there will be a need for separate resort to custom'. McLachlan, above (n 50) 390.

[53] Simma and Pulkowski present these different approaches as weak and strong forms of *lex specialis* respectively. See B Simma and D Pulkowski, 'Of Planets and the Universe: Self-Contained Regimes in International Law' (2006) 17 *European Journal of International Law* 483, 490–91.

[54] ILC Articles, above (n 1) 140, Commentary, paras 2–3.

[55] *Ibid*, 140, Commentary, para 3.

[56] ILC, 'Report of the Study Group of the ILC, Fragmentation of International Law: Difficulties arising from the Diversification and Expansion of International Law' (2006) UN Doc A/CN.4/L.682, para 102.

[57] *Case Concerning Oil Platforms (Iran v US)* (Merits) [2003] ICJ Rep 90, paras 32, 41–43 and 73. In this case, the US sought to rely on an exception for necessary 'essential security interests' as a defence to Iran's claims that US military attacks on Iranian oil platforms breached the operative provisions of the treaty. The US invited the Court to afford a 'measure of discretion' to a party's good faith application of measures of this sort. The ICJ rejected the idea that the treaty exception was intended to operate independently of relevant rules of international law on use of force. In particular, it applied the customary rules on self-defence to give content to the treaty standard that a measure was 'necessary' for essential security interests. As the test for necessity in those customary rules is both 'strict and objective', it left no room for the US' proposed claim of a measure of discretion.

to the treaty provision.[58] This type of soft *lex specialis*, where the general customary norm continues to give residual content to the treaty exception, has found recent endorsement in other areas of investment treaty adjudication.[59]

As an alternative, there is the possibility that the instrument of *lex specialis* could be taken to exclude the general law, in its entirety. This harder version of *lex specialis* would situate the treaty as contracting out of custom. But to justify this approach, an adjudicator might be expected to find clear evidence of intent to fully displace the more general norm. After all, contracting out of custom should be clear and unambiguous.[60] To my mind, the historical account traced earlier above suffices, at the margins, to discharge this burden. If so, we are then left with an outcome similar to the ILC's preferred taxonomy. The adjudicator would be obliged to apply both the obligation and exception as autonomous legal standards that would determine whether a state has committed a wrongful act of international law.

To sum up, I have put forward three potential readings on the relationship between the treaty exception and the customary plea which correlate to some degree with the models raised in the introduction to this book:

(i) primary-secondary applications, as understood in the ILC taxonomy;
(ii) the treaty exception as weak *lex specialis* (with the customary plea continuing to have residual effect); and
(iii) the treaty exception as hard *lex specialis* (which situates the treaty defence as contracting entirely out of custom).

Of these candidates, my preference is for (i) but I concede that one can also make a sensible case for (iii). These readings accurately reflect both the specific work of the ILC and the historical narrative we have explored so far. On the other hand, the soft *lex specialis* reading of (ii) could lead to a

[58] This was in fact an argument expressly made by the investor in the *Continental Award*: '[The Claimant] relies also on the ILC commentary on Art 25(1)(a) stating that the "plea is excluded if there are other (otherwise lawful) means available, even if they may be more costly or less convenient"' (ILC Commentary, para 15). This ought to be considered not only as a more precise explanation of the term 'necessary' with regard to the invocation of the defence of necessity under customary international law, *but also as a standard applicable in interpreting art XI of the BIT*' (emphasis added). *Continental Award*, above (n 32) para 191.

[59] See *Archer Daniels Midland Company and Tate & Lyle Ingredients Americas, Inc v United Mexican States* (ICSID Case No ARB/(AF)/04/5) Award (21 November 2007) para 119 (finding that '[c]hapter Eleven of the NAFTA constitutes *lex specialis* in respect of its express content but customary international law continues to govern all matters not covered by Chapter Eleven').

[60] For analysis of this point within the context of the WTO dispute settlement system and its relation to the law of state responsibility, see R Howse and R Staiger, 'United States- Anti Dumping Act of 1916 (Original Complaint by the European Communities) – Recourse to Arbitration by the United States under 22.6 of the DSU, WT/DS136/ARB, 24 February 2004: A Legal and Economic Analysis'; H Horn and P Mavroidis (eds), *The WTO Case Law of 2003* (Cambridge, Cambridge University Press, 2006) 276–77. See also Simma and Pulkowski, above (n 53) 495.

type of redundancy if the stringent customary test of means-end scrutiny is applied in residual form. After all, even if we apply the broader scope of permitted objectives in the treaty exception, if a state must prove its chosen means were 'the only way' to achieve permitted ends, it will rarely discharge that burden. In short, we will be left with a type of customary law *redux*. I explore later why this extinction of a potential source of flexibility in investment law is problematic when we consider the contemporary challenges facing adjudicators in the system.

I now turn to the actual choices made by investor-state arbitral tribunals on the relationship where, surprisingly, alternatives (i) to (iii) remain distinct minorities in the jurisprudence.

IV THE CASES

The financial losses to flow from the Argentine financial crisis have triggered dozens of claims by foreign investors alleging breach of Argentina's investment treaty obligations. Argentina has invoked defined treaty exceptions and customary law in an attempt to claim abrogation of liability for, among other things, its abrogation of the contractual rights of licensees in utility sectors to adjust tariffs in line with US inflation indices. There have been five arbitral awards that have directly considered the relationship between the customary and treaty exceptions invoked by Argentina. These cases were all initiated within the ICSID system and concern the same subject treaty, the 1991 US-Argentina BIT. There is an initial cluster of four awards; *CMS v Argentina* (May 2005),[61] *LG&E v Argentina* (October 2006),[62] *Enron v Argentina* (May 2007)[63] and *Sempra v Argentina* (September 2007).[64] The *CMS, Enron* and *Sempra* tribunals ruled against Argentina and adopt similar methods of reasoning. The *LG&E* tribunal, on the other hand, partially found in favour of Argentina on its invocation of the exceptions. What followed is the release of a ruling by an ICSID Annulment Committee on the *CMS* award. There is no formal system of appellate review on questions of law within the ICSID, but an unsuccessful party can apply for annulment on narrow grounds essentially reflecting due process failures.[65] While largely finding against Argentina, the Annulment

[61] *CMS Award*, above (n 4).

[62] *LG&E Energy Corp, LG&E Capital Corp, LG&E International Inc v Argentine Republic* (ICSID Case No ARB/02/1) Award (3 October 2006).

[63] *Enron Award*, above (n 4).

[64] *Sempra Award*, above (n 4).

[65] Convention on the Settlement of Investment Disputes Between States and Nationals of Other States (opened for signature 18 March 1965, entered into force 14 October 1966) 575 UNTS 159, art 52(1) (setting out the five grounds for annulment as: (a) tribunal was not properly constituted; (b) manifest excess of powers; (c) corruption; (d) serious departure from a fundamental rule of procedure; (e) failure to state reasons).

Committee – having adopted the language and gravitas of an appellate judicial body[66] – offered a range of targeted criticisms of the legal reasoning of the *CMS* tribunal.[67] The fifth and final instalment (to date) is the *Continental v Argentina* (September 2008)[68] award which ruled largely in favour of Argentina, with a distinct method of its own.

Of these five arbitral awards, the first three – *CMS, Enron* and *Sempra* – conflate the treaty defence with the customary plea of necessity (taken to be represented by ILC Article 25). In doing so, these tribunals ignore all of the differences inherent in the treaty exception ('public order' and so on) and instead give full priority to the stringent customary plea.

A Conflation: *CMS, Enron* and *Sempra*

There are subtle differences between the three tribunals in their adoption of this dominant methodology. The *CMS* tribunal appears to first analyze the customary exception and then separately consider the treaty clause, which might be suggestive of a *lex specialis* approach.[69] But in substance, its analysis of the constituent components of the treaty is but a mask for the application of the customary plea. The *Sempra* tribunal is more explicit in conflating the two standards:

> This Tribunal believes . . . that the Treaty provision is inseparable from the customary law standard insofar as the definition of necessity and the conditions for its operation are concerned given that it is under customary law that such conditions have been defined.[70]

Moreover, the *Sempra* tribunal gives an indication of its motivation in choosing this approach. The 'problem' for the tribunal is that 'the Treaty itself did not deal with the legal elements necessary for the invocation of a state of necessity . . . the rule governing such questions will thus be found under customary law'.[71] As discussed earlier, the ILC Articles supply the operative legal test for particular elements of the customary defence, most notably for when a chosen measure will be necessary. The stringency of

[66] One can only speculate that this is perhaps natural given the make-up and credentials of the membership of that Committee. This comprised Judge Gilbert Guillaume (a former president of the ICJ), Judge Nabil Elaraby (a former judge of the ICJ) and notably, Professor James Crawford (ILC Special Rapporteur on State Responsibility).

[67] *CMS Annulment Award*, above (n 28) paras 101–50.

[68] *Continental Award*, above (n 32).

[69] See *CMS Award*, above (n 4) paras 315–52 (reviewing the state of necessity under customary international law); 353–78 (reviewing the treaty's clauses on emergency). See also *CMS Annulment Award*, above (n 28) para 128 (noting that the *CMS* tribunal 'dealt with the defense based on customary law before dealing with the defense drawn from Article XI').

[70] *Sempra Award*, above (n 4) para 376. This approach is also adopted by the *Enron* tribunal. See *Enron Award*, above (n 4) para 333.

[71] *Sempra Award*, *ibid*, para 378.

these operative tests is linked to the generality of operation of the customary exception and to its second-order nature. This tribunal seems to simply crave the same sort of guidance in relation to the treaty exception, without even considering the construction and relationship between the two legal standards.[72] An adjudicator can, of course, seek to draw guidance by examining similarities and differences in other sources of law. But these tribunals are engaged in a very different endeavour and are allowing a distinct external norm in the form of the customary plea to override entirely the treaty norm under adjudication.

An initial consequence of this approach is a singular focus throughout these awards on the exception for 'essential security interests'. There is, on the other hand, no substantive analysis of the alternate treaty ground for exemption of measures necessary to maintain 'public order', a logical if regrettable consequence of the method chosen by these tribunals. Explicit attention to the alternate treaty exemption for 'public order' would raise an obvious, key difference between the customary and treaty standards at odds with the elected approach.

These tribunals then present what might on first view, seem to be an expansive reading of the scope of a state's 'essential security interests'. The *CMS* tribunal, for example, rejects the idea that these interests are limited to national security concerns of an international character as 'there is nothing in the context of customary international law . . . that could on its own exclude major economic crises'.[73] Yet, the ILC Articles are soon used to significantly narrow the operation of the treaty exception. The tribunals draw on the requirement that a state safeguard an essential interest against a 'grave and imminent peril' under ILC Article 25(1)(a) to find that even Argentina's severe economic crisis would not be sufficient to fall within the treaty exception. The *CMS* tribunal, for example, presents 'a major breakdown with all its social and political implications' and 'total economic and social collapse' as operative standards.[74] For the *Sempra* tribunal, Argentina's economic crisis would have had to compromise the 'very existence of the State and its independence' to attract the treaty exception.[75] Once again, it is important to clearly draw out the implications of the methodology chosen by the tribunal. There is no textual equivalent of the ILC standard of 'grave and imminent peril' in the treaty exception; these tribunals are simply importing from the customary norm an exceedingly stringent standard of operation.

Critically, the tribunals then draw on the ILC Articles to determine whether Argentina's chosen measures were 'necessary' to protect its

[72] This dynamic is also at play in the deliberations of the *Enron* tribunal. See *Enron Award*, above (n 4) para 333.

[73] *CMS Award*, above (n 4) para 359.

[74] *Ibid*, paras 319–59.

[75] *Sempra Award*, above (n 4) para 348; *Enron Award*, above (n 4) para 306.

essential security interests. As we have seen, ILC Article 25(1)(a) requires that the means chosen must be the 'only way' for the state to safeguard its interests. This highly stringent test of necessity is presented as a second ground for rejecting Argentina's defence. According to the *CMS* tribunal, Argentina's regulatory response was not the only way to deal with the financial crisis as it possessed 'a variety of alternatives, including dollarization of the economy, granting of direct subsidies to the affected population or industries and many others'.[76] The problem with this restrictive test is that it is always possible to conceive of multiple responses to a given financial crisis rendering the treaty exception largely ineffectual.[77]

There are two final uses of the ILC Articles which further illustrate the blunt matter in which these tribunals conflate the treaty exception with the customary plea. First, the preclusion of the customary defence where a state has 'contributed to the situation of necessity' under ILC Article 25(2)(b) is introduced as an operative element of the treaty exception.[78] Again, there is no reflection within the treaty text of such a limitation. Argentina's contribution to the crisis is characterized rather bluntly as 'substantial' and offered as yet another ground for rejecting its treaty defence.[79] Secondly, the tribunals draw on the ILC Articles on the question of compensation where the defending state otherwise meets the operative components of the treaty exception. This final use of the work of the ILC reveals, once again, a failure to consider the precise terms of a given Article (which is itself, a hallmark of the method of conflation). ILC Article 27(b) provides that an otherwise successful plea of necessity is 'without prejudice to *the question* of compensation for any material loss incurred by the act in question' (emphasis added).[80] In other words, the ILC Articles offer a reservation to the question of compensation, presenting this as a case by case issue to be decided between the parties concerned.[81] The *CMS* tribunal though

[76] *CMS Award*, above (n 4) para 323; *Sempra Award*, above (n 4) paras 350–51.

[77] This is, somewhat ironically, noted by the *Enron* tribunal: 'A rather sad world comparative experience in the handling of economic crises, shows that there are *always* many approaches to address and correct such critical events, and it is difficult to justify that none of them were available in the Argentine case' (emphasis added). *Enron Award*, above (n 4) para 308.

[78] *Enron Award, ibid*, paras 311–12; *Sempra Award*, above (n 4) paras 311–13.

[79] *CMS Award*, above (n 4) para 329.

[80] ILC Articles, above (n 1) art 27(b).

[81] This is made clear in the commentary to art 27(b): 'Subparagraph (b) of article 27 is a reservation as to questions of possible compensation for damage in cases covered in chapter V' and 'Subparagraph (b) does not attempt to specify in what circumstances compensation should be payable. Generally the range of possible situations covered by chapter V is such that to lay down a detailed regime for compensation is not appropriate. It will be for the State invoking a circumstance precluding wrongfulness to agree with any affected States on the possibility and extent of compensation payable in a given case'. ILC Articles, above (n 1) 86 (paras 4 and 6). This point is explicitly endorsed by the later *CMS* Annulment Committee. *CMS Annulment Committee*, above (n 28) para 147. Argentina and its expert witness use this as a key aspect in contentions in a later arbitration. *See BG Group Plc v Argentina* (UNCITRAL Arbitration) Final Award (24 December 2007) para 398 ('Objecting to BG's reliance on Article

endorses Article 27 as '[establishing] the appropriate rule of international law on this issue'[82] but mistakenly characterizes it as imposing a '*duty* to compensate' (emphasis added).[83]

We can, with confidence, reject the methodology of conflation adopted by these three cases. These tribunals ignore the clear evidence of textual difference as well as the distinct historical trajectories of these two legal norms, surveyed in sections II and II above. My conclusion here is buttressed by the findings of the *CMS* Annulment Committee. That committee characterizes the *CMS* tribunal's conflation of the customary and treaty exception as a 'manifest error of law'.[84] Interestingly, the committee also went on to present two potential readings of the relationship between the two standards, the first of which positions 'Article XI [of the BIT] as the *lex specialis* governing the matter and not [ILC] Article 25'.[85]

B The Treaty Exception as (Soft or Hard) *Lex Specialis? LG&E v Argentina*

The best candidate for a *lex specialis* approach in the jurisprudence is *LG&E v Argentina*, although there are intriguing hints in this direction in the *Continental* award as well.[86] Unlike the tribunals that adopt the conflation methodology, the *LG&E* tribunal begins its analysis with the treaty exception and also finds expressly in favour of Argentina on the treaty exception (albeit within a defined time period).[87] In fact, the tribunal seems to be giving express effect to the specialized public order component of the treaty exception.[88] The analysis of the treaty provision though is not set in isolation as much of the tribunal's reasoning draws on customary law.[89] We appear to be in the realm of this second methodology; although both the customary and treaty standards cover a similar subject area, the treaty provision is being applied as an expression of soft *lex specialis*.

We might then expect the *LG&E* tribunal to draw on the customary standard to assess whether Argentina's chosen means were 'necessary' as the

27 of the ILC Draft Articles, Argentina referred to its expert witness Prof Kingsbury, stating that the ILC Articles do not set forth that compensation should be granted in all cases where the state of necessity is alleged').

[82] *CMS Award*, above (n 4) para 390.

[83] *Ibid*, para 388.

[84] *CMS Annulment Committee*, above (n 28) para 130.

[85] *Ibid*, para 133

[86] *Continental Award*, above (n 32) para 168.

[87] *LG&E Award*, above n 62 para 229.

[88] The *LG&E* tribunal engages in an extensive if descriptive review of the consequences of the financial crisis to conclude: 'All of these devastating conditions – economic, political, social – in the aggregate triggered the protections afforded under Article XI of the Treaty to maintain order and control the civil unrest'. *Ibid*, paras 231–37.

[89] *Ibid*, para 245.

only way to maintain public order or to protect essential security interests. The tribunal though does not use the ILC Articles in this residual fashion but adopts its own rather cursory approach to 'necessity'. It is difficult to understand the precise test applied to assess the necessity of Argentina's chosen means. The tribunal characterizes Argentina's response as legitimate without explaining why this is the case.[90]

By adopting its own unprincipled approach to the test for 'necessity', the *LG&E* tribunal may be simply excluding the customary standard in its entirety. In other words, the tribunal is choosing to follow a hard contracting out approach to *lex specialis* rather than a soft approach that draws on custom in a residual fashion. The problem though is that the *LG&E* tribunal continues its analysis and finds, in a thoroughly unconvincing fashion, that the customary provisions would *also* excuse Argentina from liability. The strangest part of this later analysis is the summary finding that Argentina's measure (now characterized as an 'economic recovery package') was not just legitimate (as concluded under the treaty exception) but 'the only means to respond to the crisis'.[91]

In sum, the *LG&E* award is a candidate for a *lex specialis* approach, but it is not a convincing one. The problem lies in the internal contradiction of that award. If the treaty exception is an expression of *lex specialis*, then an adjudicator should determine the scope of priority to be accorded to the treaty text. This would mean either applying the customary norm in a residual fashion (where not in conflict) or displacing it entirely. The *LG&E* tribunal appears reluctant to choose between these approaches, perhaps recognizing the strength of the former (within the internal logic of the *lex specialis* method) but also its implications (the likely preclusion of most claims to invocation). Its own poorly conceived test of 'legitimacy' appears driven more by pragmatism rather than principle and will hardly aid in guiding successive tribunals in this difficult area.

C Separating Primary-Secondary Applications: *Continental v Argentina*

The final case considered in this chapter adopts a very different approach to the relationship between the customary plea and the treaty defence. The *Continental* tribunal is the first to pay careful attention to the text of both

[90] The *LG&E* tribunal ruled: 'Claimants contend that the necessity defence should not be applied here because the measures implemented by Argentina were not the only means available to respond to the crisis. The Tribunal rejects this assertion. Article XI refers to situations in which a State has no choice but to act. A State may have several responses at its disposal to maintain public order or protect its essential security interests. In this sense, it is recognized that Argentina's suspension of the calculation of tariffs in U.S. dollars and the PPI adjustment of tariffs was a legitimate way of protecting its social and economic system'. *Ibid*, para 239.

[91] *Ibid*, para 257.

the treaty defence and the formulation of ILC Article 25.[92] It then clearly endorses the ILC's taxonomy of separating the treaty provisions as an obligation of 'a "primary" nature' with the plea of necessity in ILC Article 25 relegated to the secondary plane.[93] The *Continental* tribunal in this respect follows that of the *CMS* Annulment Committee which also endorses the ILC's taxonomy as a means of operationalizing these standards:

> [Article XI] specifies the conditions under which the Treaty may be applied, whereas [ILC] Article 25 is drafted in a negative way: it excludes the application of the state of necessity on the merits, unless certain stringent conditions are met. Moreover, *Article XI is a threshold requirement: if it applies, the substantive obligations under the Treaty do not apply*. By contrast, Article 25 is an excuse which is *only* relevant once it has been decided that there has otherwise been a breach of those substantive obligations[94] (emphasis added).

There is of course a challenge implicit in this methodology. An adjudicator that characterizes the treaty exception as a 'primary' norm cannot simply draw on the ILC Articles as guidance in an interpretative task. It may have been this very prospect that drove the earlier tribunals to adopt the problematic but simple method of conflation. Under this very different methodology, an adjudicator must construct and defend her approach to the treaty defence across three key issues: (i) the identification and scope of 'public order'; (ii) the identification and scope of a state's 'essential security interests'; and (iii) how to test when a chosen measure is 'necessary' to achieve these purposes.

After disposing of the charged question of the relationship between the two legal norms, the *Continental* tribunal approaches these interpretative questions unlike any of the other cases we have surveyed. It clearly gives independent operation to the 'public order' ground of exemption, separate from the exclusion for 'essential security interests'.[95] We even have engagement with a critical precept of treaty interpretation – a dimension missing in the earlier arbitral awards – where an adjudicator is faced with a treaty authenticated in two or more languages.[96] By comparing the English and Spanish texts of the US-Argentina BIT, the tribunal accepts 'public order' as a synonym for 'public peace', able to be threatened by actual or even potential insurrections, riots and violent disturbances.[97] This ruling has important consequences in scenarios such as the Argentine financial crisis

[92] *Continental Award*, above (n 32) paras 162–67.

[93] *Ibid*, para 167.

[94] *CMS Annulment Committee*, above (n 28) para 129.

[95] *Continental Award*, above (n 32) para 174.

[96] Under art 33(4) of the Vienna Convention on the Law of Treaties, where there is a difference in meaning in the authenticated languages of a given treaty, the adjudicator must adopt the meaning 'which best reconciles the tests, having regard to the object and purpose of the treaty' Vienna Convention on the Law of Treaties (adopted 23 May 1969, entered into force 27 January 1980) 1155 UNTS 331, art 33(4) (VCLT).

[97] *Continental Award*, above (n 32) para 174.

which occasioned widespread rioting, looting and executive instability. Disruptive effects of this sort can engage a state's 'public order' concerns under this reading, distinct from the charged issue of whether or not such crises are covered by a state's 'essential security interests'. Even on the latter, the *Continental* tribunal interprets the scope of a state's 'essential security interests' beyond traditional and static notions of security understood as the ability of a state to counter external threats to its territorial integrity. Drawing on the Preamble of the UN Charter, the tribunal rules that the economic and social dislocations of the Argentine financial crisis also engaged Argentina's 'essential security interests'.[98]

At this stage, the *Continental* tribunal had only ruled that the downside effects of the Argentine financial crises triggered Argentina's right to maintain 'public order' and to protect its 'essential security interests' under the treaty exception. This finding goes to the scope of the permitted objectives under the treaty exception and does not, of itself, necessarily excuse Argentina's liability under the BIT. The measures actually chosen by Argentina to achieve these purposes must also be 'necessary' under the treaty exception. The necessity component of the treaty exception asks a question of the proximity or fit between the chosen means and the asserted regulatory purpose. There are though various methods of engaging in means-end inquiry. Here we find a critical difference with the earlier case law. The *Continental* tribunal discounts one candidate at the outset; the customary test that the chosen measure must be the 'only way' for the state to achieve its asserted goal. This is a logical outcome. Given that the treaty exception under its preferred methodology acts as a primary norm, there is no obligation to adopt this exceedingly stringent secondary test.

Interestingly, the *Continental* tribunal then draws on the law of the WTO in constructing its preferred test of means-end scrutiny. Citing the WTO Appellate Body's ruling in *Korea-Beef*, the tribunal adopts a reasonable less-restrictive-means (LRM) approach to the question of necessity.[99] Under this test, an adjudicator would not only identify whether there is a less restrictive alternative to the state's chosen means, but assess whether it is a *reasonable* alternative given, for example, the different costs of implementation. To be precise, a state's chosen measure will be necessary under this test if every alternative measure achieves the same level of benefit at less restriction but still requires unreasonable administration and enforcement costs. It is important to note that an alternative measure will only be assessed under this test if it achieves the *same* level of benefit as the chosen measure. There is then no possibility for the adjudicator to substitute her own judgement for that of the state as to the appropriate level of benefit to flow from the chosen measures.

[98] *Ibid*, para 175.
[99] *Ibid*, paras 193–98.

This modest approach is very different from other systems of means-end inquiry including proportionality review. In the latter, the adjudicator can determine whether the costs imposed by the measure (on the foreign investor) are excessive or disproportionate to the benefits of the policy objective. The inquiry centres on the regulatory objective, which can be abandoned depending on the adjudicator's own assessment of the benefits against attendant costs. It is highly unlikely that ad hoc arbitral panels are better assessors of such value-laden judgments and complex empirical questions than elected representatives. The *Continental* tribunal evinces a sophisticated understanding of the appropriate and modest role implicit in a reasonable LRM test, as compared with proportionality review. Consider, for example, the phrasing of its task in the following extract:

> In evaluating whether these alternatives were in fact reasonably available and would have avoided the adoption of the challenged Measures, the Tribunal is mindful that it is not its mandate to pass judgment upon Argentina's economic policy during 2001–2002, nor to censure Argentina's sovereign choices as an independent state. Our task is more modestly to evaluate only if the plea of necessity by Argentina is well-founded, in that Argentina had no other reasonable choices available, in order to protect its essential interests at the time, than to adopt these Measures.[100] (emphasis added)

The tribunal concludes with a final and critical difference – in outcome – at odds with the earlier awards (with the partial exception of *LG&E*). The *Continental* tribunal finds, in the main, that the Argentine measures are necessary under the treaty exception. As we saw earlier, the tribunals that conflated the customary plea with the treaty exception were prepared to accept that Argentina possessed a variety of speculative alternatives to its chosen strategy of abrogation of the contractual rights of foreign investors operating utility concerns. The *CMS* tribunal identified these as 'including the dollarization of the economy, granting of direct subsidies to the affected population or industries and many others'.[101] The *Continental* tribunal sensibly rejects this loose view of whether these were in fact reasonable alternatives open to Argentina. We find instead a prudent claim and one which might, if adopted in future cases, forestall conflict given state obligations under the corpus of human rights law:

> [I]n conformity with the concept of 'necessity' discussed above, we consider that the Government's efforts struck an appropriate balance between that aim and the responsibility of any government towards the country's population: it is self-evident that not every sacrifice can properly be imposed on a country's people in order to safeguard a certain policy that would ensure full respect towards international obligations in the financial sphere, before a breach of those obligations can be considered justified as being necessary under this BIT.[102]

[100] *Ibid*, para 199.
[101] *CMS Award*, above (n 4) para 323.
[102] *Continental Award*, above (n 32) para 227.

V CONCLUSION

We have now traced a range of methodological approaches on the relationship between the customary plea of necessity and the treaty exception in the US-Argentina BIT. The blunt and dominant method of conflating the treaty exception with the customary plea is clearly mistaken both on a close interpretation of the two legal standards and on a broader historical analysis of the emergence of these norms. There are serious, real-world implications that flow from this problematic methodology. Argentina is now liable for hundreds of millions in dollars damages despite objective evidence of legal error on the part of these early tribunals. If carried through, Argentine threats of non-compliance with ICSID awards will present one of the greatest challenges to the continuing viability of the system of investment treaty arbitration.

With this in mind, we face a pressing need for future adjudicators to construct a robust and defensible approach to the relation between the treaty exception and the customary plea. The choice, to my mind, really comes down to an election of reading the treaty exception as one of hard *lex specialis* or finding it be a primary norm separate from the secondary customary plea. There is little in outcome that will distinguish the two readings, at least when it comes to treaty provision such as Article XI of the US-Argentina BIT. But there may be distinct doctrinal and strategic advantages which should push us to prefer the latter over the former. The latter clearly obliges an adjudicator to give attempt to give effect to *both* the treaty exception and the customary defence. More subtly, it enables an adjudicator to avoid the temptation implicit in the *lex specialis* reading – even if drawn to the hard version – that remnants of the customary norm will continue to control the application of the treaty provision, rendering it all but inutile. Reviewing the jurisprudence to date, it is difficult to escape the sense that many arbitrators remain hard-wired to the customary test. The final methodology imposes a disciplinary boundary on an adjudicator by characterizing the treaty exception as a first-order primary norm.

There may be criticism that separating these norms into primary and secondary categories will result in redundancy of the customary defence. There is no concern as to redundancy if the treaty exception is framed more narrowly than the customary plea. Yet, given the strictness of the customary plea in ILC Article 25, it is difficult to see in what circumstances this scenario might arise. The more realistic case will approximate the Argentine disputes; where the treaty exception is likely to have a broader scope of operation than the customary defence, then invocation of the clause will *always* preclude custom. But this objection overplays the concern and ignores the different spheres of operation of these two sources of international law. Custom applies across *all* the various areas of international law. Many of these subject areas are not governed by treaties or where they are, do not have a specific preclusion clause such as Article XI of the US-Argentina BIT.[103] Where a legal dispute arises in these other areas, custom remains the mechanism by which the final question of state responsibility is assessed.[104]

Finally and perhaps most importantly, there is a critical normative dimension to my preferred methodology that would clearly separate primary (treaty) and secondary (custom) applications. This is an area of international law that has become increasingly unstable as state parties exercise both 'voice' 105 and 'exit'[106] vis-à-vis the investment treaty regime.[107] These actions have been triggered by the enormous take-up of arbitral dispute settlement in the last ten years.[108] But is not just the invocation of the system that is driving these changes; the manner in which the substantive rules have been interpreted is also part of the matrix. The evolving case law has caused serious assessment among state parties as to whether the classic model of investment treaty protection, constructed in the furnace of post-Second World War contestation between developed and developing states, places too strong a constraint on regulatory autonomy. It is though enormously difficult as a matter of pragmatics and cost not only to amend

[103] Even in the investment field, not all investment treaties have a preclusion clause such as art XI of the US-Argentine BIT. Eg, neither the UK-Argentine BIT nor the Australia-Argentine BIT has a preclusion clause for measures of 'public order' or 'essential security interests'. See, Agreement Between the Government of the United Kingdom of Great Britain and Northern Ireland and the Government of the Republic of Argentina for the Promotion and Protection of Investments (*signed* 11 December 1990) UK Doc – Argentina No 1, CM 1449 (1991); Agreement Between the Government of Australia and the Government of the Argentine Republic on the Promotion and Protection of Investments and Protocol (*signed* 23 August 1995) ATS No 4 (1997).

[104] For a precise example of this sort of case, see *BG Group*, Final Award, above (n 81) paras 369–98 (analysing the customary plea of necessity in the absence of a specific treaty exception in the Argentina-UK BIT).

[105] A range of state parties are demanding changes to both existing and newer investment treaty rules. Eg, following early NAFTA case-law adopting an additive reading of the fair and equitable standard beyond the scope of the customary minimum standard of treatment, the state parties of the NAFTA issued a binding note of interpretation confining NAFTA art 1105(1) to the 'customary international law minimum standard of treatment'. NAFTA Free Trade Commission, 'Notes of Interpretation of Certain Chapter 11 Provisions' (31 July 2001) Parts B(1) and (2). Also, new investment treaties concluded by the US have been amended to ensure that invocation of the treaty exception for 'essential security interests' is a matter of competence for signatory states alone. See, eg, Peru-US Free Trade Agreement (signed 12 April 2006) Ar 22.2.

[106] See, eg, ICSID News Release, 'Ecuador's Notification under Article 25(4) of the ICSID Convention' (5 December 2007) (detailing Ecuador's withdrawal of its consent to ICSID jurisdiction over disputes concerning, among others, its petroleum, gas and mineral sectors); ICSID News Release, 'Bolivia Submits a Notice under Article 71 of the ICSID Convention' (16 May 2007) (detailing Bolivia's denunciation of the ICSID Convention).

[107] On the interrelation between concepts of 'voice', 'exit' and 'loyalty' in various settings, see A Hirschmann, *Exit, Voice and Loyalty: Responses to Decline in Firms, Organizations and States* (Massachusetts, Harvard University Press, 1970).

[108] UNCTAD, above (n 2) at 1 (tracking exponential growth in investment treaty arbitration from 1987 to 2007).

the thousands of existing bilateral instruments in operation but to do so in a manner that anticipates every possible future contingency.[109] Investment treaties in this respect might represent a classic embodiment of the problem of incomplete contracting in economic theory.[110] This raises a key role for the adjudicator to apply existing rules in such a way as to save a contract or treaty from endemic uncertainty (and to ensure continued participation/loyalty of the parties). This could involve a more sophisticated use of the customary rules of treaty interpretation to offer contextual rulings on substantive obligations (such as the fair and equitable guarantee) to better balance the interests of key stakeholders. But for hard cases – the rare but immediate occurrence of financial crisis – express clauses that directly allow for derogation and hence flexibility will be critical in the ability of the adjudicator to adopt this broader role. As we have seen in the *Continental* award, the final methodology – by clearly divorcing the treaty exception from the stringent customary plea – offers the adjudicator an important avenue to take up this challenge.

[109] It is for this second factor that I am less convinced than Alvarez and Khamsi that simple amendment ('BIT parties can change the treaties that they ratify . . . to incorporate more sovereignty-protective provisions') offers a comprehensive solution to the problems thrown up by the Argentine cases. Alvarez and Khamsi, above (n 27) 87.

[110] There is remarkably little application of this aspect of economic theory to international investment treaties. One notable and insightful exception is Anne. See A van Aaken, 'Between Commitment and Flexibility: The Fragile Stability of the International Investment Protection Regime' (2009) 12 *Journal of International Economic Law* 507–38.

11

*Equivalent Primary Rules and Differential Secondary Rules: Countermeasures in WTO and Investment Protection Law**

Martins Paparinskis

I INTRODUCTION

THE STUDY GROUP of the ILC has noted that 'the reality and importance of fragmentation, both in its legislative and institutional form, cannot be doubted'.[1] It is less obvious that the quantitative increase in the fragmented rules and regimes and the proliferation of international adjudicators[2] always raises qualitatively new challenges. Substantive and procedural innovations on the spectrum between fragmentation and integration were well known in classical international law. In substantive terms, starting from the three bilateral treaties that created the Westphalian System,[3] 'international law has always been diverse, has always had the capacity to fragment'.[4] Indeed, in its very first contentious

* Valuable comments and criticisms of Anastasios Gourgourinis, Jürgen Kurtz, Gregory Messenger and Antonios Tzanakopoulos, the participants of the conference and particularly the editors are greatly appreciated. I am grateful to Professor Joost Pauwelyn for his question at the Society of International Economic Law 2008 inaugural conference that prompted me to consider this topic. The views expressed and the errors or omissions made are the responsibility of the author alone. Unless stated otherwise, the investment awards cited are available at icsid.worldbank.org/ICSID/Index.jsp, www.investmentlaims.com and ita.law.uvic.ca, and the Model BITs cited are available at www.unctadxi.org/templates/DocSearch.aspx?id=780 and ita.law.uvic.ca/investmenttreaties.htm.

[1] ILC, 'Report of the Study Group of the ILC, Fragmentation of International Law: Difficulties arising from Diversification and Expansion of International Law' UN Doc A/CN.4/L.682, para 9.

[2] Y Shany, *The Competing Jurisdiction of International Courts and Tribunals* (Oxford, Oxford University Press, 2003) 3–10.

[3] J Crawford, 'Multilateral Rights and Obligations in International Law' (2006) 319 *Recueil des Cours de l'Académie de Droit International* 325, 349–52.

[4] J Crawford, 'Continuity and Discontinuity in International Dispute Settlement' in C Binder et al (eds), *International Investment Law for the 21st Century: Essays in Honour of Christoph Schreuer* (Oxford, Oxford University Press, 2009) 817.

case the Permanent Court of International Justice (PCIJ) needed to grapple with the interpretative implications[5] of conflicting obligations[6] against the background of 'complexity of interstate relations'.[7] A few years later, the same Court was nearly unanimous in accepting the argument of systemic integration[8] that '[a]ucune disposition du droit écrit n'est placée dans l'espace vide. . . . C'est également le droit général international . . . qui seul peut fournir les points de vue nécessaires'.[9] In procedural terms, it is questionable whether any recent adjudicator has faced challenges similar to the 1903–05 Venezuelan arbitrations: arbitrating *pari materia* disputes against the same respondent in 11 parallel commissions[10] against the background of a controversial use of force,[11] expressly disagreeing about the most sensitive legal issue of the era,[12] and using different imaginative arguments to harmonize the case law.[13] Against this background, some caution is necessary before assuming that challenges of fragmentation and proliferation are conceptually new; often they may be traced to established classical authorities.[14] Still, one possibly new wrinkle of the debate could be provided by considering the impact of lex specialis secondary rules of state responsibility on primary Multi-Sourced Equivalent Norms (MSENs). The contours of this legal relationship will be examined on the basis of a case study of countermeasures in WTO and investment protection law.

Classical international law accepted the permissibility of otherwise wrongful acts taken for the purpose of inducing a state to comply with

[5] *Case of the SS Wimbledon* PCIJ Rep Series A No 1 16, 25–30.

[6] *Ibid* (Schücking, Dissenting Opinion) 43.

[7] *Ibid* (Anzilotti and Huber, Dissenting Opinion) 35, para 3.

[8] *Case Concerning Certain German Interests in Polish Upper Silesia (Germany v Poland)* PCIJ Rep Series A No 7, 21.

[9] *Case Concerning Certain German Interests in Polish Upper Silesia (Germany v Poland)* PCIJ Rep Series C No 11, 167 (German Pleadings by Kaufmann).

[10] Venezuela-US, Belgium, Great Britain (1903–05) 9 RIAA 111–533; Venezuela-France, Germany, Italy, Mexico, the Netherlands, Spain, Sweden, Norway (1903–05) 10 RIAA 1-770.

[11] *The Venezuelan Preferential Case (Germany, Great Britain, Italy, Venezuela et al)* (1904) 9 RIAA 99.

[12] The attribution of state responsibility for the conduct of revolutionaries was perhaps the chief normative concern underlying the Calvo Doctrine: C Calvo, 'La non-responsabilité des États a raison des pertes et dommages éprouvés par des étrangers en temps de troubles intérieurs ou de guerres civiles' (1869) 1 *Revue de Droit International* 417; C Calvo, *Le Droit International Théorique et Pratique* 6th edn vol III (Paris, A Rousseau, 1888) 137. Some Commissions attributed the conduct of revolutionaries to the state: *Kummerrow and others (Germany v Venezuela)* (1903) 10 RIAA 369, 390–41; cases referred to in *Acquatella, Bianchi et al (France v Venezuela)* (1903–05) 10 RIAA 5, 6; while other Commissions rejected the attribution: *Aroa Mines (Limited) Claim – Supplementary Claim (Great Britain v Venezuela)* (1903) 9 RIAA 402, 438–41; *Sambiaggio Case (Italy v Venezuela)* (1902) 10 RIAA 499, 516–17; *JN Henriquez Case (Netherlands v Venezuela)* (1903) 10 RIAA 713, 715–17; *Padrón Case (Spain v Venezuela)* (1902) 10 RIAA 741.

[13] Commissions considered the relevance of most-favoured-nation (MFN) clauses: *Sambiaggio, ibid*, 522–23; third party *pari materia* treaties: *Kummerrow, ibid*, 373, 376; *Henriquez, ibid*,716–17; differences in applicable law: *Guastini Case (Italy v Venezuela)* (1902) 10 RIAA 561, 578; correctness of the earlier awards: *Aroa Mines, ibid*, 443.

[14] Shany, above (n 2) 230–34, 239–42, 247–48; Crawford 'Continuity', above (n 4) 802, 816–17.

its obligations under the law of state responsibility.[15] The proposition that wrongfulness of breaching primary rules may be precluded in this manner remains valid in the contemporary legal order,[16] even if the legal and policy implications and limits of the entitlement to breach international obligations are contested.[17] Countermeasures may also be applied to MSENs, rules binding the same subjects and providing similar content while having been created through different law-making processes.[18] If the theoretical model is supplemented by *lex specialis* secondary rules on countermeasures and separate adjudicators charged with interpreting each of the MSENs, untangling the normative 'spaghetti bowl' may become quite challenging.[19] Equivalent primary rules may require similar or identical conduct, differential secondary rules may preclude wrongfulness for the breach of some but not other equivalent primary rules and adjudicators approaching the dispute from different jurisdictional perspectives may reach different conclusions about the prevailing rules and regimes.

The considerable overlap of the substantive obligations[20] and procedural mechanisms in multilateral trade law and bilateral investment protection law provides an opportunity to study this dynamic as it plays out in practice.[21] Throughout the second half of the last century, law-making

[15] F Martens, *Contemporary International Law of Civilised Nations* vol II (St Petersburg, Typography A Benke, 1905) 506–09; GS Baker (ed), *Halleck's International Law* vol 1 4th edn (London, Kegan Paul, Trench, Trubner & Co Ltd, 1908) 505–07; AP Higgins (ed), *Hall's Treatise on International Law* 8th edn (Oxford, Clarendon Press, 1924) 433–36; *Responsabilité de l'Allemagne à raison des dommages causés dans les colonies portugaises du sud de l'Afrique (sentence sur le principe de la responsabilité) (Portugal contre Allemagne)* (1928) 2 RIAA 1011 (*Naulilaa*), 1025–28; A Verdross, 'Règles générales du droit international de la paix' (1929) 30 *Recueil des Cours de l'Académie de Droit International* 271, 491–93; 'Régime des représailles en temps de paix' in *Résolutions de l'Institut de Droit International: 1873–1956* (Bâle, Editions juridiques et sociologiques SA, 1957) 167.

[16] *Air Service Agreement of 27 March 1946 between the United States of America and France* (1978) 18 RIAA 417, paras 80–98; *Gabčíkovo-Nagymaros Project (Hungary/Slovakia)* [1997] ICJ Rep 7, paras 83–87; ILC, 'Draft Articles on Responsibility of States for Internationally Wrongful Acts with Commentaries' (2001) GAOR 56th Session Supp 10 UN Doc A/56/10, 20, arts 22, 49–54.

[17] J Crawford, 'The ILC's Articles on Responsibility of States for Internationally Wrongful Acts: A Retrospect' (2002) 96 *American Journal of International Law* 874, 882–85; ME O'Connell, 'Controlling Countermeasures' in M Ragazzi (ed), *International Responsibility Today: Essays in Honour of Oscar Schachter* (Leiden, Brill, 2005); T Franck, 'On Proportionality of Countermeasures in International Law' (2008) 102 *American Journal of International Law* 715.

[18] See in this volume, T Broude and Y Shany, 'The International Law and Policy of Multi-Sourced Equivalent Norms' in T Broude and Y Shany (eds), *Multi-Sourced Equivalent Norms in International Law* (Oxford, Hart Publishing, 2011) p 1.

[19] J Pauwelyn, 'Adding Sweeteners to Softwood Lumber: the WTO-NAFTA "Spaghetti Bowl" is Cooking' (2006) 9 *Journal of International Economic Law* 197.

[20] N DiMascio and J Pauwelyn, 'Nondiscrimination in Trade and Investment Treaties: Worlds Apart or Two Sides of the Same Coin?' (2008) 102 *American Journal of International Law* 48, 49–50; F Weiss, 'Trade and Investment' in P Muchlinski, F Ortino and C Schreuer (eds), *The Oxford Handbook of International Investment Law* (Oxford, Oxford University Press, 2008); R Neufeld, 'Trade and Investment' in D Bethlehem, D McRae, R Neufeld and I van Damme (eds), *The Oxford Handbook of International Trade Law* (Oxford, Oxford University Press, 2009).

[21] G Verhoosel, 'The Use of Investor-State Arbitration under Bilateral Investment Treaties to Seek Relief for Breaches of WTO Law' (2003) 6 *Journal of International Economic Law* 493;

in international trade and investment law proceeded in markedly different ways, even though starting the normative journey from the same form of treaty bilateralism.[22] The law of free trade decisively moved towards treaty multilateralism,[23] while investment law first experimented half-heartedly with the creation of multilateral treaty rules and customary law protecting foreign investment, and finally returned to treaty bilateralism.[24] At the same time, while being adopted in different law-making contexts and addressing different issues, due to the real life overlap of trade and investment activities, trade and investment rules may also bear on the same or similar situations.[25]

This chapter does not tackle the theoretical concept of MSENs. It rather assumes that when a conduct attributable to the state under international law constitutes a breach of international obligations simultaneously under an investment treaty and WTO obligations, one is faced with a MSEN situation.[26] On the basis of a number of case studies, it will be considered how primary rules that 'point' in the same direction[27] are affected by the secondary rules of state responsibility that prima facie reflect precisely the systemic and harmonizing perspective of the international legal order.[28]

The argument is made in three steps. First, the role of countermeasures in WTO and investment protection is sketched. Secondly, the implications of a WTO-authorized countermeasure potentially breaching the injured state's investment obligations are considered generally. Specifically, the WTO-authorized suspension of TRIPS concessions[29] that may breach investment obligations regarding intellectual property (IP) rights is used as a case study.[30] Thirdly, the converse scenario of countermeasures applied against

Pauwelyn, 'Adding Sweeteners', above (n 19); J Pauwelyn, 'Trade and Investment Disputes: Complement or Conflict?' in F Ortino and S Ripinsky (eds), *WTO Law and Process* (London, BIICL, 2007) 313–19; Verhoosel, 'Trade and Investment Disputes: Complement or Conflict?', *ibid*, 304–08.

[22] RR Wilson, *US Commercial Treaties and International Law* (New Orleans, Hauser Press, 1960) 6–7.

[23] DiMascio and Pauwelyn, above (n 20) 51–53.

[24] M Paparinskis, '*Barcelona Traction*: A Friend of Investment Protection Law' (2008) 8 *Baltic Yearbook of International Law* 105, 105–33.

[25] Above (nn 20–21).

[26] 2001 ILC Articles, above (n 16) art 2.

[27] 'Report of the Study Group', above (n 1) para 15.

[28] B Simma and D Pulkowski, 'Of Planets and the Universe: Self-Contained Regimes in International Law' (2006) 17 *European Journal of International Law* 483.

[29] WTO, *EC: Regime for the Importation, Sale and Distribution of Bananas, Article 22.6 – Arbitration Decision* (24 March 2000) WT/DS27/ARB/ECU, paras 65–165; WTO, *US: Measures Affecting the Cross-Border Supply of Gambling and Betting Services, Article 22.6 – Arbitration Decision* (21 December 2007) WT/DS285/ARB, paras 4.1–4.119, 5.1–5.13; WTO, *US: Subsidies on Upland Cotton, Article 22.6 and Article 4.11/Article 7.10 of SCM Agreement – Arbitration Decision* (31 August 2009) WT/DS267/ARB/1, WT/DS267/ARB/2, paras 5.224, 5.230–5.233.

[30] See the special issue on IP rights in investment law, 'The Protection of Intellectual Property Rights through International Investment Agreements' (2009) 6 (2) *Transnational Dispute Management* (online subscription e-journal, www.transnational-dispute-management.com).

investment protection obligations that might also breach WTO rules is addressed, using the US–Mexico soft drinks disputes in NAFTA[31] and the WTO as a case study.[32] The combination of MSEN primary rules and different perceptions of invocation and implementation of responsibility for their breach through different adjudicators make clear and certain solutions unlikely. Despite the sophistication of the dispute settlement regimes created by trade and investment treaties, their focus on systemic strengthening may come at the cost of complicating the relationship and the resolution of conflicts with extra-systemic primary and secondary rules. Still, it is suggested that the existing practice permits the formulation of a framework within which states and other participants could operate.

II COUNTERMEASURES IN WTO AND INVESTMENT PROTECTION LAW

The most recent and authoritative statement on the law of countermeasures is given in the 2001 ILC Articles on State Responsibility for Internationally Wrongful Acts (hereafter 2001 ILC Articles).[33] The 2001 ILC Articles address countermeasures in two places, in Article 22 under the rubric of circumstances precluding wrongfulness, and in Articles 49–54 under the rubric of implementation of the international responsibility of the state. This approach accurately captures the dual context vis-à-vis a specific primary rule that countermeasures may occupy: both to preclude the wrongfulness of the breach of that primary rule, and as a measure undertaken to induce the state to comply with its obligations under the law of state responsibility. Countermeasures are not automatic in their application, but are rather voluntarily adopted as a reaction to wrongful acts. In general international law, countermeasures are adopted unilaterally and not through any institutionalised setting.[34] Countermeasures have to conform to certain

[31] *Archer Daniels Midland Company and Tate & Lyle Ingredients Americas, Inc v United Mexican States* (ICSID Case No ARB/(AF)/04/5) Award (21 November 2007) paras 110–84 (*ADM*); Concurring Opinion of Arbitrator Rovine; *Corn Products International, Inc v United Mexican States* (ICSID Case No ARB/(AF)/04/1) Decision on Responsibility (15 January 2008) paras 144–91; Separate Opinion of Arbitrator Lowenfeld.

[32] WTO, *Mexico: Tax Measures on Soft Drinks and Other Beverages – Panel Report* (7 October 2005) WT/DS308/R, paras 8.168–8.204; WTO, *Mexico: Tax Measures on Soft Drinks and Other Beverages – Appellate Body (AB) Report* (24 March 2006) WT/DS308/AB/R, paras 66–80.

[33] 2001 ILC Articles, above (n 16); *cf* above (nn 15–16). The ICJ has approvingly referred to the 1996 first reading version of the 2001 ILC Articles but has not had the chance to pronounce on the second reading; *Gabčíkovo-Nagymaros Project*, above (n 16) para 83. The rules on countermeasures did not substantially change between 1996 and 2001, except regarding the use of binding dispute settlement procedures by the injured state before resorting to countermeasures. The first but not the second reading required it, *cf* 1996 'Draft Articles on State Responsibility with Commentaries Thereto Adopted by the International Law Commission on First Reading art 48(2)': untreaty.un.org/ilc/texts/instruments/english/commentaries/9_6_1996.pdf; ILC Articles, above (n 16) art 52.

[34] JL Brierly, 'Sanctions' (1932) 17 *Transactions of the Grotius Society* 67, 68.

procedural and substantive rules: adoption in response to an earlier wrongful act by the particular state;[35] inapplicability to obligations not affected by countermeasures;[36] an initial call upon the wrongdoing state to comply with its obligations and an offer to negotiate;[37] and proportionality of the measure.[38]

The ILC's project 'to superimpose procedural values of rectitude and transparency on state's assessments of countermeasures options' operates in investment protection law similarly as in other areas of law.[39] Even though the role of diplomatic protection in foreign investment law has 'somewhat faded' in factual terms,[40] the investor's home state is still entitled to take countermeasures to induce the host state to comply with its obligations under the law of responsibility for the breach of investment rules. Apart from cases of express suspension of diplomatic protection through treaty law,[41] the state's right to protect its investors, *inter alia*, through the taking of countermeasures is neither affected by the conduct of investor-state arbitrations and the invocation by the investor of state responsibility nor excluded by the *lex specialis* of investment protection law.[42] Consequently, home states would be in principle entitled to protect their investors, reflecting the individualistic interplay between customary law and particular treaty law requirements of negotiations and dispute settlement.

It is less clear whether and in what circumstances the wrongfulness of countermeasures taken by a host state in breach of investment protection obligations would be precluded. Limitations for applying countermeasures to particular rules may be expressed in a number of ways, relying respectively on *lex specialis* rules, obligations not affected by countermeasures, the structure of the obligations or the limits of countermeasures. The silence of investment protection treaties, just as the silence of treaties more generally, may be read either as permitting or excluding the application of

[35] 2001 ILC Articles, above (n 16) art 49.

[36] *Ibid*, art 50.

[37] *Ibid*, art 52.

[38] *Ibid*, art 51.

[39] DJ Bederman, 'Counterintuiting Countermeasures' (2002) 96 *American Journal of International Law* 817, 819.

[40] *Case Concerning Ahmadou Sadio Diallo (Guinea v DRC)* (Preliminary Objections) [2007] ICJ Rep para 88: www.icj-cij.org/docket/files/103/13856.pdf.

[41] Such as during ICSID arbitrations, Convention on the Settlement of Investment Disputes between States and Nationals of Other States (adopted 18 March 1965, entered into force 14 October 1066) 575 UNTS 159 art 27(1); M Paparinskis, 'Investment Arbitration and the Law of Countermeasures' (2008) 79 *British Yearbook of International Law* 264, 309–17; C Schreuer, L Malintoppi, A Reinisch and A Sinclair, *The ICSID Convention: A Commentary* 2nd edn (Cambridge, Cambridge University Press, 2009) 414–32; during all investor-state arbitrations, 1994 Chile Model BIT art 8(6); 1998 Mongolia Model BIT art 8(6); Bolivia Model BIT, *International Investment Instruments: A Compendium* (vol X, New York, United Nations, 2002) 275 art 10(3); 2003 Kenya Model BIT art 10(d); 2003 Italy Model BIT art X(5).

[42] Paparinskis, 'Countermeasures' above (n 41) 281–96.

countermeasures.[43] Most authorities support the view that circumstances precluding wrongfulness are not implicitly excluded.[44] The cases dealing with necessity and non-precluded-measure (NPM) clauses may have muddled the intellectual waters a little bit, forming a spectrum between making a clear distinction between primary and secondary rules[45] to reading the treaty as a *lex specialis* secondary rule[46] or even a reference to the general secondary rule.[47] Still, none of the tribunals have thought that circumstances precluding wrongfulness were irrelevant: the controversy was about whether necessity had been given too much effect. The rules reflected in Article 50 of the 2001 ILC Articles on obligations not affected by countermeasures do not directly apply to investment obligations.[48] Countermeasures cannot be excluded by reasons of the substantive nature of investment law. The impermissibility of countermeasures regarding multilateral obligations is also inapplicable to investment law[49] that even when expressed in multilateral form remains of a bilateralisable nature.[50]

Even though the host state may in principle apply countermeasures to investment obligations, their effect and limits depend on the nature of the investors' rights. Countermeasures may not be adopted otherwise than in response to a prior breach of international law by the entity to which

[43] Simma and Pulkowski, above (n 28) 505.

[44] Regarding countermeasures, expressly in *ADM*, above (n 31) paras 116–23; implicitly in *Corn Products*, above (n 31) paras 161–79; *cf* Paparinskis 'Countermeasures', above (n 41) 345–49. Regarding necessity, *CMS Gas Transmission Company v Argentine Republic* (ICSID Case No ARB/01/08) Decision of the *Ad hoc* Committee on the Application for Annulment (25 September 2007) para 134; *Continental Casualty Company v Argentine Republic* (ICSID Case No ARB/03/9) Award (5 September 2008) paras 164–68; *National Grid Plc v Argentine* Republic (UNCITRAL Case) Award (3 November 2008) para 255; C Binder, 'Changed Circumstances in Investment Law: Interfaces between the Law of Treaties and the Law of State Responsibility with a Special Focus on the Argentine Crisis' in Binder et al (eds), *International Investment Law for the 21st Century*, above (n 4) 628–30. The *BG* tribunal left the issue open: *BG Group Plc v Argentina* (UNCITRAL Arbitration) Final Award (24 December 2007) paras 407–12.

[45] *CMS* Annulment, *ibid; Continental Casualty, ibid.*

[46] *LG&E Energy Corp, LG&E Capital Corp, LG&E International Inc v Argentine Republic* (ICSID Case No ARB/02/1) Decision on Liability (3 October 2006) paras 245–61; *Patrick Mitchell v Democratic Republic of the Congo* (ICSID Case No ARB/99/7) Decision of the *Ad hoc* Committee on the Application for Annulment (1 November 2006) para 55.

[47] *CMS Gas Transmission Company v Argentine Republic* (ICSID Case No ARB/01/08) Final Award 12 May 2005) paras 315–82; *Enron Corporation and Ponderosa Assets, L.P. v Argentine Republic* (ICSID Case No ARB/01/3) Award (22 May 2007) para 334; *Sempra Energy International v Argentine Republic* (ICSID Case No ARB/02/16) Award (28 September 2007) paras 376, 378.

[48] *Corn Products*, above (n 31) para 149; Paparinskis 'Countermeasures', above (n 41) 317–45.

[49] PM Dupuy, 'A General Stocktaking of the Connections between the Multilateral Obligations and the Codification of the Law of Responsibility' (2003) 13 *European Journal of International Law* 1053, fn 64.

[50] O Schachter, 'Entangled Treaty and Custom' in Y Dinstein and M Tabory (eds), *International Law at a Time of Perplexity – Essays in Honour of Shabtai Rosenne* (Dordrecht, Martinus Nijhoff, 1998) 735; C Carmody, 'WTO Obligations as Collective' (2006) 17 *European Journal of International Law* 419, 443; T Wälde, 'International Investment Law: An Overview of Key Concepts and Methodologies' (2007) 4 *Transnational Dispute Management* 48–49, fn 104.

the obligation is owed.[51] Investors are structurally incapable of committing such a breach of international law[52]. *Ergo*, if investment obligations

[51] 2001 ILC Articles, above (n 16) art 49(1); *cf* ILC, Draft Articles on Responsibility of International Organizations in Official Records of the General Assembly, Fifty-sixth Session, Supplement No 10/UN Doc A/64/10 19, art 50(1). Third-party countermeasures raise different issues, below (nn 148–49).

[52] To say that investors cannot breach international obligations owed to the state in a way that justifies countermeasures is not to dismiss or minimize the different important ways in which an investor's liability may be intertwined with state responsibility. The investor's liability under domestic law may lead the tribunal to dismiss its claim at the jurisdictional stage because of the lack of the state's consent, *Inceysa Vallisoletana S.L. v Republic of El Salvador* (ICSID Case No ARB/03/26) Award (2 August 2006) paras 208–57; or because the investments are not 'in accordance with' domestic law, *Fraport AG Frankfurt Airport Services Worldwide v Republic of the Philippines* (ICSID Case No ARB/03/25) Award (16 August 2007) paras 334–404; or require the rejection of the claim on the merits, *Plama Consortium Limited v Republic of Bulgaria* (ICSID Case No ARB/03/24) Award (27 August 2008) paras 130–46. In these cases, the investor's liability is used to interpret the scope or content of the primary rule and not to preclude the wrongfulness of its breach. Conversely, the US Alien Torts Statute seems to determine the existence of a domestic cause of action by reference to the content of international law, *Sosa v Alvarez-Machain* (03-339) 542 US 692, text at fn 20 (2004). Whatever its proper legal rationale, ATS is about liability to individuals and not to states. Even when investors enter into direct legal relations with states, investor-state contracts are not treaties, *Anglo-Iranian Oil Co. Case (UK v Iran)* (Jurisdiction) [1952] ICJ Rep 93, 112, and do not create international obligations per se. The state may incur international responsibility by breaching such a contract through an arbitrary use of its public powers, *Waste Management v United Mexican States (II)* (ICSID Additional Facility Case No ARB(AF)/00/3) Final Award (30 April 2004) paras 146–55; or if a treaty-based *pacta sunt servanda* clause transforms responsibility under applicable law to responsibility under international law, *Noble Ventures, Inc v Romania* (ICSID Case No ARB/01/11) Award (12 October 2005) paras 53–55. However, the converse is not the case: a breach of a contract by the investor does not breach international law and does not trigger international law remedies but only entitles the state to respond in accordance with the law applicable to contract.

Secondly, the operation of state-controlled investors, particularly Sovereign Wealth Funds, may raise different questions under different treaty rules. Under the ICSID Convention, above (n 41) art 25, it has been suggested that a state-controlled investor could make a claim 'unless it is acting as an agent for the government or is discharging an essentially governmental function', A Broches, 'Convention on the Settlement of Investment Disputes between States and Nationals of Other States' (1972) 136 *Recueil des Cours de l'Académie de Droit International* 331, 355; *Ceskoslovenska Obchodni Banka, a.s. v Slovak Republic* (ICSID Case No ARB/97/4) Decision on Objections to Jurisdiction (24 May 1999) para 17; Schreuer et al, *The ICSID Convention*, above (n 41) 161–62. However, this exclusion of certain investors from the protective scope relates only to the definition of 'investor' in the particular rule and does not necessarily apply more generally. A minority of treaties accept that states may also be investors (eg, 2004 US Model BIT art 1). Even though such an investor could breach obligations owed to the host state, it would not constitute an exception to the original proposition because of the simultaneous investor/state status of the particular entity. More broadly, in the absence of specific treaty rules, the fact that an investor exercises functions of or is directed or controlled by the home state may be relevant for the purpose of attribution of responsibility to that state, 2001 ILC Articles, above (n 16) arts 5 and 8, but it does not mean that any obligations are owed by the investor itself. In other words, even if the state-owned or controlled investor engages in conduct that breaches the obligation, it is only the home state that is bound by this obligation, incurs international responsibility and against which countermeasures may be applied.

Thirdly, it not inconceivable that such concepts as *jus cogens*, criminal responsibility and human rights obligations of non-state actors could *de lege ferenda* complicate this picture. One tribunal has remarked that 'nobody would suggest that ICSID protection should be granted to investments made in violation of the most fundamental rules of protection of human rights, like investments made in pursuance of torture or genocide or in support of slavery or are owed directly to investors, countermeasures can never preclude wrongfulness for their breach vis-á-vis investors.[53] If investment obligations are owed only to the home state, wrongfulness may be precluded provided that other substantive and procedural requirements are complied with.[54] If the latter approach is adopted, no compensation has to be paid by the host state. Even though Article 27(b) of the 2001 ILC Articles provides a 'without prejudice' clause regarding the effect of circumstances precluding wrongfulness on compensation, state practice, case law and ILC debates confirm that countermeasures (and self-defence) do not require compensation.[55]

trafficking of human organs', *Phoenix Action, Ltd v Czech Republic* (ICSID Case No ARB/06/5) Award (15 April 2009) para 78. Three lines of inquiry will be indicated without pursuing them further here. Even though prima facie this proposition relates only to a purposive interpretation of particular treaty rules, it may be important that the first three examples also occur in the ILC analysis of the impact of peremptory norms on state responsibility, ILC Articles, above (n 16) art 26 Commentaries 5–6; art 40 Commentaries 4–5. Alternatively, the passage may be read as restricting investment protection when the conduct gives rise to international criminal responsibility. The idea of holding corporations directly responsible under international law is controversial, and criminal responsibility more generally is usually not conceptualised as an obligation that an individual owes to particular states (and to the breach of which these states could respond by countermeasures). Still, the apparent lack of such practice may be explained in purely descriptive terms: individuals usually do not hold such direct international rights against states that could be subject to countermeasures, and obligations owed to individuals under human rights law cannot be suspended because of their multilateral nature. The passage may also be hinting at possible human rights obligations of corporations. The proposition that international law *de lege lata* imposes direct human rights obligations on non-state actors is controversial. There does not seem to be any host-state pleading or other practice in favour of the view that investors owe such obligations both to individuals and states, and that host states could respond to the breach of these obligations by in turn breaching their investment obligations. It remains to be seen whether and how future state practice and possible creation of new rules along these lines could affect the situation *de lege ferenda*.

53 *Corn Products*, above (n 31) paras 153–91; *ADM* Concurring Opinion Rovine, above (n 31).

54 *ADM*, above (n 31) paras 110–80.

55 The leading *Air Service Agreement* award accepted the countermeasures argument without any mention of compensation, above (n 16). The precursor of Art 27 of the 2001 ILC Articles, above (n 16), Art 35 of the 1996 ILC Articles, dealt with countermeasures and self-defence as with prejudice to compensation, above (n 33). Crawford agreed that '[i]t is clear that Article 35 should not apply to self-defence or countermeasures, since those circumstances depend upon and relate to prior wrongful conduct of the "target" State, and there is no basis to compensate it for the consequences of its own wrongful conduct', J Crawford, 'Second Report on State Responsibility' UN Doc A/CN.4/498/Add.2, para 342, generally paras 213, 229, 336–47. The ILC debate showed some uncertainty about both how the apparent acknowledgment of liability for non-wrongful acts could fit within the state responsibility project premised on wrongfulness, (1999) I *Yearbook of the ILC*, UN Doc A/CN.4/SER.A/1999 174, para 44 (Lukashuk), and whether the compensable circumstances should be those that operated as excuses and not justifications or those where the target state had not committed wrongful acts, *ibid*, para 48 (Simma). In any event, nobody argued for compensation for countermeasures, instead emphasising cases of *force majeure*, *ibid*, para 50 (Hafner), necessity, *ibid*, para 45 (Crawford) and innocent third party beneficiaries, *ibid*, para 47 (Economides), *ibid*, 176, para 68 (Crawford), or the particular circumstances of individual cases, *ibid*, 174, para 54 (Pellet). None of the states commenting on the issue suggested compensation for countermeasures to the wrongdoing state, ILC, 'Comments and Observations Received from Governments' UN Doc A/CN.4/488 79-80 (UK), 89 (Germany); ILC, 'Comments and Observations Received from Governments' UN Doc A/CN.4/515 34 (Japan, the Netherlands).

Douglas has authoritatively drawn the distinction between the perceptions of investors' rights as direct (with investment obligations owed to the investor itself) and derivative (with obligations owed only to the home state). The same point may also be made in terminologically perhaps slightly more accurate terms by distinguishing between investors as beneficiaries and investors as agents. Douglas has argued for the former approach of direct (beneficiary) rights in light of the qualitative differences between investor-state arbitration and diplomatic protection.[56] Such a reading is certainly more natural[57] than the contrary one that would see an investment treaty as an agreement between the home state and the host state to authorize the investor to exercise diplomatic protection with considerably modified content.[58] Still, the ILC did not take a position on this matter,[59] and there is no theoretical obstacle for states to confirm their intent to deal with investors only as agents through clear treaty language or through subsequent practice[60] or agreement, or even treaty amendments. While it is questionable whether this approach is in the long-term interest of traditional home states,[61] it enjoys some limited support.[62]

The WTO's rules on suspension of concessions are significantly different from the general rules on countermeasures applicable in the investment

[56] Z Douglas, 'The Hybrid Foundations of Investment Treaty Arbitration' (2003) 74 *British Yearbook of International Law* 151, 167–84; Z Douglas, *The International Law of Investment Claims* (Cambridge, Cambridge University Press, 2009) 1–38.

[57] *Corn Products*, above (n 31) para 169.

[58] Agency of exercise of diplomatic protection was recognized in the classical law, E Borchard, *Diplomatic Protection of Citizens Abroad* (New York, The Banks Law Publishing Co, 1915) 471–75; AP Sereni, 'La represéntation en droit international' (1948) 73 *Recueil des Cours de l'Académie de Droit International* 69, 112–17.

[59] Crawford, 'Retrospect', above (n 17) 888; *Wintershall Aktiengesellschaft v Argentine Republic* (ICSID Case No ARB/04/14) Award (8 December 2008) para 112.

[60] The *ADM* tribunal found such subsequent pleading practice regarding NAFTA, above (n 31) paras 176.

[61] The argument of derivative rights had a powerful short-term attraction for traditional home states that found themselves in the position of host states, enabling them to rely on restrictive rules from customary law of diplomatic protection, M Mendelson, 'Runaway Train: The "Continuous Nationality" Rule from the *Panavezys-Saldutiskis Railway* case to *Loewen*' in T Weiler (ed), *International Investment Law and Arbitration: Leading Cases from the ICSID, NAFTA, Bilateral Treaties and Customary International Law* (London, Cameron May, 2005) 124–43. One negative long-term implication of general acceptance of the argument is that it legitimises the host state's countermeasures with precluded wrongfulness and no compensation for the investor because the only obligation is owed to the home state. Another and more challenging question relates to the normative and law-making influence of the investor's practice. If the investor invokes responsibility on behalf of the home state, and if agents in general are able to change the legal relations of the principal 'as if [acts] had been personally performed by the latter', AP Sereni, 'Agency in International Law' (1940) 34 *American Journal of International Law* 638, 655, should not one – within these procedural limits – also count the investors' pleadings for the establishment of custom and subsequent practice as if they 'had been personally performed' by the home state?

[62] *Loewen v United States* (ICSID Additional Facility Case No ARB(AF)/98/3) Final Award (26 June 2003) para 233; *ADM*, above (n 31) paras 176–79; *Société Générale v Dominican Republic* (LCIA Case No UN 7927) Award on Preliminary Objections to Jurisdiction (19 September 2008) paras 108–09.

law context. The WTO Dispute Settlement Understanding (DSU) embeds the taking of countermeasures within an institutional impartial decision-making context (approved in the Dispute Settlement Body (DSB) by the de facto automatic negative consensus).[63] It provides detailed rules for the determination of inconsistency of measures adopted to comply,[64] the nature and degree of the authorized countermeasures[65] and the manner, including by reference to an arbitrator, in which the subsequent suspension of concessions is determined.[66] The absence of traditional auto-determination has led to WTO-authorized suspension of concessions being characterized as centralised countermeasures.[67] The reliance by the Appellate Body on provisions on countermeasures from the 2001 ILC Articles to confirm interpretation of WTO rules on suspension of concessions suggests that the latter are *lex specialis* of the former.[68] Further analysis will proceed on the assumption that the rules on suspension of concessions are *lex specialis* countermeasures.[69] Article 23 DSU expressly sets out rules for states

> seeking redress of a violation of the covered agreements. Article 23 restricts WTO Members' conduct in two respects. First, Article 23.1 establishes the WTO dispute settlement system as the exclusive forum for the resolution of such disputes and requires adherence to the rules of the DSU. Secondly, Article 23.2 prohibits certain unilateral action by a WTO Member. Thus, a Member cannot unilaterally: (i) determine that a violation has occurred, benefits have been nullified or impaired, or that the attainment of any objective of the covered agreements has been impeded; (ii) determine the duration of the reasonable period of time for implementation; or (iii) decide to suspend concessions and determine the level thereof.[70]

[63] In general see, Y Guohua, B Mercurio and L Yongjie, *WTO Dispute Settlement Understanding: A Detailed Interpretation* (The Hague, Kluwer Law International, 2005) 251–79; P Eeckhout, 'Remedies and Compliance' in D Bethlehem, et al (eds), *The Oxford Handbook of International Trade Law*, above (n 20) 440–42, 452–54.

[64] DSU, art 21.5.

[65] *Ibid*, arts 22.3-22.5.

[66] *Ibid*, arts 22.2, 22.6-22.9.

[67] H Lesaffre, *Le règlement des différends au sein de l'OMC et le droit de la responsabilité internationale* (Paris, LGDJ, 2007) 454–61.

[68] WTO, *US: Transitional Safeguard Measure on Combed Cotton Yarn from Pakistan – Report of the Appellate Body* (5 November 2001) WT/DS192/AB/R, para 120; WTO, *US: Definitive Safeguard Measures on Imports of Circular Welded Carbon Quality Line Pipe from Korea – Report of the Appellate Body* (8 March 2002) WT/DS202/AB/R, para 259; WTO, *US/Canada: Continued Suspension of Obligations in the EC-Hormones Dispute – Report of the Appellate Body* (14 November 2008) WT/DS320/AB/R, WT/DS321/AB/R, para 382; *cf* 2001 ILC Articles, above (n 16) art 50, Commentary 10; S Shadikhodjaev, *Retaliation in the WTO Dispute Settlement System* (The Netherlands, Walter Kluwer Law and Business, 2009) 26–47.

[69] To treat the suspension of concessions as *lex specialis* countermeasures is not to dismiss the difficult question whether its function and purpose is to induce compliance similarly to the *lex generalis*, J Pauwelyn, 'Enforcement and Countermeasures in the WTO: Rules are Rules – Toward a More Collective Approach' (2000) 94 *American Journal of International Law* 335, 337, fn 14; J Pauwelyn, 'The Calculation and Design of Trade Retaliation in Context: What is the Goal of Suspending WTO Obligations?' in CP Bown and J Pauwelyn (eds), *The Law, Economics and Politics of Retaliation in WTO Dispute Settlement* (Cambridge, Cambridge University Press, 2010).

[70] *US/Canada-Continued Suspension – Report of the Appellate Body*, above (n 68) para 371. See

Even though the application of countermeasures for the breach of primary WTO rules is elaborated in the detailed rules of the DSU, the converse situation of application of countermeasures for the breach of other (non-WTO) primary rules to WTO rules is not expressly dealt with, and therefore would be likely to give rise to greater interpretative uncertainty.

III WTO COUNTERMEASURES IN INVESTMENT PROTECTION LAW

WTO arbitrators have sometimes authorized the application of countermeasures regarding IP obligations included in TRIPS when countermeasures against GATT and GATS obligations would not be practicable and effective.[71] IP rights are protected from the trade-law perspective in TRIPS,[72] and from the investment law perspective in investment protection treaties, providing for IP rights as investments that cannot be treated unfairly, discriminated or expropriated without compensation.[73] There seems to be some overlap in the substantive coverage of the obligations under TRIPS and the investment protection rules.[74] One decision authorizing the suspension of TRIPS was taken in the *US-Measures Affecting the Cross-Border Supply of Gambling and Betting Services* dispute, and this case with slightly modified facts will be used as a case study.[75] It will be assumed that Antigua and Barbuda (Antigua) suspends TRIPS vis-à-vis US and authorises the production and sale of pirated music and software.[76] The US has no Bilateral Investment Treaty (BIT) with Antigua, but for the sake of analysis it will be assumed that a hypothetical US-Antigua BIT exists that includes IP rights among protected investments and requires states not to expropriate them without compensation and to treat them fairly and equitably and without discrimination.[77] In these circumstances, could a US investor with an investment affected by this conduct make a

below (nn 90–91) regarding the implications for the taking of countermeasures.

[71] DSU, art 22.3.

[72] CM Correa, *Trade Related Aspects of Intellectual Property Rights: A Commentary on the TRIPS Agreement* (Oxford, Oxford University Press, 2007); RC Dreyfuss, 'Intellectual Property Law and the World Trading System' in A Lowenfeld, *International Economic Law* 2nd edn (Oxford, Oxford University Press, 2008).

[73] CM Correa, 'Bilateral Investment Agreements: Agents of New International Standards for the Protection of Intellectual Property Rights?' (2004) 1 (4) *Transnational Dispute Management*.

[74] L Liberti, 'Intellectual Property Rights in International Investment Agreements: An Overview' (2009) 6(2) *Transnational Dispute Management*; J Mendenhall, 'Fair Treatment of Intellectual Property Rights under Bilateral Investment Treaties' (2009) 6(2) *Transnational Dispute Management*.

[75] *US-Gambling*, above (n 29); *cf* HG Ruse-Khan, 'A Pirate of the Caribbean – The Attractions of Suspending TRIPS Obligations' (2008) 11 *Journal of International Economic Law* 313.

[76] According to the information available at the WTO website, Antigua has not requested authorization to suspend concessions from the DSB in accordance with art 22.7 DSU: www.wto.org/english/tratop_e/dispu_e/cases_e/ds285_e.htm.

[77] A Newcombe and L Paradell, *Law and Practice of Investment Treaties: Standards of Treatment* (The Hague, Kluwer, 2009) chs 4, 6 and 7.

successful investor-state claim against Antigua?[78] The analysis is made in three steps, considering the situation in WTO law, the link between WTO law and investment protection law and the situation in investment protection law.

First, the suspension of obligations that may be requested from the DSB and determined by the arbitrator under Article 22.6 DSU relates to obligations 'under the covered agreements'. An equivalent obligation formulated in a different and unrelated rule of international law is not one 'under the covered agreements', and therefore authorization of the DSB does not apply to such obligations. The fact that other obligations require conduct similar to the WTO covered agreements that the state is authorized to breach does not affect this conclusion. The scope of authorization is identified by reference to the regime within which the obligations are expressed; it does not automatically apply to *pari materia* obligations. Even if norms expressed in different rules of international law have similar or identical content, they may have different conditions of creation, application or termination and different institutions and mechanisms that ensure their implementation.[79] The permissibility of conduct under one rule therefore does not necessarily mean its permissibility under another one.

IP treaties incorporated by TRIPS and thus binding as WTO law[80] still continue to exist as separate treaties, and a similar question has been raised whether WTO-authorized suspension would not still breach the obligations under those treaties.[81] However, the TRIPS situation is importantly different: express incorporation of IP treaties in TRIPS and the express authorization to suspend TRIPS in Article 22.3(g)(iii) DSU seem to suggest that WTO parties, even though they remain bound by those treaties, have agreed *inter se* on *lex specialis* countermeasures to the extent of incorporation. There is no such incorporation or reference by WTO law to investment obligations, and therefore the WTO-authorized breach of IP rights

[78] There is no US-Antigua BIT therefore an actual US investor could not make an investor-state claim. However, Antigua has concluded BITs with Germany and the UK, so a German or a UK investor could argue that these measures breached the relevant treaties (eg, as a shareholder of the US investor or as a co-shareholder of the Antigua investment vehicle of the US investor); *cf* interpretation of the Germany-Argentina BIT as covering indirect shareholding, *Siemens A.G. v Argentine Republic* (ICSID Case No ARB/02/8) Decision on Jurisdiction (3 August 2004) paras 136–44. To gain access to investor-state arbitration, the US investor could invest in Antigua through a UK shell company since art 1(d)(i) of the UK-Antigua BIT does not require any additional link with UK apart from incorporation; *cf* approval of 'BIT-shopping', *Aguas del Tunari S.A. v Republic of Bolivia* (ICSID Case No ARB/02/03) Decision on Respondent's Objections to Jurisdiction (21 October 2005) para 330.

[79] *Military and Paramilitary Activities in and against Nicaragua (Nicaragua v US)* (Merits) [1986] ICJ Rep 14, para 178.

[80] Agreement on Trade-Related Aspects of Intellectual Property Rights (adopted 15 April 1994, entered into force 1 January 1995) 1869 UNTS 299 arts 2(1), 9 (TRIPS); WTO, *US: Section 211 Omnibus Appropriation Act of 1998 – Report of the Appellate Body* (1 February 2002) WT/DS176/AB/R, para 238.

[81] RL Okediji, 'WIPO-WTO Relations and the Future of Global Intellectual Property Norms' (2008) 39 *Netherlands Yearbook of International Law* 69, 103.

does not authorize breach of obligations expressed in different rules of international law.

The impact of the application of WTO rules on investment protection rules may also be addressed from the opposite perspective of investment protection law. The variety of possible approaches may be illustrated on the basis of model BITs and multilateral investment treaties. Most model BITs include IP rights among protected investments without any attempt of coordination with TRIPS and WTO DSU, both in models adopted before[82] and importantly after TRIPS came into force.[83] A few treaties make limited attempts of coordination, defining the scope of some investment protection obligations by reference to the applicability of[84] or compliance with WIPO or TRIPS rules[85] or WTO law,[86] or do not apply some obligations to IP rights.[87] This treaty practice suggests that while states recognize the possibility of a MSEN situation between investment and WTO rules on IP rights, coordination is limited in number and in scope, in most cases suggesting the existence of a problem rather than fully resolving it.

The situation would be relatively uncontroversial if the only *lex specialis* aspect of WTO rules was the judicial determination of breach and the general rules were otherwise applicable. If a state is entitled to take countermeasures regarding a particular rule, then it would also be likely to be entitled to take countermeasures regarding MSEN rules.[88] Since there is no

[82] 1991 UK Model BIT art 1(a)(iv); 1991 Germany Model BIT art 1(1)(d); 1994 China Model BIT art 1(1)(d); 1994 Chile Model BIT art 1(2)(d); 1995 Switzerland Model BIT art 1(2)(d).

[83] 1997 Netherlands Model BIT art 1(a)(iv); 1998 Mongolia Model BIT art 1(2)(d); 1998 Malaysia Model BIT art 1(a)(iv); 1998 Croatia Model BIT art 1(1)(d); 1998 South Africa Model BIT art 1; 1998 Germany Model BIT art 1(1)(d); 1999 France Model BIT art 1(1)(d); 2000 Denmark Model BIT art 1(1)(d); 2000 Peru Model BIT art 1(1)(d); 2000 Turkey Model BIT art 1(2)(d); 2001 Greece Model BIT art 1(1)(d); 2001 Finland Model BIT art 1(1)(d); 2002 Mauritius Model BIT art 1(1)(A)(iv); 2002 Burundi Model BIT art 1(4)(d); 2002 Benin Model BIT art 1(1)(d); 2002 Sweden Model BIT art 1(1)(d); 2002 Thailand Model BIT art 1(1)(d); 2003 India Model BIT art 1(b)(iv); 2006 France Model BIT art 1(1)(d); 2008 Germany Model BIT art 1(1)(d).

[84] National treatment and MFN treatment obligations do not apply to WIPO procedures relating to acquisition and maintenance of IP rights, 1994 US Model BIT art II(2)(b); 1994 US Model BIT (1998 revised) art II(2)(b); North American Free Trade Agreement (adopted 17 December 1992, entered into force 1 January 1994) (1993) 32 ILM 612 arts 1108(5), 1703(3). National treatment and MFN treatment do not apply to exceptions covered by TRIPS arts 3–5, 2009 ASEAN Comprehensive Investment Agreement art 9(5): www.aseansec.org/documents/FINAL-SIGNED-ACIA.pdf.

[85] Rules on expropriation do not apply to IP rights to the extent that the conduct complies with TRIPS, 2004 US Model BIT art 6(5); on performance requirements, *ibid*, art 8(3)(b)(i); 2007 Norway Model BIT (abandoned) art 8(1)(vi)(b).

[86] States may derogate from rules on national treatment and MFN treatment in a manner consistent with WTO Agreement, 2004 Canada Model BIT art 9(4).

[87] National treatment and MFN treatment do not apply to IP rights, Energy Charter Treaty (adopted 17 December 1994, entered into force 16 April 1998) 2080 UNTS 95 art 10(10).

[88] Different dispute settlement rules, structure of obligations and possibly considerations of proportionality may influence the applicability of countermeasures to MSEN rules. Countermeasures may not be taken or have to be suspended if the dispute is pending before a court or tribunal which has authority to make decision binding on the parties, ILC

requirement for countermeasures to be reciprocal, after the determination of wrongfulness the state could *mutatis mutandis* apply countermeasures to MSEN rules.[89] If the DSU excluded only those responses to the breach of WTO law that are themselves in breach of WTO law, leaving the right to adopt countermeasures against non-WTO law unaffected, the injured state could suspend the investment treaty in accordance with its general international law rights. However, WTO rules exclude all unilateral countermeasures for the breach of WTO rules not approved in accordance with the DSU,[90] possibly extending the exclusion even to unilateral retorsions.[91] Since the scope of authorization granted by the DSB under Article 22 DSU is *ratione materiae* limited to 'covered agreements', considerations of effectiveness cannot extend this scope to unrelated rules of non-covered agreements. Consequently, while the wrongfulness of the suspending state's conduct regarding WTO rules would be a priori precluded, it would still remain bound by investment protection rules. In practical terms, a law authorizing the production of pirated music and computer programmes would not breach TRIPS rules on IP rights as falling within the authorized suspension of concessions, but would breach BIT obligations regarding discrimination and expropriation and therefore could not be adopted without incurring international responsibility. To the extent that another legal argument cannot be employed to justify non-compliance with investment protection law

Articles, above (n 16) art 52(3)(b). If the responsible state starts such proceedings regarding one MSEN rule, the injured state would only be entitled to take countermeasures regarding the other one. Countermeasures would not preclude wrongfulness if the obligations are not bilateralisable but interdependent or integral. On the distinction, see L-A Sicilianos, 'The Classification of Obligations and the Multilateral Dimension of the Relations of International Responsibility' (2002) 13 *European Journal of International Law* 1127, 1127–45; J Pauwelyn, 'A Typology of Multilateral Treaty Obligations: Are WTO Obligations Bilateral or Collective in Nature?' (2003) 14 *European Journal of International Law* 907. Eg, the wrongfulness of judicial mistreatment of property of aliens could be precluded regarding the bilateralisable customary obligations of treatment of aliens, R Phillimore, *Commentaries upon International Law* vol 3 3rd edn (London, Butterworths, 1885) 19, 31; Martens, above (n 15) 508; L Oppenheim, *International Law* vol 2 (London, Longmans, Green, and Co, 1905) 38; *Halleck's International Law*, above (n 15) 505; P Fauchille, *Traité de droit international public* (Paris, Librairie Arthur Rouseau, 1926) 692; D Bowett, 'Economic Coercion and Reprisals by States' (1972) 13 *Virginia Journal of International Law* 1, 10. Wrongfulness of similar or even identical conduct could not be precluded regarding *erga omnes partes* human rights treaty obligations of fair trial, Dupuy, above (n 49) fn 64. Finally, it is unclear whether the cumulative effect of measures on content-identical obligations arising from different sources should be additionally taken into account in assessing the proportionality of countermeasures.

89 2001 ILC Articles, above (n 16) 129, Commentary 5.

90 WTO, *US: Sections 301–310 of the Trade Act of 1974 – Panel Report* (27 January 2000) WT/DS152/R, para 7.59; WTO, *US: Certain EC Products – Panel Report* (17 July 2000) WT/DS165/R, paras 6.34–35, 6.87 (the particular point was not appealed by US and was approved by the Appellate Body; WTO, *US: Certain EC Products – Report of the Appellate Body* (10 January 2001) WT/DS165/AB/R, para 58); WTO, *US/Canada: Continued Suspension – Report of the Appellate Body*, above (n 69) para 382; Lesaffre, above (n 67) 469–72; A Lowenfeld, *International Economic Law* 2nd edn, above (n 72) 195–211.

91 WTO, *EC: Measures Affecting Trade in Commercial Vessels – Panel Report* (20 June 2005) WT/DS301/R, paras 7.187–7.207.

or preclude wrongfulness for its breach, the state would not be entitled to exercise its WTO-authorized countermeasures.

Secondly, the situation where WTO-authorized conduct cannot be exercised due to investment protection obligations suggests the possible presence of a conflict. The concept of conflict of rules in international law may be read in at least two ways. More narrowly, a conflict applies to mutually exclusive obligations.[92] There is no conflict in this sense: states can simultaneously comply with their WTO and investment protection obligations, simply by electing not to exercise the authorized right to act in breach of WTO obligations. More broadly, a conflict may be seen 'as a situation where two rules or principles suggest different ways of dealing with a problem'.[93] If this perspective is adopted, it could be possible to identify an obligation (to comply with rules regarding the treatment of IP rights as investments under BIT) and an exceptional right (to deny IP treatment under WTO rules) that 'seem to point in different directions in their application by a party'.[94]

If the broader approach to the definition of conflict is adopted, the role of the distinction between primary and secondary rules needs to be considered. The theoretical model elaborated by Roberto Ago[95] and accepted by the ILC in the 2001 ILC Articles distinguishes primary rules imposing legal obligations and 'the general conditions under international law for the State to be considered responsible for wrongful actions or omissions, and the legal consequences which flow therefrom'.[96] The existence of a conflict between primary rules is conceptually uncontroversial. Conflict between general and special rules of state responsibility is also conceptually uncontroversial, even if its resolution may be complicated.[97] The present situation seems different from the *inter se* breaches of primary and secondary rules, since rules 'point[ing] in different directions' are primary obligations to engage in certain conduct and secondary rule-based entitlements to breach other primary obligations (that are MSENs to the former

[92] CW Jenks, 'The Conflict of Law-Making Treaties' (1953) 30 *British Yearbook of International Law* 401, 451; G Marceau, 'Conflict of Norms and Conflict of Jurisdictions: the Relationship between WTO Law and Agreements and Other Treaties' (2001) 35 *Journal of World Trade* 1081, 1082–86; G Marceau, 'WTO Dispute Settlement and Human Rights' (2002) 13 *European Journal of International Law* 753, 791–94.

[93] 'Report of the Study Group', above (n 1) para 25; J Pauwelyn, *Conflict of Norms in Public International Law: How WTO Law Relates to Other Rules of International Law* (Cambridge, Cambridge University Press, 2003) 184–87; E Vranes, 'The Definition of "Norm Conflict" in International Law and Legal Theory' (2006) 17 *European Journal of International Law* 395; E Vranes, *Trade and the Environment: Fundamental Issues in International Law, WTO Law, and Legal Theory* Pt I (Oxford, Oxford University Press, 2009)

[94] 'Report of the Study Group', *ibid*, para 23.

[95] R Ago, 'Le délit international' (1939) 68 *Recueil des Cours* 419; R Ago, 'Second Report on State Responsibility' in (1970) II *Yearbook of the ILC* UN Doc A/CN.4/SER.A/1970/Add.1 177, 179, para 11.

[96] ILC Articles, above (n 16) 31, Commentary 1.

[97] Simma and Pulkowski, above (n 28).

primary obligations) with precluded wrongfulness. In other words, the conflict is not between two primary rules, or between two secondary rules arising out of the breach of the same primary rule, but between a primary rule and a secondary rule arising out of the breach of another primary rule. Even though both primary and secondary rules impose international obligations,[98] non-compliance with secondary rules would not create separate new regimes of secondary rules, being limited to reparations for the breach of the original primary rule that cannot be extended to punitive sanctions.[99]

The effect of the rules of state responsibility on the resolution of normative conflicts may be considered in the broader context of the debate about changing perceptions about the role of responsibility in the interpretation and application of international law. On the one hand, primary rules on obligations and secondary rules on circumstances precluding wrongfulness for breaches of different primary rules may be perceived as operating on analytically separate levels and therefore being logically unable of being in a situation of normative conflict. The distinction between primary and secondary rules is often given direct interpretative significance which may support such an approach.[100] On the other hand, the importance of the distinction has also been minimized to convenience of classification without additional normative significance,[101] particularly regarding rules created at the time when the form and content of Ago's project were uncertain.[102] Indeed, the internal consistency of the concept of circumstances precluding wrongfulness has been questioned in light of the ambiguous 'difference between an act which was justified, an act which was excused and an act for which responsibility did not exist'.[103]

Since the notion of countermeasures in multilateral trade may be traced to the 1947 General Agreement on Tariffs and Trade (GATT), the second perspective may have some attractiveness in the particular context.[104] In

[98] J Crawford, 'Third Report on State Responsibility' UN Doc A/CN.4/507, para 7.

[99] H Kelsen, *General Theory of Law and State* (New York, Russel & Russel, 1961) 357–58.

[100] *CMS* Annulment, above (n 44) para 134; *Continental Casualty*, above (n 44) paras 164–68; Binder, above (n 44).

[101] *Renta 4 S.V.S.A. and Others v Russia* (SCC V 24/2007) Award on Preliminary Objections (20 March 2009) paras 99–100.

[102] JE Alvarez and K Khamsi, 'The Argentine Crisis and Foreign Investors: A Glimpse into the Heart of the Investment Regime' (2008–09) 1 *Yearbook of International Investment Law and Policy* 379, 427–40; see the early criticism, RR Baxter, 'Reflections on Codification in Light of the International Law of State Responsibility for Injuries to Aliens' (1964–65) 16 *Syracuse Law Review* 745, 745–61; MS McDougal, HD Lasswell and L-C Chen, 'The Protection of Aliens from Discrimination and World Public Order: Responsibility of States Conjoined with Human Rights' (1976) 70 *American Journal of International Law* 432, 454–56.

[103] (1999) I *Yearbook of the ILC*, above (n 55) 174, para 48 (Simma); V Lowe, 'Precluding Wrongfulness or Responsibility: A Plea for Excuses' (1999) 10 *European Journal of International Law* 406; T Christakis, 'Les "circonstances excluant l'illicéités": une illusion optique?' in *Droit du pouvoir, pouvoir du droit: Mélanges offerts à Jean Salmon* (Bruxelles, Bruylant, 2007).

[104] Lesaffre, above (n 67) 454; Shadikhodjaev, above (n 68) 49–62.

the long run, one suspects that state practice and case law will increasingly adopt the vernacular of the 2001 ILC Articles in explaining obligations, whatever the theoretical perception at the time of their creation,[105] similarly to the other grand exposition of meta-rules of international law in the Vienna Convention on the Law of Treaties (VCLT).[106] Despite the controversy at the Vienna conference about the rules of interpretation[107] and the importance attributed to the non-retroactivity of the exposition,[108] the familiarity of contemporary interpreters with the textual expression of the rules[109] has proved irresistible in applying them to even nineteenth-century treaties.[110]

Assuming that the argument overcomes the two hurdles by adopting a broader approach to conflicts and being able to find a conflict between a primary rule and a secondary rule related to another primary rule, how can the conflict between the BIT obligation to protect IP rights and the WTO authorization to act in breach of IP rights be resolved? The application of Article 30 VCLT and the principle of *lex posterior* would raise familiar questions about its appropriateness in the context of multilateral treaties.[111] The perspective of *lex specialis* also does not give a clear answer as to whether trade or investment rules are more special, and it is uncertain whether the *lex specialis* nature of WTO secondary rules is relevant if the other rule in conflict is a primary rule.

If the relevant investment obligations were to prevail through their speciality or subsequence in time, they would not conflict with the TRIPS

[105] The ICJ summarily concluded that the 1948 Convention on the Prevention and Punishment of the Crime of Genocide did not refer to criminal responsibility of states since such a concept did not exist, *Application of the Convention on the Prevention and Punishment of the Crime of Genocide* (Judgment) [2007] ICJ Rep, para 170: www.icj-cij.org/docket/files/91/13685.pdf, even though it had been used in the drafting process of the Convention, *ibid*, paras 176–78, and was prominent in the postwar theoretical debates, JHH Weiler, A Cassese and M Spinedi (eds), *International Crimes of State: A Critical Analysis of the ILC's Draft Article 19 on State Responsibility* (Berlin, Walter de Gruyter, 1989).

[106] Vienna Convention on the Law of Treaties (adopted 23 May 1969, entered into force 27 January 1980) 1155 UNTS 331 (VCLT).

[107] MS McDougal, 'The International Law Commission's Draft Articles upon Interpretation: Textuality *Redivivu*' (1967) 61 *American Journal of International Law* 992; MS McDougal (1968) 62 *American Journal of International Law* 1021.

[108] S Rosenne, 'Temporal Application of the Vienna Convention on the Law of Treaties' (1970–71) 4 *Cornell International Law Journal* 1, 5–12.

[109] D Greig, 'The Time of Conclusion and the Time of Application of Treaties as Points of Reference in the Interpretative Process' in M Craven, M Fitzmaurice and M Vogiatzi (eds), *Time, History and International Law* (Leiden, Martinus Nijhoff Publishers, 2007) 207–15.

[110] *Award in the Arbitration regarding the Iron Rhine ("Ijzeren Rijn") Railway (Belgium/the Netherlands)* (2005) 10 RIAA 33, para 45. As one *Ad hoc* Annulment Committee noted, 'the Vienna Convention *qua* treaty does not apply to the BIT' (see Vienna Convention on the Law of Treaties (adopted 23 May 1969, entered into force 27 January 1980) 1155 UNTS 331, art 4 (VCLT)). But since the norms of interpretation would apply in any event this point is without incidence so far as the Award is concerned, *MTD Equity Sdn. Bhd. and MTD Chile S.A. v Republic of Chile* (ICSID Case No ARB/01/07) Decision on Annulment (21 March 2007) fn 69.

[111] J Pauwelyn, 'The Role of Public International Law in the WTO: How Far Can We Go?' (2001) 95 *American Journal of International Law* 535, 545–47.

rules pointing in the same direction but with the DSU rules authorizing the suspension of concessions. Since it is questionable whether Article 41(1)(b) VCLT would permit an *inter se* modification of DSU rules in light of their structural importance, it may be permissible to have recourse to the interpretative presumption against conflict of Article 31(3)(c) VCLT.[112] If the conflict still exists, it is not clear how it can be resolved. Conversely, if WTO rules were to prevail, the application of countermeasures would not be a unilateral attempt at implementing WTO obligations, but a WTO-authorized countermeasure that prevails over other conflicting rules.

Thirdly, assuming that a conflict exists and may be resolved in favour of the WTO rules, the consequences of this solution would need to be considered. The procedural setting most likely would be before the investor-state tribunal hearing the claim of the American investor (and having accepted the chain of arguments leading to the resolution of the conflict in favour of the WTO entitlement to breach IP rights). On the one hand, and less persuasively, the tribunal could treat WTO entitlement as primary rules that prevail over the contrary obligations under investment law, concluding that due to the modified content of the obligations no wrongful act was committed in the first place. To reach that conclusion, the tribunal would have to treat its applicable law clause[113] as permitting it to rely on other rules of international law prevailing over the particular rules it has jurisdiction to interpret.[114] If this approach is adopted, then the situation would be similar to such primary investment rules as denial of benefit clauses[115] and NPM clauses, denying protection available under the other substantive rules.[116] Since no breach has taken place, the nature of the investor's rights is irrelevant: to paraphrase Crawford's views about human rights,

[112] The German argument failed to persuade the PCIJ in its first contentious case, above (nn 5–7), but did not face any objections 46 years later at the Vienna Conference on the Law of Treaties, United Nations Conference on the Law of Treaties, Second Session UN Doc A/CONF.39/11/Add.1 57 (Fleischhauer).

[113] At least in the ICSID context, the breadth of art 42 of the ICSID Convention, above (n 41), as interpreted in the recent case law, would probably permit such a reading, E Gaillard and Y Banifatemi, 'The Meaning of "and" in Article 42(1), Second Sentence, of the Washington Convention: The Role of International Law in the ICSID Choice of Law Process' (2003) 18 *ICSID Review – Foreign Investment Law Journal* 375; *MTD* Annulment, above (n 110) paras 72–75; *CMS* Annulment, above (n 44) paras 81–85; *Azurix Corp. v Argentine Republic* (ICSID Case No ARB/01/12) Decision on the Application of Annulment (1 September 2009) paras 157–77.

[114] *Cf Questions of Interpretation and Application of the 1971 Montreal Convention arising from the Aerial Incident at Lockerbie (Libya v UK)* (Provisional Measures) [1992] ICJ Rep 3, para 39.

[115] Denial of benefit clauses entitle the host state to deny protection to shell companies. There is some controversy whether the effect can be retrospective, KJ Vandevelde, *United States Investment Treaties: Policy and Practice* (Boston, Kluwer 1992) 53, 55–57; AC Sinclair, 'The Substance of Nationality Requirements in Investment Treaty Arbitration' (2005) 20 *ICSID Review – Foreign Investment Law Journal* 357, 385–88; Douglas, *Investment Claims*, above (n 56) 470–72, or only prospective, *Plasma Consortium, Plasma Consortium Limited v Bulgaria*, ICSID Case no ARB/03/24, Decision on Jurisdiction, February 8, 2005, paras 152–65.

[116] *Nicaragua v US*, above (n 79) (Jennings, Dissenting Opinion) 528, 541; *CMS* Annulment, above (n 44) para 134; *Continental Casualty*, above (n 44) paras 164–68.

'conduct inconsistent with [investment] obligations may . . . be justified or excused . . . to the extent provided for by the applicable regime of [investment law] itself'.[117]

On the other hand, and more persuasively, the WTO-authorized *lex specialis* countermeasure could operate on the same conceptual level of secondary rules precluding wrongfulness. The tribunal would first have to respond to a *Monetary Gold* challenge that it cannot decide on rights and obligations of states that have not consented to its jurisdiction: the anterior wrongfulness of the US conduct is the first criterion for the successful argument of countermeasures.[118] However, even assuming that the *Monetary Gold* doctrine is not limited to ICJ procedure but represents a general principle of international adjudication applicable also to individual-state arbitrations,[119] the DSB authorization could be treated as an authoritative determination of wrongfulness that the tribunal may take as a given.[120]

The impact of WTO countermeasures may again be differentiated between primary and secondary rules. One of the criteria taken into account in interpreting investment obligations such as fair and equitable treatment and indirect expropriation is the reasonableness of the investor's expectations, considered against the benchmark of 'pre-existing laws and regulations'.[121] If obligations under human rights law[122] and European Union (EU) law could be counted as part of these 'laws and regulations',[123] conduct pursuant to them would arguably not frustrate reasonable expectations. Indeed, when a trader who suffered damages due to WTO countermeasures adopted by the US against the EC brought a non-contractual damage claim against the latter, the European Court of Justice (ECJ) rejected it because the economic operator exporting goods should have been aware about the WTO regime of countermeasures.[124]

[117] Crawford, 'Third Report', above (n 98) A/CN.4/507 Add.3, paras 312d, 349.

[118] *Case of the Monetary Gold Removed from Rome in 1943* (Preliminary Questions) [1954] ICJ Rep 19, 31–33.

[119] *Larsen v Hawaiian Kingdom* (UNCITRAL Arbitration) Award (5 February 2001) (2002) 119 ILR 566, paras 11.8–11.24.

[120] *Ibid*, para 11.24; Paparinskis 'Countermeasures', above (n 41) 338–39.

[121] *Gami Investments, Inc. v Mexico* (UNCITRAL Arbitration) Final Award (15 November 2004) para 94; C McLachlan, L Shore and M Weiniger, *International Investment Arbitration: Substantive Principles* (Oxford, Oxford University Press, 2007) 235–37, 302–04; R Dolzer and CH Schreuer, *Principles of International Investment Law* (Oxford, Oxford University Press, 2008) 104–06, 133–40; Newcombe and Paradell, above (n 77) 279–89, 350–51.

[122] U Kriebaum, 'Privatizing Human Rights: The Interface between International Investment Protection and Human Rights' (2006) 3(5) *Transnational Dispute Management* 8–22; B Simma and T Kill, 'Harmonizing Investment Protection and International Human Rights: First Steps Towards a Methodology' in Binder et al (eds), *International Investment Law for the 21st Century*, above (n 4) 705.

[123] T Eilmansberger, 'Bilateral Investment Treaties and EU Law' (2009) 46 *Common Market Law Review* 383, 415–18; M Burgstaller, 'European Law and Investment Treaties' (2009) 26 *Journal of International Arbitration* 181, 193–96.

[124] Joined Cases C-120/06 P and C-121/06 P *FIAMM and FIAMM Technologies v Council and Commission* [2008] ECR I-6513, para 186, also para 185.

The possibility of analogy from Union law has to be taken with a grain of salt: apart from the very specific cases regarding UN Security Council sanctions,[125] the ECJ has so far for different reasons rejected all claims about violations of the right of property.[126] There is a qualitative difference between a fluctuating market share in the ECJ case and investments made in a country protected under specific rules precluding not only frustration of expectations, but arbitrariness of decision-making.[127] As the treaty practice suggests, states sometimes coordinate the scope of content of protection of IP rights in investment and trade law but mostly do not.[128] It is unclear whether in the latter case the possibility that states could engage in conduct under another regime that would breach the particular rules should necessarily influence their interpretation, or rather simply indicate that states have wished to provide broader protection in the particular context. In any event, rules on *de jure* discrimination and direct expropriation triggered by countermeasures do not attribute such importance to expected developments and could therefore be breached.

Assuming that a breach of investment protection obligations has taken place, the impact of countermeasures would depend on the way in which investors' treaty rights are conceptualised. If the *ADM* tribunal's approach is preferred, the host state's obligations are owed only to the home state, and can therefore be suspended with precluded wrongfulness as a countermeasure; the investor's claim fails *in limine*.[129] If the *Corn Products* tribunal's approach is preferred, the host state's obligations are owed also to the investor, and due to its structural incapability to trigger the precondition of breaching an obligation owed to the state the countermeasures argument fails; the investor's claim succeeds.[130] The fragmentation and proliferation of rules, regimes and theories leads to a rather paradoxical conclusion: despite the sophistication and elegance of the WTO rules and procedures, it is precisely the focus on *lex specialis* rules intended to strengthen the multilateral system that makes it easier for non-WTO, MSEN regimes to undercut their effect. For the state to be able to lawfully exercise its WTO-authorized countermeasures in the presence of investment obligations, it has to overcome a number of complicated hurdles: showing a conflict, persuading the tribunal of its competence to consider it, resolving it in favour of WTO rules, and either having no breach of primary rules or treating the

[125] Joined Cases C-402/05 P and C-415/05 P *Kadi and Al Barakaat International Foundation v Council and Commission* [2008] ECR I-06351, paras 354-371; Case T-318/01 *Othman v Council and Commission* [2009] Judgment of 11 June 2009, paras 91–92.

[126] T Tridimas, *The General Principles of EU Law* 2nd edn (Oxford, Oxford University Press, 2006) 315.

[127] *Saluka Investments BV (The Netherlands) v Czech Republic* (UNCITRAL Arbitration) Partial Award (17 March 2006) para 307.

[128] See above, nn (82–87).

[129] *ADM*, above (n 31) para 176.

[130] *Corn Products*, above (n 31) paras 161–65.

investor only as an agent of its home state. The untangling of normative strands works in favour of the investor who – assuming that a breach of the BIT can be shown – can hope to persuade the tribunal that the rules it has jurisdiction to interpret and apply prevail in the particular dispute.

IV INVESTMENT PROTECTION LAW COUNTERMEASURES IN WTO LAW

The analysis of countermeasures and MSEN primary rules may also start from the opposite perspective of investment protection law. In the multi-faceted US–Mexican soft drinks dispute, Mexico introduced tax laws de facto discriminating against US products, allegedly as countermeasures against US breaches of NAFTA. The countermeasures triggered the prohibitions of discriminatory conduct both in NAFTA and WTO, and led to claims against Mexico in NAFTA investor-state arbitrations[131] and the WTO respectively.[132] Mexican invocation of countermeasures to respectively preclude wrongfulness and interpret the primary WTO rules was rejected in both forums. These proceedings will be taken as the basis for the case study. The argument will be made in two steps, considering in turn the situation in investment protection law and WTO law.

First, reliance on countermeasures in investor-state proceedings raises important structural challenges. As was suggested above, if the dispute comes before an investor-state tribunal, it would be put squarely before the *Monetary Gold* problem: the very subject matter of its decision about lawfulness of host state's countermeasures is the prior wrongful conduct of the home state that is not a party to the proceedings.[133] Unlike the case of WTO countermeasures, there would be no authoritative third-party determination about the wrongfulness.[134]

A tribunal could respond to the argument in four ways.[135] The *ADM* tribunal *arguendo* assumed that a breach had taken place, rejecting the countermeasures argument because of non-compliance with substantive and procedural requirements.[136] Assuming wrongfulness seems perilously close to deciding on the legal right of absent states – precisely what *Monetary Gold* was supposed to preclude – and would be ultimately unhelpful if the substantive and procedural requirements were complied with and the existence or non-existence of prior wrongfulness would be decisive. The *Corn Products* tribunal obiter dictum suggested that Mexico

[131] See above (n 31).

[132] See above (n 32).

[133] See above (nn 118–19); *cf* F Latty, 'Arbitrage transnational et droit international général (2008)' (2008) 54 *Annuaire français de droit international* 467, 495.

[134] See above (n 120).

[135] Paparinskis, 'Countermeasures', above (n 41) 337–42.

[136] *ADM*, above (n 31) paras 134–60.

had not proved the existence of the breach.[137] However, wrongfulness is a matter of legal characterization of conduct and not a question of whether the conduct has actually taken place. The decisive legal issue is the nature of the investor's rights: if the investor is a beneficiary of the rights, then the *Corn Products* tribunal is correct in concluding that countermeasures are a priori inapplicable;[138] if the investor is only an agent of its home state, the dilemma between the necessity to decide on anterior wrongfulness and the jurisdictional inability to do so may lead to a finding of inadmissibility. Whatever approach is chosen, even if the investor-state tribunal succeeds in deciding its case by evading the issue of countermeasures, it would be unlikely to produce a decision exhaustively examining and conclusively accepting or rejecting the lawfulness of countermeasures. The argument of countermeasures is different in this sense from the argument of necessity: even though the case law about necessity in the Argentinian crisis provided divergent interpretations of both facts and law,[139] the investor-state procedural setting did not affect the possibility of tribunals to decide the argument because in the law of necessity only 'interests' and not 'rights' of third parties have to be considered.[140]

Secondly, it remains to be seen what the effect of countermeasures taken for the breach of NAFTA – and lacking third-party determination regarding their lawfulness – would be in the WTO dispute settlement proceedings. For the purpose of convenience, a distinction will be drawn between primary and secondary rules of WTO law. At the level of primary rules, Mexico argued that its countermeasures fell under the general exception of Article XX(d) GATT regarding measures 'necessary to secure compliance with laws and regulations'. The Appellate Body rejected this argument both because international law in general and NAFTA in particular were not 'laws and regulations' and because deciding on it

> would entail a determination whether the United States has acted consistently or inconsistently with its NAFTA obligations. We see no basis in the DSU for panels and the Appellate Body to adjudicate non-WTO disputes . . . Accepting Mexico's interpretation would imply that the WTO dispute settlement system could be used to determine rights and obligations outside the covered agreements.[141]

While this passage has been criticized as being inconsistent with the earlier practice of reliance on non-WTO rules,[142] most of this practice

[137] *Corn Products*, above (n 31), paras 189-91.
[138] *Ibid*, paras 161–65.
[139] See above (nn 45–47).
[140] ILC Articles, above (n 16) art 25(1)(b).
[141] *Mexico-Soft Drinks – AB Report*, above (n 32) para 56.
[142] R Howse, 'The Use and Abuse of International Law in WTO Trade/Environment Litigation' in ME Janow, V Donaldson and A Yanovich (eds), *The WTO: Governance, Dispute Settlement, and Developing Countries* (New York, Juris Publishing, Inc, 2008) 659–60.

may be explained in traditional terms of interpretation of generic concepts[143] or incorporation or reference by WTO rules themselves.[144] *A contrario,* Article XX(d) does not incorporate the whole international law of countermeasures.[145]

Alternatively, it has been suggested that the Panel could have 'merely . . . decid[ed] whether Mexico *prima facie* had a strong case'[146] or 'ma[d]e a determination for its own purposes as to whether the US was acting consistently with NAFTA [as] a preliminary step in making a WTO ruling'.[147] The approach of minimising the importance of the legal argument is not entirely persuasive. The fact that the interpreter also interprets other rules of international law after making the finding of wrongfulness makes the finding no less important or conclusive. Moreover, '[a]n injured State may only take countermeasures against a State which is *responsible* for an internationally wrongful act', and to replace this criterion with prima facie perceptions would constitute a retrogressive development away from the 'objective standard of taking of countermeasures'.[148] While in the case of auto-determination the state taking countermeasures will determine for itself the wrongfulness of the other state's conduct, the situation is different for the adjudicator who has to decide on the lawfulness of countermeasures on an objective basis. The Appellate Body's unwillingness to accept the possibility of a determination of wrongfulness *en passant* seems understandable in light of the implications of this argument. Since countermeasures do not have to be reciprocal,[149] examination of the alleged anterior breach may even require the Panel to examine sensitive aspects of *jus ad bellum, jus in bello* or human rights, particularly if one goes further than the 2001 ILC Articles[150] and accepts the permissibility of third-state countermeasures *de lege lata*.[151]

[143] WTO, *US: Import Prohibition of Certain Shrimps and Shrimp Products – Report of the Appellate Body* (6 November 1998) WT/DS58/AB/R, para 130.

[144] TRIPS and IP Treaties, above (n 80); WTO, Lomé waiver, *EC: Regime for the Importation, Sale and Distribution of Bananas – Report of the Appellate Body* (25 September 1997) WT/DS27/AB/R, paras 167–78.

[145] Howse, above (n 142) 660–61. Interpretation of secondary rules would mean interpretation of all the primary rules of international law, J Crawford (ed), *The International Law Commission's Articles on State Responsibility: Introduction, Text and Commentaries* (Cambridge, Cambridge University Press, 2002) 10.

[146] P-J Kuijper, 'Does the World Trade Organization Prohibit Retorsions and Reprisals? Legitimate "Contracting Out" or "Clinical Isolation" Again?' in Janow et al (eds), above (n 142) 707.

[147] WJ Davy and A Sapir, 'The *Soft Drinks* Case: The WTO and Regional Agreements' (2009) 8 *World Trade Review* 5, 18.

[148] ILC Articles, above (n 16) art 49(1) (emphasis added), Commentary 3.

[149] *Ibid*, 129, Commentary 5.

[150] *Ibid*, art 54.

[151] S Villalpando, *L'emergence de la communauté internationale dans la responsabilité des Etats* (Paris, Presses Universitaires de France, 2005) 371–78; M Dawidowicz, 'Public Law Enforcement without Public Law Safeguards? An Analysis of State Practice on Third-Party Countermeasures and their Relationship to the UN Security Council' (2006) 77 *British*

Whatever the impact of countermeasures as a matter of primary rules of WTO law – and the *Mexico-Soft Drinks* case suggests that at least in terms of Article XX(d) GATT there is none – their role as a matter of secondary rules still needs to be considered. The *Mexico-Soft Drinks* case leaves the issue open, since Mexico curiously did not rely on the fallback argument of countermeasures as a circumstance precluding wrongfulness in case its initial argument of countermeasures as an interpretative criterion for the primary rule got rejected.[152] Whether or not primary rules additionally prescribe certain consequences from the conduct amounting to countermeasures, countermeasures would in principle always (also) operate at the level of secondary rules.[153] The jurisdiction to interpret and apply secondary rules would come from the jurisdiction regarding primary rules. Undoubtedly, to accept that countermeasures for breach of non-WTO rules could preclude wrongfulness for the breach of WTO rules would lead to significant problems in the dispute settlement process, as suggested in the previous paragraph. Still, the issue is not WTO-specific and would cause precisely the same problems for any adjudicator addressing non-reciprocal countermeasures and having jurisdiction only to interpret the rule breached by countermeasures.[154] If the argument is accepted, Panels and the Appellate Body would have to consider countermeasures as a potential circumstance precluding wrongfulness, leaving open the question about whether and how the earlier wrongfulness could be determined.

The argument against the application of countermeasures could be made in at least two ways, relying either on the structure or *lex specialis* nature of the rules. The exclusion cannot be justified in structural terms. The primary rules called 'obligations not affected by countermeasures' by the ILC do not include trade obligations.[155] It seems possible to conceptualise WTO

Yearbook of International Law 333. State practice in relation to third-party countermeasures has in practice raised issues of multilateral trade, eg, regarding Uganda, South Africa, Poland, Argentina, Iraq, Burundi, Portugal, Israel and Nicaragua; *cf* ILC Articles, above (n 16) art 53, Commentary 3; J Fernández Pons, 'Self-Help and the World Trade Organisation' in P Mengozzi (ed), *International Trade Law on the 50th Anniversary of the Multilateral Trade System* (Milano, Dott A Giuffrè Editore, 1999) 99; Dawidowicz, *ibid*, 352–54, 356–58, 368–74, 376–83, 384–86, 389–90, 399–402; E Katselli, 'Countermeasures: Concept and Substance in the Protection of Collective Interests' in KH Kaikobad and M Bohlander (eds), *International Law and Power: Perspectives on Legal Order and Justice* (Leiden, Martinus Nijhoff Publishers, 2009) 401, 426–27.

[152] Kuijper, above (n 146) 703–06.

[153] States sometimes create primary rules with content close or identical to that of secondary rules, eg, regarding distress, ILC Articles, above (n 16) art 24, Commentary 5; possibly necessity, above (nn 45–47); self-defence is both a primary rule of *jus ad bellum* and a secondary circumstance precluding wrongfulness, ILC Articles, above (n 16) art 21.

[154] In the leading cases, either countermeasures are reciprocal, *Air Service Agreement*, above (n 16); *Gabčíkovo-Nagymaros Project*, above (n 16); or the adjudicators have jurisdiction to interpret both rules allegedly breached, *Naulilaa*, above (n 15) 1016; *Responsabilité de l'Allemagne en raison des actes commis postérieurement au 31 juillet 1914 et avant que le Portugal ne participât à la guerre (Portugal contre Allemagne)* (1930) 2 RIAA 1035, 1039–40.

[155] ILC Articles, above (n 16) art 50.

obligations as bilateralisable,[156] and therefore permitting countermeasures; and in any event the existence of *lex specialis* countermeasures suggests that there is no structural impossibility in subjecting these rules to countermeasures. The argument of *lex specialis* could also be used in a different way, to suggest that states have limited not only the right to take countermeasures as a reaction to the breach of WTO law but also the right to take countermeasures against WTO rules in general, in the sense of 'renounc[ing] the possibility of countermeasures being taken [not only] for its breach, [but also] in relation to its subject matter'.[157]

The silence of the DSU and the contradictory state practice may be read in a number of ways. On the one hand, the teleology of strengthening the multilateral system through its 'system of enforcement'[158] may support excluding disruptions originating even (or a fortiori) from external sources.[159] 'Subsequent practice' may be sought in the increasing unwillingness of states in the later GATT years to justify their conduct as countermeasures, instead relying on even strained treaty-law arguments.[160] *Travaux préparatoires* show that an Indian proposal to expressly include retaliatory action in Article XX was rejected.[161] On the other hand, the practice is at best uncertain, and the preparatory materials do not explain the reason for the rejection of the Indian proposal.[162]

Whatever conclusions one may draw from the pre-WTO practice, the detailed rules that are expressly spelled out in the DSU suggest that by the Uruguay Round states knew quite well how to exclude countermeasures from applying to WTO rules. However, they chose to limit the scope of exclusion only to countermeasures adopted in response to breaches of WTO rules and not to all rules of international law. The implication of the *a contrario* argument seems inescapable. Against this background, the apparent unwillingness to confirm in express terms the even *arguendo* existing consensus excluding countermeasures in pre-WTO law suggests treating the relevance of earlier practice with a grain of salt. The Appellate Body report in *Mexico–Soft Drinks* may be read as following the same line of thinking when it criticized the implication of the Mexican argument as permitting

[156] Schachter, above (n 50) 735; Pauwelyn 'Typology', above (n 88); *contra* Carmody, above (n 50).

[157] ILC Articles, above (n 16) art 50, Commentary 10.

[158] *Ibid.*

[159] Marceau appears to take this view, suggesting that 'Article 23 of the DSU . . . prohibits trade restrictions or any remedy being taken outside the framework of the DSU', Marceau 'Conflicts', above (n 92) 1122.

[160] L Bartels, 'Article XX of GATT and the Problem of Extraterritorial Jurisdiction: The Case of Trade Measures for the Protection of Human Rights' (2002) 36 *Journal of World Trade* 353, 396–402.

[161] *Mexico: Soft Drinks – AB Report*, above (n 32) fn 175.

[162] Fernández Pons, above (n 151) 94–104; A Bianchi and L Gradoni, 'Developing Countries, Countermeasures and WTO Law: Reinterpreting the DSU against the Background of International Law' (2008) ICSTD Project on Dispute Settlement, Series Issue Paper No 5 28–40: ictsd.net/downloads/2009/02/reinterpreting_dsu1.pdf.

> WTO Members to adopt WTO-inconsistent measures based upon a *unilateral* determination that another Member has breached its WTO obligations, in contradiction with Articles 22 and 23 of the DSU and Article XXIII:2 of the GATT 1994.[163]

The Appellate Body language suggests a concern about bypassing the set of procedures created by the DSU and not about the broader teleology of a strong multilateral system requiring the exclusion of 'outside' countermeasures *in limine*. At the very least, the DSU and *Mexico-Soft Drinks* show that countermeasures are not *clearly* excluded, and at this point of analysis the presumption against an implicit waiver of rules of state responsibility could become relevant, suggesting that the legal right to take countermeasures still exists.[164]

Even if the right to take countermeasures against WTO rules for breach of other rules in principle exists, it remains to be considered whether the MSEN perspective affects this conclusion. It has been suggested that states are entitled to take general international law countermeasures against investment protection rules (even if due to the procedural context the correctness of this auto-determination would not be conclusively confirmed) but not entitled to take countermeasures for the breach of WTO law against MSEN trade rules other than in accordance with the WTO procedure. As with the earlier analysis, it may be questioned whether the distinction between primary and secondary rules permits identifying a conflict, since the relevant rules are both secondary in nature and relate to different primary rules.[165] If it is possible to identify a conflict, then a *lex specialis* secondary rule prohibiting discriminatory taxes (or rather subjecting the introduction of such taxes to a particular procedure) and a secondary rule allowing the introduction of discriminatory taxes may be said to 'pull in different directions', even if their underlying primary rules created through different law-making processes point in the same direction (prohibiting discriminatory taxes).

If the conflict exists, its resolution would depend on the interplay of the particular treaty and customary rules on the issue. NAFTA incorporates the national treatment rule from Article III GATT and any successor

[163] *Mexico: Soft Drinks – AB Report*, above (n 32) para 77 (emphasis in the original).

[164] *Elettronica Sicula S.p.A. (ELSI) (US v Italy)* [1989] ICJ Rep 15, para 50; above (n 44). Speaking in the somewhat different context of interpretation and general principles, two Panels have taken the view that '[c]ustomary international law applies generally to the economic relations between the WTO Members. Such international law applies to the extent that the WTO agreements do not "contract out" from it', WTO, *Korea: Measures Affecting Government Procurement – Panel Report* (19 June 2000) WT/DS163/R, para 7.96; WTO, *US/Canada: Continued Suspension of Obligations in the EC-Hormones Dispute – Panel Report* (31 March 2008) WT/DS321/R, para 7.336. The Appellate Body mentioned the argument but did not criticize it, possibly indicating an implicit approval, *US/Canada: Continued Suspension – AB Report*, above (n 68) para 278.

[165] See discussion above (nn 95–103).

agreement,[166] provides a priority rule for NAFTA over GATT (but at least expressly not over any successor agreement),[167] and gives the states a choice of settling disputes 'regarding any matter arising under both' NAFTA and GATT (and any successor agreements) in either forum.[168] The complex relationship between WTO rules and procedures and NAFTA rules and (at the moment non-functioning) Chapter 20 procedures is beyond the scope of this chapter.[169] If the conflict is resolved in favour of NAFTA rules, then the general proposition about applicability of countermeasures would remain valid.

If the contrary reading is correct, or in the absence of specific rules dealing with treaty conflict, a teleological reading of WTO rules could suggest that they should prevail. In light of the importance attributed in the Uruguay Round to the creation of the DSU and the abandonment of unilateral countermeasures in favour of a strong and institutionalized dispute settlement system,[170] to permit the application of countermeasures to MSENs would effectively disrupt the bargain through the normative backdoor. Reading WTO rules in a purposive light, it could be suggested that when states create a particular procedure for applying countermeasures against a particular rule, they do not escape the exclusion simply by creating a MSEN rule *inter se* and applying a unilateral countermeasure against it in a way that the dispute settlement body under the former rule would not be able to adjudicate. The *lex specialis* of WTO countermeasures would take priority over the *lex generalis* of countermeasures regarding MSEN rules, and the countermeasures could be carried out only when the more stringent WTO procedures would be complied with. If this argument is accepted, then – assuming that NAFTA did not have conflict rules – the Mexican argument should have been rejected not because Mexico had waived its customary law right to apply countermeasures to WTO rules for breaches of other rules of international law, but because it could not escape the restrictions of DSU by purporting to breach a MSEN rule.

Conversely, the teleological reasoning could be said to lead to an absurd result. states willing to apply non-reciprocal countermeasures for the breach of non-trade rules to WTO rules would be unable to do so unless they exhausted the WTO procedures first, which in turn they may be unable to do if the target state has breached only the non-WTO and not WTO obligations. A common sense compromise position would perhaps narrow the scope of the definition of conflict to reciprocal countermeasures

166 NAFTA, above (n 84) art 301.
167 *Ibid*, art 103.
168 *Ibid*, art 2005(1).
169 FM Abbott, 'The North American Integration Regime and its Implications for the World Trading System' in JHH Weiler (ed), *The EU, The WTO and the NAFTA* (Oxford, Oxford University Press, 2000) 177–89; Pauwelyn, 'Adding Sweeteners', above (n 19).
170 See above (nn 70, 90–91).

where both the original breach and countermeasure relate to MSEN rules. However, it would effectively move the perspective away from the conflict between secondary rules to the relationship between MSEN primary rules which is outside the scope of the present chapter. Consequently, even when the teleology of integrated dispute settlement is supplemented by MSEN considerations, the implications of these arguments make successful restriction of countermeasures questionable.

V CONCLUSION

To explain the impact of secondary rules on MSEN primary rules, this chapter considers two case studies of countermeasures in WTO and investment protection law. In the first case study, to apply WTO-authorized countermeasures to MSEN primary rules of investment protection, one has to overcome a number of intellectual and legal hurdles. The strengthening of the multilateral trade dispute settlement system comes at a cost of complicating the identification of relationship and the resolution of conflicts with primary rules of investment protection law and secondary rules of general international law. To be able to exercise its WTO authorization without breaching its investment protection obligations, the state faces an uphill battle: it has to demonstrate the existence of a conflict; persuade the investor-state tribunal of its authority to consider the conflict and resolve it in favour of the WTO regime (and against its own regime); succeed in showing how WTO entitlement should prevail over primary investment obligations; alternatively, persuade the tribunal that the investor is only an agent of the other BIT party. The case study shows the complexity of turning the MSEN primary rules and secondary rules in the same direction when one set of secondary rules exclusively focuses on the internal dynamic of ensuring the efficiency of its own regime.

Countermeasures breaching investment obligations and MSEN WTO rules pose opposite challenges. Due to the absence of a *ratione personae* and *ratione materiae* overlap between investor-state dispute settlement and state-state countermeasures, investor-state tribunals are unlikely to bring adjudicative clarity to the auto-determination of countermeasures. The sophistication of WTO law is similarly unhelpful, since despite the detailed rules regarding countermeasures *for* breaches of WTO law, the DSU is silent regarding other breaches *of* WTO law. One is left with two equally unattractive solutions: either constructing a waiver out of the teleology of effectiveness of WTO law (despite the *a contrario* textual indication that states knew how to limit countermeasures and chose not to draft a general waiver); or permitting the application of countermeasures with all the procedural challenges that non-reciprocal countermeasures bring to adjudicators with limited jurisdiction. Even the concept of MSEN rules is unlikely to be helpful, leaving the harmonization of the WTO *lex specialis* regime and non-reciprocal countermeasures problematic.

As was suggested in the introduction, one should not lightly assume that modern challenges are qualitatively different from the classic ones, and the proliferated adjudicators may simply be drawing attention to problems and conflicts that have latently existed for a long time. Still, the interplay of secondary rules with MSEN primary rules shows at the very least a quantitatively impressive 'spaghetti bowl' of conceptual challenges, from general issues of fragmentation, proliferation and conflicts, to more particular aspects of theory of state responsibility, role of circumstances precluding wrongfulness in different substantive and procedural settings and the multiplicity of participants in the legal process. More broadly, the case studies show the paradoxical impact that the law of state responsibility may have at different levels of analysis. The treatment of all breaches of international law as giving rise to a single regime of secondary rules is a powerful normative expression of the unity of the international legal order. At the same time, when the unity is expressed already at the level of primary rules of MSEN nature, the law of state responsibility may have the effect of turning their application in opposite directions. The pragmatic lesson may be that there is no pre-determined impact and that both unity and divergences can be expressed at the level of primary and secondary rules, leading to different interplays both *inter se* and between the categories. It may be tentatively suggested that a clearer appreciation of the contours of and linkages within the customary and treaty strata of the normative framework would be helpful to enable all the participants to engage in law-making and law-application in a creative, experimental and proliferating manner, while fully understanding the legal benchmark against which their conduct will be judged.

12

Multi-Sourced Equivalent Norms and the Legitimacy of Indigenous Peoples' Rights under International Law

Claire Charters

I INTRODUCTION

THE QUESTION ADDRESSED in this chapter is this: what is the impact of Multi-Sourced Equivalent Norms (MSENs) on the legitimacy of Indigenous peoples' rights under international law?

On the one hand, MSENs create a legitimacy deficit in the form of uncertainty about the meaning of some Indigenous peoples' rights, with nuanced differences between norms sourced in various juris-generative forums. MSENs also reflect procedural defects in international law making in that the existence of multiple sources by definition means that there is no singular, transparent or ultimate authoritative source of Indigenous peoples' rights under international law. International institutional competition between these sources of norms aggravates procedural opacity and confusion.

On the other hand, however, these legitimacy deficits are mitigated and countered by the legitimacy-positive impacts of international institutional dialogic attempts to set jurisdictional boundaries between institutions and to interpret Indigenous peoples' norms consistently. Indigenous peoples, by participating in almost all international institutions engaged in Indigenous peoples' rights, and arguing for similar rights in all of them, also facilitate cohesion across various international juris-generative forums. Moreover, analysis of MSENs in international law on Indigenous peoples illustrates that MSENs are related to the creation of more just norms relevant to Indigenous peoples and the establishment of international institutions more responsive to Indigenous peoples' needs, thereby going some way to reversing the historical discrimination against Indigenous peoples under international law.[1]

[1] A Anghie, *Imperialism, Sovereignty and the Making of International Law* (Cambridge, Cambridge University Press, 2004).

The time is ripe to analyze MSENs, and norm fragmentation generally, in specific areas of law and from an empirical perspective. Research on Indigenous peoples' rights is interesting for a number of reasons. Indigenous peoples' rights have evolved out of 'sub-systems' of international law to crystallize into a 'sub-system' in its own right,[2] reflected in the adoption of the Declaration on the Rights of Indigenous Peoples (the Declaration) in September 2007.[3] There are a number of institutions with authority to make or apply Indigenous peoples' rights, even some with little formal law-making mandate, from regional human rights bodies, to global human rights bodies, to the UN Permanent Forum on Indigenous Issues (PFII), the Expert Mechanism on the Rights of Indigenous Peoples (EMRIP) and so on. Together, the above developments have led to the creation of a plethora of MSENs on Indigenous peoples' rights.[4] For example, the UN General Assembly (UNGA), the Human Rights Council, regional and UN human rights bodies, the International Labour Organization (ILO), various Special Rapporteurs, even the World Bank, have each developed norms to regulate states' protection of Indigenous peoples' rights. While many norms point in the same direction, there are also differences in their content, sometimes because of nuanced textual differences and sometimes because of different contextual factors, meaning that they create differing levels of state obligations. Norms also differ in their bindingness under international law.

II LEGITIMACY

Legitimacy is defined here as the quality in international norms that leads states to internalize a pull to voluntarily and habitually conform to those norms, even when it may not be in their immediate interest to obey and despite the lack of formal or enforceable 'sanction', relying somewhat on Thomas Franck's theory of legitimacy.[5] He writes, that legitimacy 'exerts a claim to compliance in the voluntarist mode'.[6]

[2] See B Kingsbury, 'Reconciling Five Conceptual Approaches to Indigenous Peoples' Claims in International and Comparative Law' (2001) 34 *New York University Journal of International Law and Politics* 189.

[3] Declaration on the Rights of Indigenous Peoples, UNGA Res 61/295 (13 September 2007) UN Doc A/RES/61/295.

[4] A broad definition is taken to institutions with a law-making mandate on the basis that '[b]y examining the interactions among non-dominant native groups, Indigenous advocates, domestic governments, and international agencies, it is possible to discern whether interactions follow a particular pattern. If they do, a norm is emerging or has been established concerning the problems faced by Indigenous populations'. R Torres, 'The Rights of Indigenous Populations: The Emerging International Norm' (1991) 16 *Yale Journal of International Law* 127, 145–46.

[5] In particular in, TM Franck, *The Power of Legitimacy Among Nations* (Oxford, Oxford University Press, 1990); *Fairness in International Law and Institutions* (Oxford, Oxford University Press, 1995) and 'The Power of Legitimacy and the Legitimacy of Power: International Law in an Age of Power Disequilibrium' (2006) 100 *American Journal of International* Law 88, 91.

[6] Franck, *The Power of Legitimacy Among Nations*, *ibid*, 26.

My focus is on 'norm-based' descriptions of compliance with international law: theories that attribute conformity to norms to qualities associated with their legal character instead of political interest, the latter being more commonly associated with rational and realist international relations theory. However, I do not necessarily contest rational and realist or 'self-interest' analyses of compliance, or those that attribute compliance to domestic factors. Instead, I make the lesser claim that a norm's 'legal' quality positively influences conformity with it.

A legitimacy lens is interesting because it allows us to unpack why it is that states might realize Indigenous peoples' rights as expressed under international law. Legitimacy offers the most promising path as it is less focused on the formal legal bindingness of international norms, many Indigenous peoples' rights being found in 'soft law' instruments.[7] Knowing the factors that increase a norm's legitimacy can help us understand, measure and predict the likelihood that states will obey certain international norms. They can also help us to devise methods to increase the legitimacy of norms and thus increase the likelihood of implementation of international norms. Needless to say, obedience to international law is of critical importance for Indigenous peoples and other human rights holders. Finally, legitimacy goes some of the way towards explaining why the international legal system is indeed a legal system properly so called; why the international legal system is authoritative despite its differences from domestic legal systems with their sovereigns and sanctions.[8]

III MSENs, INDIGENOUS PEOPLES' RIGHTS AND LEGITIMACY DEFICIT

I focus on the legitimacy that attaches to norms as a result of, first, the law-making processes from which they spring and, secondly, their content. From that perspective, legitimacy problems associated with MSENs, and fragmentation more generally, include the lack of transparency and order in the law-making process, resulting in uncertainty about the content of norms when they pull in different directions and the lack of coherent, consistent and known principles underpinning the legal system as a whole.

[7] See also, O Hathaway, 'Do Human Rights Treaties Make a Difference?' (2002) 111 *Yale Law Journal* 1935, 1938: '[T]he major engines of compliance that exist in other areas of international law are for the most part absent in the area of human rights . . . Human rights law thus stands out as an area of international law in which countries have little incentive to police noncompliance with treaties or norms'.

[8] RO Keohane and JS Nye, 'The Club Model of Multilateral Cooperation and the World Trade Organization: Problems of Democratic Legitimacy' in RB Porter (ed), *Efficiency, Equity, and Legitimacy: the Multilateral Trading System at the Millennium* (Washington DC, Brookings Institution Press, 2001) 282.

A norm's legitimacy is made up of different factors; the legitimacy of each norm must be assessed individually. One norm may be legitimate because of the robustness of the processes from which it sprang, even if its content is less fair. Another norm may attract legitimacy for exactly the converse reason, because it is overwhelmingly just, even if the processes from which it sprang were unclear and confused.

A Process Legitimacy

Process legitimacy focuses on 'the procedure or source by which [a norm] was constituted'.[9] It includes not only justice in procedure, for example from its inclusion of affected voices and deliberation,[10] oftentimes associated with a norm's democratic pedigree, but appropriate procedural structure, including transparency and certainty.[11] Process legitimacy is important to 'protect against corrupt, arbitrary, or idiosyncratic decision-making or decision-executing'.[12] Process is legitimate when it is deliberative, inclusive, established, ordered and transparent.[13]

Indigenous peoples' norms under international law can suffer from process-legitimacy deficits, permitting political arbitrary manipulation, in two ways: first, when the process from which norms arise is confused, ad hoc and opaque (mechanical procedural detriments); and secondly, when it is under-inclusive, non-deliberative and non-consensual (substantive procedural injustice). The focus here is on mechanical procedural detriments.

The sheer number of horizontally-structured sources of international law on Indigenous peoples' rights highlights the lack of any singular, ordered and transparent juris-generative procedure in international law. Each source adopts its own procedure to produce juris-generative results – from multilateral negotiations to bureaucratic elite policy formation, the latter being more common in UN agencies and international banks. Even particular types of law-making processes can differ dramatically. Each multilateral forum is structurally distinct, some open to Indigenous peoples' participation and others being more restrictive. The political dynamics and incentives of multilateral law-making negotiation changes also according to institutional context; a state's assessment of its interests in

[9] I Hurd, 'Legitimacy and Authority in International Politics' (1999) 53 *International Organization* 379, 381.

[10] J Habermas, 'On Law and Disagreement. Some Comments on Interpretative Pluralism' (2003) 16(2) *Ratio Juris* 187, 190.

[11] J Webber, 'Legal Pluralism and Human Agency' (2006) 44(1) *Osgoode Hall Law Journal* 167, 170.

[12] Franck, *Fairness*, above (n 5).

[13] Habermas, above (n 10) 189.

one forum may differ from its assessment of its interests in another forum. Adjudicatory mechanisms also differ substantially with some involving an overall 'observation' on a state's compliance with international law, while others are more court-like and include the presentation of legal submissions followed by a 'judicial' determination of a specific issue.

The sources of Indigenous peoples' rights under international law include binding international treaties such as the ILO Convention 169 on Indigenous and Tribal Peoples,[14] applied by ILO monitoring mechanisms, the Convention on Biodiversity (CBD) with its Article 8(j) state obligation to protect, preserve and maintain Indigenous peoples' knowledge, innovations and practices relevant to biodiversity and international human rights treaties,[15] such as the International Convention on the Elimination of Racial Discrimination (ICERD) and the International Covenant on Civil and Political Rights (the ICCPR).[16] A string of observations from the Committee on the Elimination of Racial Discrimination (the CERD Committee) and the Human Rights Committee, coupled with decisions, in the case of the Human Rights Committee, and a plethora of findings in response to early warning and urgent action appeals, in the case of the CERD Committee, establish robust Indigenous peoples' rights to land, culture and participation in decisions that affect them. Other treaties establishing state obligations in relation to Indigenous peoples include the UNESCO treaties relating to culture and the Food and Agricultural Organization (FAO) Treaty on Plant and Generic Resources for Food and Agriculture.[17] The Declaration is the most progressive and comprehensive of international instruments detailing Indigenous peoples' rights, ranging from the right to self-determination to robust rights to lands, territories and resources. While, as a declaration, it is not formerly legally binding, it has been applied as reflecting general principles of international law.[18]

There are three human rights affiliated procedures dealing exclusively with Indigenous peoples' issues: the EMRIP, the PFII and the Special

[14] General Conference of the ILO at its 76th session (adopted 27 June 1989, entered into force 5 September 1991).

[15] Convention on Biodiversity (adopted 5 June 1992, entered into force 29 December 1993) (1992) 31 ILM 818.

[16] International Convention on the Elimination of Racial Discrimination (adopted 21 December 1965, entered into force 4 January 1969) 660 UNTS 195 (ICERD); and the International Covenant on Civil and Political Rights (adopted 16 December 1966, entered into force 23 March 1976) 999 UNTS 171 (ICCPR).

[17] UNESCO treaties include the Convention on the Protection and Promotion of the Diversity of Cultural Expression; the Convention for the Safeguarding of Intangible Cultural Heritage and the Convention Concerning the Protection of the World Cultural and Natural Heritage. UN Food and Agricultural Organisation Resolution 3/2001 (entered into force 29 June 2004).

[18] *Aurelio Cal in his own behalf and on behalf of the Maya Village of Santa Cruz et al v AG et al* Supreme Court of Belize Claim Nos 171/2007, 172/2007 (18 October 2007).

Rapporteur on Rights of Indigenous Peoples (SR on Indigenous Peoples).[19] Not one of these institutions has a formal law-making function. However the SR on Indigenous Peoples has a quasi-adjudicatory function in that he can hear communications on alleged violations of Indigenous peoples' human rights and is required to formulate recommendations on appropriate measures and activities to prevent and remedy violations of the rights and freedoms of Indigenous peoples.[20] Nonetheless, EMRIP, the PFII and the SR Indigenous Peoples are all juris-generative institutions in that their recommendations, to other international institutions as well as states, constitute authoritative interpretations of Indigenous peoples' rights. For example, the PFII has consistently made recommendations to states and,[21] recently, published a 'general comment' on the Declaration, in the same vein as human rights treaty bodies.[22] It has also encouraged the UN human rights treaty bodies, which monitor states' human rights compliance, to formulate recommendations and general comments on the rights of Indigenous peoples.[23]

Some of the most progressive jurisprudence comes from regional human rights institutions, and especially from Inter-American human rights bodies, the Inter-American Court of Human Rights (IACHR) and the Inter-American Commission on Human Rights (IAHR Commission). In a string of decisions, from *Awas Tingni v Nicaragua* to *Saramaka v Suriname*,[24] the IACHR has upheld Indigenous peoples' rights to their lands, territories and resources and set out guidelines to regulate natural resource activities involving Indigenous peoples. Equally, the African Commission on Human and Peoples' Rights (ACHPR) Working Group on Indigenous Populations and Communities is engaging increasingly in juris-generative activities, such as preparing guidelines on state reporting on Indigenous issues to input into the ACHPR guidelines for state reporting, and com-

[19] UN Economic and Social Council Resolution 2000/22 (28 July 2000) UN Doc E/2000/22 (establishing the Permanent Forum); UN Human Rights Council 'Resolution 6/36: Expert Mechanism on the Rights of Indigenous Peoples' (establishing the EMRIP) (14 December 2007) UN Doc A/HRC/6/L.42 (hereinafter UN EMRIP Mandate); and UN Human Rights Council 'Resolution 6/12: Human Rights and Indigenous Peoples: Mandate of the Special Rapporteur on the Situation of Human Rights and Fundamental Freedoms of Indigenous People' (28 September 2007) UN Doc A/HRC/Res.6/12 (extending the mandate of the SR on Indigenous Peoples) (hereinafter SR on Indigenous Peoples Mandate).

[20] SR on Indigenous Peoples Mandate, *ibid*.

[21] UN Permanent Forum on Indigenous Issues (PFII), 'Report of the Fifth Session' (15–26 May 2006) UN Doc E/C.19/2006/11 para 53.

[22] UN Permanent Forum on Indigenous Issues (PFII), 'Report of the Eighth Session' (May 2009) UN Doc E/2009/43.

[23] PFII, 'Report of the Fifth Session', above (n 21).

[24] *Mayagno (Sumo) Indigenous Community of Awas Tingni v Nicaragua* R (31 August 2001) Inter-Am Court H Rts (Ser C) No 79, para 146 (also published in (2002) 19 *Arizona Journal International and Comparative Law* 395); and *Saramaka People v Suriname* (Judgment of 28 November, 2007) para 88.

ments on situations of human rights violations in states.[25] The ACHPR has also decided important cases on Indigenous peoples' land rights.[26]

Indigenous peoples' norms are also sourced in other areas of law, including international environmental law. The Rio Declaration on Environment and Development notes the 'vital role' of Indigenous peoples in environmental management because of their traditional knowledge.[27] Agenda 21 states that efforts to 'implement environmentally sound and sustainable development should recognise, accommodate, promote and strengthen the role of Indigenous peoples and their communities'. These statements were revisited and reinforced in the final Declaration of the World Summit on Sustainable Development in 2002.[28] Moreover, specific international environmental treaties isolate Indigenous peoples for particular attention,[29] such as the International Convention for the Regulation of Whaling[30] and the International Agreement on the Conservation of Polar Bears.[31]

Trade also impacts on Indigenous peoples, as does the international regulation of trade, especially that involving traditional knowledge under the World Trade Organization's (WTO) TRIPS Agreement.[32] Representatives of Indigenous peoples, the Indigenous Interior Alliance, lodged an amicus brief in the WTO in a dispute involving alleged Canadian subsidies on trees between Canada and the United States.[33] In addition, some states have negotiated exceptions in trade treaties allowing them to take special measures in favour of Indigenous peoples.[34]

[25] 'Progress Report of the ACHPR's Working Group on Indigenous Populations/Communities: Inter-session period between 43rd and 44th ordinary sessions of the ACHPR': www.achpr.org/english/Commissioner%27s%20Activity/44th%20OS/Special%20Rapporteurs/WGIP.pdf.

[26] *Centre for Minority Rights Development (Kenya) and Minority Rights Group International on behalf of Endorois Welfare Council v Kenya* African Commission on Human and Peoples Rights (4 February 2010).

[27] Rio Declaration on Environment and Development (1992) 33 ILM 874, principle 22.

[28] 'Report of the World Summit on Sustainable Development, Plan of Implementation', UNDESA, (2002) UN Doc A/CONF.199/20. Indigenous peoples are also included in the work of the Commission on Sustainable Development, established in 1992 by the Earth Summit. See Economic and Social Council Permanent Forum on Indigenous Issues 'Information Received from the UN System, Note by the Secretariat, Addendum, Department of Economic and Social Affairs' (8 March 2006) UN Doc E/C.19/2006/6/Add.3, para 18.

[29] See the discussion in BJ Richardson and D Craig, 'Indigenous Peoples, Law and the Environment' (Oxford, Hart Publishing, 2006) 200.

[30] International Convention for the Regulation of Whaling (adopted 2 December 1946, entered into force 10 November 1948) 161 UNTS 72.

[31] International Agreement on the Conservation of Polar Bears (adopted 15 November 1973, entered into force 26 May 1976) 13 ILM 13, art 3(d).

[32] G Dutfield, 'TRIPS-Related Aspects of Traditional Knowledge' (2001) 33 *Case Western Reserve Journal of International Law* 233.

[33] A Manuel and N Schabus, 'Indigenous Peoples at the Margin of the Global Economy: A Violation of International Human Rights and International Trade Law' (2005) 8 *Chapman Law Review* 229.

[34] See, eg, the Agreement between New Zealand and Singapore on a Closer Economic Partnership (November 2000), art 74.

International banks have developed policy in line with international norms relevant to Indigenous peoples, such as the World Bank's 2005 Operational Policy and Bank Procedure on Indigenous Peoples 4.10 (OP/BP 4.10).[35] World Bank policies have the capacity to strong-arm states into compliance with Indigenous peoples' norms given that financing of projects can depend on a state's compliance with World Bank policy.

Finally, the work of international UN agencies can also be juris-generative when it is informed by international legal developments, especially when they are active in other juris-generative forums and/or put into practice policies reflecting international law on Indigenous peoples in states,[36] as the United Nations Development Programme does.[37]

Domestic jurisprudence can, of course, also influence the development of international legal norms, and many courts, executive and legislative arms of government around the world reference and rely on international law on Indigenous peoples' rights. Significantly, the Supreme Court of Belize, despite objection from the government of Belize,[38] found relevant international law persuasive 'where appropriate and cogent'.[39] In upholding Mayan land rights, the Belize Chief Justice stated that international obligations owed to Indigenous peoples 'weighed heavily with me',[40] including those expressed by the CERD Committee and under the Declaration. Other jurisdictions support international law in developing consistent jurisprudence, such as the Canadian Supreme Court's decision finding a duty to consult and accommodate First Nations interests when activities may impact on their extant aboriginal title or rights.[41]

The ongoing proliferation of international institutions further complicates the opacity surrounding Indigenous peoples' norm-making processes, as it is not necessarily clear at the start of law-generative activity, such as the negotiations on the Declaration, how it will proceed, creating confusion.

[35] World Bank, 'Operational Policy 4.10 – Indigenous Peoples' (10 May 2005); and F MacKay, 'Universal Rights or a Universe unto Itself? Indigenous Peoples' Human Rights and the World Bank's Draft Operational Policy 4.10 on Indigenous Peoples' (2002) *American University International Law Review* 527.

[36] See, eg, World Health Organization, 'WHO Traditional Medicine Strategy' (2002) and www.who.int/hhr/activities/Indigenous/en/; UN Economic and Social Council Permanent Forum on Indigenous Issues, 'Information Received from the UN System: World Health Organisation' (9 March 2006) UN Doc E/C.19/2006/6/Add.4.

[37] UNDP initiatives include, eg: assessments of activities involving Indigenous peoples, human development indicies on Indigenous peoples and supporting Indigenous involvement in dialogue on land rights in Suriname.

[38] Belize argued that the Court could not rely on the findings of the Inter-American Commission because 'that would result in the court enforcing an international treaty and would clearly fall within the bounds of non-justicability [sic])'. *Aurelio Cal*, above (n 18) para 20.

[39] *Ibid*, para 22.

[40] *Ibid*, para 126.

[41] *Haida Nation v British Columbia (Minister of Forests)* [2004] 3 SCR 511; 2004 SCC 73.

For example, the Declaration negotiations were completed by the Human Rights Commission's Working Group in February 2006, just months before its parent body, the Commission on Human Rights, was replaced by the Human Rights Council. This led to confusion in three ways. First, there was uncertainty as to whether the Declaration would be approved by the Commission on Human Rights, before it was dissolved, or by the Human Rights Council once it was established. Secondly, if the Commission on Human Rights had been retained, the Declaration would have been required to pass first through the United Nations Economic and Social Council (ECOSOC) for adoption before proceeding to the United Nations General Assembly (UNGA). In contrast, as the Human Rights Council's institutional position is higher than that of the Commission on Human Rights, and the Declaration was adopted there, the Declaration was forwarded to the UNGA directly.

Thirdly, an institutional stand-off between the Human Rights Council and the UNGA's Third Committee arose when the Human Rights Council submitted its report, including the Declaration, to the UNGA. The President of the Human Rights Council maintained that the Human Rights Council's outputs should be directly considered by the UNGA plenary rather than first by the UNGA's Third Committee, the UNGA's body responsible for reviewing human rights matters.[42] In the end, the Declaration was forwarded to the UN Third Committee, which permitted further negotiations on the Declaration before a vote was scheduled in the UNGA plenary.[43]

In sum, the procedural difficulties created by the institutional review of the UN system for those participating in the negotiation on the Declaration – states, Indigenous peoples and civil society alike – were considerable. At many points, they simply did not know what process would eventuate, and were required to operate in a state of confusion while constantly amending strategies for ever-changing possibilities.

Proliferation can lead to institutional competition, especially where more than one institution has competence over an issue. It can occur where respective institutions are mandated to apply different and at times inconsistent norms to the same or related issues or even when different bodies apply the same or similar law but interpret them differently, as is the more acute problem with the application of MSENs. These problems arise at the international legal level because of the following reasons: most institutions at the international level, and especially those associated with a specific

[42] See LA De Alba 'The Human Rights Council's Adoption of the UN Declaration on the Rights of Indigenous Peoples' in C Charters and R Stavenhagen (eds), *Making the Declaration Work: The UN Declaration on the Rights of Indigenous Peoples* (Copenhagen, IWGIA, 2009) 108.

[43] UNGA Third Committee, 'Namibia Amendments to Draft Resolution A/C.3/61/L.18/Rev.1: Working group of the Commission on Human Rights to elaborate a draft declaration in accordance with paragraph 5 of General Assembly Resolution 49/214 of 23 December 1994' (21 November 2006) UN Doc A/C.3/61/L.57/Rev.1.

treaty, may only apply their 'own' law to a dispute, not 'other' international law, with no direct requirement to interpret norms consistently;[44] resolution of an issue by one institution does not necessarily constitute the resolution of that issue within another 'system'; and, significantly, there is no higher institution to resolve international inter-institutional conflicts or to provide an interpretation of international law inclusive of all applicable norms to a dispute.[45]

The potential for institutional competition to exacerbate confusion in Indigenous peoples' rights is acute. There is a good deal of jurisdictional competition over the application of the Declaration, especially between the EMRIP, the SR on Indigenous Peoples and the PFII, which can over time contribute to an increase in the number of inconsistent interpretations of the Declaration. This is perhaps natural in that, as Hohenveldern notes, organizations defend their turf vigorously: '[o]nce established, international organizations try to continue their existence at almost any price'.[46]

Consider the mandates of the EMRIP, the PFII and the SR on Indigenous Peoples. The EMRIP has a thematic mandate – meaning it provides advice to the Human Rights Council on certain themes,[47] such as education in 2009.[48] So too does the SR on Indigenous Peoples.[49] The PFII organizes its work around particular themes each year. The EMRIP also applies the Declaration in its work, interpreting the Declaration's provisions in its work.[50] Equally the SR on Indigenous Peoples uses the Declaration as his reference point in his thematic studies, country visits and in response to communications about alleged violations of Indigenous peoples' rights.[51]

The jurisdictional competition between the EMRIP, the SR on Indigenous Peoples and the PFII was especially evident from the time when the negotiations on the EMRIP were taking place and thereafter. In a report published by the PFII – on 19 December 2007, just five days after the establishment of the EMRIP – the PFII seemed to be at pains to both support the EMRIP *and* to secure its *own* role in protecting and promoting the human rights of Indigenous peoples – that is, to ward off the institutional threat

[44] G Hafner, 'Pros and Cons Ensuing from Fragmentation of International Law' (2004) 25 *Michigan Journal of International Law* 849, 857–58.

[45] *Ibid*, 857–58.

[46] IS Hohenveldern, 'The Attitude of States towards the Proliferation of International Organizations' in NM Blokker and HG Schermers *Proliferation of International Organizations: Legal Issues* (The Hague, Kluwer Law International, 2001) 51, 60.

[47] UN EMRIP Mandate, above (n 19).

[48] UN Expert Mechanism on the Rights of Indigenous Peoples 'Study on Lessons Learned and Challenges to Achieve the Implementation of the Rights of Indigenous Peoples to Education' (26 June 2009) UN Doc A/HRC/EMRIP/2009/2 (hereinafter EMRIP Education Report).

[49] SR on Indigenous Peoples Mandate, above (n 19).

[50] EMRIP Education Report, above (n 48).

[51] See, for examples, the Office of the High Commissioner for Human Rights: www2.ohchr.org/english/issues/Indigenous/rapporteur/documents.htm.

and competition posed by the EMRIP.[52] The PFII argued for powers not explicitly anchored in its mandate and, in some cases, which seem to surpass it. This might reflect a degree of defensiveness, to ensure that it is not 'trumped' by the EMRIP, especially when one considers that the mandate of the PFII in relation to human rights is weaker than that of the EMRIP's, and the PFII functions under the ECOSOC, which has had its main human rights functions transferred to the Human Rights Council.

As the basis for its 'new function', the PFII relies on Article 42 of the Declaration, which states that:[53]

> United Nations, its bodies, including the Permanent Forum on Indigenous Issues, and specialized agencies, including at the country level, and States shall promote respect for and full application of the provisions of this Declaration and follow up the effectiveness of this Declaration.

Notably, Article 42 is not directed only at the PFII, but the UN as a whole, including the SR on Indigenous Peoples and the EMRIP and states, which makes it a questionable ground from which to argue for exceptional authority vis-à-vis the Declaration. The PFII members went on to recommend the establishment of a 'Forum Committee on the Declaration'.[54] Extraordinarily, PFII members even suggested that it take on some human rights monitoring function in relation to states, a function akin to that of the human rights treaty bodies, and undertake state visits, even though its mandate only directs it to advise and liaise with UN bodies.[55] Adopting this role would place the PFII in direct competition with the SR on Indigenous Peoples, with his mandate to hear communications based on allegations of violations of Indigenous peoples' rights under international law, including the Declaration.[56] As controversially and abovementioned, in 2009 the PFII issued a 'general comment' on the Declaration.[57]

[52] UN Permanent Forum on Indigenous Issues (PFII), 'Study on the Structures, Procedures and Mechanisms that Presently Exist and that might be Established to Effectively Address the Human Rights Situation of Indigenous Peoples and to Arrange for Indigenous Representation and Inclusion in such Structures, Procedures and Mechanism by Ida Nicolaisen and Wilton Littlechild' (19 December 2007) UN Doc E/C.19/2008/2, para 58; available on the UN Permanent Forum website: www.un.org/esa/socdev/unpfii/documents/E_C19_2008_2.pdf.

[53] See the assertion that art 42 'signals a new mandate for the Permanent Forum on Indigenous Issues' and '[t]he responsibilities conferred by article 42 constitute new functions for the Permanent Forum under is overall human rights mandate': UN Permanent Forum on Indigenous Peoples 'Report of the international expert group meeting on the role of the Permanent Forum on Indigenous Issues in the implementation of article 42 of the UN Declaration on the Rights of Indigenous Peoples' (4 February 2009) UN Doc E/C.19/2009/2 (hereinafter PFII Article 42 Report).

[54] UN Permanent Forum on Indigenous Issues 'Implementation of the Human Rights Mandate of the Permanent Forum on Indigenous Issues' (9 March 2007) UN Doc E/C.19/2007/6, para 39.

[55] PFII, 'Study on the Structures', above (n 52) para 59.

[56] SR on Indigenous Peoples Mandate, above (n 19).

[57] PFII 'Report of the Eighth Session', above (n 22).

B Substance Uncertainty

A number of scholars consider that determinacy is important to the legitimacy of international norms, including Franck, for whom it is one of the principal indicia of legitimacy.[58] He writes:

> Indeterminacy [. . .] has its costs. Indeterminate normative standards make it harder to know what conformity is expected, which in turn makes it easier to justify noncompliance. Conversely, the more determinate the standard, the more difficult it is to resist the pull of the rule towards compliance and to justify noncompliance. Since few persons or states wish to be perceived as acting in obvious violation of a generally recognised rule of conduct, they may try to resolve conflicts between the demands of a rule and their desire not to be fettered by 'interpreting' the rule permissively. A less elastic determinate rule is more resistant to such an evasive strategy than an indeterminate one.

Conflicting decisions and contradictory legal norms can exacerbate friction within the international polity. Where incoherence and uncertainty are prevalent, it is difficult for the international legal system to provide a conclusive resolution to an issue.[59] While international legal subjects can access a number of different institutions to seek resolution, otherwise known as forum-shopping,[60] those institutions, and the legal instruments they apply, may suggest different answers. In turn, norm fragmentation can lead to inequality: legal subjects may be subject to different standards and not always with sound substantive justification. Further, and particularly problematically from an Indigenous perspective, norm inconsistency can provide states with a valid argument to comply with the least onerous of applicable norms or the least onerous of competing interpretations of the applicable law. Indeed Canada, in voting against the Declaration, cited that it was open to too many different interpretations.[61]

Within the field of Indigenous peoples' norms under international law, there are numerous MSENs as well as conflicting norms. For example, there are numerous sources for a state obligation to either consult, or to acquire Indigenous peoples' consent, before undertaking projects that impact on them – in the Declaration, the ILO Convention 169, the Convention on Biological Diversity, World Bank policy, in WIPO draft principles and policies on traditional knowledge and so on. The indeterminacy arises because

[58] Franck, 'The Power of Legitimacy', above (n 5) 88, 93. The Chayes argue that non-compliance is more often a result of 'norm ambiguity and capacity limitations than from deliberate disregard'. A Chayes and AH Chayes, *The New Sovereignty: Compliance with International Regulatory Agreements* (Cambridge, Mass, Harvard University Press, 1995).

[59] Y Shany, *The Competing Jurisdictions of International Courts and Tribunals* (Oxford, Oxford University Press, 2003) 10.

[60] *Ibid.*

[61] UN Department of Public Information, 'General Assembly Adopted Declaration on Rights of Indigenous Peoples' 13 September 2007 and available at: /www.un.org/News/Press/docs/2007/ga10612.doc.htm.

the level of state obligation differs under these instruments – from participation in decision-making generally to consultation to consent, the latter more often to apply when an activity, such as resource extraction, has an impact on particular Indigenous peoples.

Indigenous peoples' rights to redress for taking of their lands in various instruments are also similar but not entirely equivalent, leading to indeterminacy and uncertainty as to the exact nature of states' obligations where more than one instrument, and more than one standard, are applicable to them. While numerous human rights treaties in the Americas and globally have been interpreted to protect an Indigenous peoples' right to demarcation of lands they still possess,[62] the position in relation to lands lost 'historically' is murkier. It is unclear whether Indigenous peoples have a right to have those lands returned where possible, under the ICERD as interpreted by the CERD Committee[63] and Article 28 of the Declaration or, less onerously, to have their spiritual relationship to those lands respected under Article 25 of the Declaration and ILO Convention 169.

In these abovementioned examples of norm inconsistency, the problem is perhaps exacerbated, rather than resolved, by the varying levels of formal bindingness of the instruments in question. On the one hand, some clarity may be derived from ranking the norms according to the authority of the instrument from which they sprang, such as, where there is norm conflict, applying the ILO Convention 169, as a treaty, over the standards expressed in the Declaration. However, this is a too simplistic solution given that the Declaration is a more recent instrument, has acquired a good deal of authority in its own right and has already influenced the interpretation of other treaties, such as the ICERD.[64]

As has been noted, indeterminacy arising from inconsistency between applicable norms can be addressed through consistent interpretation by bodies responsible for applying the law to concrete facts.[65] Moreover, international law provides some guidance in the form of rules of interpretation, such as Article 31(3)(c) of the Vienna Convention on the Law of Treaties (VCLT), which requires that in interpreting treaties there shall be taken onto account 'any relevant rules of international law applicable in the relations between the parties'.[66]

[62] See eg, the *Awas Tingni*, above (n 24).

[63] UN Committee on the Elimination of Racial Discrimination (CERD), 'General Recommendation XXIII: Indigenous Peoples' (18 August 1997) UN Doc A/52/18 annex V.

[64] UN CERD Committee, 'Concluding Observations of the Committee on the Elimination of Racial Discrimination: United States of America' (February 2008) UN Doc CERD/C/USA/CO/6, para 29.

[65] Franck, 'The Power of Legitimacy', above (n 5) 93.

[66] Vienna Convention on the Law of Treaties (VCLT) (adopted 23 May 1969, entered into force 27 January 1980) 1155 UNTS 331. See also C McLachlan, 'The Principle of Systemic Integration and Article 31(3)(C) of the Vienna Convention' (2005) 54 *International and Comparative Law Quarterly* 279.

In the case of obligations to either facilitate the participation of Indigenous peoples or consult them to obtain their free, prior and informed consent, law interpreters have gone some way towards clarifying state obligations. Institutions such as the IACHR and the SR on Indigenous Peoples are consistently interpreting it to impose an obligation for states to obtain Indigenous peoples' free, prior and informed consent where activities are likely to have a major impact on them, with lesser obligations where there is arguably no specific or serious impact on Indigenous peoples.[67] In the Human Rights Council Universal Periodic Review (UPR) Reports, states have been requested to obtain Indigenous peoples' free, prior and informed consent in matters affecting them.[68] The CERD Committee has been less exacting: in a General Comment and in response to states' reports it maintains that states must not take any measures affecting Indigenous peoples without their consent.[69]

Nonetheless, while the relatively similar interpretation of Indigenous peoples' free, prior and informed consent in international bodies demonstrates that greater clarity in the content of the norm may be possible into the future, questions still remain as to exactly when consent is required. Moreover, other bodies have yet to clarify their interpretation of these requirements, such as the Committee on Economic, Social and Cultural Rights.[70] As Hafner comments '[i]t is difficult for one institution to become acquainted with all the ramifications of the judicial reasoning of another body'.[71]

C Incoherence

Dworkin famously makes the jurisprudential case for integrity in the law, by which he means coherence and consistency with broad principles. He cites the need for the state to 'act on a single, coherent set of principles even when its citizens are divided about what the right principles of justice and fairness really are'.[72] Fraternity is the basis for Dworkin's claim that integrity is essential; because of the level of fraternity within a state's

[67] UN Human Rights Council, 'Report of the Special Rapporteur on the situation of Human Rights and Fundamental Freedoms of Indigenous peoples, James Anaya' (15 July 2009) UN Doc A/HRC/12/34; and *Saramaka v Suriname*, above (n 24).

[68] UN Human Rights Council, 'Draft Report of the Working Group on the Universal Periodic Review: New Zealand' (11 May 2009) UN Doc A/HRC/WG.6/5/L.7, paras 36 and 81(58).

[69] UN Committee on the Elimination of Racial Discrimination, 'Concluding Observations of the Committee on the Elimination of Racial Discrimination: Peru' (3 September 2009) UN Doc CERD/C/PER/C/14-17, para 14.

[70] See, eg, UN Committee on Economic and Social and Cultural Rights, 'Concluding Comments: Nicaragua' (20 November 2008) UN Doc E/C.12/NIC/CO/4.

[71] Hafner, above (n 44) 857–58. See also, JH Jackson, 'The Varied Policies of International Juridical Bodies – Reflections of Theory and Practice' (2004) 25 *Michigan Journal of International Law* 869, 875–78.

[72] R Dworkin, *Law's Empire* (Cambridge, MA, Harvard University Press, 1986) 166.

community, the polity has an obligation to apply shared basic principles coherently.[73]

MSENs can be more problematic when they 'cannot be defended together as expressing a coherent ranking of different principles of justice, fairness or procedural due process',[74] as is the case with Indigenous peoples' rights generally, demonstrated in Kingsbury's work on the competing conceptual approaches behind Indigenous peoples' rights. Kingsbury outlines the different bases, or justifications, for Indigenous peoples' claims under international law, being: human rights and non-discrimination; minority rights; self-determination; historical sovereignty and *sui generis* norms.[75] The resolution of an issue depends on the conceptual justification for the Indigenous peoples' rights accepted by the decision maker. For example, if a human rights framework is employed to address alleged discrimination against an Indigenous individual under an Indigenous peoples' customary norm, the individual's human right to equality is more likely to prevail. In comparison, under a self-determination framework, the Indigenous peoples' collective right to self-determination might trump the individual's freedom from discrimination.

The different conceptual approaches underlying Indigenous peoples' claims to rights are reflected in the Indigenous peoples' rights recognized in international law, even within the same instrument. The Declaration includes norms that reflect a human rights conceptual approach, such as the Article 2 affirmation that Indigenous peoples and individuals have the right to be free from any kind of discrimination. Likewise, it recognizes Indigenous peoples' right to self-determination, and language and cultural rights are often found in rights directed at minorities. Rights based on Indigenous peoples' historical sovereignty are reflected in the preambular paragraphs, which recognize historical injustices suffered by Indigenous peoples and describe Indigenous peoples' rights as inherent. Arguably the specific Indigenous peoples' rights to autonomy and self-government, under Article 4, are *sui generis* as they have little pedigree in international law outside the Indigenous peoples' context.

IV MITIGATING MSEN LEGITIMACY DEFICITS

The legitimacy problems outlined above associated with process, substance uncertainty and incoherence are mitigated by four factors. First, the process opacity and confusion caused by the existence of numerous law-makers in the field of Indigenous peoples' rights, and associated norm-substance

[73] D Reaume, 'Is Integrity a Virtue? Dworkin's Theory of Legal Obligation' (1989) 39 *University of Toronto Law Journal* 380.
[74] Dworkin, *Law's Empire*, above (n 72) 184.
[75] Kingsbury, 'Conceptual Approaches', above (n 2).

uncertainty and incoherence, is in part countered by the creation of new and more responsive – just – norms and institutions. Secondly, inter-institutional dialogue between institutions lessens the jurisdictional tensions between them and thirdly, shows great potential for consistent interpretation of norms in the future, lessening norm-substance indeterminacy. Finally, participation by Indigenous peoples in the various international institutions engaged in Indigenous peoples' rights provides some cohesion between MSENs as they argue for a consistent interpretation of Indigenous peoples' rights across various forums.

A Balancing Process Confusion and Norm Substance Indeterminacy with Justice

Koskenniemi and Leino are not overly perturbed by the consequences of fragmentation, suggesting that it is more important to focus on justice, stating:[76]

> If the law is unjust, or unworkable, little virtue lies in applying it coherently. If an environmental activist thinks her objective is better achieved through a 'soft' enforcement regime than by state responsibility, or if a post-conflict manager prefers a truth commission to a criminal process – one can only wonder what weight the lawyer's systemic anxiety has against their pressing concerns.

The international legal system's increasing responsiveness to the justice inhering in Indigenous peoples' claims in part counters the legitimacy loss associated with process opacity and confusion, substance indeterminacy and incoherence. This is especially true where states, international institutions and Indigenous peoples deliberately and consciously balance the competing objectives of minimizing institutional proliferation and norm fragmentation with the need for new organizations and norms.

i Increased Institutional Responsiveness

The EMRIP was established in 2007 to replace the former Working Group in Indigenous Populations (WGIP), which had functioned under the UN Commission on Human Rights prior to its dissolution in 2006. The negotiations on the EMRIP – from June 2006 until December 2007 – were intense and comprehensive. During the EMRIP negotiations, the imperative for an institution within the UN's human rights framework in Geneva was balanced deliberately and carefully with the imperative to rationalize institutions focused on Indigenous issues. Indeed, the Human Rights Council was directed, in the UNGA Resolution establishing the Human Rights Council, to 'assume, review and, where necessary, improve and rationalize all man-

[76] M Koskenniemi and P Leino, 'Fragmentation of International Law? Postmodern Anxieties' (2002) 15 *Leiden Journal of International Law* 553, 560.

dates, mechanisms, functions and responsibilities of the Commission on Human Rights',[77] reflecting the desire to both improve the UN human rights system while not overburdening it with duplicate bodies. The principal issues for discussion included: (i) whether there was a need for an indigenous-focused institution in the Human Rights Council, given the role of the PFII and the SR on Indigenous Peoples; (ii) techniques to minimize duplication between the respective bodies, as well as the UN human rights treaty bodies; and (iii) the means to ensure the requisite level of coordination between the EMRIP PFII and the SR on Indigenous Peoples.[78]

Indigenous peoples successfully argued that an Indigenous institutional presence in the Human Rights Council was necessary to 'provide specific advice to the [Human Rights Council] on Indigenous peoples' human rights issues', and was inspired 'by the need to ensure that Indigenous peoples enjoy human rights in the communities in which they live'.[79] They also stressed the need for an institution to 'facilitate the implementation of Indigenous peoples' human rights',[80] and provide a platform for direct Indigenous peoples' input into the UN's human rights framework, especially given the historical legacy of the WGIP in Geneva, in operation since 1982, and given that the PFII operates under the ECOSOC rather than the human rights machinery of the UN. The persuasiveness of these arguments is reflected in the fact that the EMRIP was indeed established.

Some Indigenous peoples' organizations countered states' concerns about duplication by pointing out that, even with the establishment of an institution devoted to Indigenous peoples' issues within the Human Rights Council, there would be net quantitative loss in the number of human rights institutions engaging with Indigenous peoples' issues when compared with the former Commission on Human Rights framework.[81] In the UN's institutional overhaul of its human rights system, the former Sub-Commission on the Protection and Promotion of Human Rights was replaced with a weaker advisory body; and the Sub-Commission had previously forcefully advanced Indigenous peoples' rights by, for example, adopting the first formal incarnation of the Declaration in 1993.[82] They

[77] UNGA 'Resolution 60/251 Human Rights Council' (3 April 2006) UN Doc A/RES/60/251.

[78] See, eg, C Charters Meeting Notes, 'Meeting with John von Kaufmann of the Canadian Mission' (9 July 2009) (on file with the author).

[79] 'Memorandum on the Indigenous Peoples Human Rights Expert Body to the Human Rights Council, submitted by the International Indian Treaty Council (IITC) and the International Organization of Indigenous Resource Development (IOIRD), July 2007' (July 2007) UN Doc IMWGIP/2007/CRP.6.

[80] IITC and IOIRD Memorandum, July 2007, *ibid.*

[81] *Ibid.*

[82] UN Sub-Commission on the Promotion and Protection of Human Rights 'Resolution adopting the draft Declaration on the Rights of Indigenous Peoples 1994/45' available at UNHCHR website: <www.unhchr.ch/Huridocda/Huridoca.nsf/(Symbol)/E.CN.4.SUB.2.RES.1994.45.En?Opendocument>.

also explained that the PFII's work would be enhanced by the creation of an entity with a mandate squarely focused on human rights, which is only one of six of the PFII's mandated areas of concern.

Nonetheless, the mandate of the EMRIP was less expansive than some Indigenous peoples had lobbied for, in part to reflect persistent concerns, especially from states, about duplication with other UN bodies engaged in Indigenous peoples' rights. It requires the EMRIP to provide thematic expertise on the rights of Indigenous peoples to the Human Rights Council with a focus 'mainly on studies and research-based advice', the latter in particular being a task that the PFII is not mandated to undertake, although the SR on Indigenous Peoples had traditionally provided such advice. A preambular paragraph in the Resolution establishing the EMRIP recalls 'that the Human Rights Council should be cognizant of the work being undertaken on Indigenous issues by other bodies in the United Nations system' and,[83]

> decides in order for the expert mechanism to enhance the cooperation and avoid duplicating the work of the Special Rapporteur on the situation of human rights and fundamental freedoms of Indigenous peoples and the Permanent Forum that it shall invite the Special Rapporteur and the Permanent Forum to attend and contribute to its annual meeting.

In contrast with the former WGIP's mandate, the EMRIP's mandate is considerably more confined. Further, the mandate of the SR on Indigenous Peoples, which was renewed and modified during the negotiations on the EMRIP, states that he or she is 'to work in close cooperation, while avoiding unnecessary duplication, with other special procedures and subsidiary organs of the Human Rights Council, relevant United Nations bodies, the treaty bodies, and the human rights regional organizations'.[84]

In sum, the example of the creation of the EMRIP illustrates a careful balance between the need for an institution within the UN's human rights structure to focus on Indigenous peoples' issues, as some of the world's most pressing human rights concerns, and the need to minimize institutional duplication and proliferation. While, indeed, the EMRIP adds a further body to the institutions engaged in Indigenous peoples' rights, and thus another body to participate in juris-generative activity in the area, this has been done in the interests of justice – to increase UN responsiveness to Indigenous peoples' issues. It has also been done deliberately, with close attention to the need to minimize and explicitly define the EMRIP's functional boundaries, thereby reducing the procedural confusion that inevitably results from the creation of a new institution.

[83] UN EMRIP Mandate, above (n 19).
[84] SR on Indigenous Peoples Mandate, above (n 19).

ii Increased Norm Justice

During more than 25 years of negotiations on the Declaration, states, international institutions and Indigenous peoples balanced the justice behind any proposed new norm against the disadvantages of the uncertainty and incoherence resulting from inconsistency with existing legal obligations. Where a new norm evolved, it reflected the conscious decision of the negotiating participants. States and Indigenous peoples argued for, or against, the inclusion of certain norms based on their pedigree in existing international legal norms.[85] UN bodies, such as the ILO and UNESCO, participated and referenced the norms from the respective Indigenous peoples' rights treaties associated with their institutions.[86]

Indigenous peoples especially made the case, with reference to massacres against them, unjust loss of land and so on, for better norms to respond to the specific types of injustice they faced. Many argued that existing norms were inadequate to produce just results. For example, the National Youth Indian Council argued that the Declaration

> constructively challenges the jurisprudential assumptions upon which many based their conceptions of rights and the relation of individuals to States. [. . .] [T]he universal declaration challenges nations containing Indigenous populations to satisfy an new and emergent international set of minimum standards of human decency that many Indigenous populations would recognize as simply the result of respectful behaviour between various groups in a larger society.[87]

Records state that

> [t]he observer for the Grand Council of the Crees reminded participants of the practical importance of articles 12, 13 and 14 and that the articles were [. . .] placed in the draft because of specific problems Indigenous peoples faced which had not been adequately protected by existing international instruments.[88]

Moreover, to the extent that there is indeterminacy in Indigenous peoples' rights, it facilitates a greater acceptance of norms, as was the case with the Declaration. States and Indigenous peoples deliberately retained some ambiguity in various provisions so that different interpretations

[85] See 'Report of the Working Group Established in Accordance with Commission on Human Rights Resolution 1995/32' (10 December 1996) UN Doc E/CN.4/1997/102.

[86] Eg, the ILO contribution in 1996 that it was 'essential that the declaration, once adopted, should not fall below the standards set in a very recent international convention, but should follow the guiding principle in the development of human rights law that each new instrument should be consistent with earlier instruments and constitute progression'. 'Report of the Working Group Established in Accordance with Commission on Human Rights Resolution 1995/32', *ibid*.

[87] National Indian Youth Council, (1990) UN Doc E/CN.4/Sub.2/AC.4/1990/3/Add.1.

[88] 'Report of the Working Group Established in Accordance with Commission on Human Rights resolution 1995/32' (10 December 1996), above (n 43) para 74.

remained possible, thereby enabling greater consensus.[89] Some flexibility in the interpretation of international norms can also be appropriate given they are to apply to such a broad array of different situations around the world.

B Dialogic Attempts to Minimize Institutional Jurisdictional Competition

Alongside the institutional competition between the various entities engaged with Indigenous peoples' norms, there are attempts by those same bodies to collaboratively mark out their respective territory in the application of the Declaration to voluntarily set themselves limitations and divide their responsibilities to minimize duplication.[90] Coupled with supportive interpretational activity by the human rights treaty bodies, the IACHR, and UN agencies and related bureaucracy, as well as states, there is reason to suggest that institutional competition will be managed to lessen process uncertainty in the context of Indigenous peoples' rights under international law. To the extent that it remains, it is useful to ensure that Indigenous peoples' rights are pervasively applied, minimizing gaps in the international system's protection of Indigenous peoples' rights.

Since 2007, the PFII, the SR on Indigenous Peoples and the EMRIP have purposefully entered into a dialogue – including meetings called specifically to address their respective mandates – to address their jurisdictional boundaries over a number of matters, including the Declaration.[91] The former chair of the EMRIP has stated that 'dialogue and discussions between the Permanent Forum, the Special Rapporteur, and the Expert Mechanism is a precondition for en effective cooperation and the best way of avoiding duplication of work (sic)'.[92] As a result of that dialogue, and criticism of the PFII's attempts to extend its mandate, the PFII appears to have

[89] B Kingsbury, 'Self-determination and 'Indigenous Peoples' (1992) 86 *Proceedings of the American Society International Law* 383, 389.

[90] L Rodriguez-Piñero notes, the 'effective implementation of Indigenous rights under the Declaration necessarily involves cooperative relations among all actors based on a responsible assumption of their respective mandates'. 'Monitoring/Implementing of Indigenous Peoples' Rights under the Declaration' in Charters and Stavenhagen (eds), *Making the Declaration Work*, above (n 42).

[91] A former chair of the EMRIP noted the 'good understanding' that it has with the SR on Indigenous Peoples and stated that the EMRIP 'looks forward also to have similar discussions with members of the Permanent Forum, on possible ways of enhancing the effectiveness of our respective efforts in promoting full and effective realization of the rights of Indigenous peoples, in line with the respective mandates and Article 42 of the [Declaration] (sic)': JB Henriksen, 'The UN Expert Mechanisms on the Rights of Indigenous Peoples' paper presented for the International Expert Seminar Implementing Indigenous Peoples Rights: The Role of the UN Mechanism with Specific Mandate Regarding the Rights of Indigenous Peoples (February 2009) (on file with the author).

[92] Henriksen, *ibid*.

now muted its forceful assertion of authority over the Declaration, watering down its claim to monitor states' compliance with the Declaration.[93] This change in tone seems to be in recognition that the EMRIP and the SR on Indigenous Peoples, as they have explained, also have a role to play in achieving implementation of the Declaration, as do the international human rights treaty bodies, and that duplication should be minimized.[94] A more consistent theme now in PFII documentation is one of shared institutional responsibility, highlighted by the statement in a PFII January 2009 report that 'coordination and collaboration among [the SR on Indigenous Peoples, the EMRIP and the PFII] was essential'.[95] It has also, notably, *not* established a formal mechanism by which it reviews state compliance with the Declaration, as it had intimated it might, although it has called on states to voluntarily provide information on their implementation of the Declaration in their reports to the PFII.[96]

The SR on Indigenous Peoples, too, in light of the EMRIP's thematic mandate, decided to make thematic studies secondary to other work he undertakes.[97] In practice, the SR on Indigenous Peoples has established an 'office' at the meetings of the PFII and the EMRIP where Indigenous peoples can direct specific complaints about states' compliance with Indigenous peoples' rights. This also serves to direct Indigenous peoples away from raising those issues within the PFII and EMRIP, which do not have the mandate to respond to specific allegations of human rights violations, as the chair of the EMRIP often reminded participants at the 2009 session.[98]

Similarly, the 2009 chair of the EMRIP has marked out its role as a human rights body with the greater proximity, relative to the PFII, to the UN's human rights machinery.[99] In delimiting its own mandate boundaries, the EMRIP chair described the EMRIP's mandate as 'strictly' thematic as opposed to that of the SR on Indigenous Peoples, supporting the SR on Indigenous Peoples' primary responsibility for hearing information and communications about alleged violations of Indigenous peoples' human

[93] See PFII Article 42 Report, above (n 53) and the 'International Expert Seminar on the Role of UN Mechanisms with Specific Mandate Regarding the Rights of Indigenous Peoples' (Madrid, 4–6 February 2009) UN Doc E/C.19/2009/CRP.17.

[94] UN Special Rapporteur, J Anaya, 'The UN Rapporteur on the Rights of Indigenous Peoples' presented for the International Expert Seminar 'Implementing Indigenous Peoples Rights: The Role of the UN Mechanism with Specific Mandate Regarding the Rights of Indigenous Peoples' (4–6 February 2009) (on file with the author). He highlights that many mechanisms are required to have a role in implementing the Declaration even though the PFII is the only body specifically mentioned.

[95] PFII Article 42 Report, above (n 53) para 54.

[96] PFII, 'Report of the Eighth Session', above (n 22) para 79.

[97] UN Special Rapporteur J Anaya, 'The UN Rapporteur on the Rights of Indigenous Peoples', above (n 94).

[98] C Charters, 'Meeting Notes UN Expert Mechanism on the Rights of Indigenous Peoples' (August 2009) (on file with author).

[99] Henriksen, above (n 91).

rights. He stated that this is 'the most significant difference between these two mandates' and that the EMRIP is not a 'complaint procedure'.[100]

This is not to say that all institutional tension and competition between the EMRIP, the SR on Indigenous Peoples and the PFII has been resolved through dialogue. For example, as mentioned, the PFII has issued a 'general comment' on the Declaration, no doubt deliberately using the term 'general comment' because it is how some UN human rights treaty bodies describe their legalistic interpretations of human rights treaties. The PFII also undertook a 'state visit' to Bolivia and Paraguay in 2009,[101] an activity usually performed by the SR on Indigenous Peoples. One PFII member has suggested that the PFII should have input into the Human Rights Council's UPR process, a role better suited for the EMRIP given its position as a Human Rights Council subsidiary body.[102] Equally, the EMRIP has shown a willingness to also extend its authority into areas beyond its mandate. Like the PFII, it has asserted some jurisdiction over the Declaration.[103] The former chair of the EMRIP has also hinted that the EMRIP would consider specific activity to seek implementation of the Declaration, like the PFII had done.[104] Contentiously, members of the EMRIP, like the PFII, 'have been discussing the possibility of developing and adopting *general comments or recommendations* on the basis of its thematic studies. General thematic comments and recommendations, similar to what the various UN human rights bodies issue, has the potential of adding value to EMRIP's thematic studies'.[105]

States and Indigenous peoples' organizations are also playing an important role in keeping the PFII, the SR on Indigenous Peoples and the EMRIP in check. Criticism has been directed at the PFII for assuming jurisdiction over the Declaration. Long-time and highly-respected Indigenous advocate Chief Oren Lyons of the Onodaga nation, Haudenosaunee, stated in his testimony to the PFII on 23 April 2008,

> [t]hat Expert Mechanism in Geneva, where the UN's human rights work has been traditionally and most successfully carried out, is, and should remain, our primary mechanism for implementing the norms contained in the Declaration. The Permanent Forum can support, but not usurp, its work. Otherwise, confusion will result, thereby jeopardizing the legitimacy of both the Expert Mechanism and the PFII.[106]

[100] *Ibid.*

[101] See the UN Permanent Forum on Indigenous Issues website: www.un.org/esa/socdev/unpfii/en/news.html.

[102] B Clavero 'International Expert Group Meeting on the Role of the UN Permanent Forum on Indigenous Issues in the Implementation of Article 42 of the UN Declaration on the Rights of Indigenous Peoples' (14–16 January 2009) UN Doc PFII/2009/EGM1/4.

[103] UN EMRIP, 'Provisional Agenda' (25 June 2009) UN Doc A/HRC/EMRIP/2009/1.

[104] Henriksen, above (n 91).

[105] *Ibid.*

[106] MC Lam 'Notes on Item 5, Human Rights, UN Permanent Forum 7th Session' (28 April 2008) (on file with the author).

Similarly, states have argued that

> the overlapping mandates could frustrate the efforts to bring to light and address allegations of human rights abuses. Building awareness of differences among mandates would hopefully reduce frustration when requests for assistance on possible human rights violations were directed to a wrong part of the system.[107]

And, Malaysia stressed that

> the cause of indigenous rights was not assisted by a de facto attempt of the Permanent Forum to change the legal understanding of the Declaration and its mandates through its General Comment. . . . As a subsidiary organ of the Economic and Social Council, the basis for any new function of the Forum required consideration through the intergovernmental process of the Council. The Forum could not assume for itself a role as treaty body, since the Declaration itself was not a treaty, nor was it legally binding. While the intention of the Forum in issuing that comment was noble, it had instead triggered debate on the credibility and roles and responsibilities of the Forum. The debate harmed and delayed acceptance of the Declaration as a set of principles, ideals and rights that all Member States could fully accept.[108]

Continuing institutional tensions is inevitable, consistent with political processes generally. As a former chair of the EMRIP pointed out:

> There is broad agreement about the need to enhance cooperation between the three core mandates on indigenous peoples' rights, and that these mandates should attempt to avoid duplicating each others work. However, it may prove difficult to avoid a certain level of overlapping due to the overlapping nature of the mandates.[109]

The point is that institutional competition is contained by the ongoing awareness that it exists and self-conscious efforts by those bodies, monitored by states and Indigenous peoples, to minimize the more serious procedural and substance problems it poses, such as confusion in the law-making process and substantive norm inconsistencies. It appears, at present, as if a balance of sorts is indeed being maintained by the PFII, the EMRIP and the SR on Indigenous Peoples.

[107] United States of America, Statement to the UNGA Third Committee (19 October 2009).

[108] Malaysia, Statement to the UNGA Third Committee (19 October 2009). Canada has stated that 'The Permanent Forum should not be acting as a treaty-monitoring body, as this was against its mandate. All UN organizations should act in accordance with their mandate'. *UN News and Media*, 'Report of 30 July 2009' available at: www.unog.ch/80256EDD006B9C2E/(httpNewsByYear_en)/34752CDF55CBBE30C12576030049AEFE?OpenDocument. The US stated 'that this year's Forum issued a General Comment, styled as an item issued by a UN treaty body. As the Forum was not a treaty body, it did not have the authority to issue authoritative interpretations of the Declaration or to develop mechanisms for reviewing countries' follow-up actions with regard to the Declaration'. *UN News and Media*, 'Report of 30 July 2009' available at: www.unog.ch/80256EDD006B9C2E/(httpNewsByYear_en)/34752CDF55CBBE30C12576030049AEFE?OpenDocument.

[109] Henriksen, above (n 91).

Moreover, the institutional competition that remains can be ultimately positive for the implementation of Indigenous peoples' rights generally. In the interests of achieving state compliance with those norms, it is certainly not a bad thing to have considerable institutional activity devoted to it. Any gaps in the implementation of the Declaration are likely to be filled by the institutional impulse to extend one's institutional mandate and prowess. Rodriguez-Piñero has written:

> The 'gap-filling' impulse has indeed historically led to the creation of fairer and more just norms: one of the reasons cited from the ILO's decision to amend the assimilationist 1957 Convention on Indigenous Peoples was because of the UN's decision to draft a declaration on the rights of Indigenous peoples. It feared that 'it would lose its historical leadership role in international action on behalf of Indigenous peoples to the United Nations'. [110]

Looking beyond the context of the EMRIP, the PFII and the SR on Indigenous Peoples, we see that many institutions engaged with Indigenous peoples' rights are also working together – dialogically – to cooperate rather than compete with one another for jurisdiction over Indigenous peoples' related issues, including the human rights treaty bodies.[111] More generally, the PFII formally liaises with other UN bodies and agencies in its annual sessions, as is required by its mandate.[112] Equally, the CBD and the WIPO collaborate on Indigenous peoples' traditional knowledge. The UN's inter-agency support group on Indigenous issues, made up of UN and other agencies engaged in Indigenous issues, provides a space for inter-institutional dialogue.[113] Other UN bodies are also taking note of the Declaration in their standard-setting activity, such as the WIPO's Inter-Governmental Committee on Intellectual Property and Genetic Resources, Traditional Knowledge and Folklore.[114]

Finally, the IACHR decision in *Saramaka v Suriname* provides an excellent example of the degree to which institutional overlap is overtly and reasonably managed.[115] The IACHR was required to consider whether Suriname's compliance with the Saramaka's land rights was an issue

[110] L Rodriguez-Piñero, *Indigenous Peoples, Postcolonialism, and International Law: The ILO Regime (1919–1989)* (New York, Oxford University Press, 2005) 273.

[111] Eg, in its concluding observations on the United States, the CERD Committee stated, despite acknowledging the United States' opposition to the Declaration that it 'recommends that the declaration be used as a guide to interpret the State party's obligations under the Convention relating to Indigenous peoples'. In UN CERD Committee, 'Concluding Observations of the Committee on the Elimination of Racial Discrimination: United States of America' (February 2008) UN Doc CERD/C/USA/CO/6, para 29.

[112] UN Economic and Social Council Resolution 2000/22 (28 July 2000) UN Doc E/2000/22.

[113] UN Permanent Forum on Indigenous Issues, 'Report of the Inter-Agency Support Group on Indigenous Issues' (5 February 2008) UN Doc E/C.19/2008/6 Annex.

[114] See, Intergovernmental Committee on Intellectual Property and Genetic Resources, Traditional Knowledge and Folklore (12th Session, 25–29 February 2008) 'UN Declaration on the Rights of Indigenous Peoples': www.wipo.int/edocs/mdocs/tk/en/wipo_grtkf_ic_12/wipo_grtkf_ic_12_inf_6.pdf.

[115] *Saramaka v Suriname*, above (n 24).

'substantially the same as one previously studied by . . . another international organization' (Article 47(d) of the American Convention), which would prevent it from hearing the matter. The Human Rights Committee and the CERD Committee had evaluated the same set of facts under their state reporting process and, in the case of the ICERD, its early warning and urgent action procedure. The IACHR found that it was not prevented from hearing the case as the issue before the Court was not substantially the same. The IACHR highlighted the differences in the processes under which the issue had been resolved and noted that the Human Rights Committee and the CERD Committee did not adjudicate on the matter, instead reviewing only the 'general situation' in Suriname. In contrast, the IACHR could adjudicate controversies and order appropriate reparations. The sensitivity to jurisdictional overlap, and the inclusion of justifications to explain why it was appropriate here to assume jurisdiction, all illustrate a containment of the worst potential consequences of institutional competition.

C Dialogic Attempts to Interpret Norms Consistently: Lessening Norm Indeterminacy

Counterbalancing the emergence of inconsistent norms, or equivalent norms where different interpretation is possible, is the increasing trend for international institutions to interpret norms with reference to other norms, even those that are not within the jurisdiction of the institution. They have focused on the norm synergies rather than differences between them. Burke-White writes 'cognizance of one another's jurisprudence and even direct conversation can help mitigate conflicting outcomes and ensure coherent rulings'.[116] Further,

> [c]ounterbalancing the danger of fragmentation is an increasingly loud inter-judicial dialogue. This dialogue has important implications for the unity of the international legal order as it provides actors at all levels with means to communicate, share information, and possibly resolve potential conflicts before they even occur.[117]

Perhaps the clearest example of this phenomenon in the context of Indigenous peoples' rights is the case law of the IACHRs and IAHR Commission, as well as that of the ACHPR. The American bodies have developed an 'evolutionary interpretation' of international human rights

[116] W Burke-White, 'International Legal Pluralism' (2004) 25 *Michigan Journal of International Law* 963, 972 and N Miller, 'An International Jurisprudence? The Operation of "Precedent" Across International Tribunals' (2002) 15 *Leiden Journal of International Law* 483, 499.

[117] Burke-White, *ibid*; and J Pauwelyn, 'Bridging Fragmentation and Unity: International Law as a Universe of Inter-Connected Islands' (2004) 25 *Michigan Journal of International Law* 903, 916.

justifying their interpretation of American human rights instruments in light of newer, more evolved international jurisprudence. They have both referenced the ILO Convention 169, the Declaration and UN human rights treaty body jurisprudence to interpret the American Convention's right to property as protective of Indigenous peoples' communal land rights under Indigenous customary law, even where the state in question has not ratified ILO Convention 169 and despite the formal non-bindingness of the Declaration.

For their part, the human rights treaty bodies have illustrated their cognizance of, and support for, outside jurisprudence on Indigenous peoples' rights on a number of occasions. It suggests that they would hesitate before coming to conflicting interpretations of relevant law on Indigenous peoples' rights, even if the respective human right treaties are comparatively not so progressive on their face. The CERD Committee, the Committee on Economic, Social and Cultural Rights and the Committee on the Rights of the Child have already all referenced the Declaration; the CERD Committee stated that it should be used as a guide to interpreting state obligations under the Convention relating to Indigenous peoples.[118] The CERD Committee in particular has also encouraged states to adopt the Declaration and consider ratifying ILO Convention 169,[119] or noted states obligations under the Declaration and ILO Convention 169.[120] States in the Human Rights Council have also referenced the Declaration in their reviews of other states, calling on them to comply with, or support, it.[121] The CERD Committee, in its review of Suriname, also endorsed the decision of the IACHR, and adopting a similar interpretation of Saramaka land rights, urgently encouraged it to comply with the Court's decision.[122] In other words, the current trend suggests that human rights treaty bodies are, whenever possible, likely to interpret human rights treaties consistently with the Declaration and Inter-American human rights jurisprudence.

[118] UN CERD Committee, 'Committee on the Elimination of Racial Discrimination Concluding Observations: United States of America' (8 May 2008) UN Doc CERD/C/USA/CO/6, para 29; UN Committee on Economic, Social and Cultural Rights, 'Committee on Economic, Social and Cultural Rights Concluding Observations: Nicaragua' (28 November 2008) UN Doc E/C.12/NIC/CO/4, para 35; and UN Committee on the Rights of the Child, 'General Comment No 11: Indigenous Children and their Rights under the Convention' (January 2009) UN Doc CRC/C/GC/11, para 10.

[119] UN CERD Committee, 'Committee on the Elimination of Racial Discrimination Concluding Observations: Canada' (25 May 2007) UN Doc CERD/C/CAN/CO/18, para 27.

[120] UN CERD Committee, 'Committee on the Elimination of Racial Discrimination Concluding Observations: Ecuador' (13 May 2008) UN Doc A/HRC/8/20, para 30.

[121] See, eg, UN Human Rights Council, 'Universal Periodic Review: Colombia' (15 December 2008) UN Doc A/HRC/WG.6/3/L.14, para 58; and UN Human Rights Council, 'Universal Periodic Review: New Zealand' (11 May 2009) UN Doc A/HRC/WG.6/5/L.7, para 81(9).

[122] UN CERD Committee, 'Committee on the Elimination of Racial Discrimination Concluding Observations: Suriname' (13 March 2009) UN Doc CERD/C/SUR/CO/12, para 14.

A complex question to emerge since the UNGA's adoption of the Declaration is how it should influence the interpretation of ILO Convention 169, and vice versa, especially in light of differences in standards that they set, as outlined above.[123] There is strong evidence to suggest that they will be interpreted consistently by international organizations, even where, as is the more common case, the Declaration sets more demanding standards and is, formally, the less binding of the two instruments.[124] However, it is not difficult to imagine an adjudicatory body facing some difficulty in reconciling respective provisions where the outcomes would be different depending on which Article of which instrument, literally interpreted, is applied. There may be limits in the extent to which a 'systematic integration' approach can resolve norm conflict.

In the future, international institutional dialogue might benefit from greater attention to clarifying guidelines to direct cross-jurisdictional dialogue – for example between the CERD Committee and the IAHR Commission when applying the non-binding Declaration in situations involving a state that has not supported it. Reference to an 'evolutionary interpretation' with little more, given the many ways such an approach can itself be applied, could aggravate rather than relieve uncertainty in the law if it is not done with some greater structure and transparency. Methodological uncertainty only confounds the problems associated with norm substance uncertainty. Miller notes, after highlighting the degree of dialogue between international institutions, that '[m]uch work remains to be done, however, to elucidate [sic] precise nature of existing relationships – especially the reasons underlying them. Until that work is done, the complacent and the critical alike will be at a disadvantage'.[125]

Of course, any interpretative methodology must not be so rigid as to weaken the benefits of flexibility in referencing 'other' norms.[126] Instead, the demand suggested here is a weaker one: norm-applying institutions should talk about interpretative methodology as well as norm meaning

[123] As Rodriguez-Piñero notes '[t]he examples of express reference to Convention No 169 by international bodies are almost too numerous to mention'. Rodriguez-Piñero, *Indigenous Peoples*, above (n 110) 330, fn193.

[124] UN Permanent Forum on Indigenous Issues, 'Information Received from the UN System and Other Intergovernmental Organizations: Office of the UN High Commissioner for Human Rights' (15 February 2008) UN Doc E/C.19/2008/4/Add.14, para 25. The PFII records that 'Participants noted that there was an emerging consensus that there was no need to reconcile the Declaration with ILO Convention No. 169. The two instruments had been negotiated at different times by different bodies and therefore diverged in a number of respects. They represented two different parts of the same body of standards and should be used as best as possible to protect, promote and fulfil the human rights of Indigenous peoples'. PFII Article 42 Report, above (n 53) para 18.

[125] Miller, 'An International Jurisprudence?' above (n 116).

[126] As Borgen notes, '[t]he challenge is to maintain a certain amount of flexibility, which is clearly required in today's politics, while simultaneously increasing the predictability of outcomes'. C Borgen, 'Resolving Treaty Conflicts' (2005) 37 *George Washington International Law Review* 573, 619–20.

and transparently express, carefully and thoughtfully, the justifications for an inclusive interpretative approach.

Potential justifications for referencing 'other' norms might include, for example, the authority of the instrument or decision and the utility in interpreting norms consistently for the system as a whole – in the interests of maintaining some unity. Institutions might cite the merits in developing human rights jurisprudence in such a way that it strives to maximize compliance with human rights obligations, achieved by interpreting older norms, such as those expressed in ILO Convention 169, consistently with newer and more demanding ones. A cacophonous dialogue coupled with the concrete application of the law to facts has the potential to better the overall quality of the law also, in the form of more creative and insightful decisions, making for 'better, more reflective opinions'.[127] Of particular note for Indigenous peoples, some scholars have posited that judicial dialogue 'can also help the *emerging* global legal culture in capturing the wisdom of a variety of legal thinking'.[128] Koch maintains that the greater the number of norms applied to a case, with norms sourced in different regimes with different cultural premises, the more accommodating the outcome will be.[129] To the extent that the Declaration reflects and voices Indigenous peoples' perspectives, as their involvement in its drafting in over 25 years would suggest it does, the inclusion of the Declaration in determining the outcome of an issue might indeed bring some multicultural jurisprudence into international law.

D The Cohesive Force of Indigenous Peoples' Participation in International Legal Forums

Indigenous peoples have played an exceptional role in international law-making.[130] Their participation has often been greater than that of civil society generally, especially in the negotiations on the Declaration, where they shared the pen along with states,[131] and the EMRIP, which would not have been established had Indigenous peoples' advocates not approved of the final resolution put forward to the Human Rights Council. This trend is consistent with the tremendous increase in the participation of Non-State

[127] A-M Slaughter, 'A Global Community of Courts' (2003) 44 *Harvard International Law Journal* 191, 201 and CH Koch, 'Judicial Dialogue for Legal Multiculturalism' (2004) 25 *Michigan Journal International Law* 879, 901.

[128] Koch, *ibid.*

[129] *Ibid.*

[130] Such as, eg, A Boyle and C Chinkin, *The Making of International Law* (Oxford, Oxford University Press, 2007) 19.

[131] See ME Turpel, 'Indigenous Peoples' Rights of Political Participation and Self-Determination: Recent International Legal Developments and the Continuing Struggle for Recognition' (1992) 25 *Cornell Journal of International Law* 579.

Actors (NSAs), and their influence, in international forums generally, as has been noted and analyzed by many.[132]

The relationship between Indigenous peoples' organizations and norm fragmentation and institutional proliferation is contradictory. On the one hand, the greater participation of Indigenous peoples' organizations has influenced the creation of new law, adding to norm fragmentation, and new institutions, increasing institutional proliferation, with the legitimacy deficits these phenomena can create.

On the other hand, institutional proliferation has also opened up further doors for Indigenous peoples, and other NSAs, to participate in international law making, utilized to great effect. One of the legitimacy positive impacts of Indigenous peoples' participation is that they can bring some cohesion to norm development in international law on Indigenous peoples' rights, given that they usually argue for the same kinds of substantive rights in almost all forums relevant to Indigenous peoples. Indigenous actors are often the same in each different international institution, which is rarely true for state representatives, with different delegations to different institutions and sometimes representing different arms, ministries or departments of the state. By way of example, one of the more active Indigenous peoples' organizations is the International Indian Treaty Council, established in 1974. It is engaged in:[133]

- the Human Rights Council and all related forums, including the EMRIP, which it lobbied hard for, and which has a relationship with the SR on Indigenous Peoples;
- the PFII;
- developments for a right to food, including at the FAO, with which it has jointly written a paper on cultural indicators of Indigenous peoples' food and agro-ecological systems;[134]
- the Stockholm Convention on Persistent Organic Pollutants, with the objective of seeking the banning of certain pollutants that particularly impact on Indigenous communities;
- UN meetings on climate change;
- the WIPO;
- CBD;
- negotiations on the OAS Draft Declaration on the Rights of Indigenous Peoples;
- the UN human rights treaty bodies (coordinating responses from Indigenous peoples' NSAs in Canada and the US to Canadian and US reports to that, and other, committees); and

[132] S Charnovitz, 'Nongovernmental Organizations and International Law' (2006) 100 *American Journal of International Law* 348, 360–61.

[133] See generally, the International Indian Treaty Council website: www.treatycouncil.org.

[134] E Woodley, E Crowley, J Dey de Pryck and A Carmen, 'Cultural Indicators of Indigenous Peoples' Food and Agro-Ecological Systems' (17 February 2009) UN Doc E/C.19/2009/CRP 3.

- initiatives to seek better respect for Indigenous peoples' rights impacted by mining and other resource extraction.

For the consistent – cohesive – message from Indigenous peoples' organizations, we only need to look at Indigenous peoples' submissions to the WIPO in its drafting of principles and policies on traditional knowledge. Consistently with the Declaration, they have:

- emphasized the need for free, prior and informed consent before traditional knowledge is used;[135]
- called for the creation of a mechanism for direct interaction between states engaged in WIPO and the PFII members;
- highlighted the need to respect Indigenous peoples' customary law;
- called for recognition that traditional knowledge rights are collective in nature;[136] and
- called on the WIPO to meet the Declaration standards.[137]

Certain IPO representatives who have acquired juris-influential roles within international institutions further facilitate norm coherence or, at a minimum, demand norm-coherence. The chairs of the EMRIP, the PFII and the SR on Indigenous Peoples are all Indigenous and have a history of advocacy in international forums for the development of Indigenous peoples' rights. Take, for example, James Anaya, the current SR on Indigenous Peoples. As well as publishing the first full and authoritative account of international legal developments relating to Indigenous peoples, he has advocated, or coordinated advocacy, for Indigenous peoples' rights in various different international forums, including in the WGIP, the Working Group on the Draft Declaration, before the former SR on Indigenous Peoples, the IACHR, the IAHR Commission and the CERD Committee. He is now in a position to apply the norms for which he has argued for decades as the SR on Indigenous Peoples, consistently with the normative claims made by Indigenous peoples, and potentially to influence the interpretations of norms on the international plane. Similarly, Vicky Tauli

[135] Submission by the Assembly of First Nations, Call of the Earth, the Aboriginal and Torres Strait Islanders Commission, Foundation for Aboriginal and Islander Research Action, Canadian Biodiversity Network, Coordinating Body of the Indigenous Organizations of the Amazon Basin, Hokotehi Moriori Trust, Rekohu, Aotearoa, Indigenous Peoples caucus of the Creators Rights Alliance, Kaska Dena Council, the Saami Council and the International Indian Treaty Council to the World Intellectual Property Organization Intergovernmental Committee on Intellectual Property and Genetic Resources, Traditional Knowledge and Folklore Sixth Session (15–19 March 2004): Agenda Item 8: the International Dimension: www.wipo.int/export/sites/www/tk/en/igc/ngo/afn_igc6.pdf.

[136] Kaska Dena Council Opening Intervention to the WIPO IGC in Traditional Knowledge (16 March 2004), www.wipo.int/export/sites/www/tk/en/igc/ngo/kdc_igc6_doc6_3.pdf (accessed 19 May 2009).

[137] Joint Statement of the Indigenous Peoples Council on Biocolonialism (IPCB), Call of the Earth/Llamado de la Tierra (COE) and International Indian Treaty Council 'General Comments' (6 December 2006, Geneva) WIPO Doc WIPOP/GRTKF/IC/10.

Corpuz, one of the leading Indigenous peoples' advocates for the UN Declaration, has until recently been the chair of the PFII, and participates in a whole range of UN institutions demanding that international institutions give effect to the Declaration.

V CONCLUSION

MSENs and international institutional proliferation contribute to some legitimacy deficits in Indigenous peoples' rights under international law. The sheer number of sources of Indigenous peoples' rights under international law makes it nearly impossible to understand the processes followed in their evolution – from multiple multilateral forums, to court-like processes, to bureaucratic policy development. In addition, the continuing proliferation of institutions, seen in the recent establishment of the Human Rights Council in 2006, EMRIP in 2007, following on from the PFII in 2000 and the SR on Indigenous Peoples in 2002, means that the procedure followed for the adoption of norms may change midway through negotiations. A related concern is the emergence of different and competing norms on a particular subject, such as Indigenous peoples' land rights, upsetting the determinacy and coherence of the law with the negative impact that can have on states' compliance with them.

On the other hand, legitimacy deficits associated with MSENs can be mitigated and countered by the international legal system, as has been illustrated in this case study of Indigenous peoples' rights. First, MSENs can also be legitimacy positive where they reflect and respond to more contemporary understandings of justice. Secondly, tensions arising from jurisdictional overlaps between institutions – as the sources of MSENs – and between the substance of norms can be constructively minimized by institutional dialogue, although the use of an express methodology would improve this process. Finally, norm beneficiaries can minimize norm incoherence by persistently and consistently demanding similar interpretations of norms across various international institutions.

13

*Multi-Sourced Equivalent Norms: Concluding Thoughts**

Robert Howse

THIS VOLUME BEGINS with the Bible – with 'righteousness' – and yet its guiding premise or idea is that one can meaningfully speak of norms and their application in a neutral language, abstracting from any specific moral or political commitment. This is of course the perspective of modern (but not postmodern) social science: norms and their operation can be studied as social 'facts' – with scholarly or scientific distance. At the same time, the world of international law in which I work and live is full of passion and struggle and conflict. International law is about punishing genocidal leaders and intervening in failed states; about who gets access to AIDS drugs and on what terms; about saving sea turtles and whales; about financial, and economic and environmental and other crises and catastrophes and who pays for the clean up. It is thus fitting that the final chapter in the volume by Claire Charters returns us to the question of 'righteousness', albeit framed in the modern idiom of 'legitimacy'. As Charters suggests, the weight or guiding power of a norm cannot be determined by its formal or general properties but depends ultimately on the rightfulness of the end that it serves and of the processes and people that created it.

What does it mean to speak of norms as 'equivalent?' As Broude and Shany indicate, equivalence does not mean sameness or even equality. But it implies some common standard against which the element of difference and thus the nature of the choice between the norms can be assessed. Consider their first example: 'The same behavior – assault, or willful killing – is often prohibited under criminal statutes and at the same time gives rise to liability under tort.' The common standard here is the wrongfulness of assault and willful killing. The basis for equivalence is a fundamental *moral* agreement. So when we turn to the world of international law

* The perspective of these remarks is based largely on recent work with Ruti Teitel, in particular, 'Cross-Judging: Tribunalization in a Fragmented but Interconnected Global Order' (2009) 41(4) *NYU Journal of International Law and Politics* 959-90.

what does it mean to observe that different norms, developed in different 'sub-systems' or through different processes (custom versus multilateral treaties for example), are 'pointed in the same direction'? One would have to presume a 'direction' – and therefore – a *telos* for international law that transcends the various divides that are connoted by the expression 'fragmentation.' As Michaels and Pauwelyn point out in their contribution, seeing international law as (ideally) a single system represents or supposes a fundamental normative choice. Drawing extensively on conflict of laws principles in domestic legal systems, Michaels and Pauwelyn raise the possibility that one can 'solve' the question of multiple norms in a truly decentralized fashion through technical rules that apply within the various regimes and through which each deals with the others. We are thus invited to imagine that international law is nothing but a universe of specific regimes that are technically coordinated. Here the sharpest contrast (at least in this volume) is with Charters, who argues that the claims of indigenous peoples have a basis in justice that is cognizable by and affects the international legal system as a whole: conceptions of rights, property, sovereignty and self-determination that cut across many 'sub-systems' and regimes of international law are affected by the recognition of the *justice* of these claims.

Teitel and I are closer to Charters' view: drawing on an argument made in extenso in her forthcoming book *Humanity's Law*, we posit that humanity and its protection is the 'concept of justice underpinning international legality [even though] this norm does not have a fixed meaning that guarantees stability or unity in interpretation across contexts.'[1] If one begins from such a common ground, and thus the possibility of normative communication between diverse actors in international law even if they differ on specific meanings, then the extent and nature of that communication will be articulated through a hermeneutics that has important sociological and political aspects.

The sociological aspect is captured to some extent by Moshe Hirsch's contribution to the volume. The international law of investor protection and that of human rights have, as it were, a common ancestry in the law of diplomatic protection of aliens. In evolving each in its own direction from that common ancestry, *both* investment law and human rights law break with the Westphalian model: both empower non-state actors to state their claims directly on the basis of international law. And yet as Hirsh notes, arbitrators in investor-state disputes have been very resistant to considering international human rights law in their decisions. The arbitrators, as he indicates, are mostly drawn from the world of international commercial law, and see themselves as agents of the 'depoliticization' of international economic relations. By contrast, those who invoke the language of inter-

[1] Ibid, 967.

national human rights in these disputes seek to 'repoliticize' economic globalization, anchoring it to the fundamental moral and political commitments upon which international human rights law is arguably grounded. But Hirsh rightly points out that the sociological differences are unstable and things can change.

One such example of change is the WTO Appellate Body. In the old GATT system, the panelist-arbitrators were part of, and saw themselves, part of, the technocratic management of trade liberalization, and were unremittingly hostile to the introduction of 'alien' values (e.g. environmentalism) through norms external to the trade liberalization *telos*, or which would complicate its technocratic management. The Appellate Body when it was first formed was mostly composed of jurists who did not come from that community of insider experts/managers. In the *Shrimp/Turtle* case, which is now widely viewed as a decisive change of direction for the multilateral trading system in relation to the environment, the Appellate Body was faced with the question of whether endangered species of sea turtles could be protected as 'exhaustible natural resources,' i.e. whether this expression in the GATT applied to non-living resources or whether it could serve the aim of biodiversity. Here the Appellate Body could simply have relied on previous decisions of the GATT panels, staffed by the insider/technocrats who found that, in cases dealing with fisheries management, stocks of fish could be regarded as 'exhaustible natural resources.' But instead the Appellate Body chose to go outside the GATT acquis and invoke the contemporary international law of biodiversity, including 'soft law' to settle the question of what are 'exhaustible natural resources.' The sociological cleavage between the insider technocrats and the AB Members (at least most of them) made possible such a move; but judicial politics alone can explain why it was necessary. The multilateral trading system was under assault by activists invoking a range of concerns of justice international legal norms related to those concerns; the legitimacy of the trading system could not be preserved, nay it would be gravely threatened, by turning them away at the door.

I am skeptical that any taxonomy of approaches or strategies, any set of rules or techniques, in dealing with MSENs could capture the hermeneutics of such choices in such pivotal moments. The bottom line pronounced by Broude and Shany that

> there is 'flexibility' that affords adjudicators (or other interpreters) the space to pursue their goals in choosing among MSENs is surely the right one. This raises the issue of whether one should be looking at all for general guidelines, rules or doctrinal structures to constrain that flexibility. And to what end?

As Pirker's contribution to this volume illustrates nicely, 'judicial borrowing' for example might enhance the legitimacy of a decision and of the decision-maker in some circumstances; while in other cases to do so would undermine it. Resolving an issue through citing the authority of another court or tribunal could be an attempt to exploit the more established or solid credentials of that other institution, or it could be an avoidance strategy, allowing a resolution of an issue that is highly controversial or divisive within a particular regime, through as it were delegating the decisive legal judgment to an 'outside' decision-maker. Or it could be a form of deference or comity.

Bartels' contribution tends to the view that jurisdictional considerations play a significant role in constraining ex ante as it were the choices of legal norms by international courts and tribunals. My sense is that judges invoke jurisdiction when they want to avoid the consideration of other legal norms based on their own hermeneutics and related conception of judicial role and legitimacy. In the *Nicaragua* case, for example, which Bartels discusses, it is true that as a *formal* matter, the ICJ was scrupulous in honoring the jurisdictional constraint that limited it to the customary rules on the use of force but substantively, since the Court was able to say that these rules have been shaped by and are reflected in the UN Charter and the *acquis* of practice and jurisprudence on the use of force under the Charter, it could legitimately allow its judgment of the matter to be shaped by this broader normative universe. Most of the Court in *Oil Platforms* took this approach even further, considering many elements of the law on the use of force, while the formal jurisdiction of the ICJ had been limited to the application of a treaty of Friendship, Commerce and Navigation. How far one wishes to go is very much a matter of the self-conception of the judge. For a bold self-conception consider the see the separate opinions of Bruno Simma in *Oil Platforms* and *Armed Activities in the Congo*, where Simma criticizes his colleagues on the court for undue caution or restraint in their interpretations and the range of norms they are prepared to entertain.[2] Contrast this with a recent arbitral award under the investor protection provisions of the NAFTA, *Glamis Gold v United States*. According to the tribunal, 'its mandate under Chapter 11 of NAFTA [is] similar to the case-specific mandate ordinarily found in international commercial arbitration.'(paragraph 3). Interpreting the NAFTA is analogous to resolving one dispute under one contract. The tribunal contrasts its own situation with that of 'a standing adjudicative body which addresses multiple disputes.'(paragraph 3). While the tribunal suggests it should take into account systemic considerations of investor protection, it is unwilling to consider the broader universe of international law beyond the 'contract' (treaty) that it is solving the dispute under. Simma himself hinted in *Oil Platforms* that the considerable legitimacy of the ICJ to pronounce on general norms of international law was related to its special status as a 'world court' and that the same might not be the case for a regional or ad hoc

[2] Here I draw on my contribution with Ruti Teitel to the Simma *Festschrift*, forthcoming.

tribunal. But I am not sure this is correct: an ad hoc tribunal without an acquis or an internal institutional legal culture to draw on might have even more need of anchoring its decisions within a broader international legal universe. The narrowness of the *Glamis Gold Tribunal* was ultimately based on the notion that it was there primarily *for the parties* and only secondarily speaking to a larger constituency.

One would hope that, having usually identified Multi-Sourced Equivalent Norms as a phenomenon of significance in international law, and demonstrated the relevance of the phenomenon to a wide and important range of contexts, this impressive volume would inspire future research on the hermeneutic issues entailed in deploying such norms and, accordingly on the philosophy of international adjudication.

Index

www.ingramcontent.com/pod-product-compliance
Lightning Source LLC
Chambersburg PA
CBHW071304180926
51613CB00001B/121